浙江省“十一五”重点教材
高等院校国际经济与贸易专业系列教材

外贸函电

第3版

主　编　赵银德
副主编　余晓泓　季　莹
参　编　尹肖妮　赵桂梅
　　　　宋海英　钱明霞
主　审　王令坤

机械工业出版社

本书共分18个单元。其中第1单元系统介绍了英文商务信函写作的基本知识；第2~15单元遵循外贸常规流程，依次介绍了建立业务关系、资信调查、询盘及回复、报价和发盘、还盘和接受、销售促销、订单及其履行、信用证、其他支付方式、包装、保险、装运、索赔与理赔、贸易方式等内容；第16单元概要介绍了当代国际贸易交往中常用的备忘录、传真与电子邮件；第17单元和第18单元分别介绍了合同和外贸单证。在内容上，除了专题简介、样函、实用语句、练习和补充阅读材料等传统组成部分之外，本书还增加了两大特色内容：一是辟专栏描述了各类信函及其回复信函的写作步骤及常用表达方式；二是对函电中出现频率较高的焦点词汇及其表达方式进行了提炼。此外，书后的附录部分给出了函电中的实用短语、缩略词、正确写作及各单元练习的参考答案。

本书可供高等院校国际经济与贸易、国际商务、商务英语专业及其他相关专业师生用作教材，也可供社会读者参考。

图书在版编目（CIP）数据

外贸函电/赵银德主编. —3版. —北京：机械工业出版社，2015.11（2024.8重印）
高等院校国际经济与贸易专业系列教材
浙江省"十一五"重点教材
ISBN 978-7-111-52033-7

Ⅰ.①外… Ⅱ.①赵… Ⅲ.①对外贸易-英语-电报信函-写作-高等学校-教材 Ⅳ.①H315

中国版本图书馆CIP数据核字（2015）第259690号

机械工业出版社（北京市百万庄大街22号 邮政编码100037）
策划编辑：常爱艳 责任编辑：常爱艳 杨 洋
封面设计：鞠 杨 责任校对：程俊巧 任秀丽
责任印制：邓 博
北京盛通数码印刷有限公司印刷
2024年8月第3版·第13次印刷
184mm×260mm·20.5印张·505千字
标准书号：ISBN 978-7-111-52033-7
定价：46.00元

电话服务 网络服务
客服电话：010-88361066 机 工 官 网：www.cmpbook.com
010-88379833 机 工 官 博：weibo.com/cmp1952
010-68326294 金 书 网：www.golden-book.com

机工教育服务网：www.cmpedu.com

序

摆在读者面前的这套"'十三五'高等院校国际经济与贸易专业规划教材"是一项凝聚了众多高校教师辛勤劳动的集体性成果。我们编写这套教材主要是基于以下两大背景。

1. 在经济全球化条件下，国际贸易作为一国参与经济全球化和国际分工的重要途径之一，其作用和重要性都大大加强

20世纪90年代以来，在经济全球化浪潮的推动下，资本的国际流动得到迅猛发展。在这种情况下，有人认为国际贸易对经济增长的作用会被削弱，其实不尽然。通过以下分析可以看出，国际贸易对一国经济增长的作用不但没有被削弱，反而在加强。

首先，在经济全球化条件下，国际分工的日益细化不但使越来越多的消费品具有了可贸易性，而且越来越多的中间产品和劳务也进入了国际交换领域，从而使贸易的范围不断扩大。

其次，在经济全球化条件下，社会化生产以及市场经济的本质并未发生根本性变化，市场交换依然是扩大再生产的前提，国际贸易仍是各国在世界范围内进行交换的主要方式和彼此间经济关系的"晴雨表"。

最后，在经济全球化条件下，虽然国际直接投资的规模越来越大，跨国公司的作用越来越显著，但是它并不排斥国际贸易，更不能取代国际贸易；相反，资本和生产的国际化不仅为国际贸易提供了更加便利的条件，而且增添了新的贸易方式和贸易动力。因为跨国资本流动规模的扩大，特别是产业资本的国际化，不仅使国际贸易的规模和发展呈现出某些新特点，而且使国际贸易出现了内部化现象，推动了以要素禀赋差异为基础的产业间贸易模式逐步向以竞争优势为基础的产业内贸易模式转变，世界范围内产业内贸易的比重不断加大。规模巨大的跨国公司在世界各地组织生产，在"全球战略"的指导下，企业内部贸易和产业内贸易发展迅速，成为世界贸易的重要组成部分。不仅如此，第二次世界大战后国际资本的流动还促使了新的贸易方式的产生，如加工贸易、补偿贸易、国际租赁业务、国际分包等。这些贸易方式是为适应资本的流动而出现的，它们与传统的商品贸易方式有很大的差别。比如补偿贸易，就是引进方首先引进国外的先进技术和设备，然后再用生产的产品直接或间接地给予技术和设备提供者补偿，这实际上已起到了国际直接投资的作用。

2. 我国加入世界贸易组织之后，对国际经济贸易人才的培养提出了更高的要求

众所周知，我国于2001年正式加入了世界三大经济组织之一的世界贸易组织，从而标志着我国已全方位地融入到经济全球化的浪潮中。"入世"不仅给我们的社会经济生活带来了巨大的影响，而且对传统的国际经济与贸易专业教育也提出了深层次的挑战。20世纪80年代，当改革开放大潮刚刚涌动之时，很多学校开设了国际经济与贸易专业，似乎只要沾上涉外的字眼，就可以"通吃天下"，但这种低层次的量的扩张在20世纪90年代中后期就遇到了"瓶颈"，许多学生毕业后找不到心仪的工作。"入世"之后，涉外色彩浓重的国际经济与贸易专业再次引起了世人的关注和青睐，但是这一次并不是上一次的简单重复，它不仅要求涉外人才量的增加，更要求涉外人才质的提升。具体来说，现在需要的涉外人才是能系

统掌握现代经济学基本原理，通晓国际经济与贸易知识及惯例，同时能熟练运用外语和计算机等现代工具的高层次的复合型人才。

经济全球化和“入世”的大背景要求我们在国际经济与贸易专业的教材编写、课程设置、人才培养等方面进行相应的变革，这套“‘十三五’高等院校国际经济与贸易专业规划教材”就是为响应这种变革所做的一项尝试。

目前，市场上国际经济与贸易方面的教材品种较多，其中不乏优秀之作，前人的优秀成果是我们编写这套教材的重要参考来源和写作基础。当然，相比较而言，我们这套教材无论在内容的编写上还是在写作的体例和形式上，都具有自身的一些重要特色。

1. 在内容的编写上

过去，人们普遍注重国际经济与贸易专业的应用性特色，而相对忽视了这个专业所具有的理论性和素质培养功能。随着我国加入世界贸易组织、更深入地融入到经济全球化浪潮中，对经贸人才的需求已从简单的操作型人才转变为高素质的复合型人才，显然，传统的教学模式和方法已很难适应时代发展的要求。我们编写的这套教材在保持传统教材重视应用性和操作性的基础上，力求吸纳和反映当代国际经济与贸易领域的最新发展实践和理论成果，凸显教材的基础性、理论性和前沿性，并与时俱进，使之更加贴近我国的改革开放实践，加强为建设和完善我国社会主义市场经济体制服务的功能，挖掘各门课程对学生素质培养的潜能，从而赋予国际经济与贸易专业新的活力和意义。

2. 在写作的体例和形式上

我们借鉴国外流行教材的经验，在内容有关之处增加了为数不少的专栏，这些专栏或者是时代背景，或者是作者小传，或者是案例，或者是对有关问题的进一步阐述，有助于拓宽学生的视野，让其更深入地了解和掌握书中内容。所列复习思考题也力求灵活多样，以启发学生做进一步的思考。另外，章中所列关键术语、学习要点、小结以及荐读书目等，不仅方便学生总领教材内容，也为其做进一步研讨提供了文献参考。

当然，作为尝试性的成果，这套教材也难免有不尽如人意之处，特别是每本教材的作者均来自不同院校，因此在编写风格方面可能会存在一些差异，这些都需要我们在以后的修订过程中进一步完善，我们真诚地期待广大读者多提宝贵意见！

北京师范大学教授、博士生导师
编审委员会主任委员　　**赵春明**

第3版前言

感谢读者对第3版《外贸函电》的关注。

秉承为教师的外贸函电课程教学和学生的外贸函电知识习得提供优质服务的理念，第3版《外贸函电》保留了为读者所认可的特质：遵循外贸常规流程的单元结构安排、描述各类信函及其回复信函的写作步骤及常用表达方式的专栏、针对外贸函电中出现频率较高的焦点词汇与实用语句的介绍、丰富的课后练习、补充阅读材料以及电子课件。

第3版《外贸函电》着力在以下两个方面进行了修订：

一是结合用户的建议，新增了“合同”和“外贸单证”两个单元，前者通过合同样例来介绍合同的主要结构、条款及实用语句，后者介绍了商业发票、装箱单、产地证明书、重量单、提单、汇票、信用证、保函等样例。

二是对补充阅读材料进行了系统化修订。本书编者一直信奉：外贸实务知识、销售技能和沟通艺术是影响函电撰写能否成功的三大因素。为此，本书围绕这三个方面编写了补充阅读材料。其中，全书各单元的Part A提供了围绕所在单元主题而选编的外贸实务类阅读材料；全书各单元的Part B与Part C按照销售知识习得的逻辑顺序进行选编，系统性地介绍了销售技能的众多核心元素；全书各单元的Part D遵循商务沟通课程的逻辑顺序，选编了众多来自商务沟通实际的、最新的、富有趣味的沟通类小案例、小品文等。

本次修订由赵银德定稿，具体修订分工如下：Unit 1、Unit 2由赵银德、季莹负责；Unit 3 ~ Unit 6由余晓泓负责；Unit 7、Unit 10由季莹负责；Unit 8、Unit 9、Unit 13由尹肖妮负责；Unit 11、Unit 12、Unit 14由赵桂梅负责；Unit 15、Unit 16由赵银德、钱明霞负责；Unit 17、Unit 18由宋海英负责；各单元的补充阅读材料、附录由赵银德、钱明霞负责。另外，包楚协助做了部分资料的收集、整理和录入工作。

再次感谢读者对第3版《外贸函电》的厚爱，请不吝赐教您在教授或学习“外贸函电”课程的过程中的成功经验。

我们为选择本书作为授课教材的老师免费提供教学电子课件（PPT），请填写书末“信息反馈表”并发至changay@126.com索取。谢谢。

编　者

第 2 版前言

与第 1 版《外贸函电》一样，第 2 版《外贸函电》秉承服务教师外贸函电课程教学和学生英文函电知识习得需要的理念，保留了为读者所认可的内容：遵循外贸常规流程的单元结构安排、描述各类信函及其回复信函写作步骤及常用表达方式的专栏、针对函电中出现频率较高的焦点词汇与实用语句的介绍、丰富的课后练习以及电子课件。不过，我们的目标在于追求卓越，为此，第 2 版《外贸函电》在以下方面采取了变革举措：一是增加了样函并且更为强调了它们之间的联系性；二是对第 16 单元进行了扩充，新设了有关商务备忘录写作的内容；三是增加了附录“正确写作”部分，毕竟商务信函写作的正确性会影响到撰写者及其所在组织的专业形象。

本次修订由主编赵银德定稿，具体修订分工如下为：Unit 1、Unit 2 由赵银德、季莹负责；Unit 3 ~ Unit 6 由余晓泓负责；Unit 7、Unit 10 由季莹负责；Unit 8、Unit 9、Unit 13 由尹肖妮负责；Unit 11、Unit 12、Unit 14 由赵桂梅负责；Unit 15、Unit 16 由赵银德负责；附录“正确写作”部分由赵银德负责。

第 2 版《外贸函电》吸收了第 1 版用户的反馈意见。如果您在讲授外贸函电课程中有什么成功经验，请不吝赐教。我们期待着！

编　者

第1版前言

外贸函电是国际经济与贸易专业及外贸英语专业的核心业务课程之一，是一门将英语与外贸业务相结合的课程。本书介绍外贸实务中各种英文业务函件、传真及电子邮件的写作格式和表达方法，对外贸易各环节的具体做法，旨在提高学生英语水平的同时，让其熟练掌握外贸业务中常用的基本术语及表达技巧，培养和提高他们的外贸业务工作能力。

本书作者长期从事外贸函电的教学，对学生想学什么、教师该如何教、教什么内容都有深刻的体验。为此，本书在结构编排和内容设置两个方面都充分考虑了教师和学生对《外贸函电》的期望。

本书共分16单元。其中第1单元系统介绍了英文商务信函写作的基本知识，第2至第15单元则遵循外贸常规流程，依次介绍业务关系建立、资信调查、询盘及回复、报价和发盘、还盘和接受、销售促销、订单及其履行、信用证、其他支付方式、包装、保险、装运、索赔与理赔、贸易方式等内容，第16单元概要介绍了当代国际贸易交往中常用的传真与电子邮件。在内容上，除了专题简介、样函、实用语句、练习和补充阅读材料等传统组成部分之外，本书还增加了两大特色内容：一是辟专栏描述了各类信函及其回复信函的写作步骤及常用表达方式；二是对函电中出现频率较高的焦点词汇及其表达方式进行了提炼。此外，书后的附录部分给出了函电中的实用短语、缩略词及各单元练习的参考答案。另外，我们为选择本书作教材的教师免费提供电子课件。

本书由赵银德担任主编并负责统稿工作，由江苏科技大学外国语学院院长王令坤教授担任主审。本书具体编写分工为：Unit 1，Unit 2 由赵银德、季莹共同编写；Unit 3-Unit 6 由余晓泓编写；Unit 7，Unit 10 由季莹编写；Unit 8，Unit 9，Unit 13 由尹肖妮编写；Unit 11，Unit 12，Unit 14 由赵桂梅编写；Unit 15，Unit 16 由赵银德编写；另外，各单元 Supplementary Reading 中 Part A 由季莹编写，Part B，Part C 及 Appendix A 由赵银德编写，Appendix B，Appendix C 由赵银德、赵桂梅共同编写。

由于编者水平有限，加上时间仓促，书中不妥之处在所难免，敬请同仁、读者不吝赐教，批评指正。

编　者

目　录

Unit 1

Fundamentals of Writing English Business Letters

英文商务信函写作的基本知识

1.1 Introduction（简介）

私人间的信函往来多是为了联络和表达感情，而企业与外界进行沟通则采用商务信函的形式。商务信函的用途十分广泛，可以用于征询信息、订购货物、商议调整、出售货物、索要价款等。在国际贸易中，交易的磋商、合同的签订大多是通过信函的方式来进行的，商务信函是具有法律效力的文件，因此，从形式到内容都必须加以重视。商务信函写得好，不仅能为公司赢得新客户，也有助于促进和发展与客户的关系。相反，如果信函词不达意，就会引起误会，并可能引发矛盾，造成客户的流失。

要写好商务信函并非易事，不仅需要具备相关的业务知识，通晓商务法规和国际惯例，还应具备扎实的语言基础，熟悉商务信函的书写形式和行文要求。因此，学习和掌握商务信函写作的基本知识就显得尤为必要。

1.2 Requirements for Writing Business Letters（商务信函的写作要求）

要写就一封成功的英文商务信函，起草人需要具备以下条件：

（1）精通英语（Good command of English）。

（2）通晓外贸理论和实务（Knowledge of business theory and practice）。

（3）通晓术语（Knowledge of technical terms）。

（4）通晓人的心理（Knowledge of psychology）。

（5）熟悉推销艺术（Skills in salesmanship）。

1.3 Seven Guidelines of Writing English Business Letters（英文商务信函写作七原则）

为了达到通过信函进行有效沟通的目的，有必要了解并掌握写好英文商务信函的原则。这些原则通常被称为“7C 原则”，即清楚、简洁、正确、具体、礼貌、体谅和完整。

1. 清楚（Clarity）

商务信函应使读者一目了然，没有晦涩难懂或容易产生误会之处。在确定了所要写的内容后，选择使用简短、熟悉和口语化的词语，构建简单、有效的句子和段落来清楚地表达目的，避免使用会产生歧义或意义不明确的词汇。如有需要，可以使用样例、插图以及其他在视觉上有助于理解的形式。

例如，As to the steamers sailing from Shanghai to San Francisco，we have bimonthly direct services. 此处 bimonthly 可以是 twice a month（一月两次地）或者 once every two months（隔月地），存在歧义，应改为：We have two direct sailings every month from Shanghai to San Francisco. 或 We have semimonthly direct sailing from Shanghai to San Francisco.

2. 简洁（Conciseness）

所谓简洁，就是指要言简意赅地表达所需表达的意思，同时又无损于书信的完整和礼貌。在书写英文商务信函时，要摈弃那些陈旧的商业术语，做到简洁明了。通过去掉不必要的词和冗长的句子，保留有效、简洁的事实信息，就可把最重要的信息呈现给对方。

例如，将 We need to act on the suggestions that our customers offer us/We wish to acknowledge receipt of your letter.../Enclosed herewith please find four copies of.../a draft in the amount of $21,000 改为 We need to act on customer suggestions/We appreciate your letter.../We enclose four copies of.../a draft for $21,000 就简洁了。

3. 正确（Correctness）

商务信函必须写得正确，因为其牵涉到双方的权利和义务，而且它还是商业单据的凭证。正确的商务信函不仅表现为语法恰当、标点符号和词汇拼写正确，还要求叙述正确、提供的事实和数字无误、写作格式规范、技巧运用恰当以及商业术语正确。

例如，My visit with the outside sales rep showed me that your schedule can change quickly. 此处 your schedule 显然并非一定为读者的 schedule，不妨改为：My visit with the outside sales rep showed that schedules can change quickly.

再如，The goods supplied are exactly equal to the samples 应改为 The goods supplied are similar in quality to the sample，这样就可避免交货时可能产生的质量方面的纠纷，毕竟交付的货物无法与样品一模一样。

4. 具体（Concreteness）

商务信函必须写得生动、具体和明确，要避免采用模糊、大概和抽象的词语和语句。在写商务信函的过程中，应尽量运用具体的事实和数字，选择形象的词，一般使用主动语态来陈述内容。

例如，将 The financial advantage of owning this equipment instead of leasing it is 10% after taxes/Selection of a program should be based on the client's needs 改为 Owning this equipment rather than leasing it will save us 10% after taxes/Select the program that best fits the client's needs 就显得生动、明确而更有分量。

5. 礼貌（Courtesy）

礼貌在商务信函中有其特殊而丰富的内涵。一封礼貌的信函可以加深与目前客户的业务关系，也有助于结交新的业务伙伴。在商务信函的写作过程中，及时是礼貌之首。此外，在撰写商务信函时，应避免使用可能激怒、伤害对方的言辞或语气，语调上要尽可能站在客户的立场上，考虑到对方的愿望和背景，做到互惠互利。

例如，Thank you for your corporation 适用于上司对下属，如用于下属对上司就不礼貌。再如，To start the scheduling process，please describe your availability for meetings during the second week of the month 就不如 Could you let me know what times you' d be free for a meeting the second week of the month 来得礼貌。

6. 体谅（Consideration）

体谅对发信人和收信人之间保持进一步联系至关重要。发信人应尽可能从收信人的立场来考虑问题，在分析对方会如何理解信息的基础上，提供其所需要的信息。简言之，体谅就是要做到为对方着想，移情于对方，在人性层面上来理解对方。此外，体谅意味着要坚持用肯定而非否定的态度。

例如，与 We are shipping your order of September 21 this afternoon 相比，The two dozen Corning Ware starter sets you ordered will be shipped this afternoon and should reach you by September 28 给对方提供了所需要的具体信息，显得十分体谅对方。

再如，与 We are happy to extend you a credit line of $5, 000 相比，You can now charge up to $5, 000 on your American Expression card 就顾及到了对方的情感。

7. 完整（Completeness）

商务信函必须力求完整，要包括写信人希望收信人作出积极反应的一切情况，或是回答来信所提出的全部问题和要求。一封完整的商务信函不仅可能会带来预期的结果，还可能建立起更好的商务关系。

例如，Our product has won several prizes 显得内容不完整，而 Our Hair Washing Machine has won first prizes in four national contests within the past three years 则提供了具体的产品名称，具体的时间，具体的奖项和数量，给对方提供关于我方产品更为完整的信息，从而传递更有说服力的信息。

1.4 Addressing Envelopes（信封的写法）

如图 1-1 所示，在寄往国外信函的信封上，收信人和收信人地址以及寄信人和寄信人地址的书写位置，都不同于国内信封的写法。

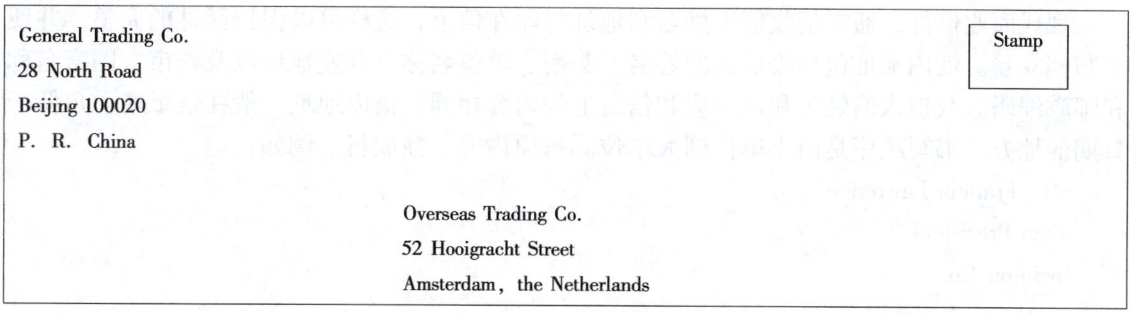

图 1-1 寄往国外信函的信封写法

其主要有以下特点：

（1）寄信人姓名和地址应写在信封的左上角，且务必与封内地址在形式和标点上一致。

（2）收信人姓名和地址写在信封中下偏右的位置，收信人的姓名和国名须分行书写。

（3）寄信人和收信人的姓名和地址的书写顺序是：先写姓名后写地址。地址的书写应由小至大，先写机构名称，再依次写门牌、街道、城市、州/省及邮政编码，最后书写国名。

（4）关于信件类别、投递方式及其他事项说明，写在信封左边寄信人地址下，或写在左下角。如怀疑信件能否送交收信人，可在信封最下边标明：IF UNDELIVERED PLEASE RETURN TO ×××，即：如无法投递，请退交×××。

1.5 Parts of English Business Letters（英文商务信函的组成部分）

1. 信头（Letter head）

信头也称为信笺抬头，由寄信人公司名称、地址、电话号码、E-mail 地址和传真构成。信头通常位于信纸的最上端。

2. 日期（Date）

日期是商务信函中至关重要的一部分。日期决定着一个合同是否生效，订单是否执行，账单是否已付款等。因此，商务信函中决不能遗漏或写错日期。日期顶边写在信纸的左边或右边，距离信头 3~4 行。书写日期时，应注意以下几点：

（1）年份必须全部写出。

（2）月份最好用英文全拼，不提倡用缩略式。

（3）日期可以用序数词或基数词。

（4）年份前要加逗号。

（5）日期切忌全部用数字表示。

3. 信函编号（Reference number）

给信函编号是为了便于往来书信的存档和查阅，一般采用 Your Ref.（你方编号）或 Our Ref.（我方编号）。信函编号通常放在日期的上方或与日期平齐靠左的位置，打印上如下字样：

Your Ref.：

Our Ref.：

4. 信内地址（Inside address）

现代商业信件，通常把收信人姓名和地址打印在信上，这样可以保持函件的完整，并便于归档立卷。信内地址包括收信人的姓名、头衔、单位名称、营业地址以及城市、国家名称和邮政编码。收信人的姓名和地址应和信封上的内容相同。信内地址一般在信纸左上角低于日期的地方。书写顺序是由小单位到大单位。每项内容单独成行。例如：

Mr. Francis Lawrence

Vice President

Swinton Co.

87 Unico Avenue

Toronto, ST 9878

Canada

5. 称呼（Salutation）

称呼写在信内地址下面空两行处。

常见的正式称呼有：Dear Mr. Smith，Dear Mrs. Smith，Dear Miss Brown，Dear Ms. White。Ms. 用于不知是否已结婚的女子姓名之前。如果称呼多个男性，则在姓名前用 Mr. 的复数形式 Messrs。Mrs. 没有复数形式，如果称呼多个女性，则在姓名前用 Mmes.，如：

Mmes. White and Gray。

写信给一家公司时，通常用 Dear Sirs，也可以用 Gentlemen（美国人经常用 Gentlemen）。称呼后用冒号或逗号均可，但前者显得更正式（Gentlemen 后常用冒号）。

6. 事由（Subject）

事由是为对方在阅读信的正文以前对信的主题、内容有一个了解，以便于登记归档和查阅。例如：

Subject：Men' s Bicycles

Re：Sales Confirmation No. 2536

Your Order No.：

Reference：

事由写在称呼下面、信的中间位置。事由下面可以画线，也可以不画线，有时可全部用大写字体。其中，Re 意为“关于，有关”，在这里做“事由”解。

7. 信函正文（Body of the letter）

信函正文是商务信函中最重要的部分。商务信函的目的是传递信息。在书写时，要遵循“7C 原则”。正文一般遵循三段式的格式。第一段一般是引入主题，第二段详细讨论，第三段以总结或建议来结束全文。当然也可以酌情增减。最好是一段表达一个意思。需两页或更多的信纸时，在前一页最后一行的右边写上 to be continued。续页应采用不带信头的信纸，并注明收信人名称、页数和日期。例如：

Mr. John Smith，Page 2，June 3，2005

8. 信尾客套语（Complimentary close）

信尾客套语是一种礼貌，是结束信函的正式方式，类似中文信函中的“此致，敬礼”等。常用的有：Sincerely，Sincerely yours，Yours sincerely，Best regards。更亲切一点的有：Cordially，Cordially yours。再正式一些的有：Yours truly，Respectfully yours，Yours faithfully。注意，只有第一个字母大写。一般打印在正文下面空一行处。

9. 签名（Signature）

签名通常在信尾客套语下空三行的位置。签名可采用不同写法，一般包括：公司名称、写信人的手写签名、写信人的打印签名、写信人的头衔。有时，也可以不写公司名称。例如：

Yours truly,

General Trading Co.

(*Signature*)

John Smith

Sales Manager

如果签名的人和打印信函的人不是同一个人，要在信中表示出来。通常在签名下面直接写上写信人和打印信函人名字的首字母缩写。如果签字的人是 John Smith，打字或起草信件的人是 Tina Edward，那么签字下面首字母缩写就是：JS/TE。

10. 经办人代号（Reference notation）

经办人代号是提供信件产生的信息资料，便于必要时查对之用。经办人代号由信件口授者和秘书的姓名首字母组成，用冒号或斜线号分开，可用以下方式书写：

FCM/HL，FCM：HL，FCM/hl，fcm：hl

11. 附件（Enclosure）

假如信封内除信纸外尚附有其他文件，可以在信中说明附件份数和内容。当附件只有一件时，注明 Enclosure 或 Encl. 即可；一件以上时，要加上编码，以便收信人识别，用 Enclosures 说明。例如：

Enclosures 3：

1. Birth Certificate

2. Visa

3. Letter of Reference

12. 抄送（Carbon copy/C. C.）

发信人若需把此信抄送给有关单位，可在附件下方即信左下端打上 C. C.，然后打上抄送单位的名称，例如：

C. C.：The Bank of China

Copies to：Directors

Cc to：CEO

Copy to：Sales Manager

13. 附笔（Postscript/ P. S.）

若写完信后还须附加项目时，就需补述，这类似于中文信中的附言。有时并非真正将忘了写的事情补上，而是为了故意引起对方的注意。附笔要放在抄送下方。在写完 P. S. 之后，有时也把签字人姓名的首字母缩写附在最后。

1.6 The Opening and Conclusion of English Business Letters（英文商务信函的开头和结尾）

1. 英文商务信函的开头

信函的开头应该直入主题，要避免空洞。根据书写商务信函的目的不同，开头一般分为两大类：一类是回复信件；另一类是主动与对方联系。

对于回复信件，可采用以下方式开头：

（1）感谢对方的来信。

We thank you for	your letter (inquiry, telex, e-mail, fax etc.) of...
Thank you for	
We appreciate	
We were pleased to receive	
Please accept our thanks for	

（2）对来信进行回复。

We are pleased to reply to	your letter (inquiry, telex, e-mail, fax etc.) of...
In answer to	
In response to	
In reply to	

（3）回复来信中的有关问题。

With reference to	your letter (inquiry, telex, e-mail, fax etc.) of...
In reference to	
Referring to	
We refer to	

（4）回复来信中提出的要求或指示。

As requested		in your letter of...
As required		
As instructed		
According to	the request/instruction	
In accordance with		
In compliance with		
In conformity with		

（5）表达满意和欣喜。

We were gratified	to learn from your letter of ... that...
We were glad	
It was a pleasure	

（6）表达遗憾和惊讶。

We regret	to learn from your letter of ... that...
We were sorry	
We were surprised	

对于主动和对方联系的商务信函，可以用以下方式开头：

（1）通过别人的介绍了解到对方。

Your company has been recommended to us by...
We have learnt from ... that...
The name of your reputable firm has come to us through...
We have had your name and address given to us by...

（2）对以前信函的补充或确认。

Further to our letter of...	对我方某月某日的信函补充如下
With further reference to our letter of...	
Confirming our letter/conversation of ...	我方确认某月某日的信函/会谈
We confirm that out letter of ... and ...	我方确认某日信函并……
With further reference to...	对……进一步补充如下

（3）通知对方一些情况。

This letter is	to inform you that ...
We are pleased	
We have the honor	
We have the pleasure informing you that...	兹荣幸地通知贵方……
We regret to inform you that...	我们遗憾地通知贵方……

2. 英文商务信函的结尾

商务信函的结尾应该简洁、中肯，与写信的主旨相符。根据是否需要对方回复把结尾分为两类。

对于期待对方回复的信件，可以用以下的方式结尾：

We shall be glad to have	a/an/your reply (answer, favorable news, comment etc.)
We hope to be favored with	
We shall be obliged for	
We are waiting for	
We shall appreciate	
We look forward to	
We trust to hear	from you about/concerning/in this respect/in this matter.
We hope to hear	
We shall be glad to hear	
Please let us hear	

对于无须对方答复的信函，可以用以下两种方式结尾：

（1）表达感谢或希望继续合作的意愿。

We thank you for the services you rendered in this matter.
Thank you for your attention to this matter.
We appreciate your patronage and hope that the pleasant relationship established between us will continue.
Your favorable cooperation will be greatly appreciated.

（2）表达歉意。

We apologize for the delay in replying to your letter.
We regret the trouble we are causing you.
Please accept our apology for the inconvenience we have caused you.
We regret that we are unable to be of assistance to you.
We regret that we can' t meet your requirements.

1.7 Useful Sentences（实用语句）

（1）回信。

We are offering a sound article at popular price, and we should appreciate an opportunity to substantiate our claims.（本公司所供物品货色优良，价格公道，感谢贵公司给我们一个机会，使我们的要求得以实现。）

In answer to your favor of the 8th June, we inform you that we are unable to take the goods offered by you.（贵公司6月8日函收悉，本公司无法承购贵公司开价的商品，此复。）

In answer to your inquiry for bran, we offer you 40 tons of the same.（关于贵公司所询麦麸一事，现可提供该货40t。）

Answering to your letter, we state that the market remains quiet.（贵函收悉，此地市场仍保持平稳。）

Kindly excuse our not replying to your favor of the 8th June until today.（至今未复6月8日贵函，甚感歉疚，还请见原谅。）

In response to your inquiry respecting Mr. Mat, we have pleasure in stating that he is a thoroughly reliable man.（关于所询Mat先生的情况，谨此高兴地告知，他是一位值得信赖的人。）

We are glad to answer your inquiry concerning T Company.（关于T公司的情况，特此欣然函复。）

Replying to your letter of the 19th respecting the account, I will send you a cheque shortly.（19日贵函关于结账一事，特此奉告，我方将很快寄去支票。）

Replying to your inquiry of the 18th inst., we are unable to offer you plates of the size you specify.（谨复贵公司本月18日函询，我们无法提供贵公司指定的那种餐盘的报价。）

In reply to your letter, we are pleased to inform you that we have shown the sample to our buyer.（贵函收悉，谨此告知，我们已将样品提交本公司的买方。）

In reply to yours of 16th July, I send herewith a cheque, valuing USD550.（贵方7月16日的来函收悉，兹寄去面额为550美元的支票一张，谨此奉复。）

（2）收讫。

We acknowledge receipt of your letter of yesterday, and gratefully accept the appointment on the terms you mention.（昨日来函收悉。谨于此按贵方所约定的条件，接受此项任务。）

We acknowledge receipt of your letter of the 15th inst.（本月15日来函敬悉。）

Kindly acknowledge receipt, and have the goods sent by the last steamer in December.（本商品将于12月最后一班轮船付运，货到时请惠予告知。）

We duly received your favor of the 25th June, contents of which we note with thanks.（贵方6月25日来信收悉，信中所谈事宜尽悉。谢谢。）

We are in possession of your favor of the 6th June, and regret having to inform you that it is impossible for us to deliver the goods.（贵方6月6日来函收悉，实难交运该货，甚感遗憾。）

Your favor of yesterday covering a cheque of USD100 is duly to hand.（贵方昨天的信和所附

来的100美元的支票均已收悉。)

I have to acknowledge with thanks the receipt of your favor of 6th June. (贵方6月6日的来函收悉，多谢。)

(3) 通知。

We inform you that I have now removed my factory to the above address. (本厂已迁移到上述地址，特此通知。)

Having established ourselves in this city as merchants and general agents, we take the liberty of acquainting you of it, and solicit the preference of your order. (我方已在本市开设贸易与总代理店，特此通知并恳请订购。)

We are pleased to inform you that our business will be turned into a limited company on the 1st August. (本公司于8月1日将改为股份有限公司，特此奉告。)

Notice is hereby given that the annual general meeting of the shareholders of our company will be held at the Bankers' Club on Mar. 8th. (公司股东年会将于3月8日在银行家俱乐部召开，特此函告。)

By this we inform you that we have today paid Mr. R. S. USD120. (今天我们已付给R. S. 先生120美元，特此告知。)

Through these lines, we intimate you that they may send you considerable orders. (通过这些渠道，他们会发来甚多订单，特此函告。)

(4) 确认。

In confirmation of my cable today, I regret to state that the factory was completely destroyed by fire last night. (谨确认今日电报，非常遗憾，该工厂于昨夜被毁于火灾。)

We confirm our call of last week respecting our offers to you. (兹确认上周本公司通过电话给贵方的报价。)

We confirm our respects of the 3rd June, and inform you that your consignment has duly arrived. (兹确认我方6月3日所发函并告知贵方，发来的货物已如期到达。)

Confirming our letter of last week, we ask you to appoint an early interview with our representative. (兹确认我方上星期致贵方函，请及早约定与我方代表面谈的日期。)

Confirming ours of the 17th May, we now hand you enclosed B/L for 50 packages. (兹确认本公司5月17日的信，随函附上50包的提单。请查收。)

We confirm our respects of yesterday, and have the pleasure to inform you that we have drawn this day on you. (兹确认昨天致贵方的信并欣告，今天我们已给你们开出汇票。)

Kindly let us have confirmation of these orders by telegraph tomorrow by 4 p. m. (贵方对我公司所提订单，请务必于明天下午四时前来电确认。)

We have much pleasure in confirming herewith the order which you kindly placed with us yesterday. (兹欣慰地告知，我方确认贵方昨天向我们提出的订单。)

(5) 愉快、欣慰。

We have the pleasure to inform you that we will forward by tomorrow' s mail to the Bank five bonds of USD500 each. (我们欣慰地告知贵方，我们将于明日给银行寄去5张面额为500美元的债券。)

We have the pleasure of enclosing herewith the documents. （随函奉上有关文件。）

We have pleasure in enclosing herewith a Bill of Lading covering 50 bales of cotton. （随信附去 50 包棉花的提单一张。）

We take pleasure in informing you that a parcel containing books and others has arrived for you from London. （兹欣慰地告知，从伦敦给您发来的书和其他东西的邮包已到达。）

We shall be pleased to enter your order at USD800 per pound. （我方愿按每磅 800 美元接受贵方订单。）

I shall be pleased to supply you with 10 cases of toys at the low price of USD900 per box. （愿提供玩具 10 箱，每箱优惠价 900 美元。）

We shall be glad if you will kindly give us a price for printing. （如蒙告知所需印刷费用，不胜欣慰。）

（6）附函。

We enclose for realization drafts as per the list at foot. （按照本函所列清单，附上应兑现的汇票。）

Enclosed please find the invoice of 80 bales wool bought by your order. （依照贵方订单，随函奉上 80 包羊毛的发票，请查收。）

Enclosed please find three orders for immediate attention. （随函附上订单三张，请立即安排。）

An order form is enclosed. Fill it out and attach your check. （随函附上订单一张，请填妥并附来支票为荷。）

Enclosed we hand you a draft, USD200, drawn on your company by our Seattle house. （随信附上我西雅图公司以贵公司为抬头的面额为 200 美元的汇票一张。）

（7）迅即。

Kindly see the empty sacks are returned as promptly as possible. （请尽快将空袋退回为盼。）

The goods are at once despatched by rail to your address. （这批货物立即由火车发往贵处。）

Please give us forwarding instructions promptly. （请尽快下达运输指令为荷。）

Please deliver these goods with all speed to the London dock. （请立即将这些货物运往伦敦码头。）

（8）依照、关于。

about/ regarding/ concerning/ as per/ as to/ as regards/ with regard to 关于

according to/ agreeably to/ conformably to/ in accordance with 依照

In accordance with your letter of yesterday, I am sending tonight 15 cases of whisky. （依照贵方昨日来函，今晚已发出威士忌 15 箱。）

Referring to our conversation of this morning, we enclose a pamphlet describing our new articles. （依照今天上午的谈话，随函呈上介绍本公司新产品的小册子一本。）

With reference to your letter of the 16th inst., we are glad to inform you that there has been a great demand for the articles. （关于贵方本月 16 日的来信，我方欣慰告知该商品的需求量甚大。）

With reference to our representative' s call, we are pleased to say that we have obtained the receipt for the goods.（关于对我方代表的电话查询，我方欣慰告知货物的收据已经收到。）

（9）期满、到期。

The steamer will be due in Yokohama on the morning of the 15th May.（该轮将于5月15日晨如期到达横滨港。）

I received in due course your letter of the 28th June.（我方已如期收到贵方6月28日的来函。）

We have duly received your valued favor of the 16th May.（我方已如期收到贵方5月16日函。）

（10）抱歉、遗憾。

to take the liberty of doing something/ to take the liberty to do something 表示抱歉

to regret/ to be sorry/ to be chagrined/ to be mortified/ to be vexed（甚感遗憾，请多包涵）

We are sorry to learn from your letter of the 10th June that your customer is still dissatisfied with the condition.（从贵方6月10日来函知，贵方客户对该条件仍表不满，甚为遗憾。）

We are sorry that we have taken the liberty in writing you prematurely on the subject.（时机尚未成熟，我们就冒昧地写信谈及此事，对此甚表遗憾。）

We are regretted to have to inform you that two cases of them are so bad in quality.（我们遗憾地告知贵方，其中两箱质量极为差劣。）

Meanwhile, I can only ask you to accept my apologies.（在此，恳请您接受我方歉意。）

We apologize you for troubling you.（麻烦不少，请您宽恕。）

Please accept our apologies for the inconvenience this matter has given you.（对此事给您带来的不便，请接受我们的歉意。）

（11）荣幸。

to have the honor of doing/ to have the honor to do 对于……甚感荣幸

We feel specially honored to be given this opportunity to meet such a nice group of distinguished people like you.（特别使我们感到荣幸的是能有机会遇到你们各位知名人士。）

Today, we feel very much honored to have Prof. Wilson with us.（今天，我们很荣幸能和威尔森教授欢聚一堂。）

（12）感谢。

We take this opportunity to thank our patrons and friends for the liberal support extended to us during our business career.（藉此机会，对凡在业务发展方面给予我们有力支持的朋友、客户表示感谢。）

We appreciate your telling us about the defective sets, and are glad to make things right.（承蒙告知该若干套不合格产品，我方愿妥善处理。）

While thanking you for your valued support, I wish to ask for a continuance of your confidence in the new company.（在感谢您过去惠予支持的同时，希望对我新公司也继续给予信赖。）

We take this opportunity of thanking you for your past valued support, and of assuring you that your orders will continue to receive our best personal attention.（藉此机会，让我们对您过去宝贵的支持表示感谢，对您今后的订单，我们将保证继续格外关照。）

We can confidently assert that any business with which you may favor us will be transacted in such a manner as will afford you the fullest satisfaction. （请相信，您所给予的任何业务，我们都会用您满意的方式执行。）

（13）提供服务。

We wish to assure you that we appreciate an opportunity afforded us for service. （请相信，我们将非常感谢贵方给予我们为您服务的机会。）

In the meantime, please be assured of our most cordially good wishes and of our desire to be of service. （同时，请牢记我们最诚挚的心愿和为您服务的热望。）

We thank you for the opportunity to be of service to you. （如有机会为您服务，我们将非常感谢。）

We are always pleased to serve you at any time. （我们随时乐意为您服务。）

（14）希望、愿望。

We hope to hear from you favorably. （盼收到您的好消息。）

We hope that you will give this matter prompt attention. （希望您能很快对此事做出决定。）

We hope this action will meet with your approval. （希望这一行动能得到您的同意。）

（15）留意签名。

We would ask you kindly to note our respective signatures given below. （惠请留意我们每个人在下面的签名。）

I request your attention to his signature, appended below. （请留意附在下面的签名。）

（16）诚请回信。

by return/ by return of post/ by return of mail 回信

Then send back the postcard and we' ll gladly tell you without a bit of obligation, of course. （届时，寄回明信片告知我们，本公司乐意奉告，当然不会增加任何麻烦。）

A postcard is enclosed for your convenience in requesting further information. （为了便于您从我们这里获取更多信息，随函附去明信片一张备用。）

Make out your check for USD50, put it in the enclosed envelope, and start it on its way to us at once. （请开 50 美元支票一张放在所附信封里，并请立即寄给我们。）

A return envelope that requires no postage is enclosed for your convenience in replying. （为方便您回信，随信附去免贴邮票的信封一个。）

1.8 Formats of English Business Letters（英文商务信函的格式）

商务信函要达到良好的沟通效果，一方面要撰写恰如其分的句子和段落，另一方面还必须运用恰当有效的信函格式。英文商务信函有三种常用的格式：缩行式（The indented form）、齐头式（The block form）和修正齐头式（The modified block form）。

1. 缩行式

如图 1-2 所示，缩行式信函的日期行、结尾客套语、作者姓名和头衔都从所在行中间偏右的位置开始写，事由行居中。每个段落的第一行从左边界空 5 个字母的位置开始，其他各行都从左边顶头写。

Letter head

Our Ref No. :
Your Ref No. :

June 1, 2005

International Investment Ltd.
77 Pearl Road
Swanton, Manchester
England

Dear Madam,

Re: ××××××

……………………………………………………………………………
……………………………………………………………………………
……………………………………………………………………………
……………………………………………………………………………

Yours sincerely,
Zhaou Hua
Zhou Hua
Manager

图 1-2 缩行式信函格式

2. 齐头式

如图 1-3 所示，齐头式信函的每一行都从左面的边界开始写，前面不留空格。

Letter head

Our Ref No. :
Your Ref No. :

June 1, 2005
International Investment Ltd.
77 Pearl Road
Swanton, Manchester
England

Dear Madam,

Re: ××××××

……………………………………………………………………………
……………………………………………………………………………

Yours sincerely
Zhou Hua
Zhou Hua
Manager

图 1-3 齐头式信函格式

3. 修正齐头式

如图 1-4 所示，修正齐头式信函类似于缩行式信函，但段落首行不缩进。

Letter head

Our Ref No. :

Your Ref No. :

June 1, 2005

International Investment Ltd.
77 Pearl Road
Swanton, Manchester
England

Dear Madam,

Re: ××××××

……………………………………………………………………………………

……………………………………………………………………………………

Yours sincerely,

Zhou Hua

Zhou Hua

Manager

图 1-4 修正齐头式信函格式

Exercises

1. Address the following envelope in English.

英国伦敦牛津街23号阳光公司 邮编：SE5，6JD

威廉·史密斯先生 收

中国北京前门大街××号
北京纺织品进出口公司
邮编 100053

2. Write down a letter with modified block form.

(1) Sender' s Name: China National Garment Corp.

(2) Sender' s Address: 260 Zhujiang Road, Nanjing 210018, P. R. China

(3) Sender' s Telephone Number: 025-83838388

(4) Date: March 13, 2005

(5) Receiver' s Name: Walkman Co.

(6) Receiver' s Address: 2561 California Avenue, Seattle, WA 889, U. S. A.

(7) Subject: Gent' s Shirt

(8) Salutation: Gentlemen

(9) The Message...

(10) Complimentary Close: Yours faithfully

(11) Signature: Dong Gang (Manager)

(12) Enclosure: Catalogue

Supplementary Reading

Part A

Effective business letter writing boils down to knowing why you are writing a business letter, understanding your customer' s needs and then clearly writing what you need to say. Every letter should be clear, human, helpful and as friendly as the topic allows. The best business letters have a conversational tone and read as if you were talking to your customer. In brief then, discover the Seven-Cs of letter writing.

When you write a letter, you are trying to convince someone to act or react in a positive way. Your customer will respond quickly only if your meaning is crystal clear. Put yourself in the reader's shoes and write in a friendly and helpful tone. Don' t represent your company as one that cannot make a mistake and must always be in the right. Try not to reply in the normal bland and defensive way of organizations—write a sincere and helpful letter.

Show you are interested in the customer' s circumstances. If he or she has mentioned something personal in the letter, refer to it in your reply. This builds a bridge between you and the customer. Read the original letter carefully and see if there is something you can put in your letter to show your interest. What do readers want from writing? They want relevant information, presented in a clear, easy-to-understand style. Therefore, getting a clear picture of your readers before you start to write helps to focus your writing to get your message across. The better picture you have of your readers, the better you can direct your writing.

Notes

1. boil down to 归结为
2. convince 使某人确信
3. crystal clear 易懂的
4. bland 冷漠的
5. defensive 防备的

Part B

Personal selling is an old and honorable profession. It has helped improve this country' s standard of living and provided benefits to individual buyers through the purchase of products. Millions of people have chosen sales careers because of the opportunity to serve others, the availability of sales jobs, the personal freedom sales provides, the challenge, the multitude of opportunities for success, and the nonfinancial and financial rewards.

A person can become a successful salesperson through company and personal training and by properly applying this knowledge while developing skills and abilities that benefit customers. Also important are believing in the product or service being sold, working hard, wanting to succeed, and maintaining a positive outlook toward both selling and oneself. In addition, a successful salesperson should be knowledgeable, able to plan, and efficient in using selling time. Effective salespeople are good listeners who provide service to customers. En route to success, salespeople develop a range of skills through study and practice, enhancing their ability to think strategically, relate to others, and understand the technical aspects of their business.

For the future, salespeople will need to be well versed in diverse international markets, able to ethically develop customer partnerships, and ready to utilize technology. The remainder of this book expands on these topics to provide you with the background either to improve your present selling ability or to help you decide if a sales career is right for you.

Part C

Order-takers Versus Order-getters

Sales jobs vary widely in their nature and requirements. Some sales jobs require the salesperson only to take orders. Order-takers may ask what the customer wants or wait for the customer to order. They do not have a sales strategy and often use no sales presentation. Order-takers must be employed to bring in additional business that the employer probably would not obtain without their efforts. Many never attempt to close the sale. They perform useful services. However, few truly create sales.

On the other hand, the creative selling of tangible goods or intangible services in highly competitive lines (or where the product has no special advantages) moves merchandise that cannot be sold in equal volume without a salesperson. These people are order-getters. They get new and repeat business using a creative sales strategy and a well-executed sales presentation. The salesperson has an infinitely more difficult selling situation than that faced by the order-taker. In this sense, the individual is a true salesperson, which is why this person usually earns so much more than the order-taker.

This salesperson has two selling challenges. First, the salesperson must often create discontent with what the prospect already has before beginning to sell constructively. Second, the salesperson often has to overcome the most powerful and obstinate resistance. For example, the prospect may never have heard of the product and, at the outset, may have no desire whatsoever to purchase it. The prospect may even be prejudiced against it and may resent the intrusion of this stranger. In other instances, the prospect may want it but may want competing products more. Frequently, the prospect cannot afford it. To meet such sales situations successfully requires creative selling of the highest order.

Creative salespeople are often faced with selling to numerous people to get one order. This is the most difficult selling situation because the representative may have to win over not only the decision maker, the one who can say yes, but also other persons who cannot approve the order but who have the power to veto.

Part D

Communication Is Key to Pay

How can you make more money at your job?

The number one way, according to *Wall Street Journal*, is to "listen to your boss". Specifically, do the work your boss wants done, follow directions, work hard, and let your boss know what you have accomplished. Employees who follow this method collect raises at a rate of 9.9%, while average performers receive 3.6% and poor performers get 1.3%, according to one survey.

Just as important is to make sure you ask your manager to define expectations. Don't assume you know what your manager wants. Make sure you understand what your manager considers an outstanding performance in your position.

Poor Customer Service Becomes Costly

A customer called AOL to cancel his service. The phone call lasted 21 minutes, including automated answering, waiting in a queue, and a five-minute conversation with a customer service representative. During the conversation, the customer service representative refused to comply with the customer's request to close his account despite 21 requests to "cancel" his service and approximately 9 "I-don't-need-it, I-don't-want-it, and I-don't-use-it" statements. To express his dissatisfaction, the customer posted the recorded conversation on the Web as a digital "documentary", which was heard by 300,000 visitors and highlighted on the *Today* show on NBC. Following the post, an AOL executive vice president e-mailed employees notifying them of the post and warning them that any of their customer interactions could be similarly posted. In addition, because of similar earlier violations, AOL agreed to pay a fine of $1.25 million and to use a third-party verification system.

Another customer service incident occurred when a customer welcomed Comcast technician into his home to replace a faulty modem. When the technician called the central office, he was placed on hold and proceeded to fall asleep on the couch after an hour of waiting. In response, the customer recorded a short documentary, *A Comcast Technician Sleeping on My Couch* and posted it to YouTube where 500,000 viewers watched the customer service blunder.

Unit 2

Establishing Business Relations

建立业务关系

2.1 Introduction（简介）

没有客户就没有生意。对任何公司来说，寻找潜在客户并建立业务关系总是关键的一步。为商品寻找有潜力的销售市场，并与该市场上销售该类商品的经营者建立业务关系，是交易开始和发展的基础。要扩大贸易往来，就必须在巩固并发展已有业务关系的基础上，不断物色新的贸易对象，不断发展新的业务关系。通常，在与客户建立业务关系之前，必须对客户的资信情况、经营范围、经营实力以及建立业务往来的意愿有所了解。

在国际贸易活动中，进口方和出口方常常远隔千山万水。在一般情况下，进出口双方可以通过以下渠道来相互了解：

（1）银行（Bank）。银行可以提供进出口商所在地的公司名称和地址。

（2）商会（Chamber of Commerce）。作为商人的组织，许多国家都成立有商会组织，其任务之一就是为会员提供商务信息和寻找新的商机。

（3）商务参赞处（Commercial Counselor' s Offices）。有时，进出口商可从商务参赞处获得必要的信息。

（4）交易会和展览会（Export Commodities Fairs & Exhibitions）。进出口商可以通过参加在国内外举行的出口商品交易会和展览会来获得有关商务信息。

（5）广告（Advertisement）。报纸和杂志上的广告也是进出口商获得信息的重要途径。

（6）商业目录（Trade Directory）。不同国家和地区的商业目录常常载有相关公司的信息。

（7）其他渠道。进出口双方还可以通过国外销售代理商（Sales Agent）的介绍、互联网（Internet）或自我介绍来获取所需要的信息。

在国际贸易商务沟通中，给新客户写信是建立业务关系的惯例。建立业务关系的信函一般应涉及以下内容：

（1）告诉对方我方是如何获悉对方的地址和经营范围的。

（2）表示我方有与对方建立业务关系和合作的强烈愿望。

（3）介绍本公司的性质、基本业务情况和经营范围。

（4）说明希望推销或购买的产品。

（5）必要时可向对方提供资信证明人，以便对方了解我方的资信情况。

（6）附寄公司简介、商品目录、价目表和小册子等，以便对方全面了解我方信息。

书写建立业务关系的信函时，应做到诚恳、真挚。回复应及时、礼貌，并按对方的要求答复，以便给对方留有一个好印象。即使不能满足对方的要求，也应及时答复并婉言说明原因，为以后可能的交易留下余地。

2.2 Writing Skills（写作技巧）

建立业务关系的信函的写作步骤及常见表达方式如下所示：

写作步骤	表达方式
1. 说明信息来源（告知对方你从何种渠道得知对方公司的情况）	Your company has been kindly introduced to us by...（贵公司由……介绍给我们。）
	We learn through/from... that...（我们通过……得知……）
	On the recommendation of ...（由……推荐……）
2. 对你的公司做简单的介绍（例如公司的业务范围等）	We wish to introduce ourselves to you as a ...（我们把自己作为……介绍给你们。）
	Our lines are mainly...（我们主要从事……）
	... fall within our business activities.（……属于我们的经营范围。）
3. 表达写信目的	We are willing to enter into business relations with you.（我们愿意和贵方建立业务关系。）
	We express our desire to ...（我方愿意……）
	We are now writing you for ...（我们现写信愿意……）
	We are desirous of ...（我方愿意……）
4. 表达与对方合作及早日收到回复的愿望	We look forward to receiving...（希望早日收到……）
	Hope to receive ...（希望收到……）
	Your early reply is appreciated.（盼早复。）
	We are anticipating your answer.（盼早复。）

回复建立业务关系的信函的写作步骤及常见表达方式如下所示：

写作步骤	表达方式
1. 感谢对方对你公司的兴趣	Thank you for ...（感谢贵方……）
	Thank you for your interest in ...（感谢贵方对……的兴趣。）
	We have received ...（我们已收到贵方……）
	Your letter of August 8 has been received with thanks.（感谢贵方8月8日的来信。）
2. 表示有与对方建立业务关系的意愿或兴趣	Your wish of establishing business relations coincides with ours.（贵方建立业务关系的愿望和我们不谋而合。）
	This is also our desire.（这也是我们的愿望。）
	We shall be very glad to enter into business relations with you.（我们将非常高兴与贵方建立业务关系。）
3. 表示采取进一步的行动	We are sending you our catalogue and pricelist...（我们将给贵方寄去我们的产品目录和价格表。）
	We shall be glad to have your specific inquiry.（我们将很高兴得到贵方的具体询价。）

2.3 Specimen Letters（样函）

Letter 1: A firm's letter to a firm concerned

Dear Mr. Peng,

Your company's name has been given to us by the Bank of China, Shanghai Branch.

We wish to buy quality tea and coffee cups and saucers[1] of different shapes fully decorated with flowers or other designs. If you can supply this type of merchandise, kindly airmail us a sample cup and saucer. Also, please enclose[2] your pricelist and all suitable illustrations.

We await your early reply.

Truly yours,
Fred Jackson

Letter 2: A reply to the above

Dear Mr. Jackson,

We have received your letter with thanks. We are glad to inform you that we can supply quality tea and coffee cups and saucers of different shapes fully decorated with flowers or other designs. We are confident that our products will meet the requirements of the market.

Enclosed please find a catalogue and pricelist[3] of the products you require. We are sending you by mail the samples you need.

Waiting for your order.

Sincerely yours,
Xianjin Peng

Letter 3: A firm's letter to a firm concerned

Dear Mr. Leeds,

We have obtained your address from Internet and are now writing to you for the establishment of business relations.

We are very well connected with[4] all the major dealers here of light industrial products, and feel sure[5] we can sell large quantities of Chinese goods if we get your offers at competitive prices.

Please let us have all necessary information concerning your products for export.

Yours faithfully,
Ping Wang

Letter 4: A reply to the above

Dear Mr. Wang,

We thank you for your letter and shall be pleased to enter into business relations with you.

As requested[6], we are sending you by another mail our latest catalogues and pricelists of our exports.

If you find business possible, please write to us.

Sincerely yours,
John Leeds

Letter 5: An exporter's to his bank

Dear Sir or Madam,

We thank you for your cooperation for our business.

Now we are keenly desirous of enlarging our trade in various agricultural products, but unfortunately have had no good connections in the southern part of Russia. Therefore, we shall be obliged if you will kindly introduce us to some of the most capable and reliable importers in the district who are interested in these lines of goods.

Your favorable information will be appreciated.

Yours faithfully,
Leon Allen

Letter 6: A reply to the above

Dear Mr. Allen,

Referring to[7] your letter, we are pleased to introduce to you the following firms:

(1) The ABC Corp., (Address...)

(2) Messrs. Wolf & Green Co., (Address...)

(3) The Pacific Co., (Address...)

We hope this information will prove useful to you.

Yours faithfully,
Mark Granger

Letter 7: A firm writes to a firm concerned

Dear Mr. Kevin,

We have obtained your name and address from Aristo Shoes, Milan, and we are writing to enquire[8] whether you would be willing to establish business relations with us. We have been importers of shoes for many years. At present, we are interested in extending our range[9] and would appreciate your catalogues and quotations. If your prices are competitive, we would expect to transact a significant volume of business. We look forward to your early reply.

Truly yours,
Per Anderson

Letter 8: A reply to the above

Dear Per,

Thank you for your letter of the 16th of this month. We shall be glad to enter into business relations with your company. In compliance with[10] your request, we are sending you our latest illustrated catalogue[11] and price list covering our export range. Payment should be made by irrevocable and confirmed letter of credit. Should you wish to place an order, please fax us.

Sincerely yours,
Kevin

Notes to the specimen letters

1. quality tea and coffee cups and saucers 优质茶具和咖啡具
2. enclose 随函附上
3. catalogue and pricelist 目录和价格表
4. be well connected with 与……有很广泛的联系
5. feel sure 相信
6. as requested 按照要求
7. refer to 谈到，涉及，有关
8. enquire 询问
9. extend our range 拓展业务范围
10. in compliance with 根据
11. illustrated catalogue 插图目录

2.4 Focal Words（焦点词汇）

benefit

n. **福利，益处，利益**

the principle of equality and mutual benefit 平等互利原则

It will be to our mutual benefit to come to an agreement. （达成协议对我们是互惠互利的。）

v. **有益于**

Both sides will benefit from this. （双方都可从中获益。）

beneficial: *adj.* **有益的**

It is beneficial to both of us to come to terms. （达成协议对我们双方都有益。）

beneficiary: *n.* **受益人**

An irrevocable L/C will be established with your company as the beneficiary. （我方将开立以贵公司为受益人的不可撤销信用证。）

deal

n. **生意**

We have come to a deal with an American customer. （我们已与一位美国客户做成了一笔生

意。）

v. 做生意；处理；和……有关

We have dealt with the company for many years. （我们与这家公司做了许多年的生意。）

Deal with a man as he deals with you. （以其人之道还治其人之身。）

The report deals with the fashion market. （该报告是有关时装市场的。）

dealer: *n.* 商人；商号

a dealer in furs 毛皮经营商

dealing: *n.* 交易，交道

Our dealings with you have been quite pleasant. （我们之间的交易一直以来都很好。）

enclose

v. 把……封上；随函附寄

We enclose a copy of our quotation. （随函附上报价单一份。）

Enclosed please find our Sales Confirmation in duplicate. （随函附上我方售货确认书一式两份，请查收。）

enclosure: *n.* 附件；装入物

The envelope contains a check for USD300 as an enclosure. （信封里有张300美元的支票。）

inform

v. 通知，告诉

We shall inform you of the name of the company. （我方会告知该公司的名称。）

He is kept informed of the fluctuations of the prices. （他知道价格的波动情况。）

information: *n.* 信息，资料，情报

We are grateful to you for all your information on the recent development in your market. （对贵方所提供的贵方市场的近来全部进展情况，谨表感谢。）

For fuller information please contact our branch in Hong Kong. （如要了解更全面的信息，请联系我们在香港的分公司。）

line

n. 行业；生意；（商品的）种类；航线；短函

best line 高级品

full line 经营各种货物

line of business 业务范围

air-line 航线

We have ample experience in all lines we handle. （对于我们所经营的各项业务，我们都富有经验。）

As soon as you reach a decision, please drop us a line. （一旦贵方做出决定，请告知我们。）

We are going to present the full line of our leather products at Guangzhou Fair in autumn this year. （我们将在今年秋季广交会上展出各式各样的皮制品。）

v. 安排

The eggs are packed in cartons with beehives, lined with shake-proof corrugated paper board, each carton containing 300 eggs. (鸡蛋用带蜂房孔的纸箱包装，内衬防震瓦楞纸板，每箱装300个。)

in line with 相一致

out of line 与……不相符合

2.5 Useful Sentences (实用语句)

(1) We take the liberty to introduce ourselves as exporters of silk piece goods, which we have been exporting to Europe and Japan. (我们冒昧地向贵方介绍，我们经营丝绸商品，并出口欧洲和日本。)

(2) We are specialized in the above business and recall that many years ago, considerable business was done with your country on such items. (我们专营上述业务，许多年前，我们同你们国家就上述商品做过大笔交易。)

(3) We shall be grateful if you will let us know whether you are interested in the above items. (贵方如能告诉我方你们是否对上述生意感兴趣，我们将深表感谢。)

(4) To give you a general idea of our products, we enclose a complete set of leaflets showing various products being handled by our corporation with detailed specifications and means of packing. (为使贵方对我公司所经营的产品有一个总体了解，现随函寄上我公司经营产品的小册子一套，内有关于产品规格及包装条件的详细说明。)

(5) You will be interested to know that for over 30 years we have been engaged in manufacturing electronic machinery of all specifications and exporting them to users all over the world, enjoying a good reputation. (贵方会乐意知悉，我公司制造各种规格的电子机械产品已有30余年历史，并一直向世界各地的客户出口，且享有良好声誉。)

(6) Thank you for your letter of July 25, in which you expressed your willingness to enter into business relations with us. (感谢贵方7月25日来信表示愿意同我们建立业务关系。)

(7) We are writing to you at the suggestion of our Commercial Counselor' s Office of the Embassy in your country. (经我方驻贵国大使馆商务参赞处的介绍，特致函贵方。)

(8) We avail ourselves of this opportunity to write to you and see if we can establish business relations with you. (我们利用此机会致函贵方以了解可否与贵方建立贸易关系。)

(9) We owe your name and address to the Paris Chamber of Commerce, through whom we have learnt you are importers of table-cloth. (承蒙巴黎商会告知贵公司名称和地址，并得知贵公司是桌布进口商。)

(10) We have the pleasure to introduce ourselves to you with the hope that we may have an opportunity of cooperating with you in your business extension. (我们有幸自荐，盼望有机会与贵方合作，扩展业务。)

(11) As you are one of the leading importers in camera, we have pleasure in contacting you in the hope of establishing business relations. (鉴于贵方是照相机的主要进口商之一，特此联系，盼能建立业务关系。)

(12) We are willing to enter into business with your firm on the basis of equality, mutual ben-

efit and exchanging what one has for what one needs.（我们愿在平等互利、互通有无的基础上与贵公司建立业务关系。）

Exercises

1. Put the following English phrases into Chinese or Chinese phrases into English.

(1) avail ourself of

(2) owe one' s name and address to

(3) on the recommendation of

(4) the line of business

(5) in the hope of

(6) 建立业务关系

(7) 在平等互利的基础上

(8) 告知

(9) 商会

(10) 专营

2. Multiple choice.

(1) We are sending you the samples ________ requested.

a. be　b. are　c. as　d. for

(2) We have been specializing ________ this line for many years.

a. in　b. on　c. at　d. with

(3) We ________ of this opportunity to approach you for the establishment of trade relations with you.

a. take　b. avail　c. avail ourselves　d. take ourselves

(4) We owe your name and address ________ Italian Commercial Bank who has informed us that you are in the market ________ table-cloths.

a. from/for　b. to/with　c. from/with　d. to/for

(5) We now have a good demand ________ the captioned item and therefore write to you in the hope of establishing trade relations.

a. for　b. with　c. on　d. in

(6) As the item ________ the scope of our business activities, we shall be pleased to establish direct trade relations with you.

a. lies within　b. fall within　c. come under　d. be within

(7) In order to obtain the needed information, the inquirer should simply, clearly and concisely write ________ he wants to know.

a. that　b. so　c. what　d. because of

(8) Your letter of May 9th addressed to our Nanjing Branch Office has ________ to us for attention and reply.

a. been passed on　b. passed　c. passed on　d. been past through

(9) In case you need more information ________ our business status, we shall be glad to an-

swer your inquiries at any time.

a. about b. in c. to d. with

(10) We take the liberty of writing to you ________ a view to establishing business relations with you.

a. in b. with c. to d. for

3. Translate the following sentences into English using the words or phrases in the brackets.

(1) 我方得悉贵公司名称，特此致函希望与贵方建立贸易关系。(establish relations with)

(2) 本公司是专营出口中国工艺品的公司。(specialize in)

(3) 贵方如能合作，我方不胜感激。(appreciate)

(4) 随函附上我方价目表两份。(enclose)

(5) 我公司欲扩大和中国的商务联系。(expand one' s business relations)

(6) 我方经营该项业务已有多年。(line of business)

4. Translate the following letter into English.

经我方驻贵国大使馆商务参赞处介绍，今写信给贵方。我方冒昧向贵方介绍，我方经营丝绸商品，向日本和欧洲出口。我方专营上述业务，望与贵方建立直接的业务关系，因为贵方是丝绸产品的进口商。贵方如能告知我方贵方是否对上述商品生意抱有兴趣，我方将深表感谢。若有兴趣的话，请告知所需数量。

5. Write a letter as per the following particulars.

You are asked to write a letter to a foreign company for establishing business relations. The letter should cover at least the following points.

(1) What information have you got about the foreign company?

(2) What is your desire?

(3) What is your business scope?

Supplementary Reading

Part A

In international trade, the importer is usually in one country and the exporter in another. They are separated sometimes by thousands of miles. Establishing business relations is the first step in the transaction in foreign trade.

Writing letters to new customers for establishment of relations is a common practice in business communications. To establish business relations with prospective dealers is one of the vitally important measures either for a newly established firm or an old one that wishes to enlarge its business scope and turnover. There are several channels through which importers and exporters can get to know each other. Generally speaking, this type of letter begins by telling the address how his or her name is known. Then, some general information should be given as to the lines of business being handled. The writer should state simply, clearly and concisely what he can sell or what he expects to buy.

Any letter of this nature received must be answered in full without the least delay and with courtesy so as to create goodwill and leave a good impression on the reader. The first impression counts heavily. Make sure that your letter follows the standard format and that it is neatly typed and error-free. To firms engaged in foreign trade, business connections are valuable. Therefore, traders must not only do everything possible to consolidate their established relations with firms having previous business but also develop and revitalize their trade by searching for new connections from time to time.

Notes

1. transaction 交易
2. prospective 预期的
3. turnover 营业额
4. courtesy 谦恭
5. consolidate 巩固
6. revitalize 使有新的活力

Part B

Most people today associate marketing with selling. Yet, the act of selling is only one part of the overall marketing activities of the firm. The task of providing products that satisfy consumers' wants forms the basis for our current marketing systems. Marketing is an exchange process between buyers and sellers, the purpose of which is to satisfy the buyer' s needs and wants through the purchase of the seller' s products.

This marketing concept evolved over the years, developing as American business matured. Initially, production-oriented American business assumed that people would buy whatever was efficiently produced. This concept gradually evolved into a sales-oriented approach in which firms generally depended on effective sales approaches to stimulate consumer demand for a product. Today' s marketing-oriented philosophy focuses on a firm' s desire to increase sales while anticipating and satisfying consumer needs. Progressive businesses today are much more consumer-oriented than firms have been in the past.

The marketing mix consists of four variables—product, price, distribution (or place), and promotion. The product variable encompasses its physical attributes. Pricing involves the marketing manager, who establishes each product' s price as well as overall pricing policies. Getting that product to the right place at the right time is the distribution variable. The promotion variable increases demand by communicating information to potential customers via personal selling, advertising, publicity, and sales promotion.

Firms must carefully consider the role of the sales force in their promotional program or promotional aspect of the marketing mix. A firm has to decide if a sales force is a viable direct-marketing tool; and if so, which types of selling activities optimally promote its products. The different levels of relationship marketing (transaction selling, relationship selling, and partnering) allow salespeople to create customer loyalty. In this manner, they can keep today' s customers while generating new customers for tomorrow.

The new consultative selling requires the salesperson to take on the roles of a team leader, business consultant, and long-term ally. By performing these three roles the salesperson can reduce the relationship gap so the customer is satisfied with doing business with the seller.

Part C

Levels of Relationship Marketing

What type of relationships should an organization have with its customers? Is the cost of keeping a relationship worth it? To answer these questions, let' s define the three general levels of selling relationships with customers:

Transaction selling: customers are sold to and not contacted again.

Relationship selling: the seller contacts customers after the purchase to determine if they are satisfied and have future needs.

Partnering: the seller works continually to improve its customers' operations, sales, and profits.

Most organizations focus solely on the single transaction with each customer. When you go to McDonald' s and buy a hamburger, that' s it. You never hear from them again unless you return for another purchase. The same thing happens when you go to a movie, rent a video, open a bank checking account, visit the grocery store, or have your clothes cleaned. Each of these examples involves low-priced, low-profit products. Also involved are a large number of customers who are geographically dispersed. This makes it very difficult and quite costly to contact customers. The business is forced to use transactional marketing.

Relationship marketing focuses on the transaction—making the sale—along with follow-up and service after the sale. The seller contacts the customer to ensure satisfaction with the purchase. The Cadillac Division of General Motors contacts each buyer of a new Cadillac to determine the customer' s satisfaction with the car. If that person is not satisfied, General Motors works with the retailer selling the car to make sure the customer is happy.

Partnering is a phenomenon of the 1990s. Businesses' growing concern over the competition not only in America but also internationally revitalized their need to work closely with important customers. The familiar 80/20 principle states that 80 percent of sales often come from 20 percent of a company' s customers. Organizations now realize the need to identify their most important customers and designate them for their partnering programs. The organization' s best salespeople are assigned to sell and service these customers. Let' s take a closer look at partnering since it is becoming so important to organizations.

Part D

Exercising Empathy for Employees and Customers

Although the concept of happy employees leading to happy customers is not new, it is experiencing a resurgence in many different industries. For example, call centers are allowing seasoned employees to work at home while a grocery chain is giving employees a profit-sharing plan that rewards them for excellent customer service.

Companies are finding creative ways to help employees identify with customers. USSA, an insurance agency for the military, provides new employees with MREs (meals ready to eat) during orientation so they will better understand the lifestyle of the members they serve.

Cabela's, an outdoor outfitter, encourages employees to use products they sell by loaning items free of charge in exchange for writing reviews on a company system. The loans are good perks for employees, and they help staff understand the issues customers may have with the products.

At Four Seasons Hotels, employees receive free overnight stays and meals at the hotel for themselves and a guest. They gain a customer's respective on the hotel, but they also grade the hotel on various services.

They companies exercising empathy for employees and customers believe their customer service helps set them apart from other organizations.

Succeeding Against the Odds

I developed my communication skills as a technique of survival. I was born in poverty and spent two years on the welfare rolls, and I learned early that I had to communicate or die. And so I talked my way out of poverty—I communicated my way to the top ...

I read and re-read books on self-improvement, success and communication. The most important lesson I learned from these books is what I call "other focusing". This means, among other things, that if we want to communicate with employees, managers, and even competitors we must ask ourselves not what we want but what they want.

This rule made me a millionaire. For the only way I got to where I am today was by persuading thousands of blacks and whites, some of whom were very prejudiced, that the only way they could get what they wanted was by helping me get what I wanted. All the law and prophecy of communication theory can be found in that formula.

Unit 3

Status Enquiries

资信调查

3.1 Introduction（简介）

资信调查在国际贸易中既必要，也十分重要。外贸企业在与从未进行过交易的国外企业做买卖前，必须先了解对方的资信状况。资信调查在国际贸易中是相互的，无论是对出口商还是对进口商来说，在进行交易前需要互相提供可供资信调查的第三方的姓名（公司名）及详细地址。这里的第三方就是商贸活动中的资信证明人。值得注意的是对方往往会挑选为其说好话的证明人，因而，应该谨慎对待来自这些证明人的报告。

资信调查主要需要获得如下信息：① 财务状况（Financial position）；② 信用（Credit）；③ 声誉（Reputation）；④ 业务做法（Business methods）；⑤ 管理能力（Management capacities）。

调查资信的方法有多种，应用最广泛的是通过银行的调查。不过，银行一般不直接回答私人查询。因此，如果卖方想得到资信证明书，就必须到自己的银行，借助于该银行来获取未来顾客的资信情况。其他的调查渠道还包括：① 商会或有关的行业工会（Chamber of commerce）；② 咨询机构（Enquiry agencies）；③ 我国的驻外商务机构（Chinese commerce agencies in foreign countries）；④ 外国的驻华商务机构（Foreign countries' commerce agencies in China）；⑤ 国内外咨询公司（Enquiry companies at home and abroad）。

资信调查信函应明确表明要求并对提供的资信情况表示感谢，同时，要保证对此进行保密。此外，为了方便提供情况者，通常可附上写明回信地址和贴好邮票的信封。

在回复这类查询信函时，回信应冠以“机密并亲启”（Private & Confidential）字样。信中应有一个说明，即此情报须保密，而且只针对接受人。不要提及被查询的公司名称，用“有关公司”“该公司”“被谈论的公司”等更安全的字样，尤其是当证明报告提供不利的信息时。除了如实提供情况和提出建议外，回信中一般还包括“对所提供情况不负任何责任”这类句子以避免可能的麻烦。

在获得调查信息后，调查者要对被调查者进行冷静、客观的分析。分析时，应遵循“3C”原则，即分析调查者的品行（Conduct）、能力（Capacity）及资本（Capital）情况。

品行是指被调查者的信誉程度和可靠性，能力是指被调查者的经营能力、管理技能和有关综合指数，资本是指被调查者的资产、盈利情况、清偿债务的能力及资金的周转速度。根据“3C”分析，最后做出客观判断：被调查者的资信状况及是否有必要与之进行交易。

因为查询资信的信函是求人帮助，所以要用礼貌和感激的语言书写。在收到信息后，无论是有利的或是不利的，必须回寄一封感谢信表示信息已经收到。这是一般应有的礼貌。

3.2 Writing Skills（写作技巧）

资信调查信函的写作步骤及常见表达方式如下所示：

写作步骤	表达方式
1. 直截了当地说明写信的意图	Our prospective customers... have given us your name as a banking reference.（我们的潜在客户……把您定为他们的银行证明人。）
	... have referred us to you that... for information concerning their standing.（……公司介绍您的目的是让我们了解他们的资信情况。）
	They state that they have done business with you for the past two years and have given us the name of your company as a reference.（他们向我们表示，他们在过去的两年中与您有过生意来往，并且指定贵公司作为他们的证明人。）
2. 说明想要调查的细节和原因	We should be very grateful to you for any information you can give us about their reputation and credit-worthiness.（我们非常感激您能给予我们有关他们的声誉和资信情况的情报。）
	We should be obliged if you would let us know ...（如果您能告知我们……我们将不胜感激。）
	Since it is our first transaction with this firm, we should greatly appreciate your advice as to what limit you consider them safe.（因为这是我们与该公司所做的首笔生意，所以非常感激您告知我们您对该公司可信任程度的意见。）
3. 保证保守秘密	Any information we receive from you, of course, will be held in strict confidence.（我们会严加保密您给的任何信息。）
	We thank you for your courtesy and assure you of strict confidence.（我们很感谢您的友好，并向您保证严守秘密。）
	For your convenience in replying, a questionnaire is enclosed, together with a stamped, addressed envelope.（为了便于您答复，特附上一张调查表和写好地址的信封。）

回复资信调查信函的写作步骤及常见表达方式如下所示：

写作步骤	表达方式
1. 感谢对方的信任，表达愿意提供信息的意愿	Thank you for your inquiry about the business standing of... we are pleased to supply you with the following information.（感谢贵方查询有关……的资信情况，我们愿意给您以下情报。）
	We can thoroughly recommend the firm you inquired about.（我们完全可以推荐贵方所打听的公司。）
	We welcome the opportunity to report favorably on....（很高兴有这次机会来报告有关……的实际情况。）
2. 有利的答复	In all these years our relations with them have been consistently and entirely satisfactory.（这些年，我们与他们的业务联系一直非常令人满意。）
	We welcome this opportunity to assure you of our complete confidence in...（很高兴有这样的机会向您保证……受到我们的完全信赖。）
	After some difficulty during the first year, the firm has met its liabilities regularly and punctually.（度过开头一年的困境之后，此公司运行正常，而且按时履行义务。）

（续）

写作步骤	表达方式
3. 不利的答复	Our own experience with them has not been satisfactory.（我们与他们打交道的经历并不令人满意。）
	Recent difficulties that seem to be due to bad management have resulted in considerable borrowing at a high rate of interest.（最近一段时间，也许是因为经营不善所带来的困难，公司借入了大量高利率资金。）
	Our records show that some of their accounts have been outstanding for long periods.（我方资料表明，他们的一些账款长期未曾结清。）
4. 希望对方对所提供的报告保密	Please consider this information for which we accept no responsibility as strictly confidential.（请贵方对此答复严格保密，我们对此不承担责任。）
	We offer this information in strict confidence and with good faith.（确信会对我们所给的答复严格保密。）
	We hope that we have been of assistance to you, and that you will recognize the importance of keeping this communication strictly private.（希望这些对贵方有用，也望贵方理解保守此秘密的重要性。）

3.3 Specimen Letters（样函）

Letter 1: Making inquiry through one's own bank

Dear Sirs,

We have received a large order from Messrs E. A. Sheen & Co., P. O. Box123, Karachi. We would therefore appreciate it if you would provide us information about the financial condition and business standing[1] of the previously mentioned firm.

The reference we have obtained is the Royal Bank, Karachi. Will you please be good enough to obtain for us the information we need?

Any information that you may provide us will be treated in strict confidence[2].

We thank in advance.

Yours faithfully,

Li Xingdong

Letter 2: A favorable reply to the above

Dear Mr. Li,

Referring to your letter of June 25, 2005, we wish to inform you that we have obtained the information you require from the Royal Bank, Karachi Branch.

The subject company was established in January 1982 with a capital of Stg. 10,000. Do business as importers and exporters in various kinds of Sewing Machines. Their balance sheets[3] of recent years enclosed will show you that their import business in this line[4] has been managed and operated[5] under satisfactory condition.

Please note that the information is provided with strict confidence and without any responsibility whatsoever on the part of this Bank.

Yours faithfully,
Wu Dongfeng

Letter 3: An unfavorable reply to the above

Dear Mr. Li,

The subject company you inquired about in your letter of June 25, 2005, from the information we have obtained from Royal Bank, Karachi Branch, we are sorry to say, has been unsatisfactory.

The company still owes an amount of money for a purchase made a year ago. They can not duly clear off[6] their balance outstanding[7].

May we ask you to treat this information as strictly confidential without responsibility on this bank or any of its officers.

Yours faithfully,
Wu Dongfeng

Letter 4: Making inquiry through a company as a trade reference[8]

Dear Sirs,

The subject firm in Newcastle with which you are now doing business has written to us that they are the leading importers in the place dealing in chemicals, and that they now wish to switch to us for the supply of the similar item, and your names were given to us as a reference. As we have no business relations with them before, we should be most grateful for any information you may obtain for us.

1. How long have you been in business relations with the company?
2. What credit limit[9] have you placed on their account?
3. How promptly are their terms of payment[10] met?
4. What amount is currently outstanding?

Any information you may give us will be treated strictly in confidence.

Sincerely yours,
Li Peichun

Letter 5: A favorable reply to the above

Dear Mr. Li,

In reply to your letter of August 15, 2005, we are pleased to tell you the subject company has been maintaining business relations with us for the past twenty years, during which they have never failed to meet their obligation[11]. The credit report of recent years enclosed will show you that their import business in chemicals has been doing well.

We believe that they owe their reputable position among the local wholesalers[12] in their area to their steady and sincere way of conducting business[13].

Please note that the information is furnished at your request without any responsibility on our part and should be held strictly confidential.

Yours truly,
J. A. Richard
Encl: Credit report one copy

Letter 6: An unfavorable reply to the above

Dear Mr. Li,

We have completed our inquiry concerning the firm mentioned in your letter of August 15, 2005 and that we must advise you to consider their request with caution.

About a year ago, an action we brought against the firm by one of its suppliers for recovery of sums due[14], though payment was later recovered in full.

Our inquiries reveal that the firm' s difficulties would seem to be due to bad management and in particular to overtrading. Most of the firm' s suppliers either give only very short credit for limited sums, or make deliveries[15] on a cash basis[16].

This information is of course supplied in strict confidence.

Yours faithfully,
J. A. Richard

Letter 7: Making inquiry through one' s own bank

Dear Sirs,

Will you please be kind enough to obtain for us all information possible respecting the financial condition and business standing of Messrs. Toyoda & Co., of Yokohama?

As we are on the point of transacting some important business with them, we should like to know exactly how their credit stands. I shall feel under great obligation if you will advise me confidentially respecting the reputation they enjoy in this line.

Any information you may give me will, of course, be treated as strictly confidential.

Truly yours,
James

Letter 8: A favorable reply to the above

Dear Mr. James,

We inform you that we can give nothing but favorable information about the firm in question.

Though they had not been long established, they stand pretty well. They command considerable funds and an unlimited credit, and the executives are thorough business men. The firm enjoys the fullest respect and unquestionable confidence in the business world.

Please consider this information for which we accept no responsibility as strictly confidential.

Sincerely yours,

Peter

Notes to the specimen letters

1. financial condition and business standing 财务状况及商业信誉
2. treat in strict confidence 严格保密
3. balance sheet 资产负债表
4. in this line 在此行业
5. manage and operate 经营
6. clear off 结清（欠款）
7. balance outstanding 欠款余额
8. trade reference 商业证明人
9. credit limit 信用额度
10. terms of payment 付款方式，支付方式
11. meet one' s obligation 履行义务
12. wholesaler 批发商
13. steady and sincere way of conducting business 经营业务稳妥、诚实
14. recovery of sums due 追讨到期货款
15. make delivery 交货
16. on a cash basis 以现金形式

3.4 Focal Words（焦点词汇）

appeal

vi. **对……有吸引力，投其所好**

We think the superb workmanship as well as the novel design will appeal to your customers.（我们认为其新颖的设计及高超的工艺会吸引贵方的顾客。）

We trust you will find that its design and color will appeal very much to your market.（其设计及色彩定会受到贵方市场的热烈欢迎。）

appealing：*adj.* **吸引人的，诱人的**

We assure you that every buyer will like the appealing appearance of the goods.（我们保证买主都会喜爱此货物的诱人外观。）

confirm

vt. **确认，证实；保兑**

We confirm (receipt of) your letter dated May 28, 2015. (2015年5月28日来信收悉。)

We hereby confirm having sold to you the following goods on terms and conditions as specified below... (兹确认已按如下条件售给贵方下列货物……)

confirmation: *n.* **确认，证实**

We thank you for your immediate confirmation of our order. (谢谢贵方迅速确认了我方订货。)

If you find our offer agreeable, please cable us your acceptance for our confirmation. (如认为我方报盘合适，请电告接受，以便我方确认。)

interest

n. **兴趣，关心；利益；利息**

Please let us have your inquiry in case of interest. (如有兴趣，请寄来询盘。)

Canned goods are of special interest to us. (我们对罐头食品特别感兴趣。)

It would be to your interest to accept our offer because you can hardly obtain similar supplies at our figure elsewhere. (接受我方报盘对贵方有利，因为贵方不可能按我方价格从别处购得类似商品。)

We are convinced that we shall be able to find a solution in the interest of both parties. (我们相信，我们会找到一种对双方都有利的解决方法。)

We charge interest on sums outstanding after 30 days. (超过30天不付的款项，我们要收利息。)

The rate of interest has gone up as high as 12% per annum. (年利率已经提高到12%。)

vt. **使……感兴趣**

What interested us most was the exquisite craftsmanship of jade-caving workers. (最使我们感兴趣的是玉雕工人的精湛技艺。)

share

n. **份额**

His company now commands a large share of trade in the European market. (现在他的公司在欧洲市场的贸易中占有很大的份额。)

There are nine major passenger car manufactures in Japan continuously competing for large shares in the world market. (日本有9家主要的小客车制造商，它们为在世界市场上取得大的份额而不断竞争。)

vt. **分担，分享**

For friendship let us share the price difference on an equal basis. (为了友谊，让我们平均负担价格差额吧!)

All the stockholders will share the profits and losses. (全部损益由股东共同承担。)

supply

n. **供应**

Present supply of wood oil is quite sufficient. (当前桐油的供应很充足。)

Supply now exceeds demand on our market. (现在我地市场供过于求。)

vt. **供应，提供**

We can supply all kinds of leather shoes. （我们可以供应各类皮鞋。）

This proforma invoice is supplied for applying for the necessary import license. （本形式发票是为申请必要的进口许可证而提供的。）

3.5 Useful Sentences（实用语句）

（1） We shall appreciate it if you will let us know their financial position. （如能告知该公司的财务状况，我们将不胜感激。）

（2） We shall appreciate it if you will give us your frank opinion on these points regarding the company. （如能坦率告知我方有关该公司的情况，将不胜感激。）

（3） Will you please be good enough to obtain for us the information possible respecting the financial standing and modes of business of ABC Company?（你们能好心为我们提供有关 ABC 公司财务状况和经营方式的资料吗？）

（4） We should appreciate it if you would provide us with reliable information respecting Messrs of J. C. Maxwell Company. We wish to know if their financial standing is considered strong. （如能为我们提供有关 J. C. 马克士威公司的可靠信息，并告知我们该公司的财务运作是否很强，我们将不胜感激。）

（5） The HP Company is now offering to present us in the sale of our Sewing Machines, and has referred us to your bank for detailed information about its credit standing, business capacity and character. （惠普公司提出要作为我公司代理，销售我们的缝纫机，并介绍我公司向贵银行了解该公司的信用、业务能力和声誉的详细情况。）

（6） The corporation trades principally in electric and electronic commodities with America and Japan. We have a high regard for their business ability and financial standing. Their reputation here is decidedly good. We hope that you will treat it as confidential. （该公司主要与美国和日本开展电器和电子商品贸易。我们对他们的经营能力和财务资信有很高的评价。该公司的名声在此地非常好。我们希望贵方把它作为机密处理。）

（7） We are at present negotiating with the firm named below about the question of agency. They have given us your name as a reference. Will you please inform us frankly whether you consider a credit to the extent of USD5, 000, 000 as a risk?（我们正在与下述公司协商有关代理问题。他们介绍你们公司为他们的资信证明人。请你们坦率地告诉我们，给该公司最多 500 万美元的信贷是否有风险？）

（8） We are glad to enter into business relations with you and hope you can give us the names of two banks as a reference. We hope to negotiate further for the specific transactions. （我们很高兴与贵公司建立业务关系，并希望你们能提供两个银行资信证明人，以便进一步洽谈具体业务。）

（9） We have much pleasure in stating that they are a small but highly respectable firm, and very old and valued customers of ours. （我们很乐于说明：该公司虽小，但信用颇好，对本公司来说，是交易甚久且最重要的一位顾客。）

（10） We regret our inability to assist you in this matter. （很遗憾我们对此实在无法提供帮

助，敬请原谅。)

(11) Please note that this information is furnished without any responsibility on our part and should be held strictly confidential. (请注意，我们对所提供的材料不负任何责任，并请对该材料严格保密。)

(12) The above information is given confidentially and without responsibility on this bank. (我方银行提供的上述信息是绝对机密的，且不承担任何责任。)

(13) 信用查询。

As we are on the point of transacting some important business with them, we should like to know exactly how their credit standing is. (因为本公司正要与该公司进行某项重要交易，所以希望事先准确了解该公司的信用状况。)

I shall feel under great obligation if you will advise me confidentially respecting the reputation they enjoy among your neighbors and correspondents. (恳请惠予告知该公司的同行与顾客对该公司的评价，本人将不胜感激。)

Any information you may give me will, of course, be treated as strictly confidential. (对于贵公司所提供的情报，无论内容如何，我们一定会严守秘密。)

It would give us great pleasure to be able to render you a similar service should opportunity occur. (如有机会，我们将乐于为贵公司提供同样的服务，作为对这次协助的报答。)

(14) 一般信用情报。

We are informed: The company is a newly-formed corporation, having been chartered in September of 1946 with an authorized capital of USD50, 000 with only USD500 recorded as having been paid in. (据我们所得到的情报：该公司为新创立的公司，1946 年 9 月创立时，其登记资本额为 5 万美元，但股东实缴金额仅为 500 美元。)

This is a strictly confidential response to a request made by the firm. (这是对该公司要求的回函，必须严格保密。)

Any statement on the part of this bank or any of its officers as to the standing of any person, firm or corporation, is given as a mere matter of opinion for which no responsibility, in any way, is to attach to this bank or any of its officers. (任何有关个人、公司以及其他任何组织的信用状况，本银行或本行职员所提供的情报无论内容如何，仅供参考。对此本银行或本行职员不负任何责任。)

(15) 信用良好的情报。

We inform you that we can give nothing but favorable information about the firm in question. (我们只能向您报告，该公司在各方面均博得好评。)

The firm enjoys the fullest respect and unquestionable confidence in the business world. (该公司在实业界颇受尊敬，信誉很高。)

In reply to your inquiry of the 1st inst., we inform you that our business relations with the firm have hitherto been most satisfactory. (贵方于本月 1 日发来的查询函收悉。本公司与该公司的交易关系到目前为止颇为顺利、愉快。特此函复。)

Replying to your letter of yesterday' s date, we are happy to inform you that the firm referred to enjoys an unlimited credit. (昨天接到贵函，我们很乐意向您报告有关查询事项。该公司博得

客户极大信赖，特此复函。）

（16）信用不佳的情报。

We are sorry we are not able to give a precise information you ask.（我们无法向贵公司提供您所需要的确切情报，对此，我们深感遗憾。）

We regret our inability to tell you anything positive concerning the firm mentioned in your letter of the 30th ult.（对于上月30日贵函所要查询的公司，我们实在无法报告确切情况，甚为遗憾。）

Exercises

1. Put the following English phrases into Chinese or Chinese phrases into English.

（1）credit standing

（2）financial status

（3）be in strict confidence

（4）modes of business

（5）open an account

（6）小额交易

（7）过额贸易

（8）商业证明

（9）定额货款

（10）拖延付款

2. Multiple choice.

（1）For information ________ our ________ we refer you to Bank of China, Shanghai Branch.

a. regards/credit standing　　b. as to/standing credit

c. involving/credit standard　　d. concerning/credit standing

（2）We should be grateful if you would say ________ they are likely ________ a credit up to USD10, 000.

a. what/to be reliable for　　b. if/to be reliable at

c. whether/to be reliable for　　d. that/to be reliable of

（3）We understand that you will treat this information as ________.

a. confidence　b. confident　c. confidential　d. confidently

（4）Any information you kindly give us will be treated in strict confidence and ________ on your part.

a. without any responsibility　　b. hasn' t any responsibility

c. is no responsibility　　d. is not to have responsibility

（5）Will you please inform us, ________, of the extent of their resources and also as to their reputation?

a. with confidence　　b. in confidence

c. as confidential　　d. of confidentially

(6) We shall appreciate ________ us ________ an opinion as to the credit standing, respectability and responsibility of the following firm.

a. your providing/with　　b. provided/by

c. to provide/with　　d. your provision to/by

(7) Will you please let us know ________ your experience ________ in your dealing with him?

a. how/are　　b. what/has been

c. which/is　　d. that/have had

(8) This firm is a ________ private company of import and export merchants, ________ in 1981.

a. high/registered　　b. height of/to register

c. highly/registered　　d. highest/to register

(9) We ________ consider the said firm quite reliable for ________ engagement as you mention.

a. should/such an　　b. with/such as

c. shall/such a　　d. would/such like

3. Translate the following sentences into English using the words or phrases in the brackets.

(1) 将与我们进行贸易往来的那家商行要我们向贵行了解有关他们的财务状况与信誉。(business standing)

(2) 你若能对上述公司的财务状况和可靠性提出意见，我们当不胜感激。(financial status and reliability)

(3) 就我们所知，他们的财状状况良好。(financial standing)

(4) 该公司声誉好，资金储备雄厚。(financial reserve)

(5) 我们劝贵方与该商行进行业务往来时务必谨慎。(deal with)

(6) 对贵方所提供的任何资料，我们都予以保密。(treat as confidential)

4. Translate the following letter into English.

我们正在考虑提供信用证给×××公司。在过去几个月的现金交易中，我们对他们了解不多。如果您能够查明他们的财务和信用情况，我们将非常感激。他们只向我们提供他们的银行——×××银行作为证明人。银行估计他们的月订货量大概是800英镑。希望您能提供帮助。

5. Write a letter as per the following particulars.

You are asked to write a letter to the Commercial Bank in your city. The letter should cover at least the following points.

(1) Ask them something about ABC Company for their financial standing.

(2) What about ABC Company' s capacity of doing business?

Supplementary Reading

Part A

Before a writer corresponds with a new customer, first, he should do credit investigations, such as capital, business activity, and financial conditions. Status enquiries are those written communications in which traders request information concerning the financial position, credit, reputation, and business methods of other firms. In business, it is of the utmost importance to obtain all the information possible respecting the firm one is about to enter into relations with.

There are various ways of obtaining such information. Instead of applying to a business friend, traders sometimes apply to banks, chambers of commerce or enquiry agencies. The information obtained from a bank or from a chamber of commerce is generally reliable. However, a bank will not give information direct to an unknown trader unless the enquiry is from one of its fellow banks. Therefore, when taking up a bank reference, the trader must do so through its own bank.

Status enquiries are generally headed "Confidential" or "Private and Confidential". These words are also written on the envelope.

Notes

1. correspond 通信
2. utmost 最大可能的
3. chambers of commerce 商务部
4. take up 从事

Part B

Ethics and social responsibility are hot topics for managers. Ethical behavior pertains to values of right and wrong. Ethical decisions and behavior are typically guided by a value system. For an individual manager, the ability to make correct ethical choices will depend on both individual and organizational characteristics. An important individual characteristic is one's level of moral development. Corporate culture is an organizational characteristic that influences ethical behavior.

Corporate social responsibility concerns a company's values toward society. How can organizations be good corporate citizens? The model for evaluating social performance uses four criteria: economic, legal, ethical, and discretionary.

Social responsibility in business means profitably serving employees and customers in an ethical and lawful manner. Extra costs can accrue because a firm takes socially responsible action, but this is a part of doing business in today's society, and it pays in the long run.

What should an individual base her or his values upon? Could the Golden Rule serve as a universal, practical, helpful standard for salespeople's conduct? What about your ethical and moral conduct?

Salespeople and managers realize that their business should be conducted in an ethical manner. They must be ethical in dealing with their salespeople, their employers, and their customers. Ethical standards and guidelines for sales personnel must be developed, supported, and policed. In the future, ethical selling practices will be even more important to conducting business profitably. Techniques for improving social responsiveness include leadership, codes of ethics, ethical structures, whistle-blowing, and establishing control systems. Finally, research suggests that socially responsible organizations perform as well as—and often better than—organizations that are not socially responsible.

Part C

Conflict of Interest?

The real estate salesperson assured the young couple that she would work hard to find them the right house. "Consider me your scout," she said. "I' ll find you the best house for the least money." The couple was reassured, and on the way home they talked about their good fortune. They had a salesperson working just for them. With prices so high, it was nice to think they had professional help on their side.

The family selling the house felt the same way. They carefully chose the broker because, they observed, with home prices all over the lot these days, they hoped a good salesperson might win them several thousand dollars more. They had another reason to choose carefully: At today' s prices, the 6 percent sales commission is a lot of money. "If we have to pay it," they reasoned, "we' re better off paying it to the best salesperson."

It happens all the time, and it can have serious consequences. How can both parties expect the best deal? How can a salesperson promise the seller the most for the money and then make the same promise to the buyer?

In the same vein, how can a salesperson whose commission rises or falls with the price of the house being sold be expected to cut into her income? Isn' t her total allegiance with the person paying her?

Confusion of this sort has existed in the marketplace for so long that critics are sometimes confounded that regulators haven' t made greater efforts to clarify matters.

Two explanations are sometimes offered. First, it is more a human than a legal problem; even if warned, buyers will continue to assume that salespeople work solely for them, rather than for the seller, who pays the salesperson a commission.

Second, a good salesperson sometimes can come close to serving the desires of both parties. The point is arguable, but the justification offered is that the salesperson' s compromises may be necessary to save a sale from falling through.

A somewhat similar situation exists in the stock market, where many small investors view their stockbroker as a confidant and adviser.

Part D

Truth Can Be Spoken in Different Ways

One Iranian told a fable of an ancient king who had an ominous dream. In the dream the king saw himself aged and afflicted, with decaying and falling teeth. Calling together his court astrologers for an interpretation, the shaken king heard the first say, "Your Majesty, I regret to tell you that the interpretation must be bad. The dream means that you will die within a year." In a rage the king threw the brash astrologer out of his court and turned to the second man.

The second astrologer said, "Your Majesty, it is good news, the very best. It means that all your programs and projects will live on after you, and all your sons and daughters will survive you." The king, who was old and knew he might die soon, nevertheless was pleased with this interpretation and richly rewarded the astrologer.

Four Ways to Say "Yes" Instead of "No"

"Yes, I want to help." Even if you have to say no personally, there is usually an alternative yes. By helping to solve someone's problem—say, by referring them to someone who might be able to help them—you keep the positive energy in motion.

"Yes, you can do better." Rather than say, "This is terrible," it is a lot more motivating to say, "You do such terrific work. I'm not sure this is up to your caliber."

"Yes, I see you." It only takes a minute to send a thank-you note or respond to an unsolicited resume.

"Yes, your talents lie elsewhere." Warren Buffet says that he's never fired anyone. He has just helped them to find the right job.

Unit 4 Enquiries and Replies 询盘及回复

4.1 Introduction（简介）

交易磋商（Business negotiation）是国际贸易业务中最重要的环节。交易磋商的一般程序分为“询盘”“发盘”“还盘”和“接受”四个环节。

询盘（Enquiry）又称询价，是指买方或卖方向对方询问以价格为中心的各种相关的交易条件，包括一般询价（General enquiry）和具体询价（Specific enquiry）。一般询价是指买方或卖方向对方索取商品目录、价目表样品等。具体询价则是指买方或卖方就指定商品要求对方发盘。

在国际贸易中，买方提出询盘是为得到所订货物的情况，如价格、目录、交货日期及其他条款。在询盘时，买方应认真考虑向哪些地区发出询盘以及在同一地区要与多少家供货商进行联系。

索取价格单或目录只需一句话即可，然而要求提供报价及其他条款可能需要较长的说明，而且这些说明必须清楚、准确。询盘时，无须用冗长和过分客气的词句。

第一次询盘，即发函的开头应先告知收信人你是如何得知他的姓名的，然后告知贵方自己的业务情况，如经营范围、所需数量、一般贸易条款及其他可能使供货人决定为你效劳的任何资料。

询盘必须简短、具体、有礼貌并且合理。而对询盘的回复，则应迅速、客气，并能对对方有所帮助。

4.2 Writing Skills（写作技巧）

询盘信函的写作步骤及常见表达方式如下所示：

写作步骤	表达方式
1. 说明信息来源（告知对方从何种渠道得知对方公司的情况）	Your name has been given us by the Chamber of Commerce/ the... Embassy/ the... bank in ...（我们从在……地方的商会/从……使馆/从……银行获悉贵方名称。）
	Your firm has been recommended to us by Bayer AG, with whom we have done business for many years.（多年来与我们有业务联系的拜耳股份公司将贵公司推荐给我们。）
	Messrs... of ... have given me your name as sole agents for...（在……的……公司向我们介绍了作为……独家代理的贵公司的名称。）
2. 直截了当地说明想要购买的货物	We are considering the purchase of...（我们打算购买……）
	We are interested in importing snooker tables but we need to have further details of the costs before making a final decision.（我们有兴趣进口台球桌，但在最后决定之前需要进一步了解有关价格的详细情况。）
	We are regular buyers of men' s knitwear.（我们是购买男用针织品的老客户。）

（续）

写作步骤	表达方式
3. 请求对方寄送目录、价格表和样品	Will you please send us your illustrated/ latest catalogue and price-list?（请贵方寄来带插图的/最新的产品目录和价格表。）
	We should like to receive a copy of your latest catalogue and full details of your export prices and terms of payment, together with samples.（我们非常希望获得贵公司的最新产品目录和有关出口价格、付款条件的详细材料以及样品。）
	Kindly let me have a description of your electric hedge trimmers.（请贵方寄来电动修剪机的说明书。）
4. 强调对方所报价格应合理和具有竞争性	If your quotation is really competitive ...（如果贵方报价具有竞争力……）
	Provided prices are right.（前提是价格便宜。）
	If your products and terms compare favorably with those of other suppliers, we shall send you an order.（如果贵公司的产品及条件与其他供货商相比有优势，我方就会下订单。）
5. 询问对方所能提供的折扣，写清你所能接受的支付条件和期望的交货时间	We should like to know if you allow discounts.（我们想知道，贵方是否给我们折扣。）
	Please let us have your lowest FOB prices, together with your terms of business, and state your best delivery date.（请告知贵公司最低离岸价和交易条件，并说明最早交货日期。）
	We require the goods delivery would be effected within six weeks of order.（我们要求在下订单后六周内供货。）
6. 表示订购货物的可能性	Will you please let us know by the 4th April so that we can place our order promptly?（请在4月4日前告知我们，以便我方及时下单订货。）
	Please let us know by return of post whether you would be interested in such an order.（请发信告知我们，贵方是否对这样的订单感兴趣。）

回复询盘信函的写作步骤及常见表达方式如下所示：

写作步骤	表达方式
1. 感谢对方的询价	Many thanks for your enquiry of ...（多谢贵方于……日的询价。）
	Thank you for your enquiry and for your interest in our products.（感谢贵方询价以及对我方产品的兴趣。）
	We thank you for your enquiry of ...（对贵方在……日的询价信深表感谢。）
2. 表示很高兴附寄……给对方	We are pleased to enclose ...（我们很高兴附寄给贵方……）
	We have pleasure in enclosing ...（我们很高兴附寄给贵方……）
	We are sending you our latest price-list and catalogue.（我们附寄给贵方我们的最新价格表和产品目录。）
3. 说明所能提供商品的详细信息及优点	We are confident you will find our products the finest on the market and considerably better than those of our competitors who supply your market at present.（我们确信，贵方将会认为我方产品是市场上最好的，大大优于竞争对手目前所供的产品。）
	The specimens sent will convince you of the excellent quality of our medical instruments.（寄去的样品会使贵方相信我方制造的医疗器械质量上乘。）

（续）

写作步骤	表达方式
4. 表明所提供的价格是合理的和具有竞争性的且说明实行价格的期限	This is the most favorable offer we can make and you will agree that none of our competitors can equal these terms.（这是我们能做到的最低报价，您会承认，在我们的竞争者中没有一家能提供与我们一样的报价。）
	Price is valid until Dec. 31.（这些价格至12月31日有效。）
	Subject to being unsold.（以未售出为前提。）
5. 阐明所能接受的付款条件和可能的交货期	Our terms of payment are cash on delivery.（我们的付款条件是货到付款。）
	We should require payment by banker's draft on receipt of our pro forma invoice.（我们要求在收到形式发票后通过银行汇票付款。）
	We can usually deliver within three weeks of receiving an order.（通常我们在收到订单后三个星期内就可供货。）
6. 希望客户对报价满意并能很快收到订单或希望未来长期开展交易	We hope you will find our quotation satisfactory and look forward to receiving your order.（我们希望贵方对我们的报价满意并期盼您的订货。）
	We look forward to doing business with you.（我们盼望与贵方洽谈业务。）

4.3 Specimen Letters（样函）

Letter 1: General enquiry

Dear Sirs,

We have been informed by the Bank of U. S. Commerce, New York, that you are one of the leading exporters of textiles in China, and that you wish to export pure silk garments to our market.

You will be pleased to note that our corporation is one of the leading importers of textile products, having over 30 years' history and high reputation[1].

We shall be able to give you considerable orders, if the quality of your products is fine and the prices are moderate. We would be obliged if you will send us some samples with the best terms[2] at your earliest convenience.

Yours faithfully,

VANCOUVER TEXTILES CORPORATION

Letter 2: A reply to the above

Dear Sirs,

We take pleasure to acknowledge receipt of your letter of January 20, from which we learn that you are interested in bringing silk garments to the New York market.

We are enclosing our quotation sheet[3] covering different sizes and colors of our pure silk garments that can be supplied from stock. We are also airmailing you two dozen sample garments in different sizes and colors. Delivery will be within 30 days after your placing an order to us. Payment of the purchase is to be effected by an irrevocable L/C at sight in our favor.

This offer is subject to your immediate reply which should reach us not later than the end of next month. The price will probably be changed once this particular offer has lapsed.

Yours faithfully,
CHINA NATIONAL TEXTILES IMP. & EXP. CORP.
SHANGHAI HOME TEXTILES BRANCH

Letter 3: A seller' s enquiry

Dear Sirs,

We are looking for companies who can help us distribute our products in new markets. We manufacture computer components. At present we export to Europe, but we would like to export to your country.

Please find enclosed our brochure, which gives details of our products.

We look forward to hearing from you.

Sincerely yours,
Jin Baicuan

Letter 4: A reply to the above

Dear Sirs,

We thank you for your enquiry of Dec. 12, 2004, as one of the largest computer companies in the Republic of Korea, we are interested in your computer components.

Please send us your latest CIF Pushan prices, together with your terms of payment, and the earliest delivery date.

Thank you in advance.

Sincerely yours,
Son Young

Letter 5: A specific enquiry

Dear Sirs,

We learn with pleasure from your letter of April 12, 2004 that you are exporters of Chinese blanket cover[4] and are willing to establish business relations with us.

At present, we are interested in blanket cover and shall be pleased if you will send us by airmail sample books and all necessary information on blanket cover, so as to acquaint us with[5] material and workmanship[6] of your supplies. Meanwhile, please quote us the lowest price CIF London, inclusive of our 3% commission, stating the earliest date of shipment.

Should your price be found competitive and delivery time acceptable, we shall place a large order with you.

Yours truly,
Leon Allen

Letter 6: A reply to the above

Dear Sirs,

Thank you very much for your letter of April 28, 2004, we are pleased to send you samples and all the necessary information on blanket cover under separate cover.

At your request,[7] we are pleased to make you an offer, subject to[8] your final confirmation, as follows:

Commodity: "Golden Cock" Brand Blanket Cover No. 21

Size: 180cm × 200cm

Color: All kinds of colors

Quantity: 1,000 pieces

Price: GBP20 each piece CIF London inclusive of 3% commission[9]

Shipment: During August/September

Payment: By 100% confirmed, irrevocable L/C in our favor payable by draft at sight to reach the sellers one month before shipment, and remain valid for negotiation in China till the 15th day after shipment[10].

As you will realize from the catalogue we sent you, our blanket cover is a perfect combination of warmth, softness and easy care. [11]We are sure that you can get benefit from[12] our products.

We look forward to your prompt reply.

Yours faithfully,
Baicu

Letter 7: A specific enquiry

Dear Sirs,

We are a leading dealer in waterproof garments in this city. Our customers have expressed interest in your raincoats and enquired about their quality.

Provided quality and price are satisfactory, so there are prospects of good sales here, but before placing a firm order we should be glad if you would send us, on fourteen day' s approval, a selection of men' s and women' s raincoats. Any of the items unsold at the end of the period, and which we decide not to keep as stock, would be returned at our expense.

We look forward to hearing from you soon.

Sincerely yours,
Anderson

Letter 8: A reply to the above

Dear Anderson,

Thank you for your letter of 10th March. We are gratified to receive your request for men' s and women' s raincoats on approval.

As we have not previously done business together, perhaps you will kindly agree to supply either the usual trade references, or the name of a bank to which we may refer. As soon as these enquiries are satisfactorily settled, we shall be happy to send you the items you mention in your letter.

We sincerely hope this will be the beginning of a long and pleasant business association. We shall do our best to make it so.

Best wishes,

Mary

Notes to the specimen letters

1. high reputation 信誉良好
2. with the best terms 以优惠条件
3. quotation sheet 报价单
4. blanket cover 被罩
5. acquaint sb. with sth. 使某人了解、熟悉某事
6. material and workmanship 材料及工艺
7. at one' s request 应某人的请求
8. be subject to 须经，以……为条件
9. inclusive of 3% commission 包括3%的佣金
10. By 100% confirmed, irrevocable L/C in our favor payable by draft at sight to reach the sellers one month before shipment, and remain valid for negotiation in China till the 15th day after shipment. 以贵方为受益人的100%保兑的、不可撤销的信用证，凭即期汇票支付，信用证必须在装运前一个月开到对方，并在装船后15天内在中国议付有效。
11. a perfect combination of warmth, softness and easy care 柔软暖和、使用方便
12. get benefit from... 从……获利

4.4 Focal Words（焦点词汇）

compare

vt. & *vi.* 比较

If you compare our products with theirs, you will agree that our price is not high at all. （如果拿我们的产品同他们的产品相比较，你们就会知道我们的价格根本不高。）

Your price of tea sets compares unfavorably with that of other origins. （贵方茶具价格高于其他公司茶具的价格。）

comparison: *n.* 比较

If you make a comparison between the two samples, you will see which is of better quality. （如将两种商品做一比较，您就会知道哪种质量较好。）

These good qualities are characteristic of our tea sets and make those of other origins pale by comparison. （这些优良品质是我方茶具所独有的，比较起来使其他产品大为逊色。）

compete

vi. 竞争

Japan competes in textiles against Britain. （日本在纺织品方面与英国竞争。）

We have to compete with a number of major producers here. （我们必须同许多本地的大生产商竞争。）

competent: *adj.* 有能力的

You should select competent workers to deal with those buyers. （你们应该挑选有能力的人员去应付那些买主。）

We are fully competent for the sales promotion of your products here. （我们完全有能力在此地为贵方推销商品。）

competition: *n.* 竞争

Competition is getting keener in the cotton market. （棉花市场的竞争渐趋激烈。）

If you would reduce the prices to meet the competition, please cable us immediately. （如为了应付这场竞争而愿意减价，请立即电告。）

credit

n. 信用，信誉；信贷，赊欠；记入贷方

We should like to know exactly how their credit stands. （我们想确切地知道他们的信用情况。）

Our products are in high credit with the customers in Australia. （我方产品在澳大利亚客户中享有盛誉。）

Please let us know whether this firm is likely to be reliable for credit up to USD5, 000. （请告知该商号在赊欠达 5000 美元的情况下是否可靠。）

We shall be happy to supply you with goods on credit. （我们乐意赊给贵方货物。）

Letter of Credit 信用证

regular

adj. 经常的

If your prices are competitive, our company will be pleased to place regular orders with you. （如果贵方价格有竞争性，我公司乐意经常向贵方订货。）

As your purchases are regular and numerous, it would be advisable for you to open a revolving L/C in our favor. （由于贵方多次大量购货，最好给我方开来循环信用证。）

sell

v. 卖；出售

The rest of the goods will be sold off at greatly reduced prices. （剩下的货物将大幅度削价出售。）

To our regret, we have to inform you of our inability to accept your order as the goods have now been sold out. （很遗憾，我们不得不告知贵方，由于该货现已售完，我方不能接受贵方订单。）

seller: *n.* 卖主，卖方；出售的货物

The seller assumes no liability hereunder for its failure to make shipments. （卖方不承担如下不能交货的责任。）

We believe that you will find our new camera a very good seller at the above competitive price.（我们相信，你们会发现我方新型照相机若按上述竞争性价格出售会是一种抢手货。）

4.5 Useful Sentences（实用语句）

（1）We have an importer enquiry for woolen blankets and would like to obtain a catalogue, price-list together with the samples as soon as possible.（我们是一家进口商，询问有关羊毛毯的情况。如能尽快向我方提供产品目录、价格表以及样品，我们将非常高兴。）

（2）Your ad in today' s *China Daily* interests us and we will be glad to receive samples with your lowest prices.（对贵方刊登在今天《中国日报》上的广告，我方甚感兴趣，如能寄来样品并附上最低价格，将不胜欣慰。）

（3）If you can supply sewing machines of the type and quality required, we may place regular orders for large quantities with you.（如果贵方能提供所要求型号和质量的缝纫机，我方就可向贵方定期大量订货。）

（4）We find that the selling prospects for your color TV of Meijia brand in our country are very good and look forward to receiving your samples and quotations as soon as possible.（我们发现贵公司产的"美佳"牌彩电在我国前景看好，盼望尽快收到贵方的样品和报价。）

（5）We should be much obliged if you could quote us the best CIFC5% Shanghai and indicate the respective quantities and various sizes that you could supply for prompt shipment.（如果贵公司能给我们上海到岸价和5%的佣金的报盘，并说明能够提供马上装运供货的各种商品的数量和规格，我们将不胜感激。）

（6）This is really the most favorable offer we can make, and we are sure that you will be pleased to accept our offer.（这是我方能给予的最优惠的报盘，我们相信贵方是会乐意接受的。）

（7）Please let us know on what terms you can supply the above goods.（请告之贵方能以怎样的交易条件供应上述商品。）

（8）The price of raw material has gone up steadily in recent three months, but we have not raised our quotation. As it is the case, we do not make any discount.（近3个月以来，原材料价一直上涨，但是我们并未提价。为此，我们不打任何折扣了。）

（9）If you are in a position to meet our demand, we shall place a large sum order from you.（如果贵方能满足我们的需求，我们将向贵方下大宗订单。）

（10）Though the quality of your textile is satisfactory for us, your quotation is not quite in line with the present market.（虽然贵方的纺织品质量让我们满意，但是贵方的报价与目前市场行情差距甚大。）

（11）We have much pleasure in enclosing a quotation sheet for our products and trust that their high quality will induce you to place a trial order.（非常高兴寄上我们的产品报价单，我们相信我们的产品质量会促使贵方试订货。）

（12）As our market is now somewhat dull and prices are generally low, you are very fortunate in making purchases at this time.（目前我方市场呆滞，货价普遍偏低，贵方此时进货，实属

有幸。）

（13）提出询盘。

We addressed our inquiry to the firm.（我们已向该公司提出询价。）

Will you please let us have a list of items that are imported by you?（敬请将贵公司的进口商品目录寄来为荷。）

Please put us on your best terms, as this order forms part of a contract.（由于这一次订购是合同的组成部分，请提供最好的条件。）

Please put us on your very best shipping terms as regards discount.（由于打折扣，请告知最好的装船条件。）

Please state your best terms and discount for cash.（请告知以现金支付的优惠条款和折扣比例。）

Kindly let us know at what price you are able to deliver quantities of best refined sugar.（敬请告知贵公司可供应的上等砂糖的数量和价格。）

We would appreciate it if you will please let us know the ruling prices of the goods.（请贵方告知该商品的现行价格为荷。）

We shall be obliged by a quotation of your lowest price for the said goods free delivered at our works.（请对上述产品报运至我方工厂交货的最低价格。）

I shall be glad if you will send me your catalogue together with quotations.（请贵方惠寄商品目录并报价，谢谢。）

（14）受理询盘。

Our terms are 2% ten days, thirty days net.（我们的条件是10日内付款为2%的折扣，30日内付款无折扣。）

Our terms are cash within three months of date of delivery, or subject to 5 percent discount if paid within one month.（我公司付款条件为交货后3个月内支付现金。1个月内付清货款者，可打5%折扣。）

My habit is to settle on the 25th all bills rendered on or before the 1st of each and every month.（每月一日以前提供的汇票，依我公司惯例应在25日全部结账。）

Terms: early delivery, and net cash payment after receipt of the material at our works, and verification of weight and quality.（条件：即期发货。在货到我方工厂，经过验讫重量及品质后，立即以现金支付。）

In reply to your enquiry of yesterday's date, we are sending you herewith several samples of wall paper closely resembling to what you want.（针对贵方昨日的询盘，现寄上与贵方来函要求相似的墙纸样品数件。）

We think you can well accord us a substantial discount off your list prices, which we see are quoted net cash.（上述价目单是以付现金拟订的，我们认为还可以打更多折扣。）

Our terms, as our invoice states, are 2% cash discount, only within ten days of date of invoice.（我公司的支付条件：以现金支付。自发票开出之日起10天内付款者，打2%的折扣。）

We shall be glad if you will quote us the best discount for cash off your list price for cash for this quantity.（对这批数量大、以现金支付的货，如贵方能从价目表中再给些折扣优待，当不胜感谢。）

Exercises

1. Put the following English phrases into Chinese or Chinese phrases into English.

（1）regular supply

（2）reasonable price

（3）special discount

（4）keen competition

（5）bulk buying

（6）向……订购

（7）即复

（8）有存货的

（9）最低价

（10）竞争价

2. Multiple choice.

（1）Please let us have details of your machine tools, ________ your earliest delivery.

a. giving us　　b. give us　　c. to give us　　d. given us

（2）We hope to receive your quotation with details ________ the possible time of shipment.

a. to include　　b. to be included

c. including　　d. being included

（3）Will you please send us your prices for the items ________ below?

a. listing　　b. being listed　　c. to list　　d. listed

（4）We shall appreciate ________ us FOB Sydney.

a. you quoting　　b. your quoting　　c. you to quote　　d. your being quoted

（5）If you can supply your goods immediately, we shall ________ to place a prompt trial order.

a. be prepared　　b. be preparing　　c. prepare　　d. preparing

（6）As we have an extensive business connection in this field, we hope ________ your special terms.

a. to give　　b. giving　　c. to be given　　d. to be giving

（7）If your prices are competitive, we are confident ________ the goods in great quantities in this market.

a. to sell　　b. to be selling　　c. in being sold　　d. in selling

（8）We confirm our cable just dispatched ________ these goods.

a. offering you firm　　b. firm offering you

c. to be offered to you firm　　d. to firm offer you

（9）As we are one of the leading importers in this line, we are ________ to handle large quantities.

a. at a position b. in a position c. on a position d. of a position

(10) Although we appreciate good quality of your goods, we are sorry to say that your price appears to be ________.

a. of the high standard b. in the high level

c. on the high side d. at the high end

3. Translate the following sentences into English using the words or phrases in the brackets.

(1) 我们对贵方生产的计算机很感兴趣，如蒙寄备有存货的计算机价格，将不胜感激。(by return)

(2) 我们相信如贵方价格有竞争力，我们能向贵方经常订购。(confident)

(3) 请报下列货物的最低价 CIF 上海，及最早交货日期。(the undermentioned)

(4) 我们要求的货物应经久耐用、色彩鲜明、富有吸引力。(durable)

(5) 如蒙告知试用我们产品后的意见，我们将非常感谢。(comment)

(6) 贵方市场另一位供应商以低于类似产品 3% 的价格向我们报盘。(supplier)

4. Translate the following letter into English.

从纽约的托马斯 H. 彭涅公司处，敬悉贵公司生产各类手工制人造皮革手套。本地区对中等价格的高品质手套向来有稳定的需求。请惠寄贵公司的手套目录一份，详述有关价目与付款条件。希望贵公司顺带惠赐样品。

5. Write a letter as per the following particulars.

You are asked to write a letter to a foreign company for a trial order of table-cloths. The letter should cover at least the following points.

(1) How did you get the information of the foreign company?

(2) What is your desire?

(3) What are the details of your want?

Supplementary Reading

Part A

An enquiry is usually a kind of letter or other kind of communication that is made to get the required information of the supply of certain product, service, or the general information. In order to obtain the needed information, the enquirer should state simply, clearly and concisely what he wants—generally information, and catalogue or price list, a sample, a quotation, etc. Enquiries should be specific and provide the necessary details to enable the receiver to answer the questions completely. When making an enquiry, begin with the question or questions you want to ask. Keep your enquiry short and to the point.

Enquiries are one of the major links in conducting business, which may be roughly classified as general enquiries and specific enquiries. General enquiries are the cases the buyers merely ask for price list, catalogues, samples, etc. Specific enquiries are the cases the buyers have a definite aim of purchasing and ask for price. When replying to such an enquiry, the writer should always remember when there is an enquiry, there is business. So such letters should be dealt with promptly, helpfully and courteously, covering all the relevant information asked for.

Notes

to the point 扼要的

Part B

As a salesperson, be knowledgeable about factors that influence your buyer' s purchase decision. You can obtain this knowledge, which helps to increase the salesperson' s self-confidence and the buyer' s confidence in the salesperson, through training and practice.

A firm' s marketing strategy involves various efforts to create exchanges that the buyer' s needs and wants. The salesperson should understand the characteristics of the target market (consumer or industrial) and how these characters relate to the buyer' s behavior to better serve and sell to customers.

The individual goes through various steps or stages in the three buying situations of routine decision making, limited decision making, and extensive decision. Uncover who is involved in the buying decision and the main factors that influence the decision. These factors include various psychological and practical buying.

Psychological factors include the buyer' s motives, perceptions, learning, attitudes, beliefs, and personality—all of which influence the individual' s needs and result in a search for information on what products to buy to satisfy them. Established strongly influence buying decisions, making satisfied customers to sell to than new prospects. Customers evaluate the information, which results in the decision to buy or not to buy. These same factors influence whether the buyer is satisfied or dissatisfied with the product.

Realize that all prospects will not buy your products, at least not all of the time, due to the many factors influencing their buying decisions. You need to uncover buyers' needs, solve buyers' problems, and provide the knowledge that allows them to develop personal attitudes toward the product. These attitudes result in positive beliefs that your products fulfill their needs. Uncovering prospects' needs is often difficult because they may be reluctant to tell you their true needs or may not really know what and why they want to buy. You can usually feel confident that people buy for reasons such as to satisfy a need, fulfill a desire, and obtain a value. To determine these important buying needs, you can ask, observe prospects, listen to them, and talk to their associates about their needs.

Part C

Awareness of Needs: Some Buyers Are Unsure

You have seen that people purchase products to satisfy various needs. Often, however, these needs are developed over such a long period that people may not be fully conscious of their reasons for buying or not buying a product. The buying decision can be complicated by their level of need awareness. Three levels of need awareness have been identified—conscious, preconscious, and unconscious.

At the first level, the conscious need level, buyers are fully aware of their needs. These are the easiest people to sell to because they know what products they want and are willing to talk about their needs. A customer might say to the salesperson, "I' d like to buy a new car and I want a BMW loaded with accessories. What can you show me?"

At the second level, the preconscious need level, buyers may not be fully aware of their needs. Needs may not be fully developed in the conscious mind. They know what general type of product they want but may not wish to discuss it fully. For example, a buyer may want to buy a certain product because of a strong ego need yet be hesitant about telling you. If you don' t make a sale and ask why, this buyer may present false reasons, such as saying your price is too high, rather than revealing the real motivation. Falsification is much easier than stating the true reasons for not buying your product—thus getting into a long conversation with you, arguing with you, or telling you that your product is unsatisfactory. You must avoid this brush-off by determining a buyer' s real needs first and then relating your product' s benefits to these needs.

At the third level, the unconscious need level, people do not know why they buy a product—only that they do buy. When people say, "I really don' t know what I want to buy," it may be true. Their buying motives might have developed years earlier and may have been repressed. In this case, the salesperson needs to determine the needs that are influential. Often, this is accomplished by skillful questioning to draw out prospective buyers' unconscious needs. An awareness of the types of needs that buyers may have will allow you to present your product as a vehicle for satisfaction of those needs. Several methods of presenting a product's benefits are available.

Part D

Warren Buffett on Ethics

In a 2008 letter to Berkshire directors, Warren Buffett says this about ethics:

"We must continue to measure every act against not only what is legal but also what we would be happy to have written about on the front page of a national newspaper in an article written by an unfriendly but intelligent reporter."

"Sometimes your associates will say 'Everybody else is doing it'. This rationale is almost always a bad one if it is the main justification for a business action. It is totally unacceptable when evaluating a moral decision. Whenever somebody offers that phrase as a rationale, in effect they are saying that they can't come up with a good reason. If anyone offers this explanation, tell them to try using it with a reporter or a judge and see how far it gets them."

"... It's very likely that if a given course of action evokes hesitation per se, it's too close to the line and should be abandoned. There's plenty of money to be made in the center of the court. If it's questionable whether some action is close to the line, just assume it is outside and forget it."

Small Companies, Large Hearts

Some small companies are building philanthropy into their business models. Hook & Ladder Brewing Company donates a portion of all sales to local burned firefighters and other burn survivors. ColorMe Company, which produces arts and crafts materials for children, gives 10% of earnings to children's charities. Toms Shoes gives a pair of new shoes to a child in need for every pair of shoes purchased from them.

Charitable contributions like these help attract and keep customers and employees and set such companies apart from their competitors.

What do you think of such philanthropic business models? What potential problems do such models have? Do you think the benefits will outweigh the pitfalls?

Unit 5

Quotation and Offer

报价和发盘

5.1 Introduction（简介）

在国际贸易中，发盘（Offer）又称发价，在法律上又称“要约”，是指买方或卖方向对方提出的各项交易条件。发盘通常是一方收到对方的询盘之后所提出的，但也可不经过对方询盘而主动向对方提出。

向一个或一个以上特定的人提出订立合同的建议，如果十分确定，并且表明发盘人（Offerer）在得到接受时承受接受的意旨，即构成发盘。由买方提出的发盘被称为买方发价或购货发盘（Buying offer），而由卖方做出的发盘被称为售货发盘（Selling offer）。发盘必须经特定的受盘人（Offeree）接受，交易才能成立。发盘是订购意旨的表示，其内容必须准确无误，不能使用意义含糊的词句。

在实际业务中，当发盘针对一个或几个特定的受盘人明示或暗示发盘人在明确、完整和最终的条件下订立合同的明确意图时，该盘就为实盘（Firm offer）。受盘人一旦在发盘的有效期内有效地表示接受，这个实盘就为不可撤销，并会对发盘人和受盘人双方产生约束力。因此，实盘又称为“有约束力的发盘”。报实盘时必须注意以下三点：

（1）发盘必须注明是实盘。

（2）发盘必须明确、清楚、完整，具有最终效力并列出所有的主要交易条件。

（3）发盘必须注明有效期。

从法律意义上讲，报价不是发盘，报价只是愿意按所列的价格等条件供应货物的一种不肯定的订约建议。对于由报价而产生的订单，卖方可自由地考虑接受或不接受该订单。在交易磋商过程中，凡是不具备以上条件的意思表示，通常只是邀请做出发盘或称发盘的邀请。没有特定的受盘人或所提建议是不确定的，如所提条件是模棱两可的，或规定须以建议人“确认为准”等保留条件的发盘都是邀请做出发盘。邀请做出发盘可以是对询盘的答复，也可径直发给对方，而且在内容上可简可繁。

完整的报价和发盘应包括以下内容：

（1）对询价表示感谢。

（2）提供所要求的所有信息，如价格、折扣及付款条件等细节。

（3）对交货期或装运期的承诺。

（4）如为实盘，应注明有效期。

（5）希望对方接受报价订购货物。

5.2 Writing Skills（写作技巧）

报价和发盘信函的写作步骤及常见表达方式如下所示：

写作步骤	表达方式
1. 对对方的询价表示感谢	Many thanks for your inquiry of . . .（多谢您于……日的询价。）
	Thank you for your enquiry and for your interest in our products.（感谢您的询价以及对我方产品的兴趣。）
	We thank you for your inquiry of . . . and are pleased to quote as follows.（我们对您在……日的询价表示感谢并愿意提供以下产品的报价。）
2. 向对方提供所要求的信息	Please note our standard terms and conditions on the reverse side of this quotation.（请注意我们列在本报价后面的交易条件。）
	We can ship your order within 3 weeks upon receipt of your order.（我们能在收到订单后三周内寄出货物。）
	It is our usual practice to supply new customers with our goods for payment within one month from date of invoice, in the first instance, and later to extend this term to three months.（我们通常的做法是：新客户首次订购我们的货物从结算日起一个月内付款交货。之后，则宽限至三个月。）
3. 表明报价的有效期	We must stress that this offer can remain open for three days only.（我们必须强调此报价只在3天内有效。）
	Subject to being unsold/ to prior sale.（以未出售为有效。）
	We cannot consider these prices firm for an indefinite period because of the situation on the coffee market.（鉴于咖啡市场的行情，我们无法长期保持这一价格不变。）
4. 表达希望对方接受所报价格早日订货的愿望	We trust you will find our quotation satisfactory and look forward to receiving your order.（相信您会满意我们的报价，盼订货。）
	We look forward to receiving your order soon.（盼尽早收到贵方订单。）
	We look forward to the pleasure of serving you.（期盼能为您服务。）

5.3 Specimen Letters（样函）

Letter 1：Request for quotation for crockery

Dear Sirs,

You have previously supplied us with crockery and we should be obliged[1] if you would now quote CIF San Francisco for the items named below. The pattern we require is listed in your 2004 catalogue as No. 8.

500 Tea cups and saucers

200 Tea plates

100 2-pint Tea-pots

When replying, please state: ①discount[2] allowable, ②terms of payment, and ③earliest possible date of delivery[3].

Truly yours,
Fred Jackson

Letter 2: Exporter's quotation

Dear Ms. Chen,

Thank you for your letter of 5th April, requesting for a further supply of our crockery[4], we are pleased to quote as follows:

Tea cups............... USD500.00 per hundred

Tea saucers............ USD200.00 per hundred

Tea plates............. USD180.00 per hundred

Tea-pots, 2-pint .... USD3.00 each

Net CIF Francisco

The above quotation is subject to our final confirmation[5]. You are allowed a discount of 5% for items ordered in quantities of 500 or more. The terms of payment are by letter of credit at sight to be opened through the Bank of China and the shipment is to be made within four weeks upon receipt of the covering letter of credit.

We hope you will find these terms satisfactory and look forward to the pleasure of your order.

Yours faithfully,
Leon Allen

Letter 3: A firm offer from the seller

Dear Sirs,

As requested in your letter of 18th April, we offer you firm as follows, subject to your reply reaching us by the end of this month.

1,000 dozen cotton shirts at USD60 per dozen CIF New York. The shipment is to be made during June. We require payment by confirmed irrevocable letter of credit[6] payable by draft at sight[7].

This is the best offer we can make[8] at present and we trust that you will accept this offer without loss of time as the demand for our cotton shirts is heavy.

For your reference, we are sending you some samples separately.

Yours very truly,
Chun

Letter 4: A non-firm offer

Dear Sirs,

We welcome your inquiry of April 17th and thank you for your interest in our Wanlida DVD. Our products are super-thin. The voice quality is better and pictures are clearer than same sort of products. We are pleased to offer you USD150 per set at CIF New York. Payment is to be made by confirmed, irrevocable L/C payable by draft at sight.

Please note that there is no commission[9] on our products, but a discount of 5% may be allowed if the quantity of your order is more than 1,000 sets.

We hope you will agree to our offer and look forward to receiving your order. Thank you again for your inquiry.

Yours faithfully,
Manager

Letter 5: A special offer

Dear Sirs,

In order to start a concrete transaction between us, we take pleasure in making you a special offer, subject to our final confirmation, as follows.

Art. No.:	81000 Printed Shirting.
Design No.:	72435 – 2A.
Specifications:	30 × 36 × 72 × 69, 35′/ 36′ × 42 yards.
Quantity:	12,600 yards.
Packing:	In bales or in wooden cases, at seller's option[10].
Price:	USDXXX per yard CIFC 5% Vancouver.
Shipment:	To be made shipment in three equal monthly installment[11]; beginning from June 2002.
Payment:	By confirmed, irrevocable L/C payable by draft at sight to be opened 30 days before the time of shipment.

We trust the above will be acceptable to you and await your trial order with keen interest.

Sincerely yours,
John Leeds

Letter 6: Exporter's quotation

Dear Sirs,

We thank you for your enquiry of 23rd September for Silk 6311. While we appreciate your efforts in pushing the sale[12] of our products, we very much regret that we are not in a position to[13] offer you the desired quality, owing to excessive demand.

However, we should like to take this opportunity to offer without engagement[14] the following material as a close substitute for your consideration: 500 pieces Silk 6103 at $4.8 per yard. CIF Hamburg, including your commission of 3%.

If you are able to close business as we propose here, please tell us as soon as possible.

Yours faithfully,
Kevin James

Letter 7: A special offer

Dear Mr. Martin,

Thank you for inquiry of June 16 for your bicycles. At your request[15], we are making you the following offer subject to your reply reaching here before July 15.

Unit Price: $250.

Payment: By irrevocable Letter of Credit in seller' s favor[16].

Delivery Date[17]: Within 90 days after receipt of your order.

The above prices are on a CIF San Francisco basis.

We manufacture and export 10 models of bicycles which are well-known for their solid frame[18], reasonable price, and attractive design[19]. If you are interested in other models, please see the enclosed catalogue.

As you know, the market is advancing recently. Please take advantage of the present situation and send us an order early.

Sincerely yours,

Per

Notes to the specimen letters

1. be obliged to sb. for sth. 感激某人做某事
2. discount 折扣
3. date of delivery 交货期
4. crockery 陶器，瓦器
5. subject to our final confirmation 以我方最后确认为准
6. by confirmed irrevocable L/C 凭保兑的不可撤销信用证
7. draft at sight 即期汇票
8. make sb. an offer 向某人报盘
9. commission 佣金
10. at one' s option 由某人选择决定
11. make shipment in three equal monthly installment 三个月分三批交货，每批数量相等
12. push the sale 推销
13. be in a position to 能够
14. without engagement 不受约束地
15. at your request 按照贵方要求
16. in one' s favor 以某人为受益人
17. delivery date 交货日期
18. solid frame 结实的框架
19. attractive design 吸引人的设计

5.4 Focal Words（焦点词汇）

advise

vt. 通知；告知

We are studying your list of commodities and will advise you of our present interest.（我方尚在研究贵方的货物列表，到时会将目前感兴趣的商品告知贵方。）

Please advise us when you will ship the goods.（请告知我方何时装运此货。）

advisable：*adj.* 可取的；明智的

It is advisable that you should ship the goods by s. s. Red Star.（你们将货装上红星号轮运来为宜。）

advice：*n.* 通知；报告

We have duly received the advice of opening an L/C.（我们已按时收到开立信用证的通知。）

certify

vt. 证明

This is to certify that we, the undersigned, have inspected the quality of the above-mentioned goods and found the result as follows.（上述商品的质量已经我们检验并签字，其结果如下，特此证明。）

When contractor shall have completed the work, he shall certify in writing, completion of the work to the owner.（承包商完成工程施工后，应向所有人出具工程完毕的书面证明。）

certificate：*n.* 证明书

The Inspection Certificate of Quality, Quantity and Weight issued by the Shanghai Import and Export Commodity Inspection Bureau shall be final.（上海进出口商品检验局所出具的品质、数量和重量检验证明书应视作最后的证明。）

offer

n. 报盘；报价

This offer will remain effective for another 10 days from 15th May.（本报盘有效期自5月15日起延续10天。）

vt. 报盘

We offer you firm 50 long tons of Tin Foil Sheets at Stg. 135 per long ton CIF Shanghai for delivery in June.（我们向贵方报出50长吨锡箔实盘CIF上海价每长吨135英镑，6月份交货。）

vi. 给予；提供

For quantities of 10 tons and over, we can offer a discount of 15% on list prices.（数量在10吨以上可以按目录价格提供15%的折扣。）

price

n. 价格

If prices are right, we should place a first order for 400 raincoats.（如果价格合适，我们第一笔将定购雨衣400件。）

vt. 定价

All our table-cloths are exquisitely made and moderately priced.（我方生产的所有台布，制作精美，定价适度。）

Our low-priced tweeds have a great market in East African Areas.（我方低价的花呢畅销于非洲东部各地。）

price list: *n.* 价格表；价目单

Will you please send us a price list of your portable transistor sets?（请寄来贵方轻便半导体收音机的价目单。）

quote

vt. 引用；复述

The buyer is always requested to quote the number of this Sales Confirmation in the L/C to be opened in favor of the seller. （买方应在向卖方开立的信用证上标明本销售确认书的编号。）

vt. 给……报价

Please quote us your lowest price. （请报贵方最低价格。）

vi. 报价

Will you please quote for the supply of approximately 100 reams of good quality white poster paper?（请对供应 100 令（2,000 刀）左右优质白色广告纸做出报价。）

5.5 Useful Sentences（实用语句）

(1) Will you please let us have an idea of your price?（请告知贵方价格为荷。）

(2) This is our latest price list. Would you like to have a look?（这是我方的最新价目表。贵方需要了解吗?）

(3) Would you please give us an approximate idea of the quantity you require?（请告知贵方大概要订多少?）

(4) In our offer, we shall make it our business to charge you the lowest possible price for any quantity you may require, in order to give you an entire satisfaction and to retain your customers. （为使贵方满意并保持贵方顾客，对贵公司的需求，我们不计较数量多少，均提供最低价格。）

(5) If your prices are most favorable than those of other suppliers, we shall send you an order.（如果贵方的价格比其他供应商更优惠，我们将向贵方订货。）

(6) This offer is firm subject to your immediate reply, which should reach us not later than the end of this month. There is little likelihood of the goods remaining unsold once this particular offer has lapsed. （上述报盘，以贵方答复在不迟于本月底前到达我方为有效。一旦此报盘过期，此货不可能存留不售。）

(7) The offer will remain firm until 31st March, beyond which date the terms and prices should be discussed anew. （报价有效期至 3 月 31 日止，此日期之后的条款及价格需重新商讨。）

(8) The stock on hand at present will be sold at a reduction of at least 50 percent, and purchasers are respectfully invited to avail themselves of this opportunity of providing themselves with articles in furniture and ironmongery at unprecedented low prices. （现减价处理库存货物，价格至少减 50%，是家具及五金制品前所未有的优惠价，请勿失良机。）

(9) As recently the goods are in extremely short supply, we regret being unable to offer the price. （因近来货源奇紧，歉难报盘。）

(10) The item is presently sold out. Therefore, we cannot send you an offer. （此商品目前已售完，因此，我们无法向贵方报价。）

(11) As requested, we are offering you the following subject to our final confirmation. (根据要求，我方就如下货物向贵方报价，但以我方最后确认为准。)

(12) On the 17th May, I venture to invite you to have a look at my shop, and wish me success. (本人冒昧地邀请贵方于5月17日前来光顾本店，请多关照。)

(13) 发盘用语。

to offer/ to make an offer/ to submit an offering 报盘

to offer firm/ to make a firm offer 发实盘

to offer subject to goods being unsold 本报盘以尚未出售为准

to hold an offer open/ to keep an offer open 留盘

to withdraw an offer/ to cancel an offer 撤销一项发盘

to alter an offer 变更报盘

to extend an offer 延长发盘有效期

(14) The size of our order depends greatly on your price. (我方所订的数量很大程度上取决于贵方的价格。)

(15) We trust that you will be able to accept our offer, which shall be kept open against reply by wire. (相信贵方能接受我们的报价，此盘有效期可到回电为止。)

(16) We are pleased to inform you that there are 50 tons of walnuts now available for export. (欣告现有50吨核桃可供出口。)

(17) We are pleased to notify you that the whole of their extensive stock of silks, velvets, ribbons, mantles, shawls, woolen and cotton goods, and haberdashery, is now on sale at prime cost. (我们正在清仓，有丝织品、天鹅绒、丝带、披风、披肩、毛制品、棉织品以及其他男士服饰，均以进货价出售，特告。)

(18) As the premises will be shortly required for other purposes, the whole of the goods must be immediately disposed of without reserve. (本店另有他用，全部货物急需清仓处理。)

(19) At your request, we now keep this firm offer open for a further ten days from 10th March. (按贵方要求，我们现将实盘有效期从3月10日起再延长10天。)

(20) Being actual manufacturers, we are able to guarantee a uniform quality and excellent workmanship of our goods, and we shall be glad to be favored, as before, with your esteemed orders, which shall have our prompt and careful attention. (作为制造商，我公司能保证产品质量和做工精美。贵公司订货若能一如既往，将不胜感激，当迅速、认真履约。)

(21) I have stocked it with up-to-date goods, and I shall regard it as a favor if you will come along and look at them. (本店现有时新商品，如能光顾，将不胜感谢。)

(22) We venture to solicit a share of your favor, as being in touch with all the leading merchants here, we are able to deal satisfactorily with any commissions with which you may entrust us. (我们与本地主要厂商均有贸易联系，所以能提供贵方所需的东西，只要贵方有吩咐，定能使贵方满意。冒昧请您关照。)

(23) I am anxious not to disappoint possible buyers in distant cities, to whom I wrote at the same time. Will you please therefore let me hear from you at once if this bargain interests you, because there are only a very few left now and we cannot get more at anything like this price? (为不

使我们的顾客失望，贵公司如对这次生意有兴趣，请迅速通知我们。因目前所剩余货不多，日后我们无法再以此价进货。）

（24）Our offer to you was open only for 5 days, but, on thinking it over, it appears to us to be only fair that buyers in distant cities should be allowed extra time.（我们的报价只有5天有效期，但为了公平起见，外地顾客应给予更多的时间研究。）

（25）Since I wrote to you a few days ago, there has been an important development as regards the offer I then made you.（数日前写给贵公司的信谅已收到，前函的发盘现又有重要进展。）

（26）Referring to your letter dated 10th July in which you inquired for plastic toys, we have pleasure in cabling you an offer as follows.（关于贵方7月10日对塑料玩具的询价函，现电报价格如下。）

Exercises

1. Put the following English phrases into Chinese or Chinese phrases into English.

（1）subject to

（2）by confirmed

（3）by draft at sight

（4）comply with one' s request

（5）have e-mail confirmation

（6）发价有效期

（7）可撤销发盘

（8）实盘

（9）免费样品

（10）发盘人

2. Multiple choice.

（1）This price will remain ________ for ten days from the date of the letter.

a. valuable　　b. valid　　c. invaluable　　d. good

（2）________ a limited supply is available at present, we would ask you to act quickly.

a. Because　　b. As　　c. On account of　　d. Since

（3）We place this order with you ________ the understanding that the discount is 10%.

a. based on　　b. with　　c. on　　d. through

（4）If your prices and qualities are satisfactory, we will place a ________ with you.

a. considerate　　b. considerable　　c. much　　d. few

（5）It is essential that you ________ competitive price.

a. quoting　　b. quote　　c. making　　d. make

（6）The firm offer creates a power of acceptance permitting the ________ by accepting the offer to transform the offeror' s promise into a contractual obligation.

a. offer　　b. offeree　　c. offeror　　d. non-firm offer

（7）We are offering you goods ________ the very high quality.

a. of　　b. at　　c. for　　d. with

(8) The purpose of a sales letter is to ________ the prospective customer's interest.

a. arouse　　b. encourage　　c. attract　　d. secure

(9) If you are interested, we will send you a sample lot ________ charge.

a. within　　b. for　　c. free of　　d. with

(10) We shall be pleased to send you the necessary information ________ our machine tools according to request.

a. on　　b. about　　c. of　　d. in

3. Translate the following sentences into English using the words or phrases in the brackets.

(1) 非常高兴收到贵方11月14日对我方自行车的询函，现回复你方询函并很高兴报盘如下。(make offer)

(2) 现报盘如下，以贵方接受复函于9月15日前抵达我处为有效。(subject to)

(3) 我们另邮寄出标有CIF阿姆斯特丹价的最新价目表，以及一份插图目录供贵方参考。(for your reference)

(4) 请说明付款条件和购买1万台以上小天鹅牌洗衣机的折扣和优惠办法。(allow discount)

(5) 相信贵方会乐于知道我们能以最低价格供应最优质的产品。(offer)

(6) 兹此电复实盘，至5月31有效。(firm offer)

4. Translate the following letter into English.

贵公司9月18日的询盘函收悉，谢谢。关于贵方所需型号的长虹彩电，我们在此向你报盘。一经收到贵方的订货，所有尺寸的彩电在下月初都能供货。贵方所需"长虹"牌34英寸彩电价格为哥本哈根到岸价，每台450美元。与其他优质彩电的报价相比，我方报价非常有竞争力。盼贵公司多订为荷。

5. Write a letter as per the following particulars.

You are asked to write an offer to a foreign company. The letter should cover at least the following points.

(1) Confirm the letter you receive on May 25, 2015.

(2) Send catalogue, price list and sample books.

(3) State condition of sale and terms of payment.

(4) Look forward to an early reply.

Supplementary Reading

Part A

In response to an enquiry, quotations may be sent. A quotation is a promise to supply goods on the terms stated. It, however, is not legally binding as a firm offer if the seller later decides not to sell.

Making an offer means one party puts forward a certain kind of suggestion orally or in written business terms and conditions to another party, and expresses the willingness to do the business just according to the stated conditions. The firm offer creates a power of acceptance permitting the offeree by accepting the offer to transform the offeror' s promise into a contractual obligation. Thus, once it has been accepted it cannot be withdrawn.

It is to be noted that unlike a quotation, a firm offer, although not legally binding, is capable of acceptance and once it has been accepted it cannot be withdrawn, but no reputable seller would risk his reputation by withdrawing his offer before the stated or agreed time.

When a buyer rejects a quotation or other offer, he should write and thank the seller for his trouble and explain the reason for rejection. Not to do so would show a lack of courtesy.

Notes

1. binding 有约束力的
2. contractual 合同的

Part B

Communication is defined as transmission of verbal and nonverbal information and understanding between salesperson and prospect. Modes of communication commonly used in a sales presentation are words, gestures, visual aids, and nonverbal communication.

A model of the communication process is composed of a sender (encoder) who transmits a specific message via some medium to a receiver (decoder) who responds to that message. The effectiveness of this communication process can be hampered by noise that distorts the message as it travels to the receiver. A sender (encoder) can judge the effectiveness of a message and media choice by monitoring the feedback from the receiver.

Barriers, which hinder or prevent constructive communication during a sales presentation, may develop or already exist. These barriers may relate to the perceptional differences between the sender and receiver, cultural differences, outside distractions, or how sales information is conveyed. Regardless of their source, these barriers must be recognized and either overcome or eliminated if communication is to succeed.

Nonverbal communication has emerged as a critical component of the overall communication process within the past 10 or 15 years. Recognition of nonverbal communication is essential for sales success in today' s business environment. Awareness of the prospect' s territorial space, a firm and confident handshake, and accurate of body language are of tremendous aid to a salesperson' s success.

Overall persuasive power is enhanced through development of several key characteristics. The salesperson who creates a relationship based on mutual trust with a customer by displaying true empathy (desire to understand the customer' s situation and environment), a willing ear (more listening, less talking), and a positive attitude of enthusiastic pursuit of lasting solutions for the customer' s needs and problems increases the likelihood of making the sale.

Part C

The Three Levels of Listening

Whenever people listen, they are at one of three basic levels of listening. These require various degrees of concentration by the listener. As you move from the first to the third level, the potential for understanding and clear communication increases.

Marginal Listening. Marginal listening, the first and lowest level, involves the least concentration, and typically listeners are easily distracted by their thoughts. During periods of marginal listening, a listener exhibits blank stares, nervous mannerisms, and gestures that annoy the prospect and cause communication barriers. The listener hears the message but it doesn' t sink in. There is enormous room for misunderstanding when a salesperson is not concentrating on what is said. Moreover, the prospect cannot help but feel the lack of attention, which may be insulting and diminishes trust. It may be funny when family members continually each other with, "Yes, dear," regardless of what is said. In real life, however, it is not funny.

Prospect: What I need, really, is a way to reduce the time lost due to equipment breakdowns.

Salesperson: Yeah, OK. Let' s see, uh, the third feature of our product is the convenient sizes you can get.

Salespeople of all experience levels are guilty of marginal listening. Beginners who lack confidence and experience may concentrate so intensely on what they are supposed to say next that they stop listening. Old pros, by contrast, have heard it all before. They have their presentations memorized and want the prospect to hurry and finish talking so the important business can continue. These traditional salespeople forget that the truly important information lies in what the prospect says.

Evaluative Listening. Evaluative listening, the second level of listening, requires more concentration and attention to the speaker' s words. At this level, the listener actively tries to hear what the prospect says but isn' t making an effort to understand the intent. Instead of accepting and trying to understand a prospect' s message, the evaluative listener categorizes the statement and concentrates on preparing a response.

The evaluative listening phenomenon is a result of the tremendous speed at which a human can listen and think. It is no surprise that evaluative listening is the level of listening used most of the time. Unfortunately, it is a difficult habit to break, but it can be done with practice.

Prospect: What I need, really, is a way to reduce the time lost due to equipment breakdown.

Salesperson: (defensively) We have tested our machines in the field, and they don' t break down often.

In this example, the salesperson reacted to one aspect of the prospect' s statement. Had the salesperson withheld judgment until the end of the statement, he could have responded more objectively and informatively.

In evaluative listening, it is easy to be distracted by emotion-laden words. At that point, you aren' t listening to the prospect. Instead, you are obsessed with the offensive word and wondering what to do about it. This is a waste of time for both you and the prospect. It increases personal and relationship tension and throws your communication off course. To avoid the problems of marginal and evaluative listening, practice active listening.

Active Listening. Active listening is the third and most effective level of listening. The active listener refrains from evaluating the message and tries to see the other person' s point of view. Attention is not only on the words spoken but also on the thoughts, feelings, and meaning conveyed. Listening in this way means the listener puts herself into someone else's shoes. It requires the listener to give the other person verbal and nonverbal feedback.

Prospect: What I need is a way to reduce the time lost due to equipment breakdowns.

Salesperson: Could you tell me what kind of breakdowns you have experienced?

In this example, the salesperson spoke directly to the prospect's concerns—not around them. Her desire to make a presentation was deferred so she could accomplish a more important task—effectively communicating with the prospect.

Active listening is a skill that takes practice in the beginning, but after a while, it becomes second nature. The logic behind active listening is based on courtesy and concentration.

Active listening is sometimes difficult to do, especially for the novice salesperson. The novice may continue to talk about a particular situation or problem. However, the salesperson must learn to listen.

Part D

Writing for International Audiences

When you're writing for readers in another country, be careful to adjust your writing style to the new culture. Even the English language changes when you leave the United States. American spelling in documents for audiences who have learned British English can be annoying to readers. Remember that spelling is cultural, so adjust your writing to suit your readers, even if that means writing *grey*, *analyse*, *colour*, *centre* and *familiarise*. Adjusting your style and your spelling for international audiences demonstrates respect for their cultures.

If you're adapting your text for an international audience, go beyond a dictionary. Localize your document by asking a native speaker from your target country (or countries) to read the document and note any problematic words, phrases, images, or examples.

Evaluating "Rules" about Writing

Some "rules" are grammatical conventions. For example, standard edited English requires that each sentence have a subject and verb, and that the subject and verb agree. Business writing normally demands standard grammar, but exceptions exist. Promotional materials such as brochures, advertisements, and sales letters may use sentence fragments to mimic the effect of speech.

Other "rules" may be conventions adopted by an organization so that its documents will be consistent. For example, a company might decide to capitalize job titles (e.g., Production Manager) even though grammar doesn't require the capitals.

Some other "rules" are attempts to codify "what sounds good". "Never use I" and "use big words" are examples of this kind of "rule". To evaluate these "rules", you must consider your audience, purposes, and situation. If you want the effect produced by an impersonal style and polysyllabic words, use them. But use them only when you want the distancing they produce.

Unit 6 Counter-Offer and Acceptance 还盘和接受

6.1 Introduction（简介）

在接到发盘后，受盘人必须对报盘内容进行认真研究。如果受盘人认为发盘价格难以接受或对其他条件不满意，既可以拒绝接受，也可以向发盘人提出建议，要求对发盘内容进行修改。这种受盘人对发盘内容进行变更的表示被称为还盘（Counter-offer），也被称为还价。事实上，还盘既是受盘人对发盘的拒绝，又是受盘人以发盘人的身份提出的新发盘。在交易磋商中，通过不断的还盘，买卖双方逐渐在贸易条件上趋向一致，直到最后达成交易。拒绝接受发盘的一方在信中应明确说明拒绝的原因，同时应表达希望日后再开展贸易的愿望。

还盘信函的写作应十分小心，双方要本着珍视友谊和未来交易机会的态度。还盘信函应包含以下内容：

（1）对发盘人的发盘表示感谢。

（2）对由于某种原因无法接受发盘表示遗憾，同时解释原因。

（3）对还盘的内容也就是己方所希望的交易条件提出建议。

（4）希望对方能够接受己方所提出的还盘建议。

如果受盘人认为能够接受发盘的全部内容和条件，那么就可向发盘人订购商品。这种买方或卖方同意对方在发盘中提出的各项交易条件，并愿意按照这些条件达成交易、订立合同的表示被称为接受（Acceptance），即法律上所称的“承诺”。作为一项有效接受，必须具备以下四项条件：

（1）接受只能由受盘人做出。

（2）接受必须是无条件的，完全同意发盘中提出的各项交易条件。

（3）接受的方式必须符合发盘的要求。

（4）接受必须在发盘规定的有效期内做出。

6.2 Writing Skills（写作技巧）

还盘信函的写作步骤及常见表达方式如下所示：

写作步骤	表达方式
1. 对发盘人的报价表示感谢	Thank you for your prompt reply and detailed quotation.（我们感谢您的及时答复和详细报价。）
	Thank you for the samples you sent in response to our enquiry of 8 June.（感谢您对我方6月8日询价的答复并寄来样品。）

（续）

写作步骤	表达方式
2. 表示无法接受发盘并说明原因	We are sorry to tell you that we cannot take you up on the offer as the price you are asking is above the market level here for the quality in question.（很遗憾地通知贵方，我方不能接受贵方的报价，因为贵方所要求的价格高于本地同等质量产品的市场价格水平。）
	I should like to point out that your choice in color and pattern is very limited and that the shades that are now fashionable are missing.（我想指出，贵方产品在颜色和样品方面选择性有限，并缺少目前流行的色调。）
3. 对所希望的交易条件提出建议	May we suggest that you could perhaps make some allowance on your quoted prices that would help to introduce your goods on this market.（我们建议，如果贵方在所报价格的基础上给予优惠，也许会有助于贵方产品的市场推介。）
	I regret that your terms are unsatisfactory and unless you can amend those terms we shall have to place our order elsewhere.（很抱歉，贵方条件不能让人满意，如果不能改变条件的话，我方只好另转订单。）
4. 希望对方能够接受你所提出的还盘的建议	It is hoped that you would seriously take it into consideration and let us have your reply very soon.（希望贵方能认真考虑我方的建议并尽快回复。）
	We hope you will consider our counter-offer most favorable, and fax us acceptance at your early convenience.（希望贵方考虑我方的还盘，并尽早发传真表示接受。）

6.3 Specimen Letters（样函）

Letter 1: An offer

Dear Sirs,

We acknowledge with thanks the receipt of your inquiry of September 5, and are pleased to make you an offer regarding our Changhong brand color TV sets in the size you required.

All sizes can be supplied by the beginning of next month subject to our receiving your order. The price for Changhong brand color TV set inch 34 is USD450 each at CIF Copenhagen.

Our price is very competitive for[1] other good quality TV sets. We look forward to receiving your large number of order[2].

Truly yours,
Fred Jackson

Letter 2: A counter-offer

Dear Sirs,

We are glad to have received your letter of September18 offering us Changhong brand color TV sets inch 34 at CIF Copenhagen USD450 per set.

In reply, we regret to inform you that your price is too high. Market information tells us that some Japanese color TV sets have been sold here at a level about 30% lower than yours.

We do not deny the quality of Changhong brand color TV sets, but the difference in price is a wide gap[3]. To step up the trade[4], we counter-offer you 10 thousand Changhong brand color TV sets inch 34 at CIF Copenhagen USD300 per set.

It is hoped that you would seriously take it into consideration[5] and let us have your reply very soon.

Sincerely yours,
Xianjin Peng

Letter 3: Acceptance

Dear Sirs,

We have received your letter of October 2. It is regretful for us to see that you cut down the price of our Changhong brand color TV sets too sharp, but regarding our long term of business relationship, we decide to accept your counter-offer on condition that cash must be paid within three months of date of delivery, or subject to 5% discount if paid within one month.

Sincerely yours,
Ping Wang

Letter 4: A firm offer

Dear Sirs,

We thank you for your letter dated June 25 covering our Jinling brand automatic washing machine inquiry.

Jinling brand is one of the best known trade marks in China. It can run 15, 000 times continuously without any breakdown. It first passed through the recognition[6] of America' s UL and the qualities have kept the first for 5 years in succession[7].

Complying with your request[8], we take a pleasure to make you a firm offer Jinling brand automatic washing machine USD120 per machine FOB Guangzhou, inclusive of your 5% commission. Your reply must reach us before 12 a. m. July 25 our time and subject to our final confirmation.

For detailed specification, please refer to the catalogue enclosed. We hope that you will be glad to place a trial order[9] with us.

We anticipate your early reply.

Truly yours,
John Smith

Letter 5: A counter-offer

Dear Sirs,

We are in possession[10] of your letter July 5 offering us Jinling brand automatic washing machine USD120 per machine FOB Guangzhou inclusive of our 5% commission.

While appreciating the quality of your lines, we made a careful study of[11] your offer. We find your prices are too high to be acceptable. In fact, the cost of raw materials has not soared in the past three months. In order to make your products more competitive in our market, we suggest that you reduce prices by 10%. If you will agree to our counter-suggestion, regular orders for large numbers will be placed. Otherwise, we will conduct our business elsewhere.

Please let us have your e-mail confirmation[12] at your earliest convenience.

Yours faithfully,

Leon Allen

Letter 6: A counter-offer

Dear Mr. Jackson,

Thank you for your letter of September 25. Although we appreciate the quality of your color TV, their price is too high for us to accept.

Referring to the S/C No. 8965, you will find that we ordered 1,000 sets of TV at the terms and conditions[13] stipulated in that S/C, but the price was 10% lower than your present price.

Since we placed the last order, price for raw materials has been decreased considerably. Retailing price[14] for your color TV here has also been reduced by 5%. Accepting your present price will mean great loss to us, let alone[15] make profits.

We would like to place repeat orders with you if you could reduce your price at least by 1.5%. Otherwise, we have to shift[16] to the other suppliers for our similar request.

We hope you take our suggestion into serious consideration and give us your reply as soon as possible.

Yours truly,

Xia Peng

Letter 7: Acceptance

Dear Mr. Jackson,

I' m sorry to learn from your letter of October 5 that you find our prices too high. We do our best to keep prices as low as possible without sacrificing quality and are constantly enquiring into[17] new methods of manufacture.

Considering the quality of the goods offered, we don' t feel that the prices we quoted are at all excessive, but bearing in mind[18] the special character[19] of your trade, we have decided to offer you a special discount of 1.5% on a first order. We make this allowance because we should like to do business with you if possible, but I must stress that it' s the furthest we can go to help you. At least I hope this revised offer will now enable you to place an order.

Sincerely yours,

Ping Wang

Notes to the specimen letters

1. be competitive for 与……相比是富有竞争力的
2. large number of order 大宗订货
3. wide gap 差距很大
4. step up the trade 促进交易
5. take sth. into consideration 考虑
6. pass through the recognition 通过认证
7. in succession 连续
8. comply with one' s request 按照某人的要求
9. place a trial order 试订货
10. be in possession 收到
11. make a study of 研究
12. have sb. 's e-mail confirmation 收到某人的电子邮件确认书
13. terms and conditions 条款
14. retailing price 零售价
15. let alone 更不用说
16. shift 转向
17. enquire into 调查，查询
18. bear in mind 记住
19. special character 特点

6.4 Focal Words（焦点词汇）

accept

vt. **接受（邀请、报价等）；承认，同意；承兑（票据）**

We cannot accept your price.（我们不能接受贵方的价格。）

We accept that we have no alternative but to replace the damaged parts.（我们同意必须无条件地替换那些已损坏的部件。）

We request you to accept the draft drawn on you.（我们要求贵方承兑你们开出的汇票。）

Our price is reasonable. Please do your utmost to accept as it will lead to further business.（我方价格合理，请尽量接受，以便进一步交易。）

acceptable: *adj*. **可接受的，合意的**

The quality is acceptable, but the time of shipment is not.（质量可以接受，但装船期不行。）

We shall place a large order for men' s shirts with you, if the time of delivery is acceptable to us.（如果交货期我方可以接受，我方会向贵方订购大量男士衬衫。）

acceptance: *n*. **接受；（票据等的）承兑，经承兑的汇票**

This time we allow you a big discount, and recommend your immediate acceptance.（此次我方给予你们很大的折扣，建议贵方立即接受。）

We shall present the draft for acceptance. (我们要呈交汇票承兑。)

contribute

vi. **有助于，促进**

You know that the appearance of the package contributes greatly to the sale of consumer goods. (你们知道，消费品包装的外观对销售有很大的促进作用。)

These measures contributed greatly to raising the quality and output of our products. (这些措施大大有助于提高我们产品的质量和数量。)

execute

vt. **执行；签署（单证，契约等）**

We always do our best to execute our contracts to the full. (我们总是尽一切可能全面地执行合同。)

In witness whereof, the parties hereto have caused this contract to be executed in duplicate by their duly authorized representatives. (为证明以上各节，双方已令其正式授权的代表签署本合同一式两份。)

execution: *n.* **执行；签署**

We hope that you will promptly accept our order and make your usual careful execution. (我们希望贵方迅速接受我方订货，并同往常一样交货时多加注意。)

Party A shall, within 30 days of the execution of this agreement, provide Party B with the list mentioned below. (本协议签订之日起30天内甲方应向乙方提供下列明细单。)

order

n. **订单，订货；定购；命令；汇票；订购（货物）**

We hope you can give us an order soon. (我们希望贵方迅速交来订单。)

We shall immediately give orders to the factory for the consignment to be prepared. (我们将立即通知工厂将货备妥。)

We suggest that for this trial order, you let us have a demand draft or a postal money order. (对这次试销订货，我们建议贵方寄给我们即期汇票或邮政汇票。)

But first, you have to give us an idea of the quantity you wish to order. (不过首先贵方得告诉我们，贵方想要订购的大概数量。)

stock

vt. **储存，备货**

We have a large tailoring department and would like to stock a new type of material. (我公司有个很大的成衣部，想要备置一种新的衣料。)

vi. **备货**

We advise you to stock up while supplies are available. (我们建议你们在供货充足时备置存货。)

adj. **库存的**

Stock offers are a touch-and-go kind of things. (现货报盘成交快，一有买主就可立即脱手。)

n. **现货，存货**

These are the only stocks available.（这些是仅有的存货。）
in stock **库存中**
out of stock **缺货，无货**

6.5 Useful Sentences（实用语句）

(1) We would very much like to place orders with you if you could bring down your price at least by 20%. Otherwise we shall switch our requirements to other suppliers.（如果贵方降价在20%以上，我们将向贵方订货。否则，将转向其他供应商订货。）

(2) You will be interested to hear that we can offer a further supply of the best quality products at the lowest price.（相信贵方会乐于知道我方能以最低价格供应最优质的产品。）

(3) You have no doubt observed an upward tendency of being maintained in the price of our products. Besides, you are also aware that there has been lately a great demand for this commodity in the world markets. Our offer is competitive, as compared with others. If you are able to accept this offer, please let us know your acceptance immediately.（无疑，贵方已观察到我们产品的价格一直保持上升趋势。此外，贵方清楚近来世界市场对该产品的需求非常大。我们的报价与其他供应商的报价相比是有竞争力的。如蒙接受报盘，请马上通知我们。）

(4) We regret being unable to make use of these goods as the price you offer is above the market level here.（很遗憾，我们不能购买这些货物，因为贵公司报价高出这里的市场水平。）

(5) Our requirements are now fully covered for some time to come, and we therefore greatly regret that we have to cancel our order with you.（很抱歉由于我公司在今后一段时间内所需货物已完全够用，因此，不得不取消此次订货，敬请谅解。）

(6) If a substantial reduction can be expected, we could reconsider your revised quotation.（如蒙贵方能将报价大幅度削减，我们可以重新考虑贵公司修改后的报盘。）

(7) This is a firm offer, subject to the receipt of reply by us before 5th April.（这是实盘，以在4月5日前收到我方答复为准。）

(8) We have here cabled to you a firm offer until May 31.（兹此电复实盘，至5月31日有效。）

(9) We offer you best CIF Paris price, subject to our confirmation upon receipt of your reply here by Friday morning our time.（我们向您报CIF巴黎最优价，在本地时间星期五上午前收到贵方答复并经我方确认此价为准。）

(10) We have none of this particular make in stock at the moment, and, owing to the great pressure at the mills, we are afraid we cannot guarantee delivery within less than three months of receipt of orders.（目前，关于此类特制品，没有存货，工厂也无法立即制造。因此，我们很担心，在接到订单后，恐怕不能保证在3个月内交货，敬请谅解。）

(11) We would remind you that the firm offer made by us last week is valid for one month from the date of our last letter.（我们提醒贵方，上周我方所发的实盘，自上封信所署日期起，有效期为1个月。）

(12) To my deep regret, the buyer of these goods has just cancelled the order, which compels

me to cancel my order with you.（非常抱歉，兹因购货人已向我公司撤销订单，迫使我公司只好向贵公司取消这一次订货。）

(13) We received your letter of the 10th inst., and thank you for your order for ...（本月10日来函收悉，感谢贵方对……的订货。）

(14) We are in receipt of your favor of the 10th May, with your order for five printing machines, which I herewith acknowledge with best thanks.（贵公司5月10日来函及五部印刷机器的订单均已收到，在此表示感谢。）

(15) We acknowledge receipt of your favor of the 10th July, and thank you for the order you have given us.（贵公司7月10日函收悉，对此次订货，我公司表示感谢。）

(16) We confirm herewith your telegraphic order of the 10th June, for 100 cwt. of the best sugar.（贵公司6月10日电报关于100英担高级砂糖订单已收到，并予以确认。）

(17) Your order for a supply of our booklet *A Wonderful Story* has not been filled, because of our inability to procure the necessary paper for printing.（由于所需印刷纸张无法解决，因此，贵公司订购我公司发行的杂志《奇闻奇事》未能安排。）

(18) We are surprised to see a steep rise in the price offered by you, but the price of raw material has been weak since the beginning of this season. We are sorry to say that as your price is too high, we will have to make our purchase elsewhere.（对贵方报价急剧上涨，我们深感吃惊。但是自本季度初以来原材料价格一直疲软，我们遗憾地说，由于价格太高我们不得不转向其他地方购买。）

(19) We regret to say that on the terms mentioned, we find it impossible to fill the same.（实在对不起，对于此次贵公司的订货条件，我公司无法供应。）

(20) We trust to be favored with your substantial orders.（我们相信会收到贵公司的大宗订单。）

(21) I regret that I have to notify you of so many orders being cancelled at the same time.（非常遗憾，我公司不得不通知，在此同一时期内，需要取消多份订单。）

(22) We are sorry to report that our buyer does not confirm this order at your price USD500; we must, therefore, ask you to cancel it.（非常遗憾地通知贵公司，因为购货人对贵公司价格500美元不予确认，因此要求贵方取消此订单。）

(23) We regret to say that there is no possibility of our cutting the price to the extent you indicated, i.e. 15%.（我们非常遗憾地说，把价降到贵方所要求的15%的程度是不可能的。）

Exercises

1. Put the following English phrases or Chinese or Chinese phrases into English.

(1) offer unacceptable

(2) offer subject to immediate reply

(3) switch to

(4) as per sample

(5) a wide gap

(6) 还盘建议

（7）达成交易

（8）削价

（9）成交

（10）市场波动

2. Multiple choice.

（1）We certainly accept your offer ________ you will ship the goods during June.

a. except　　b. provided　　c. unless　　d. but

（2）________ you make a 5% reduction, we will have to decline your offer this time.

a. When　　b. Except　　c. As　　d. Unless

（3）We offer you the following items ________ your reply reaching here by 5 p. m. May 21, our time.

a. subjecting to　　b. to subject to　　c. subjects to　　d. subject to

（4）This offer is ________ your acceptance by cable on or before January 10.

a. effective to　　b. effectively for　　c. effective for　　d. effectively to

（5）A comparison of your offer ________ our regular suppliers shows that their figures are more favorable.

a. with what of　　b. with that of　　c. with which of　　d. with this of

（6）Although we are keen on meeting your requirements, we regret that we are unable to ________ your request to reduce the prices as our prices are closely calculated.

a. comply with　　b. comply to　　c. subject for　　d. subject to

（7）________ our long business relations and our amicable cooperation prospects, we suggest that you accept our terms.

a. In that　　b. In view of　　c. For which　　d. Because of

（8）We wish to direct your attention to the good quality of our products ________ price.

a. instead of　　b. subject to

c. been past through　　d. passed on

（9）While we appreciate your cooperation ________ giving us an offer, we regret to say that we are not in the market for this commodity now.

a. about　　b. in　　c. to　　d. with

（10）We are studying your offer and hope that it will remain ________ till the end of credit payable by draft at sight.

a. open　　b. okay　　c. close　　d. order

3. Translate the following sentences into English using the words or phrases in the brackets.

（1）我们虽然赞赏贵方自行车的质量，但价格太高不能接受。（appreciate）

（2）接受贵方现实的报价意味着我们将有巨大亏损，更不用谈利润了。（speak of）

（3）我们建议贵方立即订购，以便我们保证供货，贵方也不会失去机会。（place an order）

（4）我们欣赏贵方货物的质量以及贵方对我方询盘的处理方式，并欢迎能有机会与贵方

做生意。(do business with)

(5) 我们遗憾地通知贵方，我方未能按照贵方的条件接受报价。(be in a position to)

(6) 我们希望贵方认同我方价格具有竞争力，因为我方服装质量良好。盼早日收到贵方首批订单。(be competitive)

4. Translate the following letter into English.

谢谢贵方5月18日对棉衬衫的还盘。我们很高兴地确认刚发出的电文如下：贵方5月18日电悉，还盘接受。但请注意，我们之所以特别接受贵方的要求是因为我们希望以此获得贵方未来的大量订单。盼贵方即寄正式订单，我方将予以认真关注和仔细执行。

5. Write a letter as per the following information.

You are asked to write a counter-offer. The letter should cover at least the following points.

(1) Confirm the letter you received on May 4.

(2) State the reason that you cannot accept the offer.

(3) Put forward the counter-offer suggestion.

(4) Look forward to an early reply.

Supplementary Reading

Part A

A counter-offer is virtually a partial rejection of the original offer and also a counter proposal initiated by the buyer or the offeree. The buyer may show disagreement to the price, or packing, or shipment and state his own terms instead. Such alternations, no matter how slight they may appear to be, signify that business has to be negotiated on the renewed basis. The original offerer or the seller now becomes the offeree and he has the full right of acceptance or refusal. In the latter case, he may make another counter offer of his own. And several counter-offers form the bargaining of the business just like the process of negotiating. This process can go on for many a round till business is finalized or called off. In making a counter-offer, one has to state the terms most explicitly and use words very carefully so as to avoid ambiguity or misunderstanding, the same way as one usually does in making an offer.

Acceptance means the offeree gives the expression of willingness to sign the contract according to the terms and conditions given in the previous offer within the validity unconditionally. To make an effective acceptance, the offeree should do all of the following. The acceptance should be given by the offeree within the validity of the previous irrevocable offer. And the acceptance should accept all of the content of the previous offer unconditionally.

Notes

1. ambiguity 含糊
2. irrevocable 不可撤销的

Part B

Company knowledge includes information about a firm' s history, development policies, procedures, products, distribution, promotion, and pricing. A salesperson also must know the competition, the firm' s industry, and the economy. This knowledge can even be used to improve one' s self-concept. A high degree of such knowledge helps the salesperson build a positive self-image and feel thoroughly prepared to interact with customers.

Wholesalers and retailers stock thousands of products, which often makes it difficult to support any one manufacturer' s products as the manufacturer would like. This situation may result in conflicts between members of the channel of distribution. To reduce these conflicts and aid channel members in selling products, manufacturers offer assistance in advertising, sales promotion aids, and pricing allowances. Additionally, many manufacturers spend millions of dollars to compel consumers and industrial buyers to purchase from channel members and the manufacturer.

National, retail, trade, industrial, and direct-mail advertising create demand for products and are a powerful selling tool for the salesperson in sales presentations. Sales promotion activities and materials are another potential selling tool for the salesperson to use in selling to consumer and industrial buyers. Samples, coupons, contests, premiums, demonstrations, and displays are effective sales promotion techniques employed to help sell merchandise.

Price, discounts, and credit policies are additional facts the salesperson should be able to discuss confidently with customers. Each day, the salesperson informs or answers questions customers pose in these three areas. Customers always want to know the salesperson' s list and net price, and if there are any transportation charges. Discounts (quantity, cash, trade, or consumer) represent important buying incentives the manufacturer offers to the buyer. The buyer wants to know the terms of payment. The salesperson needs to understand company credit policies to open new accounts, see that customers pay on time, and collect overdue bills.

Finally, success in sales requires knowledge of the many technologies used to sell and service customers. Computers, word processing, e-mail, faxes, pagers, cellular phones, the Internet, and the World Wide Web have quickly become part of the professional' s sales kit. Proper knowledge of the courteous manner in which these many technologies should be used is a necessity.

Part C

Sources of Sales Knowledge

Knowledge for selling is obtained in two ways: First, most companies provide some formal sales training that teaches information through preliminary training programs and sales meetings. Second, the salesperson learns by being on the job. Experience is the best teacher for the beginning salesperson.

Sales training is the effort an employer puts forth to provide the opportunity for the salesperson to receive job-related culture, skills, knowledge, and attitudes that result in improved performance in the selling environment.

Successful companies thoroughly train new salespeople and maintain ongoing training programs for their experienced sales personnel. Companies are interested in training primarily to increase sales volume, salesperson productivity, and profitability.

Like many professional careers, selling is a skill that is truly developed only through experience. Sales knowledge obtained through education, reading, formalized sales training, and word-of-mouth is helpful in enhancing overall sales ability, but actual experience is the critical source of sales knowledge. Some sales managers hire only experienced people to fill entry-level selling slots. Indeed, some corporations do not allow people to fill marketing staff positions unless they have had field sales experience with the company or a major competitor.

Sales experience improves a salesperson' s abilities by showing how buyers perceive a product or product line, revealing unrecognized or undervalued product benefits or shortcomings, voicing a multitude of unanticipated protests and objections, showing a great number of prospect moods and attitudes over a short period, and generally providing a challenge that makes selling a skill that is never mastered, only improved.

No author or sales trainer can simulate the variety of situations that a salesperson confronts over the span of a career. Authors and trainers can provide only general guidelines as a framework for action. Only actual selling experience gives a person direct feedback on how to function in a specific selling situation. The sales knowledge gained through periodic sales training and actual experience benefits the salesperson, the firm, and the customers.

Only through possessing a high level of knowledge can the salesperson provide excellent service. Knowledge is part of the golden rule of personal selling. Knowledge based upon wisdom and conveyed to the buyer truthfully builds relationships.

Part D

Cultural Differences in Document Design

Cultural differences in document design are based on reading practices and experiences with other documents. Language is one source of these differences. For example, English and other European languages are written in horizontal lines moving from left to right down the page. Hebrew and Arabic languages are read from right to left. This affects where readers of these languages look first when they see a page of text.

People in the United States focus first on the left side of a website. Middle Eastern people focus first on the right side, so websites in Arabic and Hebrew orient text, links, and graphics from right to left.

Translations also affect the layout of a document. To convey the same message, Spanish and French take up more room than English does. Writing concise text for brochures, packages, and web pages is more challenging in the wordier languages. The problem is even more complex in designing bilingual or multilingual documents. For example, a company selling in Canada must use both English and French on its packages, and the French type must be printed at least as large as the English. On some products, such as a bottle of medicine or perfume, this requirement leaves little room for fancy graphics.

Make Sure Your Website Makes the Grade

Ninety-seven percent of the 1,000-plus corporate Web sites that Forrester Research Inc. has evaluated received failing grades. Companies with bad Web sites are turning off customers and leaving money on the table. And usually it's due to common mistakes that can be broken down into four categories:

(1) Value. The first mistake that companies make is copying features from competitors.

(2) Navigation. Companies often opt for cute menus instead of clear menus.

(3) Presentations. Websites need to be easy to read and understand.

(4) Trust. People are concerned about online privacy and security. Calling attention to privacy policy can actually help sales.

Unit 7
Sales Promotion
销售促销

7.1 Introduction（简介）

在出口贸易中，促销工作对于拓展业务起着决定性的作用。促销信函是进行产品宣传和广告的形式之一，其目的是向特定顾客推销某种商品或服务。促销信函的内容因具体目的而异，既可以是介绍公司的新产品或向长期不惠顾的老客户推荐改进产品，也可以是提供特别的折扣或优惠以便吸引顾客购买等。

一封有效的促销信函必须具有以下四个特征：吸引注意（Attention）、激发兴趣（Interest）、产生购买欲望（Desire）和导致购买行动（Action）。促销信函应以诱人的开头来吸引对方的注意力，然后，通过介绍产品或服务的特征（Feature）、优势（Advantage）和利益（Benefit）来引起对方的兴趣和欲望，并最终导致对方采取购买行为。

书写促销信函的关键在于卖方通过提出聪明的建议使买方明白可从购买中获得利益。不过，如果表达得太直接，也会适得其反，因此，一定要掌握促销信函的语气和用词。一般说来，在撰写促销信函时，应注意以下问题：

（1）促销信函不可冗长，应以简短为上，否则会给人以负担。

（2）在介绍产品或服务的特征、优势和利益时，语言要清楚、简洁，态度要诚恳，切勿使用夸大的言辞，避免给人以不实的感觉。

（3）促销信函的口吻要有亲切感，多使用敬称。

（4）要使对方明了能从你所推荐的产品或服务中受益。

（5）促销信函不但在外观上要吸引人，而且信函一开头就要能引起读者的兴趣。

7.2 Writing Skills（写作技巧）

促销信函的写作步骤及常见表达方式如下所示：

写作步骤	表达方式
1. 介绍所促销的产品，使对方了解并对该产品产生兴趣	to be made of...（由……制成）
	to be moderate in price, superior in quality, excellent in craftsmanship, and novel in designs...（价格公道，质量上乘，工艺精湛，设计新颖……）
	to be beautiful in pattern, elegant in style, matching in colors and skillful in workmanship...（式样优美，款式典雅，色泽和谐，做工考究……）
	to be famous for...（以……著名）
	to be well-know for...（以……闻名）

（续）

写作步骤	表达方式
1. 介绍所促销的产品，使对方了解并对该产品产生兴趣	to sell well/fast...（销路很好）
	to meet with warm reception...（很受欢迎）
	to have/find/command a good/ready market/sale...（畅销）
	to be popular with customers...（受到顾客欢迎）
2. 进行商品比较，体现本产品的优势，进一步激发对方的兴趣	to compare favorably with...（优于）
	to be + 形容词比较级 + than...（比……要……）
	a comparison will convince... of...（比较会使人相信……）
	to make a comparison of... in respect to...（做有关……的比较）
3. 给予对方一定的优惠条件，诱发对方的购买欲望	to give... the first chance...（给予……优先）
	to offer/allow/give/grant... a... discount...（给……折扣）
4. 表述对方可以从中获益，引起对方最终的购买行为	to advise you to avail yourselves of ... in your own interest...（建议贵方……为了自己的利益）
	to deem it to one' s advantage to do...（认为……对……很有利）
	to advise... to work fast...（劝……尽早做决定）
	to be acceptable to ...（可以为……接受）

7.3 Specimen Letters（样函）

Letter 1: Product promotion

Dear Mr. Jones,

As you may know, considerable interest was shown in our new product following its recent introduction into overseas markets. We believe you may be interested in personally evaluating its outstanding qualities, and have taken the liberty of forwarding[1] under separate air shipment[2] directly to your attention.

Customers who have ordered this highly innovative machine on a trial basis[3] have praised its unique features, especially its completely automated operation, and have placed repeated order[4].

By integrating this revolutionary new machine into your manufacturing system, we feel sure[5] your production volume can be substantially increased.

We are looking forward to your reply.

Very truly yours,
Robin Williams

Letter 2: A reply to Letter 1

Dear Mr. Williams,

We are delighted to receive your letter of introducing your new product and the sample. We are very interested in the machine feature, such as the ease of operating and production efficiency. We are pleased to place a trial order with you. We expect to place further and large orders with you in the near future. Enclosed please find the detailed requirements.

Kindly confirm acceptance of our order by return.

Yours sincerely,
Rob Jones

Letter 3: Offering a discount

Dear Sir or Madam,

We are glad to have your letter of inquiry forwarded to us by the Chamber of Commerce.

We wish to inform you that we are the largest manufac-ture of cigarette lighters in China with a history of over 30 years. Our products are well-known for superior quality and prompt shipment. The quality and prices compare favorably with[6] those of other makes[7].

We deem it to your advantage to push the sales[8] of our products in your market. We are prepared to[9] give you a 10% quantity discount[10] if your order exceeds 10,000 pieces. We are sure that you will find a ready sale[11] of our products.

We are looking forward to hearing from you soon.

Yours faithfully,
Ming Wang

Letter 4: A reply to Letter 3

Dear Mr. Wang,

Thank you so much for your introduction and the discount you offered. We find both quality and prices satisfactory and are pleased to give you an order[12] for 20,000 pieces on the understanding that[13] they will be supplied from current stock. We hope to find a good market for these cigarette lighters.

Please send us your confirmation of sales in duplicate[14].

Yours faithfully,
Rob Lee

Letter 5: Recommending products

Dear Sir or Madam,

One will certainly feel pleased with ladies' dresses that are beautiful in pattern, elegant in style and reasonable in prices. These are just the characteristics of our ladies' dresses for export.

The range of our ladies' dresses is extensive. They are all made of selected fabrics and deliberately designed, cut, stitched and trimmed[15].

A catalogue has been enclosed. Please let us have your specific enquiry enabling us to dispatch samples and make quotations[16].

Yours sincerely,
Helen Chang

Letter 6: A reply to Letter 5

Dear Miss Chang,

Referring to your mail, we regret to have to disappoint you.

We just gave an order of ladies dress and don' t expect further orders for at least six months. We trust that you would be kind enough to understand our difficulty and excuse us.

Nevertheless, we are still looking forward to your offer after six months.

Yours sincerely,

Cyrille Guiilot

Letter 7: Product promotion

Dear Mr. James,

Great interest was aroused[17] at the recent Arts & Crafts product exhibition in Beijing by the largest carpet manufacture in China. Numerous enquiries and orders have also come for the beautiful hand-woven carpets.

The carpets are preferred for the following:

Appearance[18]: Elegant designs with different sizes cater for[19] the customer' s needs.

Prices: Superb quality with prices much lower[20] than those from other sources[21].

Comfort: Carpets are made from wool and silk, so they are giving the feeling of natural warmth and comfort.

You will be interested to note that our annual production is 20,000 pieces. Recently we have received enquiries from Japan, Germany, Australia and Africa. We are convinced that our carpets will be exported to more countries in the near future.

We are glad to enclose our illustrated catalogue, and will send you our best quotation as soon as we hear from you.

Sincerely yours,

Jerry

Letter 8: A reply to Letter 7

Dear Jerry,

We are delighted to receive your letter of introducing your new product and the sample and are very interested in the carpet feature. We are pleased to place a trial order with you and expect to place further and large orders with you in the near future. Enclosed please find the detailed requirements.

Kindly confirm acceptance of our order by return.

Yours sincerely,

James

Notes to the specimen letters

1. to take the liberty of doing sth. 冒昧地做某事
2. under separate air shipment 另航空邮寄
3. on a trial basis 试用阶段
4. repeat order 追加订货
5. feel sure 确信
6. compare favorably with 比……好
7. make 产品出处，牌子
8. push the sales 推销
9. be prepared to do sth. 能够并愿意做某事
10. give sb. a... discount 给某人……的折扣
11. find a ready sale 畅销
12. give an order 对……订购
13. on the understanding that 在……条件下
14. in duplicate 一式两份
15. made of selected fabrics and deliberately designed, cut, stitched and trimmed 精选衣料，精心设计、剪裁和制作
16. make quotation 报价
17. arouse great interest 引起极大的兴趣
18. appearance 外观
19. cater for 满足
20. superb quality with prices much lower 物美价廉
21. those from other sources 其他货源的同类产品

7.4 Focal Words（焦点词汇）

charge

v. **收费，索要；把……记账；使承担；指控；使充满**

He is charged 5 dollars for mending a pair of shoes.（他修了一双鞋，被索要5美元。）

The new appointed manager is charged with heavy responsibility.（新任命的经理承担了很重的责任。）

The Customs charged the company with evasion of taxes.（海关指控该公司逃税。）

The battery is charged.（电池被充满电了。）

n. **费用；掌管；责任；指控；负荷**

Samples will be sent free of charge.（免费寄送样品。）

The manager assumes full charge of the business.（经理担负全部经营事务。）

The court brought the charge of treason against him.（法院指控他叛国。）

chargeable: *adj.* **可以控诉的；应付费的；应由某人负责的**

These expenses are chargeable on him.（这些费用应由他负担。）

concern

v. 涉及，使关心

This negotiation is concerned with the payment terms. （这次谈判涉及支付方式。）

The businessman is concerned for the discount. （这位商人关心的是折扣。）

n. 利害关系；关心

It is a matter of utmost concern. （这是头等大事。）

He has shown his concern for the quality. （他表示出对质量的关心。）

concerned: *adj.* 有关的；关切的

All parties concerned should attend the meeting. （所有有关各方都要参加会议。）

concerning: *prep.* 关于

Please inform me concerning this matter. （请把关于这件事的情况告诉我。）

draw

v. 抽出，汲取；开立（票据），草拟

Samples are drawn from the bales at random. （样品是从大包中任意抽取的。）

The water is drawn from the well. （从井里取水。）

We are going to draw the L/C within this week. （我们将在本周内开出信用证。）

They will draw a document next week. （他们将在下周草拟一份文件。）

n. 抽签；有吸引力的事物；平局

This business is a great draw. （这项业务很有吸引力。）

The game ended in a draw. （比赛结果是平局。）

drawee: *n.* 受票人，汇票付款人

drawer: *n.* 抽屉；开票人，汇票发票人

pay

v. 支付；有利

How much do you pay for it?（你付了多少钱买那个东西?）

It will pay to do that business. （做那桩生意是值得的。）

n. 工资，薪金

equal pay for equal work 同工同酬

I draw my pay on the 9th every month. （我每月九号领工资。）

payment: *n.* 支付，付款

Both sides have agreed on the payment terms. （双方就付款方式达成一致。）

payable: *adj.* 可付的，应付的

payer: *n.* 付款人

payee: *n.* 收款人

stipulate

v. 规定，订定

It is stipulated that the payment should be made within a month. （按规定在一个月内付款。）

We regret to find that the goods are not packed as stipulated. （我们很遗憾地发现货物并没有按规定方式包装。）

stipulation: *n*. 规定；条款；项目

The transaction is settled down with the stipulation of direct shipment. (交易规定直接运输。)

7.5 Useful Sentences (实用语句)

(1) Our goods are moderate in price, about 10% lower than our competitors'. (我们的货物价格公道，比竞争对手的价格低约10%。)

(2) Our products have been enjoying fast sales in Europe. (我方产品在欧洲的销路一直很好。)

(3) Being moderate in price, excellent in craftsmanship, and unique in design, our products are very popular with the young. (由于价格公道、工艺精湛、设计独特，我方产品很受年轻人欢迎。)

(4) The quality and prices of our products compare favorably with those you are now using. (我方产品在质量和价格方面都优于贵方现在所用的产品。)

(5) We are giving you the first chance in view of your previous substantial orders, but we should appreciate a prompt reply. (鉴于贵方以前的大量订货，特给予优先机会，但望贵方尽快答复。)

(6) We give you this special discount for the order with the view of developing the business relations between us. (我方给贵方订单提供优惠折扣，期望发展双方的贸易关系。)

(7) To encourage you to place orders with us, we would allow for a 3% special discount for any order received at the end of September. (为了鼓励贵方向我方下订单，特对在九月底前所下的订单给予3%的优惠折扣。)

(8) As this product is now in great demand, we would recommend you to accept this offer as soon as possible. (由于此产品供不应求，我方建议贵方尽快接受此报盘。)

(9) We deem it to your advantage to avail yourselves of our offer. (我们认为贵方接受我方报盘是有利的。)

(10) We believe that the above terms are acceptable to you and await your final order with keen interest. (我们相信上述条款可为贵方接受，盼贵方最后订单。)

(11) In view of the huge demand of this product, we should advise you to work fast and place an order with us as soon as possible. (鉴于对此产品的巨大需求，请从速决定，尽快给我方下订单。)

(12) It is to our mutual advantage to meet each other half way. (彼此各让一半对双方都有好处。)

(13) We take the liberty today of sending you samples of wheat. (今天，我们冒昧送去小麦样品。)

(14) We are enclosing a copy of our recent catalogue with a few samples which may possibly interest you, and shall be glad to hear from you at any time. (现送上我公司最近发行的目录一份和样品数件，贵公司对此可能感兴趣，我方静候回音。)

(15) We have received your favor of yesterday's date, and have pleasure in enclosing you our

samples as follows...（贵公司昨日来信收悉，我方将送去下列样品。）

（16）We are sending you by this post a catalogue, containing quotations for large orders taken from our existing stock.（随信寄去目录一份，并附有批量订购现货的报价。）

（17）We have pleasure in sending herewith a copy of our illustrated catalogue of the machines suitable for your business.（现寄上一份适合贵公司业务、并附有图解的机械目录副本。）

（18）Your esteemed favor of the 28th May, with samples and price-list, is duly to hand.（贵公司5月28日寄来的样品和价目表均已收悉。）

（19）I send you my revised catalogue and price-list, in the hope that you may find something to suit you.（随信寄去新修改的目录和价目表，希望这些商品能适合贵公司的业务。）

（20）I shall be glad if you will send me your catalogue, together with quotations for large quantities.（希望能寄给我们贵公司的目录以及大批量订货的报价。）

（21）We have duly received your letter of June 1, with samples and price-list of your wines, which we have tested. The qualities are satisfactory, but your prices are considerably above our usual figures.（贵公司6月1日的来信、葡萄酒样品和价目表均已收到。经试饮，品质很好。不足的是价格比我们的通常价格高出太多。）

（22）Receiving your samples, we have shown them to their buyers.（贵公司的样品已收到，现已转给用户。）

（23）We have received your samples, with a price-list, also your scale of rebate and terms of settlement, all of which we find satisfactory.（贵公司寄来的价格表、折扣率、成交条件和样品均已收到。对以上诸方面，我们均感到满意。）

Exercises

1. Put the following English phrases into Chinese or Chinese phrases into English.

（1）meet with warm reception

（2）trial order

（3）to one' s advantage to do sth.

（4）compare favorably with

（5）trade discount

（6）满足某人的需求

（7）价格公道

（8）式样独特

（9）品质精良

（10）工艺考究

2. Multiple choice.

（1）This instrument is ________ of our manufactures, which incorporates their traditional exquisite workmanship with most advanced technology of today.

a. a new developed product　　b. a newly developed product

c. a new developing product　　d. a newly developing product

（2）We believe that the reduced prices will put you in a better position in competition

________ your business rivals.

a. at　　b. to　　c. with　　d. in

(3) We as a rule only sell commodities ________ high quality. Although their prices seem higher than those of other makes at first sight, experienced buyers prefer to purchase our products in consideration of long-term benefit.

a. at　　b. of　　c. on　　d. with

(4) We shall be glad to send you sample-cutting books and pamphlets of our new products ________.

a. with request　　b. as request　　c. upon request　　d. at request

(5) The purpose of a promotion letter is to ________ the prospective customer's interest.

a. attract　　b. arouse　　c. attend　　d. alter

(6) We specialize ________ all kinds of metals and are always ready to buy in large quantities.

a. in　　b. from　　c. on　　d. at

(7) ________ the growing needs of the fast developing market at your end, we are considering ________ a representative office in your city.

a. To meet/set up　　b. To meet/establishing

c. Thinking/setting　　d. Thinking/to establish

(8) We hope to do ________ business with you in the near future.

a. the newly　　b. fresh　　c. novel　　d. the latest

(9) Our product is durable ________ use, beautiful ________ design and rich ________ traditional Chinese art.

a. in/in/in　　b. in/to/for　　c. to/for/in　　d. for/in/on

(10) We don't think we can put the business through ________ you revise your terms and conditions.

a. unless　　b. expect　　c. only if　　d. in addition

3. Translate the following sentences into English using the words or phrases in the brackets.

(1) 我公司专营化工品的进口业务。(specialize in)

(2) 订单不断涌入，我们担心贵方采取观望态度会坐失良机。(sit on the fence)

(3) 我们的产品品质优良，价格公道，深受许多国家欢迎。(meet with a warm reception)

(4) 试销订货会使你们相信我们产品的优质。(trial order)

(5) 经过简单比较后，毫无疑问贵方会有兴趣向我方订货。(induce)

(6) 由于所需型号脱销，我们将用下列型号代替。(replace... by)

4. Translate the following letter into English.

敬启者：

关于贵方30日的询价，现确认我方各种尺码都有，数量不限。我方的丝绸以选料精良、工艺精湛、价格公道、设计独特而闻名，在世界各地都受到顾客的青睐。

随函附上报价单和最新目录。

由于本公司目前订单甚多，兹建议从速决定，尽早惠赐订单。

敬上

5. Write a letter as per the following particulars.

（1）推销新款电视机，价格公道，款式新颖。

（2）附寄插图目录和销售资料。

（3）保证一个月内交货。

Supplementary Reading

Part A

In foreign trade communication, besides business letters concerning establishment of business relations and negotiations, etc., there is, however, another type of letter, which is known as a sales promotion letter. Its purpose is to expand business, to persuade the reader to buy what the sellers are able to supply.

Sales promotion consists of those promotional activities other than advertising, personal selling, and publicity. As such, any promotional activities that do not fall under the other three activities of the promotion mix are considered sales promotion. The trade often uses the term indiscriminately. Businesspersons may use the term "promotion" when they actually mean "sales promotion". For purpose here, promotion is a broad term that encompasses sales promotion as well as the other three promotional activities.

The modern trend in sales promotion letter writing is towards making the letters more personal. A good sales promotion letter writer tries to represent the offer from the point of view of the buyer, not the seller. Keep the sales promotion letter short, otherwise it may not be read. Catch the reader's interest in the opening paragraph and give the letter an attractive look and make it as personal as possible.

Notes

1. publicity 宣传活动
2. fall under 被归入
3. indiscriminately 不加区别
4. encompass 包含

Part B

The sales process involves a series of actions beginning with prospecting for customers. The sales presentation is the major element of this process. Before making the presentation, the salesperson must find prospects to contact, obtain appointments, and plan the entire sales presentation.

Prospecting involves locating and qualifying the individuals or businesses that have the potential to buy a product. A person or business that might be a prospect is a lead. These questions can determine if someone is qualified: Is there a real need? Is the prospect aware of that need? Is there a desire to fulfill the need? Does the prospect believe a certain product can be beneficial? Does the prospect have the finances and authority to buy? Are potential sales large enough to be profitable to me?

Several of the more popular prospecting methods are cold canvass and endless chain methods, public exhibitions and demonstrations, locating centers of influence, direct mailouts, and telephone and observation prospecting. To obtain a continual supply of prospects, the salesperson should develop a prospecting method suitable for each situation.

Once a lead has been located and qualified as a prospect, the salesperson can make an appointment with that prospect by telephone or in person. At times, it is difficult to arrange an appointment, so the salesperson must develop ways of getting to see the prospect. Believing in yourself and feeling that you have a product the prospect needs are important.

Part C

Sources of prospects can be many and varied or few and similar, depending on the service or goods the salesperson sells. Naturally, persons selling different services and goods might not use the same sources for prospects. A salesperson of oil-field pipe supplies would make extensive use of various industry directories in a search for names of drilling companies. A life insurance salesperson would use personal acquaintances and current customers as sources of prospects. A pharmaceutical salesperson would scan the local newspaper looking for announcements of new physicians and hospital, medical office, and clinical laboratory openings, whereas a sales representative for a company such as General Mills or Quaker Oats would watch for announcements of construction of new grocery stores and shopping centers.

Top real estate salesperson Vikki Morrison feels that prospecting, which for her means knowing people in her neighborhood, has greatly aided her in becoming a successful salesperson. She strives to become her prospect' s friend.

"In my area, most of the people I see are wives—and any woman who tried to farm in this tract in high heels and a dress, dripping with jewelry, would never make it," she believes. "I' m not trying to impress anybody. These people either know me or they know about me from the neighbors. I'm no threat—especially in my tennies, pants, and T-shirt!"

"Usually, I never meet the husband until the actual listing—then he wants to meet me to find out if I really know what I' m doing in real estate. As far as he' s concerned, I' m just a friend of his wife' s. These are the people I care about," she explains. "If someone needs a plumber or babysitter or a dentist, they call me. If I need a closing gift and someone on the block does creative things, I call them. We' re all in this together!"

Part D

More than Words

Does the language you speak affect the way you perceive the world? Linguistic research suggests that the answer is yes—language not only reflects our thoughts, but, in many ways, shape our thoughts. Here are just a few examples:

(1) Russian speakers, who have a larger vocabulary for blues, are better able to distinguish among shades of blue.

(2) Some indigenous tribes use combinations of *north*, *south*, *east*, and *west* instead of *left* and right for direction (eg: You have a bug on your *northeast* foot.); they have superior spatial orientation, even in unfamiliar landscapes.

(3) The Pirha, an Amazonian tribe, uses words like *few* and *many* instead of number words; its people are unable to track of exact quantities.

(4) Studies conducted at Stanford found that Spanish and Japanese speakers could not remember who caused accidental events as well as English speakers could. The reason? Spanish and Japanese don't normally mention the agents of accidents: "The glass broke itself," rather than "Dana broke the glass."

Beyond Stereotypes

Learning about different cultures is important for understanding the different kinds of people we work with. However, leadership coaches Keith Caver and Ancella Livers caution that people are individuals, not just representatives of a cultural group. Based on their work with African American executives and middle managers, Caver and Livers have found that coworkers sometimes treat these individuals first as representatives of black culture, and only second as talented and experienced managers.

As an example, Caver and Livers cite the all-too-common situation of a newly hired black manager who participates in a management development activity. The new manager is prepared to answer questions about her area of business expertise, but the only questions directed toward her are about "diversity". African American clients of Caver and Livers have complained that they are often called upon to interpret the behavior of famous black Americans such as Clarence Thomas or Jesse Jackson, and they wonder whether their white colleagues would feel their race qualifies them to interpret the deeds of famous white Americans.

In this example, stereotypes make well-intentioned efforts at communication offensive. To avoid such offense, consider not only culture, but also people's individual qualities and their roles and experiences. A person who communicates one way in the role of son or daughter may communicate very differently as engineer or client.

Unit 8
Orders and Their Fulfillment
订单及其履行

8.1 Introduction（简介）

订单是指买方要求卖方按先前报盘达成的交易条件供应具体数量的货物。许多公司常常采用具有正式打印号的订货单，这样既能节省时间，又能确保不遗漏任何重要细则。不过，仍有一些公司，尤其是小公司，采用信函方式订货。必须特别指出的是，如果采用电话订购，应该通过书信加以确认。订单必须准确、清楚，否则就会带来意想不到的麻烦。一般地，订单应包括以下内容：

（1）品名和品质。应清楚地提及商品目录或目录号码，对商品质量进行必要的准确而全面的描述（如质量等级、颜色、式样等）。

（2）价格和数量。应清楚地说明所订购的每项商品的数量、重量或长度。如果没有明确的数量，则应说明最高限量与最低限量。

（3）包装和标志。

（4）装运地点、装运日期、运输方式及代理等。

（5）付款条件。

（6）单据。这包括所需的全部单据及运输指示。

（7）替代品。如果所要的商品没有现货供应，是否同意以别的商品替代。

订单一旦被接受就具有法律约束力，卖方应该严格依照订单来备货和交货。如果发现商品质量低于订单标准，买方可要求减价、换货或者取消订单，甚至索赔。如果商品符合订单要求，买方应该接受货物并在规定期限内支付货款。

收到订单后，应及时回复。在接受订单时，卖方最好在回复时重申订单条款。对于例行的小订单，使用印就的订单即可。不过，使用一封短信，明确对方所期望的交货期会更好些，而且也有助于建立良好关系。收到订单后，除非不得已，一般不宜拒绝接受订单，最好采用还盘的形式。当然，卖方有时确实会遇到必须拒绝订单的情况，如对买方的交易条件不满意、买方的信誉可疑或卖方无货可供等。拒绝订单的信函写作必须特别慎重，应着眼于建立良好的关系和发展未来的业务。

8.2 Writing Skills（写作技巧）

订单信函的写作步骤及常见表达方式如下所示：

写作步骤	表达方式
1. 表明向对方订购货物（或信后随附有订单）	We are in receipt of your letter of October 4th and are pleased to place an order with you for the following goods.（我们已收到贵方10月4日信函，并非常高兴地向贵方订购以下货物。）
	Enclosed please find our Order No. B5421.（请注意随附的我方B5421号订单。）
2. 确认双方达成的交易条件（交货期、运输方式、包装、付款条件及折扣等）	We would like to confirm that payment is to be made by irrevocable letter of credit.（我们确认以不可撤销信用证付款。）
	We would like to thank you for the 30% discount you allowed us.（非常感谢贵方给予我方30%的商业折扣。）
3. 表达进一步合作的愿望	We will submit further orders, if this one is completed to our satisfaction.（如果本次订货令我方满意，我方将继续向贵方订货。）

接受订单信函的写作步骤及常见表达方式如下所示：

写作步骤	表达方式
1. 对收到订单表示高兴，并同意订单的条件	We are pleased to confirm your order which we have accepted on the terms.（我方很高兴确认贵方订单并已接受贵方条件。）
	We are in receipt of your favor of the 10th May, with your order for five printing machines, which we herewith acknowledge with best thanks.（贵公司5月10日来函及五部印刷机器的订单均已收到，在此表示感谢。）
	We acknowledge receipt of your favor of the 10th July, and thank you for the order you have given us.（贵公司7月10日函收悉，对此次订货，我公司表示感谢。）
2. 对所订货物加以赞许	Our products are selling well in many areas.（我们的产品在许多地区销路很好。）
3. 保证对订单迅速、认真地处理	We appreciate the business you have been able to give us and assure you that your order will receive our most careful attention.（感谢贵公司照顾我们这笔交易，我们保证一定慎重办理贵方订单。）
	We are pleased to say that we have already made up your order No. 9901, and you may expect delivery within the next three days.（我们高兴地通知贵方9901号订单货已备妥，有望在三日内交货。）
4. 提醒对方注意其他可能感兴趣的商品	Besides serges we supply a wide rage of other manufactured clothes and enclose a copy of our current price list.（除了哔叽布之外，我们还供应一系列机织布，现随信附上一份最新的价目表。）
5. 希望今后收到更多订单	We appreciate your cooperation and look forward to receiving your further orders.（感谢贵方的合作，希望继续收到贵方订单。）

拒绝订单信函的写作步骤及常见表达方式如下所示：

写作步骤	表达方式
1. 对未能满足对方的需要表示歉意	We are sorry that the model required is no longer being manufactured.（非常抱歉，贵方所需型号我方已不再生产。）
	We are sorry to say that we must turn down your order as we have full order books at present and cannot give a definite date for delivery.（非常抱歉我们必须拒绝贵方订单，因为目前我们的订单排得很满，不能给你们一个确切的交货期。）
2. 若有替代品的话，建议对方使用替代品	We are sorry that your order of Model I is out of stock now. Please select a suitable substitute from the enclosed catalogue.（贵方有关I型号的订单，现在无货，深感抱歉。请从所附寄的目录中挑选合适的替代品。）
3. 希望下一次有机会合作	We regret that, owing to a shortage of stocks, we are unable to fill your order. We will, however, contact you by fax once supplying improves.（因为存货短缺，未能供应贵公司所需货品，特此致歉。一旦供应情况改善，我们将电传通知贵公司。）

8.3 Specimen Letters (样函)

Letter 1: Placing an order

Dear Sirs,

Re: Our Order No. 456

Please ship the following merchandise:

Quantity	Pattern No.	Catalogue	Prices
600 pillowcases	18	45	USD1.60 each
500 pillowcases	21	65	USD1.70 each

(All the prices are FOB Shanghai.)

Delivery: During September.

Payment: By Letter of Credit to be opened in accordance with our agreement.

Packing: Usually packing in strong bales[1], with gunny bag[2] cover and waterproof material[3]. Please acknowledge this order immediately on receipt and inform definite delivery date. This order is of no avail if it is not signed by a responsible person of our firm.

Yours faithfully,

(Signature)

Letter 2: Acknowledging an order (A reply to Letter 1)

Dear Sirs,

Re: Your Order No. 456

Thank you for your order No. 456 for pillowcases and we are happy that you are one of our customers.

We confirm with you the following order for the pillowcases at the prices stated in your letter:

Quantity	Pattern No.	Catalogue No.	Prices
600 pillowcases	18	45	USD1.60 each
500 pillowcases	21	65	USD1.70 each

(All the prices are FOB Shanghai.)

Delivery: During the first ten-day of September.

Payment: By Confirmed Irrevocable L/C[4].

Packing: Usually packing in strong bales, with gunny bag cover and waterproof material. For the above order, we enclose our Purchase Confirmation No. 216 in duplicate. Please sign and return one copy for our file[5] at your earliest convenience.

We thank you again for the above order and hope that this will lead to a long-term cooperation between us.

Yours faithfully,

(Signature)

Letter 3: Placing an order

Dear Sirs,

We thank you for your letter of July 2 and are glad to inform you that your samples are satisfactory. Enclosed please find our Order No. 237 for four of the items.

All these items are urgently required by our customers. We, therefore, hope you will make delivery at an early date.

Yours faithfully,
(Signature)
Encl.

Order No. 237

Quantity	Item	Catalogue No.	CIF Sydney NET
250	Bed Sheets, 106cm, blue	75	GBP2. 50 each
250	Bed Sheets, 120cm, primrose	82	GBP3. 00 each
500	Pillow Cases, blue	117	GBP1. 80 a pair
500	Pillow Cases, primrose	121	GBP1. 80 a pair

Packing: In cotton cloth bales.
Shipment: Prompt shipment from Shanghai.
Payment: By irrevocable L/C available by draft at sight.

Letter 4: Accepting an order (A reply to Letter 3)

Dear Sirs,

Re: Your Order No. 237

We have booked your Order No. 237[6] for bed sheets and pillowcases and are sending you herewith our Sales Confirmation No. BP-103 in duplicate. Please sign and return one copy to us for our file.

It is understood that a letter of credit in our favor covering the above-mentioned goods, will be established immediately. We wish to point out that the stipulations in the relevant credit should strictly conform to the terms stated in our Sales Confirmation in order to avoid subsequent amendments. You may rest assured that we shall effect shipment with the least possible delay upon receipt of the credit.

We appreciate your co-operation and look forward to receiving your further orders.

Yours faithfully,
(Signature)

Letter 5: Placing an order

Dear Sirs,

We acknowledge receipt of your letter of May 5, and request you to take in hand the construction of

100 pumping machines described in detail in ours of May 3, at the prices fixed by you.

GBP620.00	for No. 1
GBP580.00	for No. 2

As you make no mention of the guarantee usually given when delivering machines, we would point out to you that we must stipulate for a two year's guarantee, during which period you engage to make goods any necessary repairs free of charge[7]. Moreover, to ensure delivery of the machines on/before August 1, you are to furnish us with a 2% performance bond[8], which shall be forfeited by default on the expiration of the time specified.

Please acknowledge acceptance of our order, and confirm the conditions stated above by return of mail.

Yours faithfully,

(Signature)

Letter 6: Accepting an order (A reply to Letter 5)

Dear Sirs,

We thank you for your letter of May 17 with order for the delivery of 100 pumping machines. You may be assured that we shall do our best to execute the order to your satisfaction.

The omission of the customary guarantee in our letter of May 5 was an oversight on our part, for which please accept our apology. We hereby guarantee the 100 pumping machines ordered for two years, during which period we are prepared to repair free of charge any defects in the machines arising from faulty material. We are likewise arranging to provide the performance bond prescribed by you.

Yours faithfully,

(Signature)

Letter 7: Refusing an order

Dear Sirs,

We were very glad to receive your order of November 2 for 100 Jinxing television sets but, since you make delivery before Christmas a firm condition, deeply regret that we cannot supply you, as we have done on so many occasions in the past.

The manufactures are finding it impossible to meet current demand for this very popular set. We ourselves placed an order for twenty-four a month ago, but were informed that all orders are being met in strict rotation[9] and that our own could not be dealt with before the beginning of February.

I gather from our telephone conversation this morning that your customers are unwilling to consider other makes. I hope therefore you will be able to obtain your needs from other source. May I suggest that you try Television Services Ltd, Dalian. This I am afraid is the only suggestion I can make that is likely to be of some use.

Sincerely yours,

(Signature)

Letter 8: Refusing an order

Dear Sirs,

Thank you for your order, No. 149, which we received on May 7. Unfortunately we do not feel that we can offer the trade discounts[10] which you have asked for, viz. 35 percent as we only allow a 25 percent trade discount to all our customers regardless of the quantity they buy.

As we think you will agree, our prices are extremely competitive and it would not be worthwhile supplying on the allowance you have asked for. Therefore, in this instance, we regret that we have to turn down your order.

Yours faithfully,

(Signature)

Notes to the specimen letters

1. strong bales 大包
2. gunny bag 黄麻麻袋
3. waterproof material 防水材料
4. Confirmed Irrevocable Letter of Credit 保兑的、不可撤销信用证
5. file 档案
6. we have booked your Order No. 237 我方已接受贵方编号为 237 的订单
7. repair free of charge 免费修理
8. performance bond 履约保证金
9. all orders are being met in strict rotation 所有订单排得很紧
10. trade discount 商业折扣

8.4 Focal Words (焦点词汇)

act

n. 行为，行为过程；一幕；条例，法令

The thief was caught in the act of riffling the safe. （窃贼在盗窃保险柜时当场被抓。）

The second act was not very interesting. （第二幕没什么意思。）

Navigation Act 航海法

vt. & *vi.* 行动，办事，充任，发生作用

Why don't you make up your mind to act at once?（你为什么不下决心立即行动呢?）

We should act in a principled manner. （我们应该按原则办事。）

Who acted as chairman in her absence?（她不在时，谁担任主席?）

This medicine acts on the heart. （这种药对心脏起作用。）

These things were granted as his free act and deed. （这些东西是他自愿签约赠予的。）

act as 担任

He acted as chairman in my absence. （我不在时他担任主席。）

act in 在……方面（的）行动

I am quite sure that he acted in this matter from disinterested motives. （我十分相信，他在这个问题上这样做是无私的。）

acting：*adj.* & *n.* **代理的，演技**

an acting chairman **代理主席**

Her acting was quite first-rate. （她具有一流的演技。）

action：*n.* **行动，行为；作用；诉讼；故事**

Action speak louder than words. （事实胜于雄辩。）

They were forced to take legal action. （他们被迫提出诉讼。）

put out of action **使……失去作用**

The storm put the telephones out of action. （暴风雨使电话中断。）

take action **采取行动**

I felt that it was time for me to take action. （我认为该是采取行动的时候了。）

confirm

vt. **巩固，确定**

The latest information confirms my belief that he is to blame. （这一最新信息使我坚信他该受到责备。）

We hereby confirm acceptance of your order. （我们特此确认接受贵方订单。）

confirmation：*n.* **批准，认可，证实**

We are waiting for confirmation of the news. （我们正在等待消息的证实。）

confirmed：*adj.* **证实的，保兑的**

confirmed letter of credit **保兑信用证**

favor

n. **好感；赏识；帮忙；特权**

Would you do me a favor?（你能帮我个忙吗?）

A letter of credit in our favor will be established immediately. （需立即开立以我方为受益人的信用证。）

vt. **恩惠，给以优惠；对……有利，赞成**

Opportunities always favor those with courage. （机遇永远偏袒勇敢者。）

We trust to be favored with your order. （盼望收到贵方订单。）

favorable：*adj.* **赞成的，有利的，优越的**

We believe if you take the quality into consideration, you will find our quotation most favorable. （我方相信如果贵方将质量因素考虑在内，就会发现我方报价非常优惠。）

favorably：*adv.* **赞成地，满意地，有帮助地**

He impressed me favorably. （他给我的印象不错。）

favored：*adj.* **满意的；优惠的**

most-favored-nation treatment **最惠国待遇**

favorer：*n.* **支持者，赞成者**

in favor of **赞成，主张**

They were in favor of free trade. （他们主张自由贸易。）

in one' s favor 对某人有利

The exchange rate is not in our favor. (汇率对我们不利。)

ask a favor of sb. 求人帮一个忙

I want to ask a favor of you. (我想请你帮个忙。)

market

n. 市场，需求，销路；交易，市价

Good ware makes quick markets. (好货销得快。)

a market index 市价指数

vt. 交易，销售

The inventor is trying to market his new product. (发明者正在努力销售其新产品。)

marketable: *adj.* 适销的，畅销的

marketable goods 畅销货

marketer: *n.* 在市场上买卖的人，专营某种商品的商人或商店

a big gasoline marketer. (专营汽油的大商店。)

marketing: *n.* 买卖，营销

marketing cost. 销售费用

marketplace: *n.* 集市，市场

marketplace price 市价

register

n. 登记，记录；注册；登记册

Just sign the register here and I' ll have your bags sent up later. (请你在这儿的登记本上登记，待会儿我让人把你的包送上去。)

vt. & *vi.* 登记；注册；挂号邮寄；留下印象

Please register this letter. (这封信请挂号邮寄。)

His bearing registered me with intense fear. (他的神态给我留下极其恐惧的印象。)

registered *adj.* 登记的；注册的；挂号的

registered trademark 注册商标

registered post 挂号邮件

8.5 Useful Sentences (实用语句)

(1) In consideration of this being your initial order, we have decided to grant you 3% special discount to strengthen your position in competition with other suppliers. (考虑到这是贵方初次订单，我们决定给贵方3%的优惠折扣，以加强贵方与其他供应商的竞争地位。)

(2) We have received your letter of May 23 along with your proforma invoice No 215/1427 in triplicate and take pleasure in placing an order with you for the said items. (我们已收到贵方5月23日来信及第215/1427号形式发票一式三份，现欣然向你方订购所述商品。)

(3) We are pleased to inform you that your order No. 320 has been accepted by our manufacturers. (现欣然奉告，贵方第320号订单已被我方的厂商接受。)

(4) We hereby confirm acceptance of your order and are enclosing herewith our sales confirmation in two originals one of which please sign and return to us for our file. (我们特此确认接受贵方订单，并附上销售确认书原件两份，请签署其中一份并寄回我方存档。)

(5) We hope that this order will meet your immediate acceptance and careful execution as usual. (希望此项订单能立即为你方接受，并一如既往地谨慎履行。)

(6) Please supply the under-mentioned goods as per your quotation and samples submitted on September 5. (请按 9 月 5 日提出的报价和样品供应下述货物。)

(7) In view of our heavy bookings, we are not in a position to commit ourselves to new orders. (鉴于我方已收到大量订单，我方无法承接新订单。)

(8) Your prompt attention to this order will be highly appreciated. (请从速办理订单，不胜感谢。)

(9) Thank you again for this trial order, and we sincerely hope it will lead to further business. (再次感谢贵方此次试购，我们真诚希望这能带来进一步的交易。)

(10) We appreciate your order No. 304 for 3,000 pieces of women's shirts. We are pleased to accept your terms. Enclosed is a copy of our Sales Note No. 56. (非常感谢贵方购买 3000 件女士衬衣的 304 号订单，并十分高兴地接受贵方条件。随附一份我方 56 号售货通知。)

(11) If the first order is satisfactorily executed, we shall place further and larger orders with you in the future. (如果贵方令人满意地履行第一次订单，将来我们会继续大量地向贵方订货。)

(12) We are working on your order and will keep you informed in course of the progress. (我们正在按照贵方订单进行运作，并将进展过程随时通知贵方。)

(13) As a trial order, we are delighted to send you a small order for 80 pieces of men's shirts S/500. Please note that the goods are to be supplied in accordance with your samples. (我们乐于向贵方小批试订 80 件男衬衣，样品 500 号，请注意所供货物应与样品一致。)

(14) As soon as the purchase is made, and the price ascertained, I will inform you at what they will be invoiced. (当我们查明何时有货，价格多少时，将立即通知贵公司可按什么价格成交。)

(15) We shall gladly join with you in the purchase of 100 bales of wool, to be shipped in moieties by two different vessels, to sail about a month apart. (我们很乐意协同贵公司采购 100 包羊毛，分两条船装运，中间相隔约一个月。)

(16) We have been able to execute the whole of your indent except the pepper. (除胡椒无货不能采购外，贵公司所订购的其他商品，均可购入。)

(17) On the adjoining page we hand you an indent for various lines, which please ship at once. (我们已将委托购买的各种商品在附页列明，请立即发运。)

Exercises

1. Put the following English phrases into Chinese or Chinese phrases into English.

(1) a trial order

(2) duplicate order

(3) outstanding order

(4) close business
(5) order sheet
(6) 第一次订货
(7) 存货清单
(8) 接受订单
(9) 取消订单
(10) 执行订单

2. Multiple choice.

(1) Please ship the ten chests of tea ________ our order No. 2213 at an early date.
a. covered by　　b. covering
c. to be covered　　d. which covered

(2) We are pleased that we have booked ________ 2, 000 pieces of bicycles.
a. your order　　b. with you
c. an order with you　　d. an order with you for

(3) We assure you that any further orders you may ________ will always be carefully attended to.
a. place us　　b. place with us　　c. make us　　d. make with us

(4) We find your terms ________ and now send you our order for the following items.
a. satisfied　　b. satisfaction　　c. satisfactory　　d. satisfy

(5) The buyer suggested that many important orders ________ follow.
a. may　　b. will　　c. would　　d. should

(6) Your prompt attention ________ our order will be much appreciated.
a. of　　b. for　　c. to　　d. in

(7) Please keep us ________ of the despatch of the goods ordered.
a. informed　　b. inform　　c. advising　　d. informing

(8) We trust that you will ________ our order with special care.
a. refer to　　b. deal in　　c. dispose of　　d. attend to

(9) We suggest that shipment of our order ________ effected in May instead of June.
a. is　　b. will be　　c. is to be　　d. be

(10) The shipping date ________ in your order No. 2356 is now under consideration.
a. referring to　　b. referred to　　c. mentioning　　d. stating

3. Translate the following sentences into English using the words or phrases in the brackets.

(1) 作为试订单，我们欣然小量订购贵公司 AC106 号空调机 150 台，请注意货品必须与样品一致。(trial order)

(2) 鉴于贵公司常年惠顾，虽然现时市价较前调升，但本公司仍会按以往订单所列条件接受此次订单。(accept the order)

(3) 由于我们对质量和价格都满意，现就以下货物向贵方订货。(place an order)

(4) 现给贵方寄去我们的 123 号销售合同，一式两份，以供贵方签名。请签署后退回一份留作我方查存之用。(for our file)

(5) 很遗憾，由于需要此商品的订单已接受到今年年底，我们今年之内无法接受新的订单。(book, fresh order)

(6) 我们希望此次订购是建立长期的、愉快的业务关系的第一步。(the first step)

4. Translate the following letter into English.

事由：加拿大燕麦

感谢贵方 1998 年 11 月 10 日来信以及第 P/756 号订单确认书，订购 1000 吨加拿大燕麦。

随信附上我方第 FM-4321 号合同的正副件各两份，供贵方签署。请回签并退回签署的合同正副本各一份，供我方存档。

关于交货期问题，我方将竭力迅速地全部装运，只是贵方信用证必须及时寄达。因此，为了使我方能尽早装船，要求贵方尽快安排开立信用证。

我们借此机会对于你们对我公司的信任表示谢意。

5. Write a letter as per the following particulars.

(1) 感谢对方 7 月 12 日寄来的印花棉布的样品。

(2) 对价格和质量都满意，订购下列货物：

Quantity	Pattern No.	Prices (net)
300 yards	72	33p per yard
450 yards	82	38p per yard
300 yards	84	44p per yard

CIF Lagos

(3) 货物需从现货供应。

(4) 希望将来能向对方大量订货。

(5) 请对方寄给我们一式两份的售货确认书。

Supplementary Reading

Part A

An order is a request to supply a specified quantity of goods. It may result from an offer or an enquiry with subsequent quotations. An order may be given by letter or memorandum, by telex or telegraphic message, or orally at a meeting. Usually, buyers use printed order forms and seller use printed acknowledgements.

The essential qualities of an order are accuracy and clarity. An order should include full details of description, quantities, mode of packing, shipment and prices and quote article numbers and other important terms agreed upon in preliminary negotiation. According to commercial law, the buyer's order is an offer to buy and the arrangement is not legally binding until the seller has accepted the offer. After that, both parties are legally bound to fulfill their agreement. Sellers should deliver goods exactly of the kind ordered at the agreed time and buyers should accept the goods supplied and then pay for them.

Part B

Most salespeople agree that careful planning of the sales call is essential to success in selling.

Among many reasons why planning is so important, four of the most frequently mentioned are that planning builds self-confidence, develops an atmosphere of goodwill, creates professionalism, and increases sales. By having a logical and methodical plan, you can decide what to accomplish and then later measure your accomplishments with your plan.

There are four basic elements of sales call planning. First, you must always have a sales call objective—one that is specific, measurable, and beneficial to the customer. Second, as a salesperson, you must also develop or review the customer profile. By having relevant information about your customer, you can properly develop a customized presentation. You can find information on the background, needs, and competitors of your potential buyer by reviewing your company' s records or by personally contacting the buyer and the company.

The third step in planning your sales call involves developing your customer benefit plan. To do this, look at why the prospect should purchase your product and develop a marketing plan to convey those reasons and the benefits to your prospect. Then, develop a business proposition by listing your price, percent markup, return on investment, and other quantitative data about your product in relation to your prospect. Lastly, develop a suggested purchase order and present your analysis, which might include suggestions on what to buy, how much to buy, what assortment to buy, and when to ship the product.

Finally, plan your whole sales presentation. Visual aids can help make your presentation informative and creative. In making your call, think in terms of the phases that make up a purchase decision—the mental steps: capturing the prospect' s attention, determining buying motives, creating desire, convincing the person that your product is best suited to her or his needs, and then closing the sale.

By adhering to these guidelines for planning your sales presentation, you may spend more time planning than on the actual sales call. However, it will be well worth it.

Part C

The Selling Process and Examples of Prospect' s Mental Thoughts and Questions

1. Prospecting. A salesperson locates and qualifies prospects.

2. Preapproach. The salesperson determines sales call objective and develops customer profile, customer benefit program, and selling strategies. Customer' s needs are determined.

3. Approach. The salesperson obtains interview, meets prospect, and begins individualized sales presentation. Needs are further uncovered.

Prospect' s Mental Steps: Attention due to arousal of potential need or problem. Interest due to recognized need or problem and the desire to fulfill the need or solve the problem.

Prospect' s Potential Verbal and Mental Questions: Should I see salesperson? Should I continue to listen, interact, devote much time to a salesperson? What' s in it for me?

4. Presentation. The salesperson relates product benefits to needs, using demonstration, dram-

atizations, visuals, and proof statements.

Prospect' s Mental Steps: Interest in information that provides knowledge and influences perceptions and attitude. Desire begins to develop based on information evaluation of product features, advantages, and benefits. This is due to forming positive attitudes that product may fulfill need or solve problem. Positive attitudes brought about by knowledge obtained from presentation.

Prospect' s Potential Verbal and Mental Questions: Is the salesperson prepared? Are my needs understood? Is the seller interested in my needs? Should I continue to listen and interact? So what? (to statements about features) Prove it! (to statements about advantages) Are the benefits of this product the best to fulfill my needs?

5. Trial Close. The salesperson asks prospect' s opinion on benefits during and after presentation.

Prospect' s Mental Steps: Desire continues based on information evaluation.

6. Objections. The salesperson uncovers objections.

Prospect' s Mental Steps: Desire continues based on information evaluation.

Prospect' s Potential Verbal and Mental Questions: Do I understand the salesperson' s marketing plan and business proposition? I need more information to make a decision. Can you meet my conditions?

7. Meet Objections. The salesperson satisfactorily answers objections.

Prospect' s Mental Steps: Desire begins to be transformed into belief. Conviction established due to belief the product and the salesperson can solve needs or problems better than competitive products. Appears ready to buy.

Prospect' s Potential Verbal and Mental Questions: Let me see the reaction when I give the salesperson a hard time. I have a minor/major objection to what you are saying. Is something nonverbal being communicated? Did I get a reasonable answer to my objection?

8. Trial Close. The salesperson uses another trial close to see if objections have been overcome or, if presentation went smoothly before the close, to determine if the prospect is ready to buy.

Prospect' s Mental Steps: Conviction becomes stronger.

Prospect' s Potential Verbal and Mental Questions: Can I believe and trust this person? Should I reveal my real concerns?

9. Close. The salesperson has determined prospect is ready to buy and now asks for the order.

Prospect' s Mental Steps: Action (purchase) occurs based on positive beliefs that the product will fulfill needs or solve problems.

Prospect' s Potential Verbal and Mental Questions: I am asked to make a buying decision now. If I buy and I am dissatisfied, what can I do? Will I receive after-the-sale service as promised? What are my expectations toward this purchase? Why don' t you ask me to buy? Ask one more time and I'll buy.

10. Follow-up. The salesperson provides customer service after the sale.

Prospect' s Mental Steps: Satisfaction-Dissatisfaction.

Prospect' s Potential Verbal and Mental Questions: Did the product meet my expectations? Am

I experiencing dissonance? How is the service associated with this product? Should I buy again from this salesperson?

Part D

Make the Most of Your Brainstorming

Matt Bowen, president of the Aloft Group Inc., marketing and PR agency, has advice on running successful brainstorming meetings:

(1) Identify a clear, concrete goal before you start. That allows you to establish some boundaries for ideas—about practicality or cost, for example—and helps you keep your brainstorming session focused.

(2) Let everyone involved in the meeting know what the goal is ahead of time. That gives everyone a chance to have ideas ready when they come to the meeting: if people "pre-brainstorming," you can focus your brainstorming on refining ideas.

(3) Set limits on meeting size and duration. Bowen recommends limiting a brainstorming meeting to seven participants. An hour is enough time for a focused discussion, and it's easier for everyone to participate and be heard in a small team.

(4) Let the ideas flow freely. Bowen recommends practicing active listening skills that encourage people both to share their ideas and to build on each other's ideas.

(5) Remember that there are no bad ideas: any idea, however important, might inspire the best solution, and spending time weeding out weak ideas can stifle creativity.

(6) Brainstorm with a diverse team. The best ideas come out of teams with very different perspectives.

Being Taken Seriously

It's frustrating to speak in a meeting and have people ignore what you say. Here are some tips for being taken seriously:

(1) Link your comment to the comment of a powerful person, even if logic suffers a bit. For example, say "John is saying that we should focus on excellence, and I think we can become stronger by encouraging diversity."

(2) Show that you've done your homework. Laura Sloate, who is blind, establishes authority by making sure her first question is highly technical: "In footnote three of the 10K, you indicate..."

(3) Find an ally in the organization and agree ahead of time to acknowledge each other's contributions to the meeting, whether you agree or disagree with the point being made. Explicit disagreement signals that the comment is worth taking seriously: "Duane has pointed out..., but I think that..."

(4) Use the style of language that powerful people in your organization use.

(5) Repeat your ideas. Put important ideas in a memo before the meeting.

Unit 9
Letter of Credit
信用证

9.1 Introduction（简介）

信用证（Letter of Credit）是国际贸易中最常用的支付方式，不仅适用于个别交易，也适用于系列交易。信用证的开证程序始于进口方。进口方通知开证行（Issuing Bank）开立以出口方为受益人（Beneficiary）的信用证。信用证包含进出口双方达成交易的详细内容。信用证开出后，由开证行将信用证寄给出口方所在地的通知行（Notifying Bank）。接到信用证后，银行和出口方会对信用证进行审核。根据审核无误的信用证，出口方就可备货装运。装运后，出口方就可以缮制符合信用证要求的单据，再据此向议付行（Negotiation Bank）交单议付，取得货款。

有时，进口方由于某种原因而未能按合同规定的时间开立信用证，这时，出口方应催促进口方迅速办理开证手续（Urging Establishment of L/C），特别是大宗商品或进口方要求特制的商品，更应结合备货情况及时进行催证。催证信函的写作得讲究技巧，其目的是劝说对方给予紧密合作并履行其义务。如果催证信函措辞不当，就有可能激怒进口方，造成不愉快的后果。因此，除特殊情况外，不应在催证信函的一开始就强烈地指责对方没有履行合同，而应用礼貌的语气告诉对方货已备妥，但是相关的信用证还未开到。如果第一封信没有回音，紧接着，就要写第二封信，此时可向对方表示失望和惊讶。

如果出口方在审证时发现信用证条款存在与合同内容不相符的地方，这时就需要改证。改证要求一般是由出口方提出的。有时，出口方发现信用证条款需要修改也会提出改证要求。改证的一般程序是先由出口方征得进口方的同意，再由进口方向开证行申请修改信用证。出口方有时会由于某些原因，而不能在信用证规定的装运期内装运，这时出口方必须要求延长信用证的装运期和有效期。无论是信用证修改，还是信用证展期，对应信函的写作都要注意采用礼貌的语气。因为信用证的修改或展期耗时耗费，对进出口双方来说都是烦恼的事情。

9.2 Writing Skills（写作技巧）

催证信函的写作步骤及常见表达方式如下所示：

写作步骤	表达方式
1. 提醒买方我方货已备妥待运或交货期已临近，但尚未收到相关信用证	In regard to 25,000 yards of cotton prints under the Sales Confirmation No. 789, we would like to draw your attention to the fact that the date of delivery is approaching, but up to now we have not received your relative Letter of Credit.（我们提醒贵方注意，789 号售货确认书项下 25，000 码印花布的交货期已临近，但我方至今尚未收到相关信用证。）

（续）

写作步骤	表达方式
2. 向对方说明需及时开立信用证的原因（或重要性）	We wish to remind you that it was agreed when placing the order, that you would establish the required L/C upon receipt of our Confirmation.（我方提醒贵方注意，订货时双方约定，一接到我方确认书，贵方就开立信用证。）
3. 请对方尽快开证	As the goods have been ready for shipment for quite some time, it behooves you to take immediate action, particularly since we cannot think of any valid reason for further delaying the opening of the credit.（货已备妥多日，贵方应立即开证，我们不知道贵方有何合理理由迟迟不开证。）

改证或信用证展期信函的写作步骤及常见表达方式如下所示：

写作步骤	表达方式
1. 告诉对方已收到信用证	We wish to acknowledge receipt of the L/C No. 3450 for the amount of USD5, 000 covering your order No. 987.（贵方987号订单项下金额5，000美元的3450号信用证已收到。）
2. 指出信用证与合同不符而需修改的地方（说明需要展期的原因）	We find that the following two points do not conform to the contract.（我方认为条款中有下列两点与合同不符。）
	In connection with shipment, we are very sorry to advise that the goods cannot be ready before the end of May, because of delay of our manufactures.（关于装运问题，我方深表歉意，由于厂商的延误，该货无法在5月底前备妥。）
3. 希望对方给予合作	Your prompt attention to the matter will be much appreciated.（请尽快办理，不胜感激。）
	We are confident that you will give us cooperation by extending the shipment date to June 10, and the negotiation validity to June 25, 2005 respectively.（相信贵方会予以合作，将装运期和议付期分别延期到2005年6月10日和6月25日。）

9.3 Specimen Letters（样函）

Letter 1: Urging establishment of L/C

Dear Sirs,

Please open a credit[1] of GBP30, 000 with your correspondents in London in favor of[2] the Universal Clothing Co. London, to be available to the company until July 31 against a shipment of waterproof clothing by S. S. Cathay leaving London for Tokyo on July 24.

When the consignment is shipped the company is to draw on your correspondents at 60d/s. The documents to accompany the draft are the bill of lading, commercial and consular invoices and insurance policy. Kindly ask your correspondents to see that the insurance policy gives full cover before they accept the draft.

Yours faithfully,

(Signature)

Letter 2: Importer notifying L/C arrangement

Dear Sirs,

Re: Order No. 7766

We enclose an order for 2,000 (two thousand) waterproof raincoats and have made arrangements with the Bank of Japan, Tokyo, to open a credit in your favor. The credit is valid until July 31 and will be confirmed[3] to you by the Bank's London office, Gresham Street, EC2P 2EB. Please draw on them at 60 d/s. It is understood that the goods will be shipped by S. S. Cathay, sailing from London on July 24.

Carton containing the goods should be marked S. M. The amount of our credit has been fixed to provide adequate cover for your invoice, which should provide for all charges, including insurance to Tokyo.

Please notify us when the goods are shipped.

Yours faithfully,
(Signature)

Letter 3: A reply to Letter 2

Dear Sirs,

Your order No. 7766 of July 1 has now been completed and taken on board the S. S. Cathay which, we are informed, will be sailing tomorrow.

Shipping documents, including original invoice, have been passed to the London Branch of the Bank of Japan, upon whom we have drawn at 60 d/s for the net amount due, namely GBP2,651.44. From the copy invoice enclosed you will notice that we have allowed a special quantity discount of 2.5% and, provided you give us a liberal share of your business, we shall be happy to allow a similar discount on future large orders.

We trust the consignment will reach you safely and prove satisfactory.

Yours faithfully,
(Signature)

Letter 4: Urging establishment of L/C

Dear Sirs,

With reference to the goods under our Sales Confirmation No. 5354, we wish to draw your attention to the fact that the date of delivery is approaching, but we have not yet received the covering L/C to date. Please do your utmost to expedite the L/C, so that we may execute the order smoothly. In order to avoid subsequent amendment, please see to it that the L/C stipulations are in exact accordance with the terms in the Confirmation.

Hope to hear favorably from you soon.

Yours truly,
(Signature)

Letter 5: Seller asking buyer to extend L/C

Dear Sirs,

Re: Letter of Credit No. AG8432

We have received your Letter of Credit No. AG8432 for the amount of USD2, 960 to cover your order No. 806 for 20 metric tons of mineral fertilizer.

The said credit calls for shipment on or before the 31st of December. As the earliest steamer sailing for your port is the S. S. Peace scheduled to leave Shanghai on or about the 3rd of January, it is, therefore, impossible for us to effect shipment at the time you named.

This being the case, we have to ask you to be so kind as to extend the date of shipment to the 15th of January, under cable advice to us. We understand that cable amendment is costly, but this is a matter over which we can exercise no control.

Yours faithfully,

(Signature)

Letter 6: Buyer' s refusal of extending L/C (A reply to Letter 5)

Dear Sirs,

We received your letter of 15th October requesting us to extend our L/C owing to the fact that you are unable to make shipment within the stipulated time, we shall not be able to fulfill our contract with our clients. Besides, such delay will certainly cause us a lot of unnecessary inconveniences and expenses.

We would, therefore, ask you to try your utmost to effect shipment according to the original schedule. In the event of your failing to do so, we will have to ask you to compensate us for any loss arising therefrom.

We are awaiting your immediate reply.

Yours faithfully,

(Signature)

Letter 7: Requesting amendment to L/C

Dear Sirs,

We are in receipt of your letter on July 20 requesting us to ship all the 20 sets of safety pin machines[4] in September. Unfortunately we are unable to comply with[5] your wishes.

When we offered the machines, it was expressly stated that shipment would be effected in October. If you desire early delivery, we can only make a partial shipment[6] of ten machines in September and the remaining ten in October. We hope this arrangement will be agreeable to you. Should this be so, please amend the covering credit to allow partial shipment under advice to us.

Please cable us your confirmation so that we can request the manufacturers to expedite delivery[7].

Sincerely yours,

(Signature)

Letter 8: On amount in L/C and time of shipment

Dear Sirs,

Re: L/C No. 12345 Issued by Barclay' s Bank

We hereby acknowledge with thanks receipt of[8] the captioned L/C for the amount of[9] USD2, 500 covering your order No. 215 for rapeseeds.

It appears that the amount of your L/C is insufficient, as the correct total CIF value of your order comes to[10] USD2, 650 instead of USD2, 500 with a difference of USD150.

Furthermore, when we booked your order, we made it clear that delivery should be made within one month after receipt of your L/C. Now you are allowing us only half a month. As you may be well aware, it is impossible for us to get the shipment ready in such a short period of time.

In view of the above, you are requested to increase the amount of your L/C by USD150, making a total of USD2, 650, and also to extend the time of shipment to 31st October. Your prompt attention to this matter will be appreciated.

Yours faithfully,

(Signature)

Letter 9: Requesting amendment to L/C

Dear Sirs,

Re: Letter of Credit No. 789

We thank you for your L/C No. 789 covering your order No. 0089 for 10 metric tons of Zinc Oxide.

You failed to mention in the L/C that the quality of the material is to be based on the certificate of quality issued by China Commodity Inspection Bureau[11], as you agreed when placing the order.

On the contrary, you inserted in the L/C two clauses to the effect that inspection of the material will be made at the port of destination and that you have the right to lodge claims against us within 10 days after arrival of the shipment.

We are sorry to say that we cannot agree to such terms, and believe that their being contrary to our agreement has perhaps escaped your attention[12]. Your prompt amendment to the L/C and deletion of the two clauses is urgently requested.

Yours faithfully,

(Signature)

Letter 10: On amount in L/C

Dear Sirs,

We wish to acknowledge receipt of L/C for the amount of $2, 500 covering your order No. 315 for 8 metric ton walnut-meat.

It appears that the amount in your L/C is insufficient, as the correct total CIF value of your order comes to $2, 960 instead of $2, 500, the difference being $460.

In view of the above, please increase the amount of your L/C by $460. On receipt of your amendment we shall arrange shipment without fail[13].

Sincerely yours,
(Signature)

Notes to the specimen letters

1. open a credit 开立信用证
2. in favor of 以……为受益人
3. confirm 由……保兑
4. safety pin machines 安全别针机
5. comply with 满足
6. partial shipment 部分装运
7. expedite delivery 加速装运
8. acknowledge receipt of 收到
9. for the amount of 金额为
10. come to 等于
11. China Commodity Inspection Bureau 中国商品检验局
12. escape your attention 贵方的疏忽
13. without fail 立即

9.4 Focal Words（焦点词汇）

account

n. **账目，账户；理由**

We shall credit the difference, totaling GBP5,000 to your account. （我方将把差额总数5，000英镑记入贵方账户贷方。）

Our bank does not keep an RMB account with the Bank of China, Head Office, Beijing. （我方银行没有在北京的中国银行总行开立人民币账户。）

We wish to give you a brief account of some flexible measures we adopted. （我们愿意扼要说明一下我方采取的若干灵活措施。）

vi. & *vt.* **报账；认为**

These expenses of different kinds should be separately accounted for. （这些不同种类的支出应分别列账。）

All of them account these lines are profitable fields of investment. （他们所有人都认为这些行业是有利可图的投资领域。）

for one's account **由……代理，为……代购（销）**

We hereby open an irrevocable L/C No. 123 in favor of... for account of ... 兹开立第123号不可撤销信用证，受益人为……开证申请人为……

We usually allow a commission of 5% on an order placed by a commission agent for account of his customer who opens L/C direct to us.（凡代理商代其客户订货并由客户向我方直接开出信用证者，我方通常给 5% 的佣金。）

on account **作为部分账款；以赊账方式；作为部门偿还**

He owed USD100 and sent me USD50 on account.（他欠 100 美元，先给我寄来 50 美元作为部分偿还。）

on account of **由于……**

We both understand our slippers are very popular in your market on account of their superior quality and competitive price.（我们双方都知道我方拖鞋因价廉物美而畅销于贵方市场。）

on one' s own account **自己承担风险**

They do not feel able to make purchase on their own account.（他们不能自负盈亏来购进货物。）

amount

n. **数量，金额**

We have been doing an increasing amount of business with the firm mentioned in your letter in the recent years.（近年来，我们与贵方信中所提及的那家公司的交易量越来越大。）

We would like to give you a sample order to an amount of about USD3, 000.（我们愿意给贵公司一个样品订单，金额为 3000 美元。）

vi. **合计，共计**

The total value of the machines amounts to USD2, 000, 000.（这些机器的总价值达 200 万美元。）

Your reply amounts to a refusal of our request.（贵方的答复等于拒绝了我方的要求。）

cover

vi. & *vt*. **包括，涉及；偿付，弥补；投保**

Carriage is not covered by quotation.（报价中不包括运费。）

The compensation will cover the whole loss.（此项赔款足以抵偿全部损失。）

Please open a letter of credit to cover the order.（请开具这笔订单的信用证。）

Insurance is to be covered of by the buyer.（保险由买方投保。）

n. **封袋，保险**

Under separate cover, we are sending you the counter samples as requested.（按照贵方要求，我们把复样另邮你处。）

We have decided to arrange the necessary insurance cover.（我们已决定办理必要的保险。）

coverage：*n*. **保险范围，投保总额，保证金**

He has fire and theft coverage on his store.（他给自己的商店投保了火险和盗窃险。）

Regarding insurance, the coverage is for 110% of the invoice value up to the port of destination.（关于保险，按发票金额的 110% 投保，至目的港为止。）

issue

vi. & *vt*. **发行；开立；出版；收益**

We have arranged with our bankers to issue an L/C in your favor.（我们已请我方银行开立以贵方为受益人的信用证。）

to issue securities（banknotes, cheques, stamps）发行证券（钞票、支票、邮票）

The magazine is issued once every week.（这份杂志每周发行一次。）

Little money issued from the stocks.（股票收益甚微。）

n. 发行；出版；期刊；问题；收益

Stockholders usually have the right to buy additional stock from a new issue before it is made available to general public.（股东通常有权在向社会公开发行新股前增购股票。）

The buyer skirts the real issue.（买主在回避实质问题。）

issuer：*n.*（证券等）发行人，（信用证）开证银行，签发人，发布人

issuing：*adj.* 发行的；开证的；发货的

value

n. 价值，价款，价格

These articles are really of good value.（这些商品确实货真价实。）

They imported goods to the value of USD50, 000.（他们进口了价值5万美元的货物。）

Insurance is to be covered by the sellers for 110% of the invoice value.（由卖方按发票金额的110%投保。）

vi. & *vt.* 估价；评价

Intangible assets are very hard to value properly.（无形资产很难恰当估价。）

We value your enquiry very much.（我们非常重视贵方的询盘。）

valuer：*n.* 估价人，评价人

value on 向……开出汇票

You may value on us for the invoice amount at 60 days' sight.（贵方可按照发票金额向我方开出60天期的汇票。）

9.5 Useful Sentences（实用语句）

（1）We have opened an L/C in your favor against contract No. GF805 available by documentary draft at sixty days' sight.（我们已根据GF805号合同开立以贵方为受益人、见票60天付款的跟单信用证。）

（2）According to the stipulation of S/C No. 2035, you should establish the covering L/C before April 20.（根据第2035号销售确认书的规定，贵方必须在4月20日前开立有关信用证。）

（3）We have made arrangement with Bank of Japan, Tokyo, to open a credit in your favor. The credit is valid until May 31, and will be confirmed by the Bank's London Office.（我们已安排位于东京的日本银行开立以贵方为受益人的信用证。该信用证有效期到5月31日，并将由该行的伦敦分行保兑。）

（4）You must expedite the covering L/C, otherwise we shall be unable to effect shipment before the end of this month.（贵方必须从速开立信用证，否则，我们就不能在本月底以前装船。）

（5）The 100 pieces motors are scheduled to be loaded onto S. S. Flying Cloud on April 12.

Please extend your L/C to the end of April. （100 台电动机定于 4 月 12 日装上“飞云”轮。请将信用证的有效期延长到 4 月底。）

（6） With regard to L/C No. 705, we have already instructed the opening bank to extend the dates of shipment and validity to May 15 and May 30 respectively. （关于第 705 号信用证，我方已指示开证行将装船期及有效期分别延到 5 月 15 日和 5 月 30 日。）

（7） Your L/C No. 595 stipulates for a Certificate of Origin to be visaed by your consul. We regret being unable to accept this clause. （贵方第 595 号信用证规定原产地证书必须由贵方领事签准。我方不能接受此条款，深表遗憾。）

（8） With reference to your amendment to L/C No. 903 changing the assortment of the goods, we regret having to give it a refusal, because the goods have been packed already. （关于贵方提出修改第 903 号信用证——改变商品的品种搭配一事，因为货物已经包装完毕，我方不能同意，深表遗憾。）

（9） You are requested to notify your client to increase the L/C amount to USD578,000. （要求你们通知贵方客户将信用证金额增加到 57.8 万美元。）

（10） Please amend L/C No. 526 allowing transshipment and partial shipment, so that we may effect shipment without delay. （请修改第 526 号信用证，允许转船和分装，以便我方马上装船。）

（11） We have surrendered to the Bank of China, Fuzhou, the clean, shipped on board B/L in complete set together with other documents according to the terms of your L/C No. 999. （我们已根据贵方第 999 号信用证条款，将全套清洁提单连同其他单据提交中国银行福州分行。）

（12） The original shipping documents have been presented to the negotiating bank here for payment. （装船单据正本已提交这里的议付行支付货款。）

Exercises

1. Put the following English phrases into Chinese or Chinese phrases into English.

（1） to cable a credit

（2） to amend a credit

（3） to extend a credit

（4） to increase a credit

（5） recourse repudiation

（6） 保兑信用证

（7） 可转让信用证

（8） 有追索权信用证

（9） 信用证余额

（10） 通过银行开立信用证

2. Multiple choice.

（1） ________ yesterday did we receive your L/C.

a. Until　b. Not until　c. Until not　d. No until

（2） we must point out that ________ your L/C reaches us before the end of this month, we shall not be able to effect shipment within the stipulated time limit.

a. if　　b. unless　　c. in case　　d. in case of

(3) Payment is to be made ________ sight draft drawn under an irrevocable letter of credit.

a. on　　b. upon　　c. against　　d. for

(4) ________, we require payment by L/C.

a. If business is resulted　　b. If business is materialized

c. If business finalizes　　d. If business results

(5) In accordance with our agreement, we have ________ at 30 day' s sight for the amount of the enclosed invoice.

a. drawn on you　　b. written to you　　c. called on you　　d. advised you

(6) You must be responsible for all the loss ________ from your delay in opening the covering L/C.

a. arising　　b. rising　　c. arousing　　d. have arisen

(7) We could manage to arrange the shipment in July, subject to your L/C ________ us not later than June 15.

a. reaches　　b. being reached　　c. reaching　　d. reach

(8) Please open your L/C immediately to facilitate ________.

a. our shipping arrangement　　b. for shipment

c. to arrange shipment　　d. us to arrange shipment

(9) The stipulations of the L/C should ________ those of the contract.

a. agree to　　b. agree in　　c. agree on　　d. agree with

(10) The amount in your L/C appears insufficient. The correct total CFR value of your order comes to USD9, 328. 00 instead of 3, 928. 00, the difference ________ USD5, 400. 00.

a. be　　b. is to be　　c. being　　d. been

3. Translate the following sentences into English using the words or phrases in the brackets.

(1) 请尽快修改信用证，以便我们安排装运。(make amendments)

(2) 我们被请求已开出以贵方为受益人的信用证，特此通知。(in one' s favor)

(3) 4月17日到期的第357号信用证已被展期至5月2日。(expire)

(4) 请贵方将信用证做如下修改：“吨”前删去“长”字，加入“公”字。(delete, insert)

(5) 考虑到我们多年的友好关系，这笔交易我们接受60天期的信用证。(in consideration of)

(6) 我们多次催促贵方开证，但至今未收到贵方的信用证。(urge sb. to do sth.)

4. Translate the following letter into English.

敬启者，

事由：地方银行开立的第4654号信用证

贵方8月6日的来信收阅，对于标题信用证上所出现的错误我方深表抱歉，该失误完全是由于粗枝大叶所造成的。

今天上午我方已通知银行用电报修改第 4654 号信用证，并相信信用证修改书不久将会到达贵方。由于我方急需该货，如蒙安排即期装运，我方将不胜感谢。

如客户满意这批货的话，不久将有可能续订。

对于贵方在这方面的紧密合作我们预致感谢。

谨上

5. Write a letter as per the following particulars:

（1）贵方 4 月 5 日的来信收到，内容已悉。

（2）信用证第 20888 号，已通知开证行展延装船期和信用证有效期分别为 5 月 15 日和 5 月 30 日；有关展期的电报想必现在已到达贵方。

（3）请马上与轮船公司联系，订好舱位，务必在 5 月 15 日前发运。

（4）如果用户满意这批货，我们可以保证将大量续订。

（5）感谢贵方在这方面的合作，同时我方等待贵方电开装船通知。

Supplementary Reading

Part A

Paying for goods supplied in domestic trade is fairly simple matter because payment can be made either in advance or within a reasonably short period after delivery. But this problem is much more complicated in foreign trade. Must the seller wait perhaps several months for his money or shall the buyer pay several months before he not even sees his goods? Clearly, the seller runs certain risks of non-payment if he surrenders goods before payment has been made. As it is not often possible for the seller personally to collect payment before delivery, the appointment of agents for this purpose in the importers' countries becomes necessary. This function is usually entrusted to the banker, who has branches or correspondent banks in most towns or cities overseas.

The most generally used method of payment in the financing of international trade is the letter of credit （L/C）, which is reliable and safe method of payment, facilitating trade with unknown buyers and giving protection to both sellers and buyers. The L/C consists of a promise by the opening bank that he will honor drafts drawn by the seller of merchandise, provided that the seller surrenders to the bank a complete set of documents evidencing that the goods shipped are in accordance with the contract and that all stipulations in the L/C have been complied with. The process of issuing a letter of credit starts with the buyer. He instructs his bank to issue an L/C in favor of the seller for the amount of the purchase. The buyer' s bank sends to its correspondent bank in the seller' s country the L/C, giving instructions about the amount of the credit, the beneficiary, the currency, the documents required, and other special instructions. On arrival of it, the correspondent bank advises the seller of the receipt of the credit. Sometimes, a seller required a confirmed L/C. In this case, the correspondent bank usually adds its confirmation, becoming a confirming bank and advises the seller of the same; the seller will then dispatch the goods accordingly.

Notes

1. surrender 提交

2. entrust 委托
3. confirmed 保兑的

Part B

To improve your chances of making a sale, you must master the art of delivering a good sales presentation. An effective presentation will work toward specifically solving the customer' s problems. The sales presentation method you select should be based on prior knowledge of the customer, your sales call objective, and your customer benefit plan.

Because prospects want to know how you and your product will benefit them and the companies they represent, you must show that you have a right to present your product because it has key benefits for them. Many different sales presentation methods are available. They differ from one another depending on what percentage of the conversation is controlled by the salesperson. The salesperson usually does most of the talking in the more structured memorized and formula selling techniques, while more buyer-seller interaction occurs in the less structured methods.

In the memorized presentation, or stimulus-response method, the salesperson does 80 to 90 percent of the talking, with each customer receiving the same sales pitch. Although this method ensures a well-planned presentation and is good for certain nontechnical products, it is also somewhat inflexible, allowing little prospect participation. The formula presentation, a persuasive selling presentation, is similar to the first method, but it takes the prospect into account by answering questions and handling objections.

The most challenging and creative form of selling uses the need-satisfaction presentation. This flexible method begins by raising questions about what the customer specifically needs. After you are aware of the customer' s needs, you can then show how your products fit these needs. You must be cautious because many people don' t want to open up to the salesperson.

When selling highly complex or technical products like computers or insurance, a problem-solution presentation consisting of six steps is a good sales method. This method involves developing a detailed analysis of the buyer' s specific needs and problems and designing a proposal and presentation to fit these needs. This customized method often uses a selling team to present the specialized information to the buyer.

In comparing the four presentation methods, there is no one best method. Each one must be tailored to meet the particular characteristics of a specific selling situation or environment.

Part C

The Need-Satisfaction Presentation

The need-satisfaction presentation is different from the memorized and the formalized approach; it is designed as a flexible, interactive sales presentation. It is the most challenging and creative form of selling.

The salesperson typically starts the presentation with a probing question such as, “What are you looking for in investment property?” or “What type of computer needs does your company have?" This opening starts a discussion of the prospect' s needs and also gives the salesperson an opportunity to determine whether any of the products being offered might be beneficial. When something the prospect has said is not understood by the salesperson, it can be clarified by a question or by restating what the buyer has said. The need-satisfaction format is especially suited to the sale of industrial and technical goods with stringent specifications and high price tags.

Often, the first 50 to 60 percent of conversation time (referred to as the need-development phase) is devoted to a discussion of the buyer' s needs. Once aware of the prospect' s needs (the need-awareness phase), the salesperson begins to take control of the conversation by restating the prospect' s needs to clarify the situation. During the last stage of the presentation, the need-fulfillment (or need-satisfaction) phase, the salesperson shows how the product will satisfy mutual needs.

Should you have to come back a second time to see the prospect, as is often the case in selling industrial products, you would use the formula sales presentation method in calling on the same prospect. You might begin with a benefit statement such as this:

Mr. Pride, when we talked last week, you were interested in saving your executives time and energy in getting to and from your plant, and you felt the Dyno Electric Cart could do this for you. (You could pause to let him answer or say, "Is that correct?")

From the buyer' s response to your question, you can quickly determine what to do. If the buyer raises an objection, you can respond to it. If the buyer requests more information, you can provide it. If what you have said about your product has pleased the buyer, you simply ask for the order.

Be cautious when uncovering a prospect' s needs. Too many questions can alienate the prospect. Remember, initially many prospects do not want to open up to salespeople. Actually, some salespeople are uncomfortable with the need-satisfaction approach because they feel less in control of the selling situation than with a canned or formula presentation. A good point to remember is that you are not a performer on a stage, but rather, your job is to meet your prospect' s needs—not your own. Eventually, you can learn to anticipate customer reactions to this presentation and learn to welcome the challenge of the interaction between you and the buyer.

Part D

A Positive Message That Backfired

Sharing good news is often considered the easiest part of a writer' s job. However, just as with any message, writers must craft positive messages carefully and pay attention to their audience and the situation.

In March 2011, Transocean issued its annual report to its shareholders and the United States Securities and Exchange Commission. As the largest offshore oil drilling contractor in the world, Transocean had enjoyed a profitable year with, according to standard industry measures, an exemplary safety record. In the filing, the company stated, "We recorded the best year in safety performance in our Company' s history."

Unfortunately, Transocean is the owner of Deepwater Horizon, the oil rig that exploded in the Gulf of Mexico, April 2010. The accident killed 11 workers, injured another 17, and triggered the largest—and most publicized—oil spill in the history of the United States. Millions of barrels of oil gushed into the ocean over three months, causing an environmental disaster.

But in its report, Transocean attempted to minimize the Deepwater Horizon accident to place greater emphasis on its good news: "Notwithstanding the tragic loss of life in the Gulf of Mexico, we achieved an exemplary statistical safety record as measured by our total recordable incident rate and total potential severity rate."

The strategy backfired. News articles about the report focused on the phrase "the best year in safety performance" and the six-figure bonuses and salary increases for the executives, all only months after the disaster in the Gulf of Mexico. Days after the annual report's filing, Transocean apologized for the wording.

By failing to craft its positive annual report with sensitivity to the situation and public opinion, Transocean saw a positive message turned into another negative strike against the company.

Compliment Carefully

Compliments can be valuable for building goodwill in informative messages. But too often they offer backhanded compliments. Consider these examples:

(1) "That dress looks better on you every year."

(2) "You short people sure are intelligent."

(3) "You must have been really pretty when you were young."

If you decide to use a compliment in your message, proceed carefully. Make sure you are being sincere and specific and that your compliment can't be misunderstood. You should also limit your compliments to those that will be most significant to your reader. Using compliments correctly can help you build goodwill and good relationships with others.

Unit 10

Other Terms of Payment

其他支付方式

10.1 Introduction（简介）

在国际贸易中，除了上一单元所讨论的信用证之外，另外两种重要的支付方式分别是汇付（Remittance）和托收（Collection）。

汇付和托收都是以商业信用为基础的支付方式，分别表现为先货后款或先款后货的卖方信用或买方信用。

汇付是最简单的国际货款结算方式。采用汇付方式结算货款时，出口方将货物直接交付给进口方，由进口方径自通过银行将货款汇给出口方。汇付方式有三种：电汇（Telegraphic Transfer or T/T）、信汇（Mail Transfer or M/T）和票汇（Demand Draft or D/D）。

托收是出口方委托银行向进口方收款的一种支付方式。托收分为光票托收和跟单托收。光票托收是指出口方仅把金融单据委托银行代为收款。跟单托收是出口方发运货物后开立汇票连同货运单据，委托出口地银行通过其在进口地的分行或代理行向进口方收取货款。跟单托收又分为承兑交单（Documents Against Acceptance or D/A）和付款交单（Documents Against Payment or D/P），付款交单又可分为即期付款交单（D/P at sight）和远期付款交单（D/P after sight）。

付款方式信函的内容通常包括：介绍付款方式、要求更有利的付款方式或者变更付款方式等。

10.2 Writing Skills（写作技巧）

其他付款方式信函的写作步骤及常见表达方式如下所示：

写作步骤	表达方式
1. 提示合同或相关的货物	We refer you to Contract No. . . .（关于第……号合同）
	Referring to . . .（关于……）
	With regard to our contract of . . .（关于我们……的合同）
	With reference to the contract of . . .（关于……的合同）
2. 提出具体付款的方式及理由	As . . . we shall be glad if you . . .（因为……如果贵方……我们将不胜感激。）
	As you know. . . , we suggest that . . .（正如你所知……，我们建议……）
	Owing to. . . , we would appreciate it if you . . .（由于……如果贵方……我们将不胜感激。）
3. 表示希望对方同意的愿望	We wish you can accommodate us in this respect.（希望贵方在这方面给予照顾。）
	We hope to receive your favorable reply.（望收到贵方肯定的答复。）

回复其他付款方式信函的写作步骤及常见表达方式如下所示：

写作步骤	表达方式
1. 说明收到信函	We have received your letter of ... （收到贵方……的来信。）
	Thank you for your letter of ... （感谢贵方……的来信。）
2. 说明自己的意见（同意或不同意），并阐明理由	We agree to ... （我们同意……）
	We want to make it clear that... （我方想澄清一点……）
	With regard to ..., we regret being unable to accept... （关于……很遗憾我们不能接受……）
3. 说明自己为此做出的努力以及做生意的意愿	It is in view of our friendly relationship that we extend you this accommodation. （鉴于我们的友好关系，我们才给予贵方此照顾。）
	We sincerely hope that we can ... （诚挚地希望我们能……）

10.3 Specimen Letters（样函）

Letter 1: Ask for easier terms of payment

Dear Mr. Deng,

We' ve studied the specifications and price-list of our new paints and now wish to place the enclosed order with you. As we are in urgent need of several of the items, we should be glad if you make up and ship the order as soon as you possibly can.

In the past, we have dealt with you on sight credit basis. Now, we would like to propose a different way of payment, i. e.[1], when the goods purchased by us are ready for shipment and the freight space booked[2], you cable us and we will remit[3] you the full amount by T/T. The reasons are we can thus more confidently assure our buyers of the time of delivery and save a lot of expenses on opening the letter of credit. As we feel this would not make much difference to you but would facilitate our sales, we hope you will grant our request.

We look forward to your confirmation of our order and your affirmative reply to our new arrangements of payment.

Yours faithfully,
Alexander Tunk

Letter 2: A reply to Letter 1

Dear Mr. Tunk,

We are pleased to acknowledge your order for our new paints.

The arrangements you proposed to meet outstanding accounts are quite satisfactory. All items included in your order can be supplied from stock and will be packed and shipped immediately your remittance by T/T is received.

Yours sincerely,
Xiang Deng

Letter 3: Request for payment by D/A

Dear Mr. Liu,

Thank you for your letter of 4th of June, which arrived this morning.

We are pleased that you have been able to ship our order in good time[4] but we are surprised that you still demand payment against documents. After long years of satisfactory trading we feel that we are entitled to easier terms. Most of our suppliers are drawing on us at 60 d/s[5], documents against acceptance, and we should be grateful if you could grant us the same terms.

We are looking forward to your favorably reply.

Yours faithfully,
Billy Singh

Letter 4: A reply to Letter 3

Dear Mr. Singh,

We have received your letter in which you ask for an easier term of payment.

In consideration of the very pleasant business relationship we have had with your firm for more than 15 years, we have decided to agree to your suggestion. We shall, therefore, in future draw on you at 60 d/s, documents against acceptance, and trust that this term will suit your requirements.

We hope that our concession will result in a considerable increase of your orders and assure you that we shall always endeavor to execute them to your complete satisfaction.

Yours faithfully,
Mark Liu

Letter 5: Propose to pay by D/P at sight

Dear Sirs,

We wish to place with you an order for 100 leather handbags.

For this particular order we would like to pay by D/P at sight. Involved about USD2,000, this order is comparatively a little one. It goes without saying[6] that we very appreciate the support you have extended us in the past. If you can do us a special favor[7] this time, please send us your contract, upon receipt of which we will establish the draft[8] of D/P.

Yours faithfully,
Wan Wang

Letter 6: A reply to Letter 5

Dear Mr. Wang,

We are in receipt of your letter of August 22.

Having studied your suggestion for payment by D/P at sight for USD2,000, it is quite difficult for us to accept that. As our usual practice goes[9], we require payment by confirmed and irrevocable letter of credit[10]. That is to say, at present, we can' t accept D/P terms in all transactions with our customers abroad. I regret to say that we must adhere to[11] our usual practice and hope that this will not affect our future business relations.

Yours sincerely,
Don Torend

Letter 7: Request for payment by D/A

Dear Mr. Liu,

We are the largest supermarket in Canada and have recently received a number of enquiries for your bicycles. We think there are good prospects for the sale of this product, but at present it is little known[12] here and as we can't count on[13] regular sales we don't feel able to make purchases at our own expenses[14].

We are therefore writing to suggest that you send us a trial delivery for sale at 60 d/s on D/A terms. We make the proposal hoping to place firm orders[15] when the market is established.

We believe our proposal offers good business opportunities and hope you will be willing to accept.

Sincerely yours,
Billy Singh

Letter 8: A negative reply to Letter 7

Dear Mr. Singh,

Thank you for your letter asking for a change in payment terms. There is nothing unusual in our current arrangement.

I regret to say that we can't accept your change and must adhere to our usual practice and sincerely hope this won't affect our future business relations.

Sincerely yours,
Mark Liu

Notes to the specimen letters

1. i. e. 即
2. the freight space booked 预订舱位
3. remit 汇款
4. in good time 适时
5. d/s = days after sight 见票后若干天付款
6. it goes without saying 毋需多说
7. do... a favor 帮助……做某事
8. draft 汇票
9. as our usual practice goes 按照我们常规的做法
10. confirmed and irrevocable letter of credit 保兑的、不可撤销的信用证

11. adhere to 坚持
12. little known 了解甚少
13. count on 依靠，指望
14. at one’ s own expenses 由某人付费
15. place firm orders 稳定订货

10.4 Focal Words（焦点词汇）

due

adj. **适当的，预期的；应支付的**

The contract has been signed in due form.（已按适当形式签订了合同。）

The negotiation is due to begin from next Monday.（定于下周一正式开始谈判。）

We are going to pay the amount due to you within one month.（我们将在一个月内付清所欠的款项。）

n. **应得物；（复）应付款**

You should give him his due.（你应该给他应得的。）

These are harbor dues.（这些是入港税。）

due to **由于，应归于**

Due to our mistake, we can’ t book shipping freight space in time.（由于我方的失误，我们无法及时订到舱位。）

All is due to the bilateral efforts.（所有这些都应归于双方的努力。）

file

n. **文件夹；档案；锉刀**

Take out the file we need and copy those documents.（请把我们所需的文件夹拿出来并复印那些文件。）

These are files of all the previous contracts.（这是以前合同的卷宗。）

v. **把……归档；提出（申请）；排成纵队行进**

Please file away these documents.（请将这些文件归档。）

He has filed an application with the authorities.（他已经向有关当局提出申请。）

The court has filed a suit against him.（他已被起诉。）

They filed out of the room.（他们从房内鱼贯而出。）

means

n. **方法；财产，资产**

This company has left no means untried to expand the foreign markets.（为了开拓国外市场，该公司已用尽了一切办法。）

This foreign firm has not much means.（这家国外公司并没有多少资产。）

This firm is reliable. It never does business beyond its means.（这家公司比较可靠，在经营上一直量入为出。）

by all means **尽一切办法，务必**

This plan must be realized by all means. （这个计划一定要实现。）

by any means **无论如何**

By any means, we have to ensure that the goods will reach in perfect condition. （无论如何，我们都要确保货物安然无恙地到达。）

by means of... **用……；依靠……**

He succeeded by means of perseverance. （他依靠坚持而获得成功。）

oblige

v. **迫使，以契约束缚；答应……的请求；（用被动语态）使感激**

The company was obliged to sign the contract. （公司被迫签订了合同。）

The boss obliged himself to settle his company' s bills. （老板根据契约代公司清账。）

Will you oblige me by closing the window?（劳驾您替我关上窗户，可以吗?）

obligee：*n.* **债权人**

obliging：*adj.* **乐于助人的，有礼貌的**

obligor：*n.* **债务人**

outstanding

adj. **杰出的；未完成的，未付款的**

He has made outstanding contributions to the company. （他为公司做出了卓越的贡献。）

There is still an outstanding issue. （仍然有一个悬而未决的问题。）

We don' t know how to deal with an outstanding check. （我们不知该如何处理这张未兑现的支票。）

n. **（复）未偿清的贷款**

10.5 Useful Sentences（实用语句）

（1）We are prepared to accept payment for your trial order on D/P basis. （对贵方这批试购的货物，我方准备接受付款交单的支付方式。）

（2）In order to save a lot of expenses on opening the L/C, we will remit you the full amount by T/T when the goods purchased by us are ready for shipment and the freight space is booked. （为了节省开立信用证的大量费用，我们将在我方购买的货物已备齐待运，舱位已订下时，电汇全部金额。）

（3）We regret that we are unable to consider your request for payment under D/A terms. （对贵方要求以承兑交单方式付款一事，我们歉难考虑。）

（4）In view of the amount of this transaction being very small, we are prepared to accept payment by D/P at 60 days sight for the value of the goods shipped. （鉴于此笔交易金额甚小，我方愿意接受60天远期付款交单方式来支付货款。）

（5）In compliance with your request, we exceptionally accept D/A, but this should not be regarded as a precedent. （按照贵方要求，我们破例接受承兑交单的支付方式，但下不为例。）

（6）On receipt of your remittance for USD20,000 as per the enclosed invoice, we will release your order to the forwarders. （一收到根据附寄发票寄来的2万美元汇款，我们会立即向运输

商发送贵方订货。)

(7) We propose to pay by Bill of Exchange at 30 days, documents against acceptance. Please confirm if this is acceptable to you. (我们建议凭 30 天的承兑方式付款。若贵方接受这一协议，请予以确认。)

(8) We were pleased to receive your bank check. It has been credited to your account, which is now completely clear. (很高兴收到贵方的银行支票。我们已将此款记入贵公司账户的贷方，现已完全结清。)

(9) As business has been rather slack, we would ask you to alter your terms. (由于生意相当萧条，故要求贵方改变付款条件。)

(10) We will specially grant you a draft at 90 days' under D/A. (兹特别允许贵方见票后 90 日付款的承兑交单条件。)

(11) Considering the long business relationship between us, we agree to change the terms of payment to D/A or D/P. (考虑到我们之间长期的业务关系，我方同意将付款方式改为承兑交单或付款交单。)

(12) We shall greatly appreciate your kindness in giving priority to the consideration of our request and giving us an early favorable reply. (如蒙贵方能优先考虑我方的要求并尽早回复，我方将不胜感激。)

(13) 结算用语。

This account is under examination, and if found correct, it shall be carried to a new account, in conformity with your instructions. (所开账目现正核对，如无错误，将遵照贵公司的指示转入新开的账户内。)

Enclosed we hand you a statement of account to date, showing a balance of USD20,000 in our favor, which we trust will be found in order. (到目前为止，我公司应收账款尚有 2 万美元。兹奉上结算报告书一份，敬请查收为荷。)

Your favor of yesterday was duly received, and we hand you herewith a statement of your account as requested, which we hope you will find correct. (贵方昨日函敬悉。兹遵照贵方请求，随函附上结算报告书，敬请查收。)

(14) 请求付款。

With these facts before you, we feel sure that you will send us your check by return mail. Thank you. (有鉴于此，相信贵方将随复函寄来支票，特此致谢。)

Please let us have your check for the USD60 now past overdue. (迟付的 60 美元，请速予寄来为荷。)

Why not settle this matter now? Just attach your check to this letter, and send it by today's mail. (何不立即对此案做一结算？请在今日将支票随函发出即可。)

We urge that you make this settlement without delay. (我们恳求速予结账。)

(15) 催告付款。

We wish to state that if the account be not paid by next Monday, we shall be forced to place the matter in the hands of our solicitors. (如下周一前未能结清本款项，我方将不得不委托我公司顾问律师来处理。)

In spite of your repeated promises to let us have a cheque, we are still without a settlement of your outstanding account, and therefore, unless same is settled by the end of this month, we shall be compelled to hand over the matter to our solicitor.（贵方虽多次答应付款结账，但迄今尚未结清。如在本月底以前仍未能结清，我方只好委托我公司顾问律师来处理。）

（16）汇票汇款。

I send you herewith a cheque, value USD250, 000, receipt of which please acknowledge.（兹奉上面额25万美元的支票一张，敬请交付收据为荷。）

（17）付款已收到。

We acknowledge receipt of your cheque, USD100, 000, in settlement of the charges on the consignment, and pass this sum to your credit, with best thanks.（为结清委托销售，我方已收到面额10万美元支票一张，现已转入贵贷方账户，非常感谢。）

We are duly in receipt of your favor of the 16th May, enclosing a draft, value USD51, 250, to balance your account.（我方已收到贵方5月16日函及随函附寄的面额51，250美元的汇票一张，用以结清贵方账款。）

（18）开立汇票。

We advise you that we have drawn on you this day for USD100, 000, at 3m/s, to the order of yourself, which we commend to your kind protection.（我方已于本月开出由贵方所指定的人于见票后3个月付款的面额为10万美元汇票一张，请惠予承兑，特此通知。）

We have the pleasure to inform you that we have drawn this day on you for USD500, 000, at 3m/s for which we have credited you as usual.（我方于本月向贵方开出见票后3个月付款的面额为50万美元的汇票一张。对此，我们依惯例，记入贵贷方账内，特此通知。）

We have this day drawn the following bill of exchange on your esteemed firm, No. 223, USD500, 000, payable at sight.（我方于本日向贵公司开出第223号面额50万美元汇票一张，见票即付。）

For your reimbursement, you will draw on me at sixty days' sight, and at the most favorable exchange, furnishing me at the same time, with an invoice, bill of lading and insurance policy.（为收回款项，请依照最有利的汇率，向我方开出见票后60日付款的汇票，并请同时提供发票、提单及保险单为荷。）

（19）请求承兑汇票。

Enclosed we hand you a draft, USD300, 000, drawn on you by our London house. Kindly accept same and return.（我公司伦敦分公司开出面额30万美元的汇票一张，兹同函奉上，请承兑后寄还为荷。）

We have taken the liberty of drawing on you today against this consignment for USD500, 000 at sixty days' sight, which please protect on presentation.（兹向贵公司开陈这批货见票后60日付款、面额50万美元汇票一张，请予承兑为荷。）

（20）寄汇票。

Enclosed is a sight draft for USD26. 15 on Messrs. Robert & Sons, which clears off our indebtedness to you.（随函奉上以Robert & Sons公司为付款人、面额26. 15美元的即期汇票一张，用以清偿所欠贵方债务。）

Enclosed you will receive first of exchange for USD500 at sixty days' sight, on George Bury & Co., with which you will please to do the needful, and credit my account accordingly. (随函奉上以 George Bury 公司为付款人、面额 500 美元见票后 60 日付款的第一联汇票一张，请办理手续取款后，记我的贷方账户为荷。)

(21) 承兑汇票。

Your three drafts on Martin & Co., to my order, have been accepted by Smith & Co.. (贵方由本人指定以 Martin 公司为付款人的三张汇票，已由史密斯公司承兑。)

I am favored with your esteemed letter of the second Sept., enclosing USD500 in a bill at sixty days' sight, on George Bury & Co., which, having been duly honored, will appear to your credit at maturity. (贵方 9 月 2 日函及所附以 George Bury 公司为付款人、面额 500 美元见票后 60 日付款的汇票一张均已收悉，现已获得及时承兑，到期后将记入贵方贷方账户。)

(22) 无法承兑汇票。

We state that your draft, No. 3345, for USD2,500,000, duly accepted by Mr. Wang, has been dishonored by non-payment. (由王先生承兑的贵方汇票第 3345 号、面额 250 万美元，已遭拒付，特此声明。)

We regret to state that the bill for USD560,000 on Mr. George, has been dishonored by non-payment, and we shall be obliged by your remitting us USD567,500, amount of same and charges incurred. (我们很遗憾地声明，以乔治先生为付款人的票面 56 万美元的汇票已遭拒付，我们不得不要求贵方汇寄 56.75 万美元及由此而产生的费用。)

(23) 延期付款。

I shall be very much obliged if you will give me a little more time to settle your account due 3rd July. (对 7 月 3 日应付款项，如果能延些时间，我将非常感谢。)

Owing to the serious depression of trade now prevailing, we shall be unable to meet our acceptance for USD1,500, which matures for payment on the 28th Oct. (由于目前生意普遍不景气，由我公司承兑、10 月 28 日到期、面额 1500 美元的汇票将无法兑现。)

(24) 往来账目。

Enclosed I now wait on you with your account current, leaving a balance of USD500 in my favour, which if found correct, you will be so good as to pass to a new account. (随函奉上贵方的往来账，我方顺差 500 美元，如核查无误，请列入新账为荷。)

I hand you, enclosed, your account current, showing a balance in my favor of USD500. (随函寄上贵方的往来账，账上显示我方顺差 500 美元。)

(25) 分期付款。

As the machine was hired to you on the understanding that regular payments would be made, we must ask that in future the terms of the agreement should be strictly adhered to. (我们约定分期付款而将该机械租给贵公司使用。我们希望贵公司对此协议能严格履行。)

The customer pays the installments direct to us, after delivery of the goods and we send him the receipts. (我们送货后，顾客直接向我们办分期付款。我们收款时，要将收据交付顾客。)

(26) 付款日通知。

The account is subject to 10% discount if settled within fifteen days of rendering, after which it is strictly net.（提交清算书后15日内付款可打10%的折扣，超过15日，依全额付清。）

Please note that our pay day for Town Accounts is Wednesday of any week, between the hours of 11 a. m. and 3 p. m.（敬请留意，我公司对市区的付款日，订于每周三上午11时到下午3时止。）

Exercises

1. Put the following English phrases into Chinese or Chinese phrases into English.

(1) document against payment (D/P)

(2) document against acceptance (D/A)

(3) bill of exchange

(4) terms of payment

(5) draw on...

(6) 破例

(7) 一收到

(8) 更有利的条件

(9) 鉴于

(10) 在各方面

2. Multiple choice.

(1) Mr. Ying could agree ______D/P terms.

a. with　　b. to　　c. that　　d. from

(2) Payments should be made ______sight draft.

a. at　　b. upon　　c. by　　d. after

(3) Documentary collection is to be made with the documents to be ______to the draft.

a. enclosed　　b. attached　　c. together　　d. along with

(4) The draft established by you through the Bank of China will ______at the end of this month.

a. due　　b. be due　　c. mature　　d. expire

(5) As instructed, we will draw ______you a sight draft for collection through the Bank of China.

a. for　　b. against　　c. on　　d. from

(6) We regret ______unable to accept your terms of payment as mentioned in your last mail.

a. to be　　b. being　　c. to　　d. for being

(7) Please be informed that your request for payment by D/P has ______our attention.

a. received　　b. been received　　c. obtained　　d. been receiving

(8) Taking into consideration our long-standing business relations with you, we accept ______ by D/P.

a. enquiries　　b. invitations　　c. installment　　d. payment

(9) In order to promote business between us to our mutual advantage, we shall consider ______your suggestion.

a. accepting b. accept c. to accept d. acceptance

(10) Our terms of payment ______ been stipulated in the relative sales contract.

a. having b. has c. have d. had

3. Translate the following sentences into English using the words or phrases in the brackets.

(1) 关于第25号合同，我们同意付款交单的支付条款。(with regard to)

(2) 考虑到我们多年的友好关系，这笔交易我们接受电汇的方式。(in consideration of)

(3) 我们很抱歉不得不谢绝贵方一切承兑交单的付款方式。(decline the request)

(4) 根据贵方要求，我们将破例同意以30天的承兑交单方式交货。(as an exceptional case)

(5) 如同意在支付方面做出让步，如即期付款交单，我们将不胜感激。(make a concession)

(6) 我方将另函寄送承兑交单见票后60日付款的汇票。(by separate posts)

4. Translate the following letter into English.

我们是印度最大的超市，目前收到大量购买贵方自行车的订单。我们认为销售此商品很有前途，不过，目前对这里市场了解甚少。因为无法确定能否定期销售该产品，故我们难以自己承担全部费用。

为此，我们写信建议贵方寄给我们一批试订货，承兑交单付款。希望在市场建立起来后，再稳定订货。

希望我们的建议能带来良好的生意机会，并希望贵方愿意接受。

5. Write a letter as per the following particulars.

(1) 我方欲按贵方的报价，订购500台计算机。

(2) 考虑到双方的长期合作关系，希望采用付款交单方式。

(3) 承蒙贵公司一向照顾，若能继续给予优惠，不胜感激。

(4) 如同意上述建议，请寄合约。

Supplementary Reading

Part A

Payment is sometimes made by collection through banks under the terms of Documents against Payment (D/P) or Documents against Acceptance (D/A). In this case, the banks will only do the service of collecting and remitting and will not be liable for non-payment of the importer, while in the case of an L/C the opening bank offers its own credit to finance the transaction. D/P calls for actual payment against transfer of shipping documents. There are D/P at sight and D/P after sight. The former requires immediate payment by the importer to get hold of the documents. In the latter condition, the importer is given a certain period to make payment at 30, 45, 60 or 90 days after presentation of the documents, but he is not allowed to get hold of the documents until he pays. D/A calls for delivery of documents against acceptance of the draft drawn by the exporter. D/A is always after sight.

As far as the seller's benefit is concerned, L/C is better than D/P. D/P at sight is better than

D/P after sight, whereas D/P is better than D/A. In international trade, payment through collection is accepted only when the financial standing of the importer is sound or where a previous course of business has inspired the exporter with confidence that the importer will be good for payment.

Notes

1. remit 传送
2. draft 汇票
3. standing 身份，名望
4. sound 可靠的

Part B

As the first step in your sales presentation, the approach is a critical factor. To ensure your prospects' attention and interest during a memorized or formula mode of presentation, you may want to use a statement or demonstration approach. In more technically oriented situations in which you and the prospects must agree on needs and problems, a questioning approach (SPIN, for instance) is in order. Generally, in developing your approach, imagine your prospects asking themselves, "Do I have time to listen to, talk with, or devote to this person? What' s in it for me?"

Words alone will not ensure that you are heard. The first impression that you make on a prospect can negate your otherwise positive and sincere opening. To ensure a favorable impression in most selling situations, dress conservatively, be well groomed, and act as though you are truly glad to meet the prospect.

Your approach statement should be especially designed for each prospect. You can choose to open with a statement, question, or demonstration by using any one of the techniques. You should have several alternative approaches ready in case you need to alter your plans for a specific situation.

Carefully phrased questions are useful at any point in a sales presentation. Questions should display a sincere interest in prospects and their situations. Skillfully handled questions employed in a sales approach can wrest a prospect' s attention from distractions and center it on you and your presentation. Questions are generally used to determine prospect wants and needs, thereby increasing prospect participation in the sales presentation. Four basic types of questions are direct, nondirective, rephrasing, and redirect questions.

In using questions, ask the type of questions that you can anticipate the answer to. Also, remember to allow prospects time to completely answer the question. Listen carefully to their answers for a guide as to how well you are progressing toward selling to them. Should you determine that your prospect is not listening, do something to regain attention. Techniques such as offering something or asking questions can refocus the prospect' s attention long enough for your return to the presentation.

Part C

Openings that use demonstrations and drama are especially effective because of their ability to force the prospect into participating in the interview. Of the two methods discussed here, the product approach is more frequently used alone or in combination with statements and questions.

In the product approach, the salesperson places the product on the counter or hands it to the customer, saying nothing. The salesperson waits for the prospect to begin the conversation. The product approach is useful if the product is new, unique, colorful, or if it is an existing product that has changed noticeably.

If, for example, Pepsi-Cola completely changed the shape of its bottle and label, the salesperson would simply hand the new product to the retail buyer and wait for a reaction. In marketing a new pocket calculator for college students, the Texas Instruments salesperson might simply lay the product on the buyer' s desk and wait. It is possible to effectively combine the product approach with the showmanship approach.

The showmanship approach involves doing something unusual to catch the prospect' s attention and interest; this should be done carefully so that the approach does not backfire, which can happen if the demonstration does not work or is so flamboyant that it is inappropriate for the situation.

"Ms. Rosenburg, our paper plates are the strongest on the market, making them drip-free, a quality your customers will appreciate." (The salesperson places a paper plate on her lap and pours cooking grease or motor oil onto it while speaking to the prospect.)

As she hands the buyer a plate from a new line of china, she lets it drop to the floor. It does not break. While picking it up, she says, "Our new breakthrough in treating quality china will revolutionize the industry. Your customers, especially newlyweds, will love this feature. Don' t you think so?"

The salesperson selling Super Glue would repeat the television advertisement for the prospect. In the prospect' s office, the salesperson glues two objects together, such as a broken handle onto a coffee cup, waits one minute, hands the cup to the buyer for a test, and then begins the sales presentation. The mended cup can be left with the buyer as a gift and a reminder.

The life insurance salesperson hands the prospect a bunch of daisies, saying, "Steve, when you' re pushing daisies, what will your family be doing?" (This is probably too tactless to use on anyone except a close friend, but you get the picture.)

Part D

Delivering Cancer News

Oncologists, doctors who specialize in treating cancer, have one of the toughest jobs when it comes to delivering negative news. These doctors often inform patients that they have a difficult battle to face or that there is almost no hope and death may be imminent.

Some medical schools now insist that students learn how to deliver bad news to patients, particularly those suffering from cancer. These medical programs have added classes where students learn to give the negative news through verbal and nonverbal forms of communication. Some of these schools also use role-playing with patient actors. The medical students have to inform the actors of an unwanted diagnosis and appropriately deal with the actor's response. Some studies suggest that the manner in which bad news is presented to a patient has significant effects on their overall health.

As an additional resource for doctors to be upfront with their patients, the American Society of Clinical Oncology has developed a booklet. It helps patients understand their options when they learn they have cancer. The goal is to help improve their quality of life, maximize their remaining time, and plan for end-of-life care. The society believes that currently less than 40% of patients have conversations with their doctors about their options.

Turning Tables on Complaints

While consumers have many avenues for complaining, the organizations that are complained about may feel a bit powerless. However, the Alamo Drafthouse, a movie theater in Austin, Texas, found a way to turn the tables on one complainer.

The movie theater has one simple rule: don't text or use a phone during the movie. One woman broke this simple rule and was kicked out of the theater. She then called the theater to complain about the situation; she believed they were ripping her off.

The theater now uses this woman's ridiculous message as a public service announcement that shows before all movies begin to remind movie goers of the one simple rule. In other words, instead of allowing the customer, who was clearly in the wrong, to create negative publicity, the theater owners created a positive situation for their business.

In another instance, a pizza shop in New York turned the tables by printing T-shirts for employees with the negative reviews they received online at Yelp. The strategy helped increase business and create more loyal customers.

What do you think? Are the actions of these businesses justified? How else can organizations gain power in this electronic age when it is so easy for anonymous consumers to complain?

Unit 11 Packing 包 装

11.1 Introduction（简介）

一般地，进入国际流通领域的货物不但要经过长途运输，而且要经过多次转运和储存。因此，出口货物的包装要求比国内贸易要严格得多。进出口双方在签订合同时，一般要对包装问题进行洽商并做出具体规定。包装条件是进出口贸易合同的一项要件，是构成货物说明的重要组成部分。

在国际贸易中，包装分为两类。一类是运输包装（Transport packing），又称大包装或外包装（Outer packing），是指将货物装入特定容器，或以特定方式成件或成箱的包装。运输包装的作用在于保护货物在长时间和远距离的运输过程中不被损坏或丢失，同时，又可方便货物的搬运，起到减少运费、节省租仓和方便计数的作用。另一类是销售包装（Selling packing），又称小包装或内包装（Inner packing），是指对制造出来的商品以适当的材料或容器所进行的初次包装。销售包装除了保护商品的品质外，还有美化商品、宣传商品、方便陈列、吸引顾客、促进销售、提高商品价值以及方便消费者识别、选购、携带和使用商品的作用。目前，商品的包装呈现小型化、透明化和实用化的倾向。

常见的运输包装有：箱，如木箱（Wooden case）、铁箱（Iron case）、板条箱（Crate）、纸箱（Carton）等；桶（Drum），如木桶（Wooden drum）、铁桶（Iron drum）、塑料桶（Plastic drum）等；包（Bale）；袋（Bag），如布袋（Cloth bag）、麻袋（Gunny bag）、纸袋（Paper bag）、塑料袋（Plastic Bag）等；瓶（Bottle），如钢瓶（Cylinder）、长颈瓶（Flask）等；坛（Jar）；盒（Box）；篓（Basket）；托盘（Pallet）；集装箱（Container）等。

此外，也有少数商品不采用包装，仅仅采取散装（In bulk）和裸装（Nude packed）方式。

有关包装的信函要写得简洁明了。书写这类信函时，出口方可以向进口方详细描述其习惯包装方式（Customary packing），同时也可说明可以接受进口方的包装要求（Packing Instruction），但额外费用应由进口方承担（At the expense of the buyer）。进口方也可以通知出口方意想不到的包装要求或对包装的担心。如果要更改有关包装的任何条款，都必须在装运前经双方商讨同意后确定。

11.2 Writing Skills（写作技巧）

包装信函的写作步骤及常见表达方式如下所示：

写作步骤	表达方式
1. 告知对方写信的目的（关于包装问题的洽谈）	We thank you for your letter of . . . （感谢贵公司……日来函。）
	We are pleased to inform you that . . . （很高兴告诉贵方……）
	We are now writing to you in regard to the packing of . . . （我方来函告知关于……的包装问题。）
2. 说明包装方式、包装材料等包装要求	The relative clause should be . . . Packing: . . . In addition, directive marks should be . . . （相关条款如下……包装材料（方式）为……此外，指示性标记为……）
	We write to you in regard to the packing of . . . , and we would like you to have the goods packed in . . . （兹去函告知关于……的包装要求。我们希望采用以下包装方式……）
3. 表示希望对方能够接受此包装要求并予以关注，盼早日回复	Kindly let us know whether these requirements could be met. （请告知此包装要求是否能够得到满足。）
	We hope you will find it in order and pay special attention to the packing. （希望贵方会发现该包装方式是恰当的，并能给予特别关注。）
	We should be grateful if you let us have your opinions about these requirements. （如果贵公司能告知我方对此包装要求的看法，我方将不胜感激。）
	We await your early reply. （期盼早日回复。）

回复包装信函的写作步骤及常见表达方式如下所示：

写作步骤	表达方式
1. 感谢对方来函并告知对方回信的目的	We have received your letter of . . . （我方已收到贵方……日来函。）
	We regret to inform you that . . . （很遗憾地告知贵方……）
	Thank you for your packing instructions, but regret our inability to comply with your request for special packing. （感谢收到你方的包装指示，但很遗憾我们不能满足贵方对特殊包装的要求。）
2. 提出有关包装的参考意见和解决办法	We shall pack. . . in. . . instead of in . . . as. . . （由于……我们将用……包装来代替……包装。）
	In order to. . . , we would like to make the following suggestions for your consideration. （为了……特提出以下意见供贵方参考。）
3. 表示希望对方能够确认此包装意见和办法	We hope to have your confirmation on the packing. （希望得到贵方对此包装的确认。）
	We hope you will accept our packing and assure you of our sincere cooperation. （希望贵方能够接受我方包装，并向贵方保证我方的合作诚意。）

11.3 Specimen Letters（样函）

Letter 1: Negotiation on carton packing

Dear Sirs,

We are pleased to inform you that for your future orders we shall pack our garments in cartons instead of in wooden cases, as packing in cartons has the following advantages.

(1) It will prevent skillful pilferage, for the traces of pilferage will be more in evidence.

(2) It is fairly fit for ocean transportation.

(3) Our cartons are well protected against moisture by plastic lining[1].

(4) Cartons are comparatively light and compact, so they are more convenient to handle.

Our comments above come from a comparative study of the characteristics of the two modes of packing, i. e. carton packing and wooden case packing, as well as the results of shipments already made.

We hope you will accept our carton packing and assure you of our sincere cooperation.

With best wishes.

Yours faithfully,

(Signature)

Letter 2: A reply to the above

Dear Sirs,

We have received your letter of July 29 with pleasure and immediately approached our clients about the packing. After our repeated explanation, they say they will have no objections to[2] your packing of the garments in cartons if you guarantee that you will pay compensation in all cases wherein they cannot get indemnification from[3] the insurance company for the reason that the cartons used are not seaworthy.

We deem it our duty to inform you of this and consider it a tacit understanding that you would hold yourselves responsible for the losses our clients might sustain on account of[4] your using such cartons if the insurance company refuses compensations.

We think you will understand that our candid statements are made for our mutual benefits as packing is a sensitive subject, which often leads to trade disputes.

We appreciate your cooperation.

Yours sincerely,

(Signature)

Letter 3: Shipping marks requirements

Dear Sirs,

Re: Sales Confirmation No. 99A/782

We thank you for your letter dated October 10, enclosing the above Sales Contract in duplicate but wish to state that the packing clause in the contract is not clear enough. The relative clause should be read:

Packing: Seaworthy export packing[5], suitable for long distance ocean transportation.

The shirts under the captioned contract should be packed in plastic bags, five dozen to one carton, 20 cartons on a pallet, and 10 pallets in FCL container[6]. On the outer packing please mark our initials: JHCL in a triangle, under which the port of destination and our order number should be stenciled. In addition, directive marks like WATERPROOF[7], etc. should also be indicated.

We have made a footnote on the contract to the effect and are returning herein one copy of the contract, duly countersigned by us. We hope you will find it in order and pay special attention to the packing.

We look forward to receiving your shipping advice soon and thank you in advance.

Yours faithfully,

(Signature)

Letter 4: Asking for improving packing

Dear Sirs,

Thank you for your Quotation No. 293 about Round Steel Bars.

We regret to inform you that among the five lots of Round Steel Bars arrived here per S. S. Mary on May 11, 2014 were six bundles of different grades, which were in scattered and mixed condition because their packing was not sufficiently strong and their iron hoops were broken in transit. Since it was very difficult to assort them, inconvenience and losses occurred. Although we had in time notified you of such unfortunate things occurred before, the present case has shown that our comments were ignored, for no improvements in packing has been made.

Therefore, we must have your promise to take effective measures to improve your packing[8] before we could book this new order with you.

We await your early reply.

Yours sincerely,

(Signature)

Letter 5: Packing instruction

Dear Sirs,

Re: Our Order No. 168

With reference to the shipment of our Order No. 168 for 100 cases of chinawares, we wish to draw your attention to the following.

As the goods are susceptible to[9] be broken, the chinawares must be packed in wooden cases capable of withstanding rough handling[10].

Please mark the cases with our initials in a diamond, under which comes the destination with contract number and stencil conspicuously the words FRAGILE, HANDLE WITH CARE on both sides of the cases.

We trust that the above instructions are clear to you and that the shipment will give the users entire satisfaction.

Yours faithfully,

(Signature)

Letter 6: Container packing

Dear Sirs,

We thank you for your inquiry of May 28th and are pleased to provide you with our information about the container service by our company. The shipping containers we can provide are of two sizes, namely[11] 20ft and 40ft respectively.

They can be opened at both ends, thus making it possible to load and unload at the same time. For carrying goods liable to be spoiled by dampness or water, they have great advantages of being both watertight and airtight[12]. Containers can be loaded and locked at the factory, if necessary. So pilferage can be therefore impossible.

Being temperature-controlled, our containers are provided for any cargo that needs a special care. This lends its full benefits in shipping. There is also a saving on freight charges. When separate consignments intended for the same port of destination are carried in one container, there will be charged less and an additional saving on insurance because of lower premium charged for container-shipped goods.

We enclose a copy of our tariff and look forward to receiving your instructions.

Yours faithfully,

(Signature)

Letter 7: Asking for better packing

Dear Sirs,

Taking into account the specialty of this article, we request you to pack this cargo with your best care. So as to withstand the hazards of ocean transportation[13], it must be water-proof and against the tropical climate[14].

Please note that each cargo is requested to be wrapped up in oil paper and packed in a zinc-lined case[15]. Also please stencil our shipping marks five inches high[16] and give gross and net weight, port of destination, country of origin and a B in the rectangle as the main mark of each case.

Sincerely yours,

(Signature)

Letter 8: Packing instruction

Dear Sirs,

Please pack this machine in a strong wooden case and wrap and pad generously all polished parts of the machine to avoid scratches and knocks[17] against the container.

Also please put the machine in a case of about 10 cubic meters covered with waterproof cloth and strapped vertically and horizontally with metal bands[18] and cut vent holes[19] in the case to minimize condensation.

Sincerely yours,

(Signature)

Notes to the specimen letters

1. our cartons are well protected against moisture by plastic lining 纸板箱垫有一层塑料能防潮

2. have no objections to... 不反对……
3. get indemnification from... 从……中得到赔偿
4. on account of... 由于……
5. seaworthy export packing 适合于海运的出口包装
6. in FCL container 整集装箱装运；（FCL：Full Container Load）
7. WATERPROOF 防水
8. take effective measures to improve your packing 采取措施改进包装方式
9. be susceptible to... 容易受……的影响
10. withstanding rough handling 经受得住粗鲁搬运
11. namely 即，也就是
12. watertight and airtight 防水的和不漏气的
13. withstand the hazards of ocean transportation 应付海运时的危险
14. against the tropical climate 防止潮湿的热带气候
15. a zinc-lined case 钉锌条的箱子
16. stencil our shipping marks five inches high 刷上5英寸高的装船标志
17. scratches and knocks 摩擦和碰撞
18. strapped vertically and horizontally with metal bands 用金属带纵横捆绑
19. vent hole 气孔

11.4 Focal Words（焦点词汇）

avail

v. **有用于；有利于**

I' m afraid these articles of the contract will avail you only little of nothing. （我担心合同中的这些条款对您不会有什么帮助。）

avail oneself of sth. （=take advantage of）**利用……**

You should avail yourself of this opportunity to promote your products. （你要充分利用这次机会推销自己的产品。）

available：*adj.* **可利用的，可得到的；有效的，可支付的**

I' m afraid that these dresses are not available in your size. （我担心这件衣服没有适合你的尺码。）

We will cable you as the goods are available. （一旦有货我们即刻电告贵方。）

The license for the export of the product is available for 5 months. （该产品的出口许可证有效期为5个月。）

availability：*n.* **可用性，有效性**

distribute

v. **分配，分发，分销**

Like universities, congress distributes power according to its rules and customs. （正如大学一样，国会也是按照它的规则和惯例来分配权力的。）

The teacher distributed the examination papers to the class. （教师将试卷分发给学生。）

The agent distributed the goods among the buyers. （代理商把货物批发给买方。）

distribute to/among **分配，分发**

distribute over **散布，分布**

distribution：*n.* **分配；配给物；散布，分布；销售，经销**

They could not agree about the distribution of the profits. （他们不同意这种利润分配办法。）

The pine-tree has a very wide distribution. （松树分布很广。）

We have a good product, but distribution is bad. （虽然我们产品的质量很好，但销路不佳。）

distributive：*adj.* **分配的，分发的，分送的，经销的**

pack

v. **包装**

It is our usual way to pack these goods in cartons. （我们通常采用纸板箱包装。）

pack away **把……装起来**

All the chinaware was carefully packed away in cases and stored in the warehouse. （所有瓷器都被小心地包装起来，并储藏在仓库里。）

pack off **寄出，包装发往**

We have packed the samples off to you. （我们已将样品寄给贵方。）

常用的"包装方式"表示方法有：

(1) in... **表示用某种容器包装**

Walnuts are packed in double gunny bags. （核桃用双层麻袋包装。）

(2) in... of... each **表示用某种容器包装，每一容器内装若干**

Men's shirts are packed in wooden cases of 10 dozen each. （男式衬衫用木箱装，每箱10打。）

(3) ... in... each containing... **用某种容器包装，每一容器内装若干**

Nylon socks are packed in wooden cases, each containing 50 dozen. （尼龙袜用木箱包装，每箱装50打。）

(4) ... to... **表示将若干件装于某一容器内**

Folding chairs are packed 2 pieces to a carton. （一个纸板箱装两把折叠椅。）

(5) each... in... and... to... **表示先将每单位装入某种容器，再将若干单位装另一种较大的容器**

Each pair of nylon socks is packed in a plastic bag and 12 pairs to a box. （每双尼龙袜装一个塑料袋，12双装一盒。）

(6) ... to... and... to **表示先将若干单位装某种容器，再把若干此种容器装另一种较大的容器**

Pens are packed 12 pieces to a box and 200 boxes to a wooden case. （12只钢笔装一盒，200盒装一木箱。）

packing：*n.* **包装；包装材料；包装方法；包装费**

The packing must be seaworthy. （该包装必须适合于海洋运输。）

We need a lot of packing to protect these glasses. （我们需要大量的包装材料以保护这些玻璃器皿。）

We offer these shirts at USD20 each, plus postage and packing. （这些衬衫我方报价为每件20美元，外加邮资和包装费。）

packing charges **包装费用**

packing instruction **包装指示，包装要求**

packing list **装箱单**

neutral packing **中性包装**

customary packing **习惯包装**

inner packing **内包装**

outer packing **外包装**

package：*n.* **中小型的包裹（指包、捆、束、箱等）；“一揽子”交易**

Each package should be marked “Fragile”. （每件包装上都要标明“易碎品”。）

The computer is sold with a printer and software as part of the package. （这台计算机与打印机和软件一并销售。）

packet：*n.* **小包（=a small package）；（计算机）数据包，信息包**

The packets of tea are intact. （该批茶叶的包装完好无损。）

repack：*v.* **重新包装，改装**

source

n. **源泉，来源，出处，消息来源，原始资料**

The explorers searched for the source of the river. （探险人员找到了这条河的源头。）

Idleness is the source of all evils. （懒惰乃万恶之源。）

The brain is the ultimate source of ideas. （人脑是思想的根本源泉。）

Sources of supply are essential if you want to export in quantities. （如果想大量出口，货源是至关重要的。）

The financial difficulty of the firm can be traced to their inability to find a source of funds. （该公司的财务困难归结于他们无法找到资金来源。）

We learn from reliable sources that the price of coal will rise considerably. （根据可靠的消息来源，煤价将大幅度上涨。）

specify

v. **规定，指定，详述，载明**

The contract specifies the terms of payment. （合同规定了支付条款。）

He specified the airfield to which I should come. （他指定了我应该降落的机场。）

John forgot to specify the place where we should meet. （约翰忘了具体说明我们见面的地点。）

Please specify your requirements so as to enable us to make you offers accordingly. （请详细说明贵方的要求，以便我方进行相应的报盘。）

The contract specifies payment by sight L/C. （合同载明，凭即期信用证付款。）

11.5 Useful Sentences（实用语句）

（1）The packing of this article features novel design and diversified styles. （该产品的包装特点是设计新颖，形式多样。）

（2）The new packing of the porcelain is in Chinese national style and suitable for display in supermarkets. （这些陶瓷的新包装具有中国特色，适合在超级市场展销。）

（3）The inner packing must be attractive and helpful to the sales. （内包装必须具有吸引力，能够促进销售。）

（4）The goods are to be packed in wooden cases containing 20 dozen each. （货物用木箱包装，每箱20打。）

（5）Packing charges are excluded in the quoted prices. （报价不包含包装费用。）

（6）The packing must be seaworthy and strong enough to stand rough handling. （包装必须适合海运，足够牢固，经得住野蛮搬运。）

（7）No name of country or trademark is to appear on the outside containers. （外箱上不得出现国名和商标。）

（8）We must make it clear that with the different packing material, the packing expenses will be different. （我们必须说清楚：采用不同的包装材料，包装费会不一样。）

（9）All the cartons are lined with plastic sheets, so they' re absolutely waterproof, I can assure you. （所有纸箱都内衬塑料纸，我可以保证绝对防水。）

（10）The dimensions of the carton are 17cm high, 30cm wide and 50cm long. The volume then is about 0.026 cubic meter. （该纸板箱高17厘米，宽30厘米，长50厘米，容积约为0.026立方米。）

（11）Because the goods will be transshipped, I hope each case will be marked with details of weights, symbols of warnings and directions, as well as your own marks. （货物要转船，所以我希望每个箱体上标注重量说明、警告性标志、指示性标志以及你们自己的标志。）

（12）Actually, this packing is both shockproof and moistureproof. Nevertheless we have still marked the cartons with warnings like "FRAGILE", "USE NO HOOK" and "DO NOT DROP". （实际上，这种包装既防震又防潮。尽管如此，我们仍在箱上刷上了像"易碎""切勿用钩"和"轻搬轻放"的标志。）

Exercises

1. Put the following English phrases into Chinese or Chinese phrases into English.

（1）waterproof

（2）wooden case

（3）in sound condition

（4）registered trademark

（5）packing instructions

（6）standard export packing

（7）装箱单

（8）以毛作净

（9）习惯包装

（10）中性包装

（11）适合海运的包装

（12）运输标志

2. Multiple choice.

（1）Pens are packed 12 pieces ______a box and 200 boxes ______a wooden case.

a. to, in b. in, to c. to, to d. to, of

（2）Please see to it that the ______is suitable for a long sea voyage.

a. packing b. package c. pack d. packed

（3）We would suggest that you ______the carton with double straps.

a. will secure b. securing c. secure d. are secured

（4）Packing charges ______in the price, and we can make delivery whenever you wish.

a. in included b. are included c. include d. included.

（5）We give you on the attached sheet full details regarding packing and marking, which must be strictly ______.

a. abide by b. observed c. submitted d. seen

（6）We are confident that the package of our products will ______the roughest handling in transit.

a. stand up to b. stand to c. suffer from d. put up

（7）This container can be easily opened ______both ends.

a. by b. on c. at d. in

（8）The adoption of containers facilitated ______to a great extent.

a. us to load and unload b. to have loaded and unloaded

c. us to loading and unloading d. the loading and unloading

（9）We give you on the attached full details ______packing and working.

a. regarding b. be regarded c. regarded d. regard.

（10）We regret that we have suffered heavy loss ______your improper packing.

a. resulted from b. resulting from c. resulted in d. resulting in

3. Translate the following sentences into English using the words or phrases in the brackets.

（1）水泥要用双层牛皮纸袋包装，每袋装50千克。(be packed in, each containing)

（2）请严格遵守包装及标记的细则。(be strictly observed)

（3）请确保用防漏包装。(leak-proof packing)

（4）所有的袋子都设计得很精美，符合你们当地市场的喜好。(come in line with)

（5）跟以往一样，箱子上要刷制一个菱形标志，上面写我公司的首写字母。(be marked with)

（6）我们的包装方式已经被其他客户广泛接受，到目前为止，还没有任何投诉。(be

widely accepted by)

4. Translate the following letter into English.

敬启者:

很遗憾通知贵方,贵方2月12日发往迪拜(Dubai)的200箱铁钉(Iron nails)中,有20箱受到严重的损害,当然,这不是贵方的过错。

我方不得不写信来与贵方谈论有关铁钉包装之事。我方认为有必要向贵方表明我方今后交易的包装方法,以避免今后的交易中再发生类似的损失。

发往迪拜的铁钉须用木箱装,净重112磅,每箱内装重量各为7磅的16袋铁钉。发往马耳他(Malta)的铁钉用双层麻袋(double gunny bags)包装,每袋重50~60千克。英国市场上,客户喜欢装25千克的纸板箱。

请贵方告知能否满足这些要求。

真诚的,

马克

5. Write a letter as per the following particulars.

(1) 贵方包装指示收悉。

(2) 今歉告,我方难以满足贵方的特殊包装要求。

(3) 为使你我双方的首次交易获得成功,我方愿意提出以下建议,供贵方考虑:

1) 床单8打装一盒,6盒装一纸板箱,10纸板箱装一板条箱。

2) 将贵公司名称缩写印在菱形内。

3) 将货物生产国名标在纸板箱和板条箱上,而不是标在每一个盒子上。

4) 将特别提示和警告印在板条箱上,而不是印在每一个纸板箱上。

(4) 请以电传方式告知贵方的意见。

Supplementary Reading

Part A

Packing is an art. It needs more care in export trade than in domestic trade. The real art of packing is to get the contents into a nice, compact shape that will stay the way during the roughest journey. Every buyer expects that his goods will reach him in perfect condition. Nothing is more infuriating to a buyer than to find his goods damaged or part missing on arrival. It should go without saying that the seller must try to pack the goods in such a way that they will go through the ordeal of transport unscathed.

Packing is the continuation of the goods' production. Packing can keep the goods safe and complete and prevent loss and leakage in their whole circulation, and it can raise its value, save the cost and labor, and promote the sales. Generally, we can divide packing into transport packing and sales packing.

Transport package is also called shipping mark. It is generally made up of a few simple geometric figure, letters, numbers or words. In most cases, it is written or pressed on the top or side of the container being shipped, and it is designed that the consignor or the consignee can identify the goods easily.

Notes

1. infuriating 令人发怒的
2. go without saying 理所当然
3. ordeal 折磨
4. unscathed 未受伤的
5. leakage 渗漏
6. geometric 几何的
7. consignor 发货人
8. consignee 收货人

Part B

The sales presentation is a persuasive vocal and visual explanation of a proposition. While there are numerous methods for making a sales presentation, the four common ones are the memorized, formula, need-satisfaction, and problem-solution selling methods. Each method is effective if used for the proper situation.

In developing your presentation, consider the elements of the sales presentation mix that you will use for each prospect. The proper use of persuasive communication techniques, methods to develop prospect participation, proof statements, visual aids, dramatization, and demonstrations increases your chance of illustrating how your products will satisfy your prospect' s needs.

It is often not what we say but how we say it that results in the sale. Persuasive communication techniques (questioning, listening, logical reasoning, suggestion, and the use of trial closes) help to uncover needs, to communicate effectively, and to pull the prospect into the conversation.

Proof statements are especially useful in showing your prospect that what you say is true and that you can be trusted. When challenged, prove it by incorporating facts in your presentation on a customer' s past sales—guaranteeing the product will work or sell, testimonials, and company and independent research results.

To both show and tell, visuals must be properly designed to illustrate features, advantages, and benefits of your products through graphics, dramatization, and demonstration. This allows you to capture the prospect' s attention and interest; to create two-way communication and participation; to express your proposition in a clearer, more complete manner; and to make more sales. Careful attention to development and rehearsal of the presentation is needed to ensure it occurs smoothly and naturally.

Always prepare for the unexpected, such as a demonstration that falls apart, interruptions, the prospect' s questions about the competition, or the necessity to make your presentation in a less ideal place, such as in the aisle of a retail store or in the warehouse.

The presentation part of the overall sales presentation is the heart of the sale. It is where you develop the desire, conviction, and action. By giving an effective presentation, you have fewer objections to your proposition, which makes for an easier sale close.

If you want to be a real professional in selling, acquire or create materials that convey your message and convince others to believe it. If you try to sell without using the components of the sales presentation mix, you are losing sales not because of what you say but how you say it. Exhibits, facts, statistics, examples, analogies, testimonials, and samples should be part of your repertoire. Without them, you are not equipped to do a professional job of selling.

Part C

One of the best ways to convince a prospect that a product is needed is to show the merits of the product through a demonstration as George Wynn did. If a picture is worth a thousand words, then a demonstration is worth a thousand pictures. Therefore, it is best to show the product, if possible, and have the prospect use it. If this is not feasible, then pictures, models, videotapes, films, or slides are the best alternatives. Whatever the salesperson is attempting to sell, the prospect should be able to see it.

Psychological studies have shown that people receive 87 percent of their information on the outside world through their eyes and only 13 percent through the other four senses. What this says to the salesperson is to make a product visible. Also, let the prospect feel, see, hear, smell, and use the product. The dynamic demonstration appeals to human senses by telling, showing, and creating buyer-seller interaction.

Demonstrations are part of the dramatization and fun of your presentation. Do not underestimate their ability to make sales for you, no matter how simple they may appear. For example, a glass company once designed shatterproof glass. This was not standard equipment in automobiles at the time, as it is now. The company had its salespeople going around the country trying to sell shatterproof glass. One of the salespeople completely outsold the rest of the sales force. When they had their convention, they said, "Joe, how come you sell so much glass?" He replied, "Well, what I' ve been doing is taking little chunks of glass and a ball-peen hammer along with me on sales calls. I take a little chunk of glass, and I hit it with the hammer. This shows that it' s shatterproof. It splinters, but doesn' t shatter and fall all over the ground. This has helped me sell a lot of glass."

So, the next year they equipped every salesperson with a ball-peen hammer and little chunks of glass. But an interesting thing happened. Joe still far outsold the rest of the sales force. So when the convention occurred the next year, they asked, "Joe, how is it you' re selling so much? You told us what you did last year. What are you doing differently?" He replied, "Well, this year, I gave the glass and the hammer to the customer to let them hit it." You see, the first year Joe had dramatization in his demonstration; the second year he had dramatization and participation. Again, it' s often not what you say but how you say it that makes the sale.

Part D

It Came from Where?

New companies face an uphill battle to persuade people to trust them and their products. The problem is even worse if the new companies are located in a country not usually associated with the product they are selling. Take chocolate, for example. Although the cocoa beans used to produce the world's best chocolate come from South America and Africa, consumers associate fine chocolate with European companies.

Companies from emerging markets employ several different strategies to deal with consumer perceptions. Some try actively to change perceptions, by playing up their countries on product labeling. Others hide their countries of origin or use companies in the United States or Europe as their primary labels.

The most successful, however, work for years to establish their brand by producing quality products and offering excellent service. Carmakers like Toyota, Nissan, and Honda established themselves through years of investment and quality improvement to become some of the most trusted brands in the auto business.

Face-to-face Persuasion

When you present your persuasive message in a spoken, face-to-face format, remember that your personal interactions are an important part of your message. A recent study of successful retail salespeople identified some strong techniques you can use when you're speaking persuasively:

(1) Use their name. People respond well when you show that you care enough about them to use their name.

(2) Show your interest. Build goodwill and rapport by asking about, noticing, and remembering details about your audience's history and preferences.

(3) Identify mutual interests. Turn your persuasive pitch into a conversation by inviting stories from your audience and sharing your own in return.

(4) Be polite and honest. Many people react to persuasive messages by being on guard against potential dishonesty. Demonstrate your respect for your audience by backing up your claims with evidence: show them, don't tell them, and invite them to judge for themselves.

(5) Give and seek information. Take the pressure off your persuasive message by changing it into an informative message instead of sales. Building rapport by inviting your audience to share their knowledge with you.

Unit 12
Insurance
保　险

12.1 Introduction（简介）

保险与外贸业务紧密相连。国际贸易中的货物往往需要从出口国运至进口国，货物在长途运输中，包括装卸和存储都可能会遇到难以预料的风险（Risks），导致货物发生损失（Loss）。为了消除贸易商对运输风险的后顾之忧，进口商或出口商在货物装运前向保险公司（Insurance company）为货物投保，以转嫁和规避这种风险或损失。

货物运输保险是指投保人（Insured）在货物装运前向保险人（Insurer）投保，即办理保险手续（Insurance formalities）、选择保险险别（Coverage）、确定保险金额（Insurance amount）、支付保险费（Premium）并领取保险单证（Insurance documents）的过程。此后，如果投保货物在运输中遇险而发生损失，则承保人应负责对投保险别范围内的损失进行经济补偿。

保险合同（Insurance contract）常采用大保单（Insurance policy）的形式，是指保险合同的保险人同意接受风险而向投保人提供风险保障，在投保人支付一定的保费后，保险人同意被保险货物受损时支付合同中规定的金额或比例。保费（Premium）是由被保险人支付的一笔钱，一般是货物金额的一定比例。对于 FOB 和 CFR 交易，由进口方对货物投保、办理投保手续并支付保险费用。对于 CIF 交易，习惯上由出口方按发票金额（Invoice value）的 110% 投保一切险（All risks），即 100% 是 CIF 发票总值，10% 是合理的利润和其他费用。有时，进口方要求投保的金额会超过 110%，此时，额外保险费应由进口方承担（For the buyer' s account）。

一旦投保货物在运输中发生投保险别范围内的损失，须向保险公司或其代理人立即提出保险索赔（Insurance claim）。为了落实货物的正常索赔，保险索赔时需要提交以下文件：保险单（Insurance policy）或保险凭证（Insurance certificate）、提单（Bill of lading）、原始发票（Original invoice）、检验报告（Survey report）、船长声明书（Master' s protest）和索赔报告书（Statement of claim）等。

在书写保险类信函时，应做到简洁、清晰和明了，应明确投保要求及保险费的支付办法，以便对方及时办理投保手续。回复保险信函时，应做到及时而有礼貌，并清楚地表明己方的保险要求或提出合理性建议。

12.2 Writing Skills（写作技巧）

进口方写给出口方请其代办保险信函的写作步骤及常见表达方式如下所示：

写作步骤	表达方式
1. 说明某合同项下来函	We wish to refer you to...（请参阅……）
	We are pleased to inform you that...（很高兴告知……）
2. 说明所投保的险别，确定投保的金额	Please see to it that the insurance is covered for...% of the invoice value against...（请务必保证，该批货物投保金额为发票金额的……%，投保险别为……）
	As we now desire to have the consignment insured at your end, we shall be much pleased if you will kindly arrange to insure the goods on our behalf against...at invoice value plus...%, amounting to...（我们希望在你处投保，如果贵方能够代我方按照发票金额加成……%，投保……（险别），总计金额为……我方将不胜感激。）
3. 告知保险费的支付办法	We shall of course refund the premium to you upon receipt of your debit note.（当然，一收到贵方的还款通知，我方立即将保险费退还贵方。）
	If you like, you may draw on us at sight for the amount required.（如果贵方愿意，贵方可以开立一张该金额的即期汇票向我方索款。）
	As we understand that as per your customary practice, you only insure the shipment for 10% above the invoice value, the extra premium for additional coverage shall be for our account.（我们知道按照贵方的惯例，贵方仅对货物发票金额加一成投保，而附加险的额外保险费将由我方承担。）
4. 进一步提出办理保险的要求	We sincerely hope that our request will meet with your approval.（我方希望此要求能得到贵方同意。）
	Please arrange insurance according to our request.（请按我方要求办理投保。）

出口方回复进口方请其代办保险信函的写作步骤及常见表达式如下所示：

写作步骤	表达方式
1. 确认对方要求办理保险的来函	This is to acknowledge receipt of...requesting us to effect insurance on the shipment for your account.（收到贵方……日来函，要求我方对该批货物代办保险。）
	We have received your letter of..., asking us to insure the goods for an amount of...% above the invoice value.（我方已经收到贵方……日来函，要求我方对该货物按发票金额加成……%投保。）
2. 告知对方保险条款、投保险别、保险金额、保险单据等	We are pleased to inform you that we have covered the shipment with... against...for...（很高兴告知，我方已向……办理投保手续，投保……（险别），投保金额为……）
	Although it is our usual practice to take out insurance for the invoice value plus 10%, we are prepared to comply with your request for getting cover for 130% of the invoice value.（尽管我们的惯例是按照发票金额110%投保，但是此次我们准备同意贵方要求对该批货物按发票金额的130%投保。）
3. 说明保险费的偿付问题	The policy is being prepared accordingly and will be forwarded to you by next Tuesday together with our debit note for the premium.（我方准备将相应的保单及我方关于保险费的索款通知单，于下周二寄送贵方。）
	The extra premium will be for your account.（额外的保险费将由贵方负担。）

投保人写给保险公司信函的写作步骤及常见表达式如下所示：

写作步骤	表达方式
1. 说明写信的目的（关于保险信息或要求特惠保险费率等）	We have known that your company is the largest insurance company in China. （我们已得知贵公司是中国最大的一家保险公司。）
	We write this letter to you in the hope of getting some information about the special rate of insurance. （特致函，希望获得有关特惠保险费率的信息。）
2. 提出保险要求（保险险别、保险金额、保险费率等）	We wish to insure with your company a shipment of... valued at... against ... （我们希望就……（货物），货值为……向贵方办理投保……（险别）。）
	Would you please tell us whether you can cover All Risks for the consignments? （请告知能否对该货物投保一切险？）
	We wish to know whether you can issue a special rate for shipments. （我们希望知道贵公司能否对该货物给予特惠保险费率。）
3. 希望对方同意保险要求，并盼早日回复	We shall appreciate it if the goods could be insured at favorable rate. （如蒙该货物能以优惠保险费率投保，我们将不胜感激。）
	We are awaiting your early reply. （盼贵方早日回复。）

保险公司回复投保人信函的写作步骤及常见表达式如下所示：

写作步骤	表达方式
1. 确认对方来函收悉	We have acknowledged receipt of your letter of... and are pleased to note your readiness to insure with us a shipment of... （我们已经收到贵方……日来函，很高兴得知贵方就……（货物）向我方投保。）
	We are pleased to receive your letter of... in regard to insurance. In reply, we would like to inform you of... （很高兴收到贵方……日关于保险的来函，在此，我们欣然告知……）
2. 告知保险条款及保险要求（保险险别、保险金额、保险费率等）	The prevailing rate for the shipment against... is ... %, subject to *Ocean Marine Cargo Clauses*. （目前，根据《海洋运输货物保险条款》规定，该货物投保……险的保险费率是……%。）
	Generally we cover insurance... in the absence of definite instructions from our clients. If you desire to cover..., we can provide such coverage at a slightly higher premium. （通常，如若没有客户的明确指示，我方承保……如果贵方希望投保……我方将以稍高一点的保险费率承保。）
3. 表示希望对方及时确认	If you find our rate acceptable, please let us know. （如果贵方认为我方的保险费率可以接受，请告知。）
	We trust the information will serve your purpose and await your further news. （相信该信息能满足贵方要求，等候贵方的进一步消息。）

12.3 Specimen Letters（样函）

Letter 1: The importer asks the exporter to cover insurance

Dear Sirs,

Re: Our Order No. 101. Your S/C No. 013 Covering 500 Cases Electronic Toys

We wish to refer you to[1] our order No. 101 for 500 cases electronic toys, from which you will see that this order was placed on CFR[2] basis.

As we now desire to have the consignment insured at your end, we shall be much pleased if you will kindly arrange to insure the goods on our behalf[3] against All Risks[4] at invoice value plus 10%, that is, USD2, 200. 00.

We shall of course refund the premium to you[5] upon receipt of your debit note[6] or, if you like, you may draw on us at sight for the amount required.

We sincerely hope that our request will meet with your approval.

Yours truly,
(Signature)

Letter 2: A reply to the above

Dear Sir/ Madam,

Re: Your Order No. 101 for 500 Cases Electronic Toys

This is to acknowledge receipt of your letter dated July 20, requesting us to effect insurance on the captioned shipment for your account[7].

We are pleased to inform you that we have covered the above shipment with the People's Insurance Company of China against All Risks for USD2, 200. 00. The policy is being prepared accordingly and will be forwarded to you by next Tuesday together with our debit note for the premium.

Yours sincerely,
(Signature)

Letter 3: The requirement to increase the rate of insurance

Dear Sirs,

We refer to the 4, 000 cases of iron nails under Sales Contract No. 214 and are pleased to inform you that we have established with the Bank of China, New York Branch the confirmed, irrevocable L/C No. 231 in the amount of USD6 813, valid up to May 15th.

Please see to it that the above-mentioned goods are to be shipped before May 15th and the insurance is covered for 130% of the invoice value against All Risks. As we understand that as per your customary practice, you only insure the shipment for 10% above the invoice value, and the extra premium for additional coverage shall be for our account.

Please arrange insurance according to our request and meanwhile we are expecting your shipping advice.

Yours faithfully,
(Signature)

Letter 4: A reply to the above

Dear Sirs,

We have received your letter of January 23, asking us to insure the captioned goods for an amount of 130% above the invoice value.

Although it is our usual practice to take out insurance for the invoice value plus 10%, we are prepared to comply with your request for getting cover for 130% of the invoice value.

But the extra premium will be for your account.

Please take note of the above.

Yours faithfully,
(Signature)

Letter 5: Application for insurance

Dear Sirs,

Knowing that your company is the largest insurance company in China with branches and sub-branches throughout the country and survey and claim settling agents in major ports of the world. We, China Arts and Crafts Import and Export Corporation, wish to insure with your company a shipment of Chinese porcelain valued at USD 780, 000 on board the vessel Hongyuan against All Risks, bound from Shanghai to[8] Genoa sailing on 20th March.

We shall appreciate it if the goods could be insured at favorable rate.

Yours truly,
(Signature)

Letter 6: A reply to the above

Dear Sirs,

We have acknowledged receipt of your letter of 20th and are pleased to note your readiness to insure with us a shipment of Chinese porcelain from Shanghai to Genoa by sea.

The prevailing rate for the proposed shipment against All Risks including War Risks is 0.5%, subject to our own Ocean Marine Cargo Clauses and Ocean Marine War Risks Clauses[9]. Copies thereof are enclosed herewith for your reference[10].

If you find our rate acceptable, please let us know, preferably, by cable, the details of your shipment so that we may issue our policy[11] accordingly.

Yours truly,
(Signature)

Letter 7: Asking for the information about special rate of insurance

Dear Sirs,

We write this letter to you in the hope of getting some information about the special rate of insurance[12].

Regularly we arrange consignment of chinaware to Sydney, Australia by both passenger and cargo liners of the International Shipping Line[13]. Would you please tell us whether you can cover All Risks for the consignments and, if so, on what terms? Particularly, we wish to know whether you can issue a special rate for the promise of regular monthly shipments.

We are awaiting your early reply.

Yours faithfully,
(Signature)

Letter 8: A reply to the above opening rate

Dear Sirs,

We are pleased to receive your letter of June 25 in regard to insurance. In reply, we would like to inform you of the following.

(1) All Risks. Generally we cover insurance WPA and War Risks in the absence of definite instructions from[14] our clients. If you desire to cover All Risks, we can provide such coverage at a slightly higher premium.

(2) Breakage. Breakage is a special risk, for which an extra premium will have to be charged. The present rate is about 5%. Claims are payable only for that part of the loss which is more than 5%.

(3) Value to be insured. We note that you wish us to insure shipments to you for 10% above the invoice value, which is having our due attention.

We trust the information will serve your purpose and await your further news.

Yours truly,
(Signature)

Notes to the specimen letters

1. refer sb. to sth. 参看，参照
2. CFR 价格术语，为 cost and freight（成本加运费价）的缩写。该术语下，保险由买方办理
3. arrange to insure the goods on our behalf 代我方办理该批货物的保险
4. All Risks 一切险，是中国人民财产保险股份有限公司（PICC）制定的中国保险条款（China Insurance Clauses 略称 C. I. C.）中的《海洋运输货物保险条款》所包括的三个基本险别之一，其他两个险别为平安险（Free from Particular Average，FPA）和水渍险（With Particular Average，WPA）。除以上三种基本险别外，还有附加险（Extraneous Risks），包括一般附加险、特殊附加险和特别附加险。

   常见的一般附加险有 11 种，分别为：

   Theft, Pilferage and Non-Delivery Risks（简称 T. P. N. D. 或 TPND）偷窃、提货不着险
   Fresh and/or Rain Water Damage Risks 淡水雨淋险
   Shortage Risk 或 Risk of Shortage 短量险
   Intermixture and Contamination Risks 混杂、玷污险
   Leakage Risk 或 Risk of Leakage 渗漏险
   Clash and Breakage Risks 碰损、破碎险
   Hook Damage Risk 钩损险

Rust Risk 或 Risk of Rust 锈损险
Breakage of Packing Risk 包装破裂险
Sweating and Heating Risks 受潮受热险
Taint of Odor Risks 串味险
常见的特殊附加险有 2 种，分别为：
War Risk 战争险
Strikes Risk 罢工险
常见的特别附加险有 6 种，分别为：
Failure to Delivery Risk 交货不到险
Import Duty Risk 进口关税险
On Deck Risk 舱面险
Rejection Risk 拒收险
Aflatoxin Risk 黄曲霉素险

Fire Risk Extension Clause for Storage of Cargo at Destination Hong Kong, including Kowloon or Macao 出口到港、澳地区（包括九龙）的货物存仓火险

5. refund the premium to you 将保险费退还贵方
6. debit note 索款通知单
7. for one' s account 由某方付费，由……负责
8. bound from ... to... 从……驶往……
9. Ocean Marine Cargo Clauses 海洋运输货物保险条款
   Ocean Marine War Risks Clauses 海洋运输战争险保险条款
10. for your reference 供贵方参考
11. policy 保单，同于 insurance policy
12. the special rate of insurance 特惠保率
13. the International Shipping Line 国际班轮运输
14. in the absence of definite instructions from... 没有……的明确指示

12.4 Focal Words（焦点词汇）

assure

v. **向……保证，使确定，使……确信，给……保险**

assure sb. of sth. **向某人保证某事**

We assure you of the reliability of the information. （我们可向你们保证该信息的可靠性。）

We assure you of the best quality and moderate prices of our goods. （请放心，我方商品质量好，价格公道。）

assure sb. that **向某人保证……**

We assure you that we shall do our best to expedite shipment. （请确信我们会迅速装运。）

be assured of sth. **请确信某事**

Please be assured of our continued cooperation. （请确信我方仍将继续合作。）

be assured that 请确信……

You may be assured that we will contact you as soon as our fresh supply comes in. (请确信一有新货到来，我方定会立即与贵方联系。)

You may be assured that our trade contract is being successfully carried out. (请放心，我们的贸易合同正在顺利地实施。)

assure... with ... 给……保险

He assured his life with that company. (他向那家保险公司投保了人寿险。)

assurance: *n.* 把握，信念，保证

They have signed the contract, without any assurance of getting payment. (他们在没有把握获得付款的情况下就签订了该合同。)

We obtained an assurance from our regular customers that they would demand a large supply of our products. (老客户向我们保证，他们会大量求购我方产品。)

assured: *adj.* 感到放心的

attach

vt. 附加，随附上；认为……有（重要性）

There is no need to attach any new stipulation to the contract. (没有必要在合同中附加任何新的条款。)

We attach a catalogue of our commodities for your consideration. (随附我方商品目录单一份，供贵方考虑。)

They attach great importance to packing. (他们很重视包装。)

attachment: *n.* 附件；查封，扣押

effect

v. 实施，实行，实现

Please effect the following insurance against WPA. (请办理投保水渍险。)

We shall effect shipment without delay. (我方将迅速发运。)

Payment is to be effected by irrevocable L/C. (以不可撤销的信用证付款。)

n. 实施，生效；结果，效果；财物

The new tax regulations were brought into effect last week. (新税法上周开始实施。)

This situation has adverse effects upon us. (这种情况给我方带来不良后果。)

The whole company is her personal effects. (整个公司都是她的财产。)

in effect 实际上，实质上；有效的

The committee agreed to a reduction in the hourly wage in effect. (委员会同意了实质上是减少每小时工资的办法。)

The old system of taxation will remain in effect until next May. (旧税制在5月前仍然有效。)

take effect 开始生效

The agency agreement will take effect from July 1. (代理协议将于7月1日起生效。)

with effect from 自……生效，自……实行

Price is increased 5% with effect from January. (价格自1月份来上涨了5%。)

effective: *adj.* 有效的，生效的

The agreement becomes effective from the 15th of May. （该协议从 5 月 15 日开始生效。）

Take effective measures. （采取有效措施。）

insure

v. **投保，保险**

Please insure against Shortage Risk. （请投保短量险。）

Please insure the goods against All Risks and War Risk. （请将此批货物投保一切险和战争险。）

Every company insures itself against loss or damage to its property. （每个公司都进行投保以免自己的财产受损。）

insurance：*n.* **保险**

I would like to have the insurance of the goods covered at 110% of the invoice value. （我们希望货物能够按照发票金额的 110% 投保。）

在表示“投保”“办理保险”时，常与 insurance 搭配的动词或动词词组有：to arrange / cover / effect / provide / take out insurance。

insurance on + 所投保的货物，如 insurance on the 100 tons of wool。

insurance against + 投保的险别，如 insurance against FPA。

insurance with + 所投保的保险公司，如 insurance with the People' s Insurance Company of China。

insurance for + 投保金额，如 insurance for 110% of the invoice value。

insurance at + 保险费或保险费率，如 insurance at the rate of 5% 。

insurance company **保险公司**

insurance agent **保险代理人**

insurance certificate **保险凭证**

insurance coverage **保险范围**

insurance amount **保险金额**

insurer：*n*，**保险公司，保险人，保险业者，同 underwriter（保险公司）**

refer

v. **谈到；参照；提交；接洽**

We refer to our letter of March 8th. （兹谈及我方 3 月 8 日函。）

We refer you to our letter of June 8th. （请参阅我方 6 月 8 日函。）

Your enquiry for bicycles has been referred to our sister corporation for attention. （贵方有关自行车的询价已交由我兄弟公司办理。）

We have referred them to you for their requirements. （我们已请他们就相关要求与贵方进行接洽。）

reference：*n.* **参阅；关于；参考；证人**

Please make reference to our cable of June 4th. （请参阅我方 6 月 4 日电报。）

With reference to your letter of May 4th, we will take the matter into serious consideration. （关于贵方 5 月 4 日来函，我方将认真考虑此事。）

for your reference **供……参考**

For your reference, we enclose a copy of our latest catalogue. (随函附寄我方最新目录一份，供贵方参考。)

12.5 Useful Sentences（实用语句）

(1) We can arrange insurance on your behalf. (我们可以为贵方代办保险。)

(2) We shall take out insurance at this end under open policy. (我们将在我地办理预约投保。)

(3) We have covered the goods against All Risks and TPND. (我们已为货物投保了一切险和偷窃、提货不着险。)

(4) We shall cover the shipment for 10% above the invoice value. (对于该批货物我们将按发票金额的10%投保。)

(5) Since the premium varies with the extent of insurance, extra premium is for the buyer' s account, should additional risks be covered. (因为保险费随保险范围的不同而不同，如果买方要求投保附加险，额外的保险费则应该由买方负担。)

(6) The cargo is to be insured as per warehouse-to-warehouse clauses. (这批货物将实行“仓至仓”保险。)

(7) Insurance is to be effected by the sellers for 110% of the invoice value against All Risks and War Risks as per the relevant Ocean Marine Cargo Clause of the People' s Insurance Company of China, dated January 1st, 1981. (由卖方根据中国人民保险公司1981年1月1日颁布的《海洋运输货物保险条款》按发票金额的110%投保一切险和战争险。)

(8) In the absence of definite instruction from our clients, we generally cover insurance against WPA and War Risks; if you desire to cover FPA, please let us know in advance. (在我方客户没有具体要求时，我们通常投保水渍险和战争险。如果贵方想要投保平安险则请事先告知。)

(9) If you wish to secure protection against TPND, it can be easily done upon the payment of an additional premium. (如果贵方想要求我方投保偷窃、提货不着险，非常容易办到，只要支付附加保险费即可。)

(10) Please see to it that the above-mentioned goods should be shipped before the 15th May and the goods should be covered for 150% of invoice value against All Risks. We know that according to your usual practice, you insure the goods only for 10% above invoice value, therefore the extra premium will be for our account. (请注意上述货物必须确保于5月15日前装出。保险须按发票价格的150%投保一切险。我们知道按照贵方一般惯例贵方只按发票价格加成10%投保，因此额外保险费由我方负担。)

(11) We will get an insurance policy as soon as we' re through with all the formalities. (我方办完所有手续就可得到一份保险单。)

(12) FPA covers total losses resulting from both natural calamities and accidents, and partial losses caused by accidents. (平安险承保自然灾害和意外事故所造成的全部损失，以及意外事故所造成的部分损失。)

Exercises

1. Put the following English phrases into Chinese or Chinese phrases into English.

(1) on sb.' s behalf

(2) for one' s account

(3) refer sb. to sth.

(4) refund the premium to you

(5) in the absence of definite instructions

(6) 免赔率

(7) 保险费

(8) 办理保险

(9) 保险凭证

(10) "仓至仓"条款

2. Multiple choice.

(1) Will you please ______ to take out All Risks insurance for us on the following consignment?

a. help b. arrange c. cover d. insure

(2) Please insure ______ invoice value plus 10%.

a. for b. with c. at d. against

(3) Please insure ______ Leakage (Breakage, Fresh Water Damages).

a. on b. at c. with d. against

(4) Please insure ______ 10% above invoice value.

a. for b. at c. on d. with

(5) We shall provide such insurance at your ______.

a. account b. behalf c. risk d. cost

(6) We will refund the premium ______ you ______ receipt of your debit note.

a. to, upon b. with, upon c. to, at d. with, at

(7) Would you please draw ______ us ______ sight for the above-mentioned amount?

a. for, in b. against, with c. on, at d. to, at

(8) We are writing to request you to effect insurance ______ the captioned goods ______ our account.

a. under, in b. against, for c. at, in d. on, for

(9) ______ will be added to invoice amount together with freight charges.

a. Coverage b. Insurance c. Premium d. Rate

(10) Insurance is to be ______ by the buyer if a transaction is concluded on FOB or CFR basis.

a. taken b. covered c. done d. made

3. Translate the following sentences into English using the words or phrases in the brackets.

（1）破碎险的保险费率为5%，如果贵方愿意投保破碎险，我们可以代为办理。（on one' s behalf）

（2）请按照我们的要求办理保险，同时，我们等候贵方的装运通知。（as per one' s request）

（3）我们将在我地办理预约投保。（under open policy）

（4）如果贵方愿意，可以开立一张该金额的即期汇票向我方索款。（draw on... at sight）

（5）如果没有你们的明确指示，我们将按一般惯例投保平安险和战争险。（in the absence of definite instructions）

（6）我们知道按照你们的惯例，你们只按发票金额加10%投保，因此额外的保险费由我们负责。（for one' s account）

4. Translate the following letter into English.

敬启者：

关于我们购货确认书123号项下的500条白兔牌毛毯，现通知贵方，我们已由花旗银行开立了保兑的、不可撤销的信用证第567号，总金额为4,400美元，有效期至8月31日为止。

请注意上述货物必须在8月底前装运，保险须按发票金额的130%投保一切险。我们知道，按照你们的一般惯例，你们只按发票金额另加10%投保，因此额外保险费由我方负担。

请按我方要求办理保险，我方等候贵方的装船通知。

谨上

5. Write a letter as per the following particulars.

（1）我方刚刚收到贵方用以支付墙壁瓷砖（wall tiles）的第157号信用证。

（2）请注意，对此货物我方不投破碎险（Risk of Breakage）。因此，贵方必须将“破碎险”从信用证中删除。

（3）此外，我方要指出的是，像窗户玻璃、陶瓷等货物，即使已经投保额外的破碎险，保险时仍有5%的免赔率。换句话说，如果破损率低于5%，此损失得不到赔偿。

（4）我方相信，贵方已经清楚地了解这些情况，请立即电报修改信用证。

Supplementary Reading

Part A

Insurance is distinguished from gambling, because the gambler desires the event to occur on which he gambles. He stands to gain if it does so. In insurance no one desires the event to occur; if it does so, the insured person receives an indemnity for the loss sustained. The idea of insurance is to obtain some indemnity in the event of any happenings that cause loss of money; insurance is against risk. It provides a pool or fund into which many contribute and out of which the few who suffer loss are compensated.

Originally, insurance was applied to losses at sea, where risks were always great. Now it has become a vast subject, entering into almost every activity of human beings. As a large percentage of our trade in and out of this country goes by ship, what mainly concerns us is still the marine insurance. Marine insurance covering an international transaction may be arranged by either the seller or the buyer, depending on the terms of sale.

A contract of insurance, which is generally made in the form of an insurance policy, is one between a party who agrees to accept the risk and a party seeking protection from the risk. In return for payment of a premium, the insurer agrees to pay the insured a stated sum should the event insured against occur. The premium, being the name given to the sum of money paid by the insured, is quoted as a percentage of the sum insured.

Notes

1. gamble 赌博
2. indemnity 赔偿
3. premium 保险费

Part B

People want to buy, but they do not want to be misled, so they often ask questions or raise objections during a sales presentation. Your responsibility is to be prepared to logically and clearly respond to your prospect' s objections whenever they arise.

Sales objections indicate a prospect' s opposition or resistance to the information or request of the salesperson. Basic points to consider in meeting objections are to ① plan for them, ② anticipate and forestall them, ③ handle them as they arise, ④ listen to what is said, ⑤ respond warmly and positively, ⑥ make sure you understand, and ⑦ respond using an effective communication technique.

Before you can successfully meet objections, determine if the prospect' s response to your statement or close is a request for more information, a condition of the sale, or an objection. If it is a real objection, determine whether it is minor or major. Respond to it using a trial close, and if you have answered it successfully, continue your presentation based on where you are in the sales presentation. For example, if you are still in the presentation, then return to your selling sequence. If you have completed the presentation, move to your close. If you are in the close and the prospect voices an objection, then you must decide whether to use another close or return to the presentation and discuss additional benefits.

Be aware of and plan for objection. Objections are classified as hidden, stalling, no-need, money, product, and source objections. Develop several techniques to help overcome each type of objection, such as stalling the objection, turning the objection into a benefit, asking questions to smoke out hidden objections, denying the objection if appropriate, illustrating how product benefits outweigh the objection drawbacks, or developing proof statements that answer the objection.

Welcome your prospect' s objections. They help you determine if you are on the right track to uncover prospects' needs and if they believe your product will fulfill those needs. Valid objections are beneficial for you and the customer. A true objection reveals the customer' s need, which allows a salesperson to demonstrate how a product can meet that need. Objections also show inadequacies in a salesperson' s presentation or product knowledge. Finally, objections make selling a skill that a person can improve constantly. Over time, a dedicated salesperson can learn how to handle every conceivable product objection—tactfully, honestly, and to the customer' s benefit.

Part C

Forestalling the objection has the salesperson discussing an objection before the prospect raises it. It often is better to forestall or discuss objections before they arise. The sales presentation can be developed to address anticipated objections directly.

For example, take an exterior house paint manufacturer' s salesperson who learns that an unethical competitor is telling retail dealers that his paint starts to chip and peel after six months. Realizing the predicament, this salesperson develops a presentation that states, "Three independent testing laboratories have shown that this paint will not chip or peel for eight years after application." The salesperson has forestalled or answered the objection before it is raised by using a proof statement. This technique also can prevent a negative mood from entering the buyer-seller dialogue.

Another way to anticipate objections is to discuss disadvantages before the prospect does. Many products have flaws, and they sometimes surface as you try to make a sale. If you know of an objection that arises consistently, discuss it. If you acknowledge it first, you don' t have to defend it.

On the other hand, a customer who has an objection feels compelled to defend that objection. For example, you might be showing real estate property. En route to the location you say, "You know, before we get out there, I just want to mention a couple of things. You' re going to notice that it needs a little paint in a few places, and I noticed a couple of shingles on the roof the other day that you may have to replace." When you arrive, your customer may take a look and say, "Well, those shingles aren' t so bad and we' re going to paint it anyway." Yet, if you reached the house without a little prior warning of small defects, those items are often what a customer first notices.

A third way of using an anticipated objection is to brag about it and turn it into a sales benefit. A salesperson might say, "I want to mention something important before we go any further. Our price is a high one because our new computerized electronics provide technology found in no other equipment. It will improve your operation and eliminate the costly repairs you are now experiencing. In just a minute, I want to fully discuss your investment. Let' s first discuss the improvements we can provide. Take a look at this."

This takes the sting out of the price objection because you have discussed it. It is difficult for a buyer to come back and say, "It' s too high," because you have mentioned that already. So, there are times when you can anticipate objections and use them advantageously.

Part D

What Employers Want

You can increase your odds of getting an interview by understanding what hiring managers are thinking while they evaluate your resume. The following are questions managers ask themselves:

1. Can this applicant fill the needs of the company? Your resume should stress all of your most relevant skills and experience which match the position opening. Rather than submitting a generic resume for every position you apply for, create a customized resume based on your review of the job

opening.

2. Will this applicant stay with the company long term? Managers seek employees who are most likely to stay with a company long term because the hiring process is long, difficult, and costly. The cost of replacing an employee averages $13,355 according to a study conducted by the Environment Policy Foundation. To avoid costly turnover, managers look at your resume to see if you have a stable work history.

3. Will this applicant be professional? Your resume represents your ability to communicate. Unfortunately, managers will eliminate resumes for the slightest problems since they may receive hundreds of resumes for one position. Make sure your resume is easy to follow and doesn't contain types or grammatical mistakes.

Play Safe

Before posting your job application online, you should verify the site is safe. Here are some criteria:

1. Have you heard of the site? If not, be careful. Look for online reviews of the site.

2. Does it ask you to register before you can search for jobs? This is a big red flag. Try a different site.

3. Does it have a comprehensive privacy policy? Read the policy to see if they sell or rent your information. Putting up your job packet on a nonprivate forum could affect your identity in the future. Do not assume the site is protected if it has a privacy seal.

4. Can you limit access to your personal contact information? Identity theft is a growing problem. Good sites allow you to protect personal contact information.

5. Does it let you delete your resume after you get a job? Safe websites should allow you to delete your documents or make them inactive while you are not conducting a job research. You don't want your new boss to think you are still on the job market for an even better position.

Unit 13 Shipment 装　运

13.1 Introduction（简介）

装运（Shipment）是国际货物买卖合同中不可缺少的一项条款。合同签订之后，负责装运的一方必须履行安排运输的义务。在实际中，装运业务通常包括以下环节：通关、租船订舱、缮制装运单据、发出装船通知等。

装运条款（Terms of shipment）一般包括装运时间、装运港及目的港、装船时间、装运单据、分批装运或转船装运等。

装运时间通常是指将货物装上运输工具的时间或期限。在按 FOB、CFR 和 CIF 条件成交的情况下，卖方的装运时间以提单上签署的日期为依据。如果提单日期在合同规定的装运期内，卖方就履行了合同的交货义务。

在货物装运之前，有时买方会给卖方一个书面通知，即“装运须知”（Shipping instructions），用来明确装运要求、装船方式、包装规定和货物标记等。

卖方完成货物装运后，应履行合同规定并及时写信通知买方，即寄送装船通知（Shipping advice）。装船通知一般包括合同（或订单）号码、商品名称、数量、货值、船名及其启航日期等。寄送装船通知的目的是让买方及时办理保险并做好接货准备。

卖方完成发货后，必须向买方提供装运单据（Shipping documents）。装运单据是卖方履行合同及取得货款的重要依据。装运单据的种类和份数，由买卖双方根据每笔交易的具体情况协商决定。

书写装运事项信函的目的一般是敦促卖方尽快装运、修改装运条件、寄送装运通知、寄送装运单据等。此外，利用通知对方有关装运事项的机会，一方可以表达与对方进一步发展业务关系的愿望。

13.2 Writing Skills（写作技巧）

进口方给出口方的装运信函的写作步骤及常见表达方式如下所示：

写作步骤	表达方式
1. 简要说明交易货物及有关装运条件（敦促出口方尽快装运、说明装运条件、等待装运通知）	We refer to Contract No. CT8898 signed between us on 20th December, 2004 for 1,000 metric tons of cotton, which is stipulated for shipment in March, 2005.（2004 年 12 月 20 日签订的 CT8898 号合同规定，1,000 公吨棉花原定于 2005 年 3 月装运。）
	We are very anxious to know about the shipment of our order for 5,000 cases of tin plates.（我们急于知道 5,000 箱马口铁订货的发运消息。）

（续）

写 作 步 骤	表 达 方 式
1. 简要说明交易货物及有关装运条件（敦促出口方尽快装运、说明装运条件、等待装运通知）	For some special reason, we request you to advance shipment of the consignment under order No. 579 from October to September.（由于某种特殊情况，我们要求贵方将579号订单项下货物的装运期从10月提前到9月。）
2. 陈述事实，说明理由	As we are in urgent need of the goods, we find it necessary to stress the importance of making punctual shipment within the validity of the L/C.（由于我们急需这批货，所以我们认为有必要强调在信用证有效期内按时装货的重要性。）
3. 表明我方观点或建议及愿望	In case you should fail to effect delivery in April, we will have to lodge a claim against you for the loss and reserve the right to cancel the contract.（如果你们4月份尚不能交货，我们只好向贵方提出损失索赔并保留取消合同的权利。）
	We should appreciate prompt shipment and hope to establish a regular connection for the future if this first consignment proves to conform to the samples supplied.（非常感谢贵方的及时装船，如果首批货物与所供样品一致，我们希望将来进行经常性的业务联系。）

出口方给进口方的装运信函的写作步骤及常见表达方式如下所示：

写 作 步 骤	表 达 方 式
1. 开头语	We are pleased to notify you that the cargo has been shipped by ...（我们高兴地通知贵方，货物已装……）
	We felt apologetic that we really have no way to make shipment on ..., because of ...（由于……我方实在无法于……装运货物，谨向贵方表示歉意。）
2. 结束语	The shipment will reach you within 5 days.（货物将于5天内到达贵方。）
	We appreciate the business you have been able to give us and assure you that all your future orders will continue to receive our most careful attention.（感谢贵公司这次照顾我们这笔交易，今后贵公司所有订单我们保证一定慎重办理。）
	We should be obliged if you would kindly understand the situation and you would comply with our request.（对我方处境请予谅解，并盼答应我方要求，我方不胜感激。）

13.3 Specimen Letters（样函）

Letter 1: Request for expediting shipment

Dear Sirs,

Re: Zinc Sheets

Referring to our previous letters in respect of our order No. 1165 of January 22nd for 1,000 metric tons of zinc sheets, we have to call your attention to[1] the fact that so far we have not had any definite information from you as to when we may expect delivery, although these goods are contracted for shipment before the end of last month, and our relative L/C was opened with the Bank of China as early as in February 2004.

Needless to say, we have been put to no little inconvenience by the delay in delivery. It is therefore imperative that you notify us by fax immediately of the earliest possible date of shipment for our consideration without prejudice to our right of cancellation of the order and/or lodging claims for losses thus sustained.

Please look into the matter at once and let us have your definite reply by fax without any further delay.

Yours faithfully,
Xiaofeng Wang

Letter 2: A reply to the above

Dear Mr. Wang,

Re: L/C No. 4468 under Your Order for Zinc Sheets

Kindly accept our thanks for your extension of your L/C No. 4468 and we are now pleased to inform you that we have this day shipped the above goods on board m/v[2] PEACE which sails for your port tomorrow.

Enclosed please find one set of the shipping documents covering this consignment as follows:

(1) One non-negotiable[3] copy of B/L[4].

(2) Invoice in duplicate.

(3) Packing list in triplicate.

(4) One copy of Manufacturer' s Certificate of Quality[5].

We are glad to have been able to execute your order after long delay and trust that the goods will reach you in good time to meet your urgent need and that they will turn out to your entire satisfaction.

Availing ourselves of this opportunity, we assure you of our most prompt and careful attention in executing your future orders and will try our best to avoid any recurrence of such delay in future.

Yours truly,
Tom Jackson

Letter 3: Insisting on shipments by designated steamers

Dear Sirs,

With reference to our order No. 56 and 74 for a total of 400 metric tons of peanut oil, we have today received a fax from our buyers, M/S Black & White Corporation Ltd. , regarding delivery of these orders.

We wish to draw your attention once again to our letter of 8th, in which we have given you our instructions as to how order No. 56 and No. 74 should be shipped. To meet their requirements, it is of great importance to our buyers that the arrival dates of these orders should be confirmed as early as possible. The main reason for our insisting on shipments being carried by steamers of K-lines is that their steamers offer the shortest time for the journey between Hong Kong and Hamburg. We shall appreciate it if you will endeavor to ship the consignments as follows:

Order No. 56: By s. s.[6] Montreal due to[7] sail from Hong Kong on September 18 or at latest by s/s Victorial due to sail from Hong Kong on September 28 arriving in Hamburg on October 8 and October 18 respectively[8].

Order No. 74: Either by the above steamers or the latest by s. s. Mondeal due to sail from Hong Kong on October 8 arriving in Hamburg on October 29.

We shall appreciate very much your close cooperation in this respect and shall always find opportunity to reciprocate[9].

Yours faithfully,
Ling Yang

Letter 4: A reply to the above

Dear Mr. Yang,

Re: Your Orders No. 56 and 74

We have received your faxes of 8th and 12th of August, requesting us to ship the goods under the captioned orders by either s. s. Victorial, Mondeal or Montreal.

In this regard, we wish to point out that it is not our practice to effect shipment by vessels designated by our clients, but incidentally as the steamer you have named is the very one on which we intend to ship your order, we have no objection to complying with your wishes.

For your information, we have got in touch with the K-lines and have now succeeded in booking the required shipping spaces on s/s Montreal scheduled to sail from Hong Kong to Hamburg around the middle of next month.

The goods will go forward on s. s Dong Feng leaving Guangzhou for Hong Kong on September 5, where they will be transshipped by s. s. Montreal for onward freight to Hamburg.

We trust that everything is now in order.

Yours truly,
Glen Washington

Letter 5: Advice of shipment to importer

Dear Sirs,

We forward you the goods ordered on April 8, per m. v. South Seas, sailing today from Guangzhou. The details are as follows:

Our Contract No.: S05JA52088
Your Order No.: 05GZ056
L/C No.: 0588DFE0986
Invoice No.: F05JA2086

B/L No.: VS05-0086

Quantity: 300 cartons, 6,800 dozen

Invoice Amount: USD21,000.98

Commodity: 100% cotton men' s long sleeve shirts, standing up collar, garments washed

Vessel: South Seas V.1068

ETD Guangzhou[10]: May 18

ETA Kobe/Osaka[11]: May 25

We have taken every care in packing and handling the goods, so that they will reach you in good order and condition[12]. In order to facilitate your checking the goods, all the cartons have been marked with the cardinal numbers which are corresponding to those indicated in the packing lists, where the color and size assortments have also been stated.

We trust that this consignment will turn out to your entire satisfaction, and hope that we shall have many opportunities in future to demonstrate[13] our ability to handle orders promptly and carefully.

Yours faithfully,

(Signature)

Letter 6: Explaining the reason for late delivery

Dear Sirs,

Re: Your Order No. 918 for 200 Bicycles

We have for acknowledgment your letter of November 20, asking for definite news of shipment of the subject goods.

Inasmuch as[14] we ourselves are still waiting for a reply from the local shipping agents concerning the matter of space, we regret being unable to give you any good news at the moment. You may, however, have the satisfaction of knowing that although we are not the only exports here that are having great difficulties in obtaining ocean freight space, we are doing our utmost to get the goods off[15] before the relative credit expires[16]. In the next few days, we expect to let you know by fax the result of our efforts.

We realize that you have been inconvenienced to a certain extent by the delay occasioned[17] by the shortage of shipping space, but we trust nevertheless you will appreciate that not only is this a rare case of its kind between us so far, but also it is entirely beyond our help[18].

Yours truly,

(Signature)

Letter 7: Sending shipping instructions

Dear Sirs,

We are in receipt of your letter of 15th May, from which we understand that you have booked our order for two Model 790 Machines.

Our confirmation of order will be forwarded to you in a few days.

Since the purchase is made on FOB basis, you are to ship the goods from Liverpool on a steamer to be designated by us. As soon as the shipping space[19] is booked, we shall advise you of the name of the steamer, on which the goods are to go forward. For further instructions, please contact our forwarding agent[20], ABC Company, Liverpool, who has hitherto taken care of shipments from you.

As some parts of the machines are susceptible to shock, the machines must be packed in seaworthy cases capable of withstanding rough handling[21]. The bright metal parts should be protected from water and dampness in transit[22] by a coating of slushing compound[23] that will keep out dampness, but will not liquefy and run off[24] under changing weather conditions.

We trust that the above instructions are clear to you and that the shipment will give the users entire satisfaction.

Yours faithfully,

(Signature)

Notes to the specimen letters

1. call your attention to 提醒你注意
2. m/v (= motor vessel) 汽船
3. non-negotiable 不可议付的
4. B/L (= bill of lading) 提单
5. Manufacturer's Certificate of Quality 厂商品质证明书
6. s. s. (= steamship) 轮船
7. due to (do something) 预定，约定
8. respectively 各自地，分别地
9. reciprocate 互换，往复
10. ETD Guangzhou 预计离开广州时间，ETD 是 estimated time of departure 的缩写
11. ETA Kobe/Osaka 预计到达神户/大阪时间，ETA 是 estimated time of arrival 的缩写
12. in good order and condition 情况良好
13. demonstrate 表明，证实
14. inasmuch as 因为，由于
15. we are doing our utmost to get the goods off 我方正尽全力将货物运出
16. expire 到期
17. occasion 引起，造成
18. it is entirely beyond our help 我方完全无能为力
19. shipping space 舱位
20. forwarding agent 运输代理行
21. capable of withstanding rough handling 能够经得起野蛮搬运
22. in transit 运输途中
23. slushing compound 防止光亮金属部件生锈的润滑油

24. run off 从……流掉，使……流掉

13.4 Focal Words（焦点词汇）

ship

vt. 装运，装上船

The goods will be shipped in one lot.（这些货物将一次装运。）

n. 船

shipbuilding：*n.* 造船业

shipment：*n.* 装运；装运期限；到货

Please arrange shipment as soon as possible.（请尽快安排装运。）

Please extend shipment 30 days.（请将装运期限延长30天。）

Quality must be the same as your last shipment.（品质应与上次到货一致。）

shipping：*n.* 船舶，船舶总吨位数，航运，装运

The shipping space for sailing to London up to the end of this month has been fully booked up.（本月底驶往伦敦的舱位已订满。）

Their shipping exceeds that of any other country.（他们的船舶总吨位数超过任何其他国家。）

shipping service 航运业

shipping instruction 装运须知

We await your shipping instruction.（我们等待贵方装运须知。）

shipper：*n.* 发货人，托运人，货主

forward

adj. 前部的，向前的，前进的，远的

Our cabin was in forward part of the ship.（我们的舱位在船的前部。）

In practice, the forward rate is not always directly applicable.（事实上，远期汇率并不总是适合的。）

adv. 向前；提出

At the meeting he brought forward the question of pricing.（在会议上他提出了定价问题。）

vt. 送发，寄去；转交

Would you be so kind as to forward my letter?（你能帮我寄封信吗？）

forwarding：*n.* 运送，运输业；转运

If there arises any problem, please contact our forwarding agent.（如果出了任何问题，请与我们的运输代理联系。）

a forwarding merchant 转运商

a forwarding station 发送站

look forward to 盼望

She was looking forward to being an economist.（她希望成为经济学家。）

regard

vt. **认为；尊重**

I regard this market as one with great potential.（我认为这个市场很具潜力。）

He is very highly regarded by his students.（他深受学生的尊重。）

n. **考虑，关心；尊敬**

He shows no regard for other people.（他不关心他人。）

regardful：*adj.* **尊重的，信守的**

He was regardful.（他信守诺言。）

regarding：*prep.* **关于，有关**

Would you please tell me or direct me to someone with whom I can speak regarding loans?（你是否可以告诉我或找其他人跟我谈谈关于贷款的事?）

regardless of **不注意，不顾**

Regardless of the wind or rain, they will go.（不管刮风下雨，他们都要走。）

regards：*n.* **致意，问候**

He sent his best regards to you.（他向你问好。）

regret

vt. **后悔，遗憾**

He who will not learn when he is young will regret it when he is old.（少时不学，老来后悔。）

I regret the loss of her friendship.（失去她的友谊，我深感遗憾。）

n. **懊悔，遗憾**

I left my home with some regret.（我带着遗憾离开了家。）

regrets：*n.* **致歉，礼貌辞谢邀请的回帖**

He could not come to the party, but he sent his regrets on a postcard.（虽然他不能来参加晚会，但寄来了致歉的明信片。）

regrettable：*adj.* **抱歉的，可惜的，不幸的**

As is regrettable, business has stopped.（很遗憾，已经停止营业了。）

regretful：*adj.* **后悔的，遗憾的，抱歉的**

She gave a regretful smile.（她歉意地一笑。）

regretfully：*adv.* **深感遗憾的是**

Regretfully, we have had to turn down your offer.（深感遗憾的是，我们不得不拒绝贵方发盘。）

13.5 Useful Sentences（实用语句）

(1) We are glad to inform you that the goods ordered by you are ready packed for delivery. Shipment can be made immediately after receipt of L/C.（我们高兴地通知贵方，贵方订购的货物已备妥待交，收到信用证就可以装船。）

(2) As the shipment date stipulated in the L/C is July 31 and cannot be further extended, the goods must be shipped not later than the above date.（由于信用证上规定的装船日期是7月31

日，而且不能再延长，因此，货物必须不迟于上述日期装船。）

（3） Our shipment terms are shipment within three months after receipt of L/C. （我方的装船条件是收到信用证后3个月内装运。）

（4） One of our customers placed an order for 30,000 dry batteries for shipment in five equal lots at intervals of three months. （我们的一位客户订购了3万节干电池，分五批装运，每批数量相等，间隔时间为3个月。）

（5） The earliest shipment possible is December. We hope this will be acceptable to your customers. （预期最早的装船期是12月，希望这能为贵方客户所接受。）

（6） Owing to the delayed arrival of the scheduled steamer, we have failed to effect shipment within the L/C validity. Would you please extend the shipment of the L/C for one month, enabling us to proceed with shipment as quickly as possible? （由于预定轮船晚到，我们未能在信用证有效期内完成装运。请贵方将信用证的装船期延长一个月，以便我方能尽快着手装船。）

（7） We shall certainly cable you in due course the name of the chartered steamer and its approximate date of arrival at your port, enabling you to make prearrangement for shipment. （我们一定及时将租船船名和到达贵方港口的大约日期电告贵方，以便贵方能预先安排接船。）

（8） The equipment will be ready for shipment by the end of this month, please notify us at an early date of the name of the chartered steamer and its date of arrival at our port. （设备到本月底将备好待运，请早日通知我方租船船名和抵达我港日期。）

（9） As most of the items on this order are not yet ready for shipment, we would ask you to permit partial shipments in your L/C, enabling us to ship first the part which is already available. （由于此项订单的大部分商品尚未备妥待运，我们要求贵方在你们的信用证中允许分装，以便我方先装运已有的货物。）

（10） Enclosed please find one set of the shipping documents covering this consignment. （随函附上有关该货的装运单据一套。）

（11） Your delay in the shipment of our customer' s order No. 543 has made us get into a great deal of trouble with him. So you are requested to let us know definitely when the goods can be shipped. （贵方延误了我方客户第543号订单的装船，导致我方与该客户卷入很大的纠纷。因此，我们要求贵方告诉我们货物能装船的确切时间。）

（12） We must reiterate that prompt shipment must be regarded as an essential condition for all our orders. （我们必须重申，迅速装运是我方下所有订单的一个重要条件。）

（13） 请求发货指示。

The above order is now ready. Please give us forwarding instructions as soon as possible. （上述订购货物已备齐，请早日指示如何发运。）

Please send us by return full instructions for the five cases for London, as to contents, value, consignee and who pays all the charges. （请回信告知，这次运往伦敦的5箱货物的详细内容、价值、收货人以及费用由谁负担。）

（14） 发货指示。

In reply to your letter of the 25th May, please send ten bales of our goods, marked... 1-10, by rail as soon as possible to our address, and the other ninety bales afterwards by next steamer. （复

贵公司5月25日来函，请将本公司的10包货物，尽快用火车运来，并请标注唛头……1～10。其余90包，请用下次轮船运出。）

Please ship my thirty bales cotton, now kept in your warehouse, to Messrs. T. T., and forward B/L to me. （请将保管在贵公司仓库的30包棉花运交T. T. 公司，并将提单寄本公司。）

Please ship as soon as possible seventy bales of goat skins, kept in your warehouse, to Messrs. White & Co. in London, and send me the Bill of Lading. （请速将保管在贵公司仓库的70包山羊板皮运交伦敦的怀特公司，并将提单寄交我处。）

（15）装运通知。

We herewith send you the goods ordered last week, and hope you will find same satisfactory. Your further orders will receive our prompt attention. （上周所订购的货物已发运，希望贵公司会感到满意。愿继续为您服务。）

The goods are being prepared for immediate delivery and will be ready for shipment tomorrow. （该货可以立即交付，准备明日装船。）

We are sending you today by the American Railway Express, prepaid, the following books. （我们已于今日，将下列书籍通过美国铁路快运运达您处，运费已付。）

（16）卸货转运。

These goods will be unloaded in 2 hours. （两小时后即可卸货。）

The cargoes were discharged at San Francisco. （货轮已于旧金山港卸货。）

I inform you that the cargo of the Adelaide has been landed and warehoused here, and the vessel is undergoing the necessary repairs. （“阿德雷得”号货轮所装货物已全部装卸完毕并已入库存放。目前，该轮正在进行必要维修，特此通知。）

（17）发票、提单、保险单。

We have the pleasure to enclose the invoice amounting to USD500,000, together with the bill of lading, both of which you will find in order. （随函寄去总额50万美元的发票与提单各一份，请查收为荷。）

Enclosed please find the invoice of eighty bales cotton bought by your order, and shipped to Kobe per Shanghai, as per the enclosed B/L. （根据贵公司的订单，已将80包棉花装于驶往神户的“上海”号货轮。随函寄去发票及提单各一份，请查收。）

（18）包装运费及贴补。

The goods are to be packed in tin-lined cases, and the contents of each case clearly marked on the outside. （货物均须用内衬马口铁或锡纸的木箱包装，且外壳必须清楚标明其内装物品。）

I have settled the freight and primage with Captain Smith, as per the account enclosed, and have debited you, in your account, USD500 for balance paid him. （运费及贴补已依照同函账单交付史密斯船长，付款后所余500美元已记入贵公司借方账户。）

（19）运输代理人、租船等。

For your information, we enclose a copy of the letter received from the Charterers' Agents with regard to stowage of the cargo. （关于装船一事，谨寄上从租船代理商处收到的装载报告书副本一份，请收悉。）

Our special arrangements with large transport institutions put us in a position to offer you considerable reductions for large shipments. （我公司与大型运输公司订有特别协定，尤其对大量货物的运输，可以有较大的折扣。）

We offer you our services as forwarding and customs agents, and you should decide to avail yourself of them, you may rest assured that we should always act to the best of your interests. （我公司为运输报关代理，恳请惠顾。只要有所吩咐，我们将全力为贵公司服务，绝不辜负您的信任。）

Exercises

1. Put the following English phrases into Chinese or Chinese phrases into English.

(1) demurrage rate
(2) despatch money
(3) discharging port
(4) loading port
(5) booking note
(6) freight prepaid
(7) partial shipment
(8) 通知书准备就绪
(9) 租船契约
(10) 唛头
(11) 已装船提单
(12) 班轮运输
(13) 运费到付
(14) 班轮运费表

2. Multiple choice.

(1) Our advice of despatch was mailed to you three days ago and you no doubt ______ it by now.

a. will receive　　b. will have received
c. received　　d. have had received

(2) We give you on the attached sheet full details regarding packing and marking, which must be strictly ______.

a. observed　　b. abide by　　c. submitted　　d. seen

(3) Rope or metal handles should be fixed to the boxes to ______carrying.

a. make　　b. easy　　c. convenient　　d. facilitate

(4) The said L/C ______shipment on or before September 15.

a. calls for　　b. calls about　　c. asks about　　d. requires for

(5) We look forward to ______the goods in the fourth quarter.

a. delivery of　　b. your delivery　　c. deliver　　d. delivery

(6) Damage ______the goods was caused by heavy rain in transit.

a. of　　b. to　　c. for　　d. on

(7) ______any change in the date of delivery, please let us know in advance.

a. There should be　　b. Should there be

c. There would be　　d. Would there be

(8) For all the remaining items the stated dates of delivery are approximate, but ______would these dates be exceeded by more than ten days.

a. in no case　　b. in any case

c. under any circumstances　　d. by all means

(9) We have to point out that the postponement of the fulfillment of the contract ______caused us certain expenses.

a. had　　b. have　　c. has　　d. having

(10) ______our S/C No. 7904 dated August 8, we wish to say that the goods will be shipped by the end of next month.

a. With reference to　　b. Refer to

c. Referring　　d. With refer to

3. Translate the following sentences into English using the words or phrases in the brackets.

(1) 合同规定一旦货物装船，卖方须电告装运通知。(shipping advice)

(2) 我方不得已而要求贵方同意在巴黎转船。(transshipment)

(3) 由于某种特殊情况，我方要求贵方将579号订单项下的货物的装运期从10月提前到9月。(advance shipment of)

(4) 在收到贵方信用证修改通知书以后，我们立即预订该船的舱位。(book shipping space)

(5) 我方将尽力在下个月装运这批货物。(make delivery of)

(6) 我们会按要求将清洁的、已装船、空白抬头提单一式三份交由米兰银行转交贵方。(hand over, forward)

4. Translate the following letter into English.

贵方4月4日来函收悉。

关于剩余的500吨钢板，由于眼下租船极为困难，我们一时无法告知贵方船离开的确切日期。如果贵方能为我方租船，我们可以早日装货。否则，请申请延长贵方的进口许可证。我们一旦租到船，会马上告知贵方。

5. Write a letter as per the following particulars.

(1) 8901号订单已于2015年10月17日装上“天谭”号，该船预计10月27日到达利物浦。

(2) 我们已通知贵方代理 Eddis Jones。

(3) 一旦贵方承兑我方汇票，我方银行代理 Westorland Bank Ltd., High Street, Nottingham，将向你们提交提单（No. 517302）、发票（No. EH3314）和保险凭证（AR1184531）。

(4) 希望这批货使贵方满意。

Supplementary Reading

Part A

The effectuation of shipment signifies the seller' s fulfillment of the obligation to make delivery of the goods. So far as foreign trade is concerned, shipment is mostly made by ocean vessels, tramp or liner. A tramp vessel is a freight-carrying vessel that has no regular route or schedule of sailings. It is first in one trade and then in another, always seeking those ports where there is a demand at the moment for shipping space. A liner is a vessel with regular sailings and arrivals on a stated schedule between specified ports.

The ocean bill of lading is an essential document in making a shipment. It presents three aspects. First, it is a receipt of the goods. Second, it is a contract for the performance of certain services upon certain conditions. Third, it serves also as evidence of ownership of the goods described, and when made out to order, it becomes in practice a negotiable instrument, used as security for loans and other purposes.

With the expansion of international trade, the container service has become popular. The use of containers provides a highly efficient form of transport by road, rail and air, though its fullest benefits are felt in shipping, where costs may be reduced as much as one half.

Notes

1. effectuation 实现，完成
2. tramp vessel 不定期货船
3. liner 班轮
4. ocean bill of lading 海运提单
5. container 集装箱

Part B

Closing is the process of helping people make decisions that will benefit them. You help people make those decisions by asking them to buy. The close of the sale is the next logical sequence after your presentation. At this time, you finalize details of the sale (earlier, your prospect was convinced to buy). Constantly look and listen for buying signals from your prospect to know when to close. It is time to close the sale any time the prospect is ready, whether at the beginning or end of your presentation.

As you prepare to close the sale, be sure you have presented a complete story on your proposition and that your prospect completely understands your presentation. Tailor your close to each prospect' s personality and see the situation from the prospect' s viewpoint. Remember that you may make your presentation and close too early, which causes a prospect to say no instead of "I don' t understand your proposition and I don' t want to be taken advantage of." This is why you should never take the first no. It is another reason to use a trial close immediately before the close. But, no matter when or how you close, do so in a positive, confident, and enthusiastic manner to better serve your prospect. Learn and follow the 12 steps to a successful closing.

Plan and rehearse closing techniques for each prospect. Develop natural closing techniques or consider using closes such as the alternative, compliment, summary, continuous-yes, minor-decision, assumption, T-account, or the standing-room-only close. Consider the situation and switch from your planned close if your prospect' s situation is different from anticipated.

A good closer has a strong desire to close each sale. Rarely should you accept the first no as the final answer. If you are professional, you should be able to close a minimum of three to five times.

Do not become upset or unnerved if a problem occurs when you are ready to close. Keep cool, determine any objection, overcome them, and try to close again—you can' t make a sale until you ask for the order!

Part C

No matter when or how you close, remember that when you ask for the order, it is important to be silent. Do not say a word. If you say something—anything—you increase the probability of losing the sale.

You must put the prospect in a position of having to make a decision, speak first, and respond to the close. If you say anything after your close, you take the pressure off the prospect to make that decision.

Imagine this situation: The salesperson has finished the presentation and says, "Would you want this delivery in two or four weeks?" The average salesperson cannot wait more than two seconds for the prospect' s reply without saying something like, "I can deliver it anytime," or starting to talk again about the product. This destroys the closing moment. The prospect does not have to make the decision. There is the time to think of reasons not to buy. By keeping quiet for a few seconds, the prospect cannot escape making the decision.

All individuals experience the urge to say no, even when they are not sure of what you are selling or when they may want what you propose. At times, everyone is hesitant in making a decision. To help the prospect make the decision, you must maintain silence after the close.

The professional salesperson can stay quiet all day, if necessary. Rarely will the silence last more than 30 seconds. During that time, do not say anything or make a distracting gesture; merely project positively nonverbal signs. Otherwise, you will decrease your chances of making the sale. This is the time to mentally prepare your responses to the prospect' s reaction.

It sounds simple, yet it is not. Your stomach may churn. Your nerves make you want to move. You may display a serious look on your face instead of a positive one. You may look away from the buyer. Worst of all, you may want to talk to relieve the uncomfortable feeling that grows as silence continues. Finally, the prospect will say something. Now, you can respond based on the reaction to your close.

Constantly practice asking your closing question, staying silent for 30 seconds, and then responding. This will develop your skill and courage to close.

Part D

Unfortunate Cover Letter Statements

1. "Please find my resume." Did you look under the couch?
2. "I have integrity so I will not steal office supplies and take them home." Good to know.
3. "Please, please, please hire me for this job. I will be waiting by the phone." Don't wait too long.
4. "What interested me about this job is that it's with a prestigious company." Glad to hear it.
5. "After perusing my resume, I am looking forward to hearing from you soon." If you don't mind, we'd appreciate the opportunity to peruse it ourselves before we get back to you.
6. "I'm submitting the attached copy of my resume for your consumption." Yum.
7. "I perform my job with effortless efficiency, effectiveness, efficacy, and expertise." And an awful lot of alliteration.
8. "The interview you schedule will undoubtedly reveal my unmatched talent and suitability for the position." Uh, don't count your chickens...

You(r) Attitude Matters

If you find getting a job difficult, your attitude may be the reason. Here are four common career-blocking attitudes and response to them:

Attitude: I deserve a good job because I went to school for four years.

Response: Employers are looking for who is best for a job, not who "deserves" a job.

Attitude: I am open to any job. I have no idea what I want to do.

Response: Employers want workers who are focused.

Attitude: I don't have experience because no one will give me a chance.

Response: Employers don't employ people to give them a "chance". Employers are concerned with what an applicant can do for them.

Attitude: I am so down on myself that it's hard to keep looking for a job.

Response: Get professional help, because this attitude is poisonous to your life as well as your career.

Unit 14

Claim and Settlement

索赔与理赔

14.1 Introduction（简介）

在合同的执行过程中，签约双方应该严格履行合同义务。任何一方如果不能履约就会给另一方带来麻烦，有时还会使另一方遭受经济损失。一旦发生这种情况，受损方有权根据合同规定要求责任方赔偿或是采取补救措施。受损方所采取的这种行动称之为“索赔”（Claim）；责任方就受损失一方提出的要求进行处理，叫作“理赔”（Settlement）。

索赔时，应根据事实和有关证明分清责任，向责任方、轮船公司（Shipping company）或保险公司（Insurance company）提出索赔；理赔时，应根据事实和有关证明，该赔则赔，不该赔则拒绝赔偿。在国际贸易业务中，当因进口方拒开或迟开信用证、不按时派船或无理毁约而致使出口方遭受损失时，就会发生出口方向进口方索赔的情况。更为常见的情况是进口方向出口方提出索赔。例如，当进口方在收货时发现货物破损或者货物的质量不符合合同规定要求等问题时，进口方就会向出口方提出索赔。

在书写索赔及理赔信函时，应注意以下几点：

（1）迅速及时。索赔必须在（合同规定的）索赔期限内提出，否则对方有权不予受理。理赔者对索赔期内提出的索赔要求，应予重视，按照国际惯例迅速进行调查研究，弄清事实，并及时给予答复。

（2）详细明确。索赔时往往会信函与电报、电传或传真并用。为争取时间，首先发出电报、电传或传真，明确提出要求，紧接着通过发送信函来详细申述理由以使对方信服，必要时或根据合同规定，附以有关证件（如检验证明等）来支持信函中提出的论点和要求。提出的要求或解决办法一定要明确，切忌含糊其辞。

（3）语气婉转。书写索赔信函时，说理要充分，信心要坚定，语气要客气婉转而不失礼貌。处理索赔事件时，要防止感情用事，避免情绪激动。激动的情绪非但无助于问题的解决，而且还会起反作用。

14.2 Writing Skills（写作技巧）

索赔信函的写作步骤及常见表达方式如下所示：

写作步骤	表达方式
1. 对货物提出索赔，并表示遗憾	Much to our regret, about...（对提出……表示遗憾。）
	We regret to say that ...（我们很遗憾地告知……）

（续）

写作步骤	表达方式
2. 说明要求索赔的原因	We have just received the Survey Report from... evidencing that...（我们已经收到由……开来的检验报告，证明……）
	We immediately invited qualified surveyors to the spot to look into the case, and their findings show that ...（我们立即邀请专业检验人员到现场检查，结果表明……）
3. 说明由此而造成的不便，并请求对方解决	The inferior quality of... causes us considerable difficulty and it is hard for us to dispose of it.（该货物品质不合格给我们带来相当大的困难，使得我们很难处理。）
4. 提出解决索赔的建议、办法或要求	We must ask you to arrange for the dispatch of replacements at once.（我们要求贵方必须立即替换货物。）
	We think we can reserve the right to lodge a claim against you for the loss we have suffered.（我方保留对贵方给我们造成的损失提出索赔的权利。）
	On the basis of the Survey Report, we hereby register a claim with you for... in all.（以检验报告为依据，我们在此向贵方提出总金额为……的赔偿要求。）
5. 表示希望对方及时解决或告知处理办法	We are awaiting your prompt reply.（盼即复。）
	We are enclosing the Survey Report and look forward to settlement at an early date.（我们随函附寄了检验报告，希望贵方能够尽快解决。）
	We would like you to inform us of what you decide to do regarding our losses.（对于我方的损失，请贵公司告知贵方的处理办法。）

回复索赔信函（索赔有理由的情况下）的写作步骤及常见表达方式如下所示：

写作步骤	表达方式
1. 对该索赔事件表示遗憾	Thank you for your letter of... but it was with great regret that we heard ...（感谢贵公司……日来函，我们对……事件深表遗憾。）
	With reference to your claim for... we wish to express our much regret over the unfortunate incident.（对于贵方就……问题的索赔，我们对此不幸事件遗憾。）
2. 说明正在对索赔事件进行调查	On going into the matter we find that ...（经对此事件的调查，我们发现……）
	After a check-up by our staff, it was found that... thus resulting in... for which we tender our apologies.（经过我方人员的核查，发现由于……问题而导致……对此我们致以歉意。）
3. 表示将对该索赔事件采取解决措施	We have arranged... at once.（我们立即采取……解决办法。）
	In view of our long-standing business relations, we will make payment for... into your account.（鉴于我们之间长期的业务关系，我们将支付……金额款项给贵方作为赔偿。）
4. 对于给对方带来的不便表示歉意	We regret the inconvenience you have sustained.（对于贵方所承受的不便，我方深表歉意。）
	Please accept our apologies for the trouble caused to you.（对于给贵公司带来的不便，请接受我们的歉意。）
5. 表示希望此种解决方式能让对方满意	We trust that the arrangement that we have made will satisfy you.（相信我们的安排将会使贵方感到满意。）

回复索赔信函（索赔没有理由的情况下）的写作步骤及常见表达方式如下所示：

写作步骤	表达方式
1. 表示对收到对方……日索赔信函感到遗憾或惊讶	We feel deeply sorry that... in your letter of...（贵公司……日来函收悉，对于……事件，我方深表遗憾。）
	We are sorry to learn from your letter of...（对于贵方……日来函，我方深表遗憾。）
2. 经过调查发现该事件另有原因	After going into the matter carefully we estimate that... might be due to...（经过认真调查，我们估计……事件可能是由于……原因所致。）
	We can assure you that the goods in question were in perfect condition when they left here. We have the clean B/L to support what we say. Maybe the damage complained of must have occurred in transportation.（我们保证该批货物发货时状况良好，有清洁提单证明。由此，该损害可能是在运输过程中产生的。）
3. 表示该损失应由其他当事人承担	The responsibility should rest with either of the parties concerned.（对此损失应该由相关任何一方当事人负责。）
	This being the case, we would like to advise you to claim on the shipping company who should be held responsible.（对此情况，我们告知贵方应向船运公司索赔，应该由其负责。）
4. 对该损失再次表示遗憾或提出拒绝赔偿	Consequently we find no ground to compensate you for the loss.（由此，我们没有理由向贵方赔付。）
	We think we are apparently not liable for the damage.（显然，我们不应对此损失负责。）
	At any rate, we deeply regret about the unfortunate incident.（无论如何，我们对此不幸事件深表遗憾。）

如果未能对索赔进行及时、有效的处理，则应立即告知对方信已收到，并说明正在调查此事，以后会给出充分的答复。

回复此类索赔信函的写作步骤及常见表达方式如下所示：

写作步骤	表达方式
1. 表示收到对方……日索赔函感到遗憾或惊讶	We are very surprised to learn from...（对于……我方深表惊讶。）
2. 表示要对此事件进行澄清或说明	We want to have the problem clarified without any delay.（我们希望毫不延迟地澄清此问题。）
3. 表示正在调查此事	We have sent our representative to your end to investigate the matter in detail.（我们已经派代表到你处详细调查此事。）
4. 表示将会给对方合理的答复	You may be assured that the matter will be settled in a reasonable manner to our mutual benefits.（请相信我方将以互利的方式合理地解决此事。）

14.3 Specimen Letters（样函）

Letter 1: Claim on wrong goods

Dear Sirs,

Re: Our Order No. 123

We duly received the documents and took delivery of the goods on arrival of s/s Prince at Hamburg.

We thank you for your prompt execution of this order. Everything appears to be correct and in good condition[1] except in case No. 3.

Unfortunately when we opened this case we found it contained completely different articles, and we can only presume that a mistake was made and the contents of this case[2] were for another order.

As we need the articles we ordered to complete deliveries to our own customers, we must ask you to arrange for the dispatch of replacements[3] at once. We attach a list of the contents of case No. 3, and shall be glad if you will check this with our order and your copy of your invoice.

In the meantime, we are holding the above-mentioned case at your disposal[4], and please let us know what you wish us to do with it.

Yours faithfully,
(Signature)

Letter 2: A reply to the claim on wrong goods

Dear Sirs,

Re: Your Order No. 123 per s/s Prince

Thank you for your letter of November 11. We were glad to know that the consignment was delivered promptly, but it was with great regret that we heard case No. 3 did not contain the goods you ordered.

On going into[5] the matter we find that a mistake was indeed made in the packing, through a confusion of numbers[6], and we have arranged for the right goods to be dispatched to you at once. Relative documents will be mailed as soon as they are ready.

We have already cabled to inform you of this, and we enclose a copy of the telegram.

We shall be grateful if you will keep case No. 3 and contents until called for by the local agents of World Transport Ltd., our forwarding agents, whom we have instructed accordingly[7].

Please accept our apologies for the trouble caused to you by the error.

Yours faithfully,
(Signature)

Letter 3: Complaint for low quality

Dear Sirs,

The green beans under S/C No. AB046 dispatched on November 4, 2002 have arrived at our port yesterday. The Commodity Inspection Bureau has carefully examined the quality of the beans, and we regret to say that they found it is far low the standard stipulated in the S/C. The covering Inspection Certificate is going to be airmailed to you as soon as it comes to hand.

We think you will look into the matter at once and take immediate measures to correct the mistakes and ensure that nothing like this will happen in the future.

The inferior quality of these beans has caused considerable difficulty to us and it is hard for us to dispose of [8] it, even at a rather low price. We think we can reserve the right to lodge a claim against you for the loss we have suffered.

Yours faithfully,
(Signature)

Letter 4: A reply to the above

Dear Sirs,

We are very surprised to learn from your letter of December 30th, 2015 that the green beans dispatched November 4, 2015 were below the standard stipulated in the contract and that you are reserving the right to lodge a claim against us.

Naturally we hope that the transaction will be concluded to your satisfaction. Now that you have found the quality of the beans do not comply with that stipulated in the contract, we want to have the problem clarified without any delay. So we have sent our representative to your end to investigate the matter in detail. We would not give any comment before our representative inspects the goods. We will soon let you know the date of this visit and hope you will give him your best cooperation.

You may be assured that the matter will be settled in a reasonable manner to our mutual benefits.

Yours faithfully,
(Signature)

Letter 5: Claim on the seller for the damaged goods

Dear Sirs,

Re: Your S/C No. 2A-667B

We have been informed by our agents in Beijing that 200 Tea Sets under the above S/C by S/S Great Wall arrived at Port Amsterdam on July 8. Much to our regret, about 20% of the packages was seriously damaged with contents shattered to pieces and the outer bands broken.

We immediately invited qualified surveyors to the spot to look into the case, and their findings show that this was due to poor packing. A detailed survey report will be dispatched to you subsequent to their further study of individual case.

In accordance with the stipulations of the above Sales Confirmation, we think the tea sets should have been packed in strong seaworthy wooden cases suitable for long distance ocean voyages. We are obliged to hold you are responsible for the damage and claim on you for the compensation for the loss thus incurred.

Meanwhile our buyers are urging us to settle the case immediately. Therefore, we would like you to inform us of what you decide to do regarding our losses.

We are awaiting your prompt reply.

Yours faithfully,
(Signature)

Letter 6: A reply to the above

Dear Sirs,

We feel deeply sorry that the 200 tea sets under the above S/C by S/S Great Wall arrived at Port Amsterdam on July 8 with 20% of the packages damaged as mentioned in your letter of October 11, 2001.

You may be aware that our tea sets have been sold in a number of markets abroad for quite a long time, and all our customers have been satisfied with our packing. Each shipment of our exports is strictly inspected by our shipping departments before loading, and each package is subject to a careful examination. So we think that the goods were in perfect condition when they were shipped, and individual packages were clearly marked with Handle With Care, Fragile and other necessary care marks. The clean B/L supports these facts.

After going into the matter carefully, we estimate that damage might be due to rough handling in transportation or during loading and unloading. We consider it a matter for you to take up with the shipping company or the insurers who have covered you on the said consignment against Risk of Breakage. The responsibility should rest with[9] either of the parties concerned. Consequently, we find no ground to compensate you for the loss.

Yours faithfully,
(Signature)

Letter 7: Claim for short weight

Dear Sirs,

Re: Our Order No. 234 for 10 M/T Chemical Fertilizer

We have just received the Survey Report from Shanghai Commodity Inspection Bureau evidencing that the captioned goods unloaded here yesterday was shortweight[10] 1,120kg. A thorough examination showed that the short weight was due to the improper packing, for which the suppliers should be definitely responsible.

On the basis of the SCIB's Survey Report[11], we hereby register a claim with you for GBP270.00 in all.

We are enclosing the Survey Report No. (98) 607 and look forward to settlement at an early date.

Yours faithfully,
(Signature)

Letter 8: The settlement of the claim for short weight

Dear Sirs,

Re: Your Claim No. 145

With reference to your claim No. 145 for a short weight of 1,120kg chemical fertilizer, we wish to express our much regret over the unfortunate incident.

After a check-up by our staff, it was found that 28 bags had not been packed in 5-ply strong paper bags as stipulated in the contract, thus resulting in the breakage during transit, for which we tender our apologies.

In view of our long-standing business relations, we will make payment by check for GBP270.00, the amount of claim, into your account with the Bank of China, upon receipt of your agreement.

We trust that the arrangement we have made will satisfy you and look forward to receiving your further orders.

Yours faithfully,

(Signature)

Letter 9: Arbitration award

Dear Sirs,

We are pleased to see that, regarding our disputes under Contract No. 0471, both of us are satisfied with the fair and reasonable arbitration award which was rendered by the Foreign Economic and Trade Arbitration Commission[12] of CCPIT[13] after they had thoroughly examined every aspect of this case. The award is being carried out by both sides. What pleases us most is that our friendly relationship has not been harmed by these disputes which had to be resolved by arbitration. On the other hand, this case has deepened the mutual understanding and confidence between us.

We highly appreciate your cooperation and expect further development of business between us.

Yours faithfully,

(Signature)

Notes to the specimen letters

1. everything appears to be correct and in good condition 一切似乎都是正确完好的
2. the contents of this case 箱内（所装）货物
3. to arrange for the dispatch of replacements 安排货物更换事宜
4. at your disposal 任你使用，任你处理
5. go into 调查，仔细审查
6. through a confusion of numbers 由于号码混淆（through 为介词，表示原因之意）
7. We shall be grateful if you will keep case No. 3 and contents until called for by the local agents of World Transport Ltd., our forwarding agents, whom we have instructed accordingly. 请将第3号箱和所装货物代为保存，等候世界运输公司驻你地代理人前来领取。世界运输公司是我们的运输代理行，我们已委托该公司代为办理。
8. dispose of 处理，处置
9. rest with 取决于，归于
10. shortweight 短重，也可以写作 short-weight。例如：We lodge a claim against you for a short

weight of 4.82 M/T. （我方为短重4.82公吨向贵方提出索赔。）

short 短少，短缺，不足。可以与许多名词或过去分词构成复合词，例如：

short delivery 缺交，短交

short-delivered 短交，缺交

short shipment 短装，装载不足

short shipped 短装，装载不足

short-landed 短卸

short-paid 少付

short-invoiced 发票少开

short-established 少开

11. Survey Report 检验报告

Survey Report on Quality 品质鉴定证明

Survey Report on Weight 重量鉴定证明

12. the Foreign Economic and Trade Arbitration Commission 对外经济贸易仲裁委员会

13. CCPIT（the China Council for the Promotion of International Trade）中国国际贸易促进委员会

14.4 Focal Words（焦点词汇）

claim

n. **索赔，赔偿要求**

claim for 表示索赔原因，索赔的金额，例如：claim for damage，claim for USD10,000。

claim on 表示对某批货物索赔，例如：claim on the goods。

claim against 表示向某人索赔，例如：claim against the underwriters（保险公司）。

表示"提出"索赔的常用动词有：lodge，file，raise 和 put in。此外，还可用 make，issue，register，render，enter，set up 等。

表示"为某事向某人提出索赔"的常用句型：lodge a claim against（with/on/upon）sb. for sth.，例如：We shall lodge a claim against the insurance company for the goods damaged during transit.（对于货物在运输途中的损坏，我们将向保险公司提出索赔。）

accept a claim **同意索赔**

entertain a claim **受理索赔**

reject a claim **拒绝索赔**

settle a claim **解决索赔**

waive a claim **放弃索赔**

withdraw a claim **撤回索赔**

vt. **索赔，要求赔偿**

to claim USD50,000.00 索赔5万美元。

to claim USD50,000.00 for damage 因损坏索赔5万美元。

to claim USD50,000.00 on the goods 对该货物索赔5万美元。

to claim USD50, 000. 00 from the underwriters 向保险公司索赔 5 万美元。

We should claim USD2, 500. 00 from you for the loss caused by improper packing. （对于不合格包装所造成的损失，我们应向贵方索赔 2,500. 00 美元。）

compensate

vt. **补偿，赔偿**

The success will compensate you for your efforts. （成功将补偿你的努力。）

You should compensate us for the loss caused by the late delivery. （贵方必须向我方赔偿因迟交货物所引起的损失。）

compensation: *n.* **补偿，补偿；报酬**

You will get compensation for what you have done. （对于你所做的一切，你会得到补偿。）

The buyer claimed a compensation for USD1, 200 for the damage. （对于货物的损坏，买方要求赔偿 1200 美元。）

claim compensation from sb. for sth. **就某事向某人要求索赔**

We reserve the right to claim compensation from you for any damage. （我方将保留就损害而向贵方要求索赔的权利。）

What compensation can you offer for my work per week? （你一周能支付给我多少报酬?）

compensation trade **补偿贸易**

full compensation **全额赔偿**

complain

vi. **诉苦，申诉，抱怨**

complain to sb. of /about sth. **因某事而向某人表示不满**

The buyers complained to the seller of the excessive moisture contained in the minerals. （买方因矿石中水分含量过多向卖方表示不满。）

The buyers complained about the excessive moisture of the minerals. （买方对矿石中水分含量过多表示不满。）

The buyers complained that the minerals contain too much moisture. （买方对矿石中水分含量过多表示不满。）

complaint: *n.* **抱怨，申诉，投诉**

We have noted your complaint and will do our best to avoid a repetition. （我们已经注意到贵方的抱怨，将尽力避免再出现此事。）

make (lodge / file / lay) a complaint against sb. for sth. **因某事而向某人表示抱怨**

This being the case, we have to lodge a complaint against you for the inferior quality. （既然如此，我们不得不就质量低劣问题向贵方申诉。）

settle

vt. **解决；清偿，结算**

Any dispute that may arise from under this contract shall be settled by arbitration. （本合同项下的任何争议应通过仲裁解决。）

We will ask the Bank of China to help us settle payment. （我们将请中国银行协助解决付款问题。）

Please settle this long outstanding account without further delay. （请清偿这笔长期未清的账款，勿再拖延。）

We are requested to settle your account within one week. （要求我方于一周内与贵方结账。）

settlement：*n.* **解决；清偿，理赔**

We hope we can reach an amicable settlement before long. （我们希望尽快达成和解。）

For a settlement of our account of USD300, please send us your cheque. （请寄支票，以清偿我方的300美元账款。）

settlement of disputes **解决争端**

settlement options **索赔选择权**

arbitrate

vi. & *vt.* **仲裁，公断，裁决**

Both sides agreed to arbitrate. （双方同意提交仲裁。）

The two parties hereby agree to arbitrate their disputes if any. （双方同意如果有争端将提请仲裁。）

arbitration：*n.* **仲裁**

This is the maximum concession we can afford. Should you not agree to accept our proposal, we would like to settle by arbitration. （这是我方所能做出的最大让步。如果贵方不同意接受我方建议，我们将通过仲裁解决。）

When no settlement can be reached through negotiations, the disputes shall be submitted for arbitration. （如果协商不能解决，将把争议提交仲裁。）

arbitration clause **仲裁条款**

arbitration award **仲裁裁决**

arbitration application **仲裁申请**

arbitration procedure **仲裁程序**

arbitrator：*n.* **仲裁员，仲裁人**

refund

vt. **归还，偿还**

refund the excess on a tax **归还多收的税款**

refund the goods to the seller **把货物归还卖方**

n. **归还额，偿还额**

obtain a refund of a deposit **获得保证金退款**

The shipping company will give you a refund of freight if the goods are lost. （如果货物丢失，船运公司将退还运费。）

refundable：*adj.* **可归还的，可偿还的**

The bid bond is refundable to those bidders who are not the winner. （对于未中标者，投标保证金予以退还。）

refundment：*n.* **归还，偿还，退款**

14.5 Useful Phrases and Sentences（实用语句）

(1) We have just received the survey report from the Shanghai Commodity Inspection Bureau (SCIB) evidencing the short weight of 1, 800lbs.（我们刚收到上海商检局的检验报告，证明短重1800磅。）

(2) The inspection report shows a difference of 35 tons between the actual landed weight and the invoiced weight.（检验报告显示实际卸货重量和发票重量之间相差35吨。）

(3) The quality of your shipment for our order No. . . . has been found not in conformity with the agreed specification. We must therefore lodge a claim against you for the amount of. . . The SCIB' s survey report is forwarded herewith and your early settlement is requested.（我方第……号定单发来的货物的质量与协议的规格不符，因此，必须向贵方提出索赔，金额为……随附上海商品检验局的检验报告，请早日解决此索赔案。）

(4) The goods have not turned out to our satisfaction, the quality being so poor as to render them unsuitable for the requirements of this market. As the whole parcel is quite useless to us, we must ask you to refund us the invoice value and the inspection fee as per the statement of claim enclosed. We trust that our claim will draw your prompt attention, and as soon as settlement is made, we shall return the goods to you at your expense.（该货不能令我方满意，质量如此低劣，以致不合此地市场需求。由于全部货物对我方毫无用处，务必请贵方退赔发票金额和检验费，详见所附索赔清单。希望贵方立即处理我方索赔，一旦解决，我们就退回货物，费用由贵方负担。）

(5) With reference to your telex of 17th June, we are surprised to learn that the tea sets reached you in a damaged condition, as they were very carefully packed as usual before dispatch. We have had no previous occasion for complaint that our goods have been damaged in transit.（贵方6月17日电传中提到茶具到货受损，我方很惊讶，因在发货前与通常一样很小心地予以包装。我方货物因途中运输受损而接到申诉还是首次。）

(6) We' ll make a thorough investigation to find out where the responsibility actually lies. But before that we can' t promise anything.（我们要进行彻底调查，以查明责任所在。但是在这以前，我们不能做出任何承诺。）

(7) We will make payment by check of GBP980.00, the amount of the claim, into your account with the Bank of China, upon receipt of your agreement.（一旦贵方同意，我们一定将索赔金额980英镑以支票付入贵方的中国银行账户。）

(8) We regret to tell you that your claim can' t be entertained as it is raised far beyond the time limit stipulated in the contract.（我们很遗憾地告诉你们，贵方索赔不能被受理，因为它已远远超过合同规定的索赔期限。）

(9) We, therefore, suggest that you lodge a claim against the shipping company for compensation.（因此，我们建议贵公司向有关船运公司提出索赔。）

(10) We wish to settle this dispute fairly, so we suggest that we submit it to arbitration.（我们希望公平地解决我们的争端，所以我们建议将其提交仲裁。）

（11）关于申诉/抱怨的用语。

to make a complaint against a person 对某人提出申诉/抱怨

to complain of something to a person 对某人提出某种申诉/抱怨

to have a complaint on 关于……的申诉/抱怨

to receive a complaint on 收到关于……的申诉/抱怨

to repeat complaints about 重提关于……的申诉/抱怨

to report a complaints on 提出关于……的申诉/抱怨

to have a cause for complaint 有提出申诉/抱怨的正当理由

to have no complaint to make 无瑕疵可议

to have something to complain of to a person 对某人提出关于……的申诉/抱怨

to acknowledge an error 承认错误

to correct an error 改正错误

to adjust a dispute 解决纠纷

（12）关于索赔的用语。

to claim for indemnity 要求索赔

to have a claim on 对……有索赔权

to send in one' s claim for compensation/to enter one' s claim for compensation/to put in one' s claim for compensation 提出索赔

to lodge one' s claim with a person for/to file one' s claim with a person for/to submit one' s claim to a person/to place one' s claim before a person 对某人提出索赔

to lay claim to 主张对……索赔

to enter a claim for... with/to file a claim for... with/to put in a claim for... with 对……提出索赔

to satisfy one' s claims 满足某人的索赔

to accept one' s claim/to meet one' s claim/to entertain one' s claim 接受某人的索赔

to avoid a claim/to obviate a claim 排除索赔

to withdraw a claim/to waive a claim/to abandon a claim 撤回索赔

（13）关于赔偿的用语。

to compensate for losses to a person with/ to compensate a person for losses with/ to recompense a person for losses with 依……对……赔偿损失

counter-claim 反索赔

（14）关于质量的用语。

We regret to have to inform you that the tins of lobster which you sold me on 29th June have caused numerous complaints.（我们不得不遗憾地向贵公司报告：贵公司6月29日售给我公司的虾罐头质量太差，使我们收到不少申诉。）

We regret to say that a part of the goods, indeed, nearly half, have lost a good deal of their quality by wetting from sea-water.（我们实感遗憾，贵方货物中一部分（几乎一半）受海水浸蚀，质量降低很多，特此报告。）

（15）关于与样品不一致的用语。

The goods submitted do not correspond with the sample sent.（到货与惠送样品并不相同。）

We find every bale weighs short.（我们发现每包重量都不足。）

We greatly regret to say that the goods are not in accordance with your sample.（非常遗憾，到货确与样品不完全相同。）

（16）关于包装不合格的用语。

With regard to the fruit, I am astonished to learn that it arrived in such a bad order, every precaution having, as I considered, been taken to insure its preservation.（为保持该批水果的质量，我曾经采取了良好的预防措施，而今到达贵地时竟如此恶化，实在意想不到。）

We regret to find on opening up 20 cases of the glass delivered here yesterday that 15% of the sheets are broken, 45% show bubbles, and nearly all are badly scratched.（我方打开昨天运到的 20 箱玻璃，非常遗憾地发现有 15% 破损，45% 呈泡沫状，几乎都有明显划痕。）

We are sorry to learn that this shipment has not given full satisfaction, and we cannot understand how it should have gone out of condition during so short a voyage.（我方获知这批货物未能让贵方满意，甚感遗憾。我公司对在这样短的海运时间内会发生如此不良的后果深感不解。）

（17）关于商品更换、退还的用语。

They say they are to receive the compensation money from the company.（他们说要从公司获得补偿金。）

We must ask you to replace them with good salable ones.（我们必须请求贵方以适于销售的货物更换该货。）

Please let us have a marketable lot in exchange for them.（请允许我们收到适于销售的货物并将原货寄回。）

（18）关于折扣或补贴的用语。

As much of this consignment will be practically useless, kindly allow me a liberal discount upon the price agreed upon.（由于这批寄售的商品中有很多无法使用，所以请对原来商定的价格做一次大幅度的折扣优惠为荷。）

Would you kindly let me know if you will take them back, or allow me to sell them at a discount of 50%?（对本货物，贵公司是否可考虑同意退货，或者按 50% 的折价由本公司脱手，请回复。）

The inconvenience thus caused is very great, and I hold the owners responsible for any loss which may accrue through this delay.（因延迟到货所造成的诸多不便及一切损失，应由发货人负全部责任。）

（19）关于说明与辩解的用语。

It is a practical impossibility to weave such a cloth in the length you now require.（这种布料实际上不可能按贵公司要求的长度纺织。）

Our communications of the 3rd May and 20th inst., will, we trust, remove the unfavorable opinion you appear to have formed.（我们相信，本公司 5 月 3 日及本月 20 日的函件能消除贵公司的疑虑。）

We have never received a bill of lading or invoice from you, and if any of your letters to us contained such documents, they must, in some way, have been miscarried.（我们未收到贵公司所寄的提单及发票。如果贵公司在给我们的信函中确实包含了这些文件，那么一定是被误送到其他地方了。）

Exercises

1. Put the following English phrases into English or Chinese phrases into English.

（1） CCPIT

（2） on going into the matter

（3） to hold no liability for sth.

（4） take up the matter

（5） at sb.'s disposal

（6） make compensation for sb.'s losses

（7） 公证行

（8） 不可抗力

（9） 仲裁裁决

（10） 无追索权

（11） 承担责任

（12） 国际贸易仲裁委员会

2. Multiple choice.

（1） We have ______the drums one by one and found that most of them are leaking.

a. examined　b. tested　c. rolled　d. traced

（2） We have to file a claim against you ______USD20, 000. 00.

a. of the amount　b. to the amount of

c. about　d. equal to

（3） The analysis of the first shipment is not satisfactory ______certified by the China Commodity Inspection Bureau.

a. after　b. has been　c. as is　d. which is

（4） Fifty cases of green tea you sent us were found to be badly damaged. This was apparently attributable to ______packing.

a. domestic　b. outer　c. inferior　d. faulty

（5） We trust you will do your best ______this matter settled at once.

a. to have　b. to put

c. to make　d. to be responsible

（6） The answer ______a claim letter is easy if you are agreeing to the customer's request.

a. to　b. of　c. for　d. in

（7） If there were any delay in delivery, we would cancel the order and reserve the right to ______a claim against you.

a. give　b. lodge　c. have　d. get

（8） The report of survey revealed that the damage is ______improper packing.

a. because　　　　　　　　　　b. because of
c. contributed to　　　　　　　d. attributed to

(9) Complaints ______ if the contract is not fulfilled in some way, amounting to a breach of conditions.

a. is made　　b. will be made　　c. will make　　d. were made

(10) It was found upon examination that early 15% of the packages ______, which was obviously attributed to improper packing.

a. was broken　　　　　　　　b. broken
c. had been broken　　　　　　d. been already broken

3. Translate the following sentences into English using the words or phrases in the brackets.

(1) 经检验，我们发现虽然箱子本身并无损坏迹象，但很多货物已严重损坏。(upon examination)

(2) 我们以上海商检局的报告为依据，特此向贵方提出索赔。(on the basis of)

(3) 现向贵方就短重及质量低劣提出索赔。(lodge/register a claim with)

(4) 我们提出合同价格减去30%是公平合理的，否则，按照合同规定办事，买方有权退货并提出索赔。(lodge a claim)

(5) 自从你们提出申诉之后，我们已经采取措施以克服缺点。我们现在已确实弄清楚，货物在装箱之前是完好的。(in sound condition)

(6) 将有缺陷的设备运交你们，非常抱歉。今天另运出12台替换设备，希望贵方对这批新货感到满意。(send a replacement of)

4. Translate the following letter into English.

敬启者:

事由：贵方关于100公吨化肥的索赔

贵方9月6日函就化肥短重1,800磅一事提出索赔，对此不幸事件 (unfortunate incident) 我方深表遗憾。想必你们在履行贵方客户订货方面已遇到很多困难。

经过我方仓库工作人员核查，发现约有40袋未按照合同规定，用五层坚固纸袋 (5-ply strong paper bags) 包装，致使在运输途中发生破损。这完全是仓库主任 (warehouse managers) 的疏忽 (negligence) 所致。对此，我们作为出口商向贵方致以歉意。

兹随函寄去支票一张，计1,146美元，用以最终并全部了结此索赔案。收到后请及时函告我方。

我们希望这一不幸事件不会影响我们之间的良好关系及今后的交易。

真诚的，
迈克尔·曼

5. Write a letter as per the following particulars.

(1) 订单123号50箱瓷器收到。

(2) 其中7只箱子破裂，内装瓷器损坏。

(3) 检验报告证明损坏是不良包装所致。

（4）要求赔偿损失费及检验费计8,650美元。

Supplementary Reading

Part A

In ideal business conditions everything should be done so carefully, with details of offers and orders checked, packing supervised, handling of goods carried out expertly, that no mistakes are made and nothing damaged. Unfortunately as in other walks of life, nothing goes so well as that. Errors occur and goods are mishandled. Accidents happen usually because of hurry, lack of sufficient supervision; shortage of staff owing to illness or holidays; shortage of sufficiently trained staff; resultant haste and overwork, etc. So the mistakes creep in. The above results may lead to subsequent complaints or claims of different characters. Generally there are differences between the goods delivered and the goods ordered; inferior quality; missing or shortage from the delivery; delay of the shipment; bad packing, and so on. In order to keep the business relations developed to the entire satisfaction, we must make complaints or claims in a restrained and tactful way.

Any disputes arising from the execution of the contract can be not settled through friendly negotiation, so we can use other different ways to solve the problems. It is almost a truism to state that arbitration is better than litigation; conciliation is better than arbitration; and prevention of legal disputes is better than conciliation. Generally speaking, friendly negotiation or mediation is the best way of all and beneficial to both parties. In case disputes can' t be settled through mediation, they should be submitted to arbitration if it has been agreed upon beforehand in the contract or sign another afterwards. Each of the disputing parties select arbitrators first, and then appointed selected the umpire to form the Arbitration Tribunal. The arbitration award is final. It has the force of law and binding upon both parties.

Notes

1. walks of life 行业
2. creep in 悄悄混进
3. tactful 有策略的
4. truism 不言而喻
5. litigation 诉讼
6. conciliation 调解
7. umpire 首席仲裁员
8. Arbitration Tribunal 仲裁庭

Part B

Salespeople increase sales by obtaining new customers and selling more product to current customers. Customer referrals are the best way to find new prospects. Thus, it' s important to provide excellent service and follow-up to customers. By building a relationship and partnership, you can provide a high level of customer service.

Customers expect service. When you deliver service, customers are satisfied and continue to buy; this results in retention and loyalty. Providing service to customers is important in all types of selling. Follow-up and service create goodwill between salesperson and customer that allows the salesperson to penetrate or work throughout the customer' s organization. Account penetration helps the salesperson to better serve the account and uncover its needs and problems. A service relationship with an account leads to increases in total and major brand sales, better distribution on all product sizes, and customer cooperation in promoting your products.

To serve customers best, improve account penetration. Contact each customer frequently and regularly; promptly handle all complaints. Always do what you say you will do, and remember to serve customers as if they were royalty. Finally, remember to sincerely thank all customers for their business, no matter how large or small, to show you appreciate them.

If customers begin to buy from a competitor or reduce their level of cooperation, continue to call on them in your normal professional manner. In a friendly way, determine why they did not buy from you, and develop new customer benefit plans to recapture their business.

Always strive to help your customers increase their sales of your product or to get the best use from products that you have sold to them. To persuade a customer to purchase more of your products or use your products in a different manner, develop a sales program to help maximize sales to that customer. This involves developing an account penetration program; increasing the number and sizes of products the customer purchases; maintaining proper inventory levels in the customer' s warehouse and on the shelf; achieving good shelf space and shelf positioning; clear communication with persons who directly sell or use a product; a willingness to assist wholesale and retail customers' salespeople in any way possible; a willingness to help customers; and an overall effort to develop a positive, friendly business relationship with each customer. By doing these eight things, your ability to help and properly serve each customer increases.

Today' s professional salesperson is oriented to service. Follow-up and service after the sale maximize your territory' s sales and help attain personal goals.

Part C

Providing good service to customers in today' s competitive marketplace is not enough—service must be excellent. Excellent service often requires technology and automation. Here is an example of how companies are improving customer service.

For the Livingston Group, a Toronto-based logistics company that sells such services as freight forwarding and distribution to importers and exporters, the question was how to spend no more than USD80, 000 to make their eight salespeople more effective in working with their customers. The division' s goals were ① to make account executives accessible to customers and each other no matter where they were; ② to create presentations on the road that could be shared internally; and ③ to be sure account executives could manage their accounts easily while eliminating the administrative tasks that take up considerable selling time.

InteGain set up the following integrated application for Livingston Group: Each account executive received an IBM Thinkpad, loaded with GoldMine for Windows Software (produced by ELAN

Software Corporation of Pacific Palisades, California), Microsoft Windows for WorkGroups 3.11, WinFax Pro 4.0, and WinCIM (which allows access to CompuServe). They each also received a Hewlett-Packard DeskJet portable printer and a Nokia portable telephone. Each account executive was equipped with the MyLine telephone service from Call America Business Communications based in San Luis Obispo, California. This service provides account executives with their own 800 numbers and directly connects inbound calls to them wherever they are via their portable or home office phones.

The program works like this: At the end of each business day, account executives use their laptops to send new data or presentations collected and created during the day to a CompuServe mailbox. As part of an automated process, a system at Livingston Trade Technologies' home office automatically dials into this Compu-Serve mailbox, retrieves the uploaded information, consolidates it, prepares reports, and redistributes the consolidated information to each of the executives in several minutes. InteGain's integrated application is called TARGET.

Automating allows salespeople to work independently out of their cars and to spend less time on administrative tasks. And, because management is kept informed, it can make quick decisions on facts relating to customer service.

Part D

What Not to Wear at an Interview

CareerBuilder.com surveyed hiring professionals to discover the top fashion mistakes interviewees make:

(1) Too-short skirts.

(2) Overly bright or vividly patterned clothing.

(3) Wrinkled or stained clothing.

(4) Poorly fitted clothing.

(5) Socks that are too short, or don't go with the shoes.

(6) Patterned hosiery or bare legs.

(7) Scuffed or inappropriate footwear, including sneakers, stilettos, sandals, and open-toed shoes.

(8) Extra buttons or tags attached to a new suit.

(9) Earrings on men; multiple sets of earrings on women.

(10) Visible tattoos, tongue jewelry, and facial piercings.

(11) Heavy makeup.

(12) Long or bright fingernails.

(13) Unnatural hair colors or styles.

(14) Strong aftershaves, perfumes, or colognes.

(15) Backpacks, fanny packs, or purses (use a brief case).

(16) Sunglasses on top of your head or headphones around your neck.

Interview Checklist

Here is a checklist for a surefire attitude from Judi James, author of *You're Hired! Intervies: Tips and Techniques for a Brilliant Interview*.

(1) Sell yourself to yourself. If you don't believe in yourself, chances are the interviewer won't believe in you either.

(2) Show, don't tell. Prepare short stories of your accomplishments; they are more convincing than simply stating you are a good leader or problem solver. Keep your information relevant to the job.

(3) Avoid JBY syndrome. An interview is not the place to Just Be Yourself (JBY). Interviews are formal events; reflect that formality in your attire and behavior.

(4) Be vivid. Energy, enthusiasm, and charisma help you stand out.

(5) Avoid body language "leakage". Nervous habits such as fidgeting and fiddling can send negative signals.

(6) Make a good entrance. Stand tall, smile, look confident. Practice a firm handshake and making eye contact.

(7) Look the part. Dress appropriately for the company and job.

Unit 15
Modes of Trade
贸易方式

15.1 Introduction（简介）

在对外贸易中，最为常见的是单边出口和单边进口方式。只要交易双方就各项交易条件达成一致，签订合同，并按合同规定履行了各自的义务，交易就告完成。然而，在实际业务中，由于商品之间存在差异，市场也各具特点，所以，许多灵活多样的贸易方式就应运而生。

1. 代理

代理（Agency）是指出口人通过签订代理协议，将商品委托给国外客户（代理人），委托其在一定地区和一定时间内为出口人代售商品、招揽生意或处理有关事宜的一种贸易方式。

代理是国际贸易中常见的方式，在运输、保险、广告等行业也活跃着为数众多的代理人，全球贸易有一半左右是通过代理商来完成的。根据委托人授权程度的不同，代理可分为总代理（General agency）、独家代理（Exclusive or sole agency）和佣金代理（Commission agency，也称一般代理）。

与代理相关函电的主要内容通常涉及代理类型、被代理商品的名称、代理地区范围、代理期限、代理数量和金额、代理佣金等，还可能涉及非竞争条款、商标保护、广告宣传和市场报导等。

2. 加工与装配贸易

加工与装配贸易（Processing & assembling trade）是指由国外委托方提供原材料、零部件或元器件，委托国内企业（承接方）按一定的技术、质量标准加工成成品并交还委托方，委托方再对国内企业支付工缴费的贸易方式。

加工与装配贸易方式和进出口紧密结合，有“两头在外”之称。这种贸易方式有利于一国通过利用外国原材料、零部件或元器件来增加本国的生产和出口，扩大就业，增加财政收入，有利于本国企业及时掌握出口商品在国际市场的信息，也有利于本国企业引进国外先进的技术设备、提升技术水平和管理水平。

有关加工与装配贸易函电的主要内容包括：合同标的，来料来件的数量，加工装配期限，关于成品、工缴费、运输和保险、付款方式的规定，预防性和约束性条款，违约与赔偿，不可抗力规定等。

3. 补偿贸易

补偿贸易（Compensation trade）是在信贷的基础上一方从另一方输入技术、机器设备或劳务，然后在一定时期内用产品或双方商定的商品清偿价款的一种贸易方式。从偿付的办法来看，有直接补偿、间接补偿、劳务补偿、收益分期补偿、综合补偿等形式。

补偿贸易对进出口双方都有利，有利于出口方扩大技术和设备的出口、抢占市场、降低出口经营风险并获得稳定、廉价的回头产品，也有利于进口方利用外资信贷扩大技术和设备的进口、获取国外先进的管理经验、利用外商销售能力开拓市场并建立起本国的进口替代与出口导向产业。

4. 合资企业

合资企业（Joint venture）指的是以盈利为目的，由不同国家的投资人共同投资建立并经营的企业。实际中，合资企业主要分三种：股权式合资企业（Equity joint venture）、契约式合资企业（Contractual joint venture）和共同开发（Joint exploration）。

合资方式有利于合资一方引进国外资本、提升技术水平，有利于向发达国家或地区学习先进的管理经验。鉴于合资企业的合同内容较为复杂，所以，在创建合资企业的函电来往中，一般没有必要一一涉及，只需表明意向并对一些关键内容（如投资额、产品种类、企业选址、预期产量等）加以确定就可。待双方达成意向后，再进入合同的创立阶段。

15.2 Specimen Letters（样函）

Letter 1: Application for agency

Dear Sirs,

We know from A&J Corporation that you are looking for a reliable firm with good connections in the cotton piece goods trade to represent you in Canada.

Having already had experience in marketing[1] cotton piece goods similar to your own, we are familiar with customers' needs and are confident we could develop a worthwhile market for you in Canada. We have well-equipped showrooms in Vancouver, Quebec and experienced sales staff who make regular calls on customers.

We should appreciate your letting us know as soon as possible whether you are interested in our offer and on what terms you would be willing to reach an agency agreement. If it does[2], we would suggest you meeting with Mr. Stockton to discuss details of an agreement to both of us.

Yours faithfully,
Island Pty, Ltd.
(Signature)
General Manager

Letter 2: A reply to the application for agency

Dear Sirs,

We thank you for your letter of February 20, in which you proposed to sell our products on agency basis.

We are deeply impressed by your kindness in submitting this proposal to us, and your application is now under our careful consideration. However, before going further into this arrangement, we would like to know your market consumption, the definite quantities you require quarterly or annually, your plan to push the sales of our products, and your bank references, etc.

Last but not least[3], the whole matter hinges upon[4] the question of the amount of commission you would require on orders obtained and executed. And as your Mr. Stockton intends visiting Tianjin at the end of February, we shall be pleased to discuss the possibility of coming to an arrangement with him personally.

We are looking forward to your early reply and awaiting Mr. Stockton' s call.

Yours sincerely,
Tianjin Textiles Imp. /Exp. Group
(Signature)
Director

Letter 3: An initial proposal for processing after sample with supplied materials

Dear Sirs,

After several months' negotiation, we have finally succeeded in reaching an agreement on the proposed contract for processing after sample with supplied materials. Now we enclose a summary of those essential points of our proposition with this letter for your perusal[5] and hope to have your comments.

Please give the propositions of your best consideration and if you fall in with us on these essential points[6], let us have your prompt reply so that we can move to the next stage.

Awaiting with keen interest your early reply.

Yours sincerely,
Nova Motor Group
(Signature)
General manager

Letter 4: A confirmation letter to Letter 3

Dear Sirs,

We take pleasure in confirming the following arrangements in connection with processing after sample with supplied materials[7] agreed upon between Mr. Smith, manager of your company and us during his visit to this city.

You are to supply raw materials, samples and technical drawings, and we are to process the materials according to the drawings into finished products, which shall fully conform to your samples and bear a brand designated by you[8]. We have studied the matter with our manufacturers and it is estimated that they will be able to produce 500 sets each month as required by you, to be delivered in two lots of 250 sets each. In order to enable our manufacturers to trial produce the products, we would request you to send us the samples and technical drawings six months ahead of the required shipment.

As to the rate of spoilage[9] of the raw materials, it is rather difficult to make a close estimate at present stage of trial manufacture. Accordingly, we propose not to lay down any rate until the end of this stage when we shall figure out the rate according to the actual spoilage.

If you should have any different views of any other problems, please do not hesitate to communicate with us.

Yours sincerely,
(Signature)

Letter 5: A proposal letter for compensation trade

Dear Mr. Riddick,

Please accept our thanks for your prompt response to our fax dated March 20 in connection with the above subject. We have also received your counter sample of the men's poplin shirt.

Having carefully examined the counter sample, we find everything satisfactory except for the stitches, which are not what we expected. We attribute this shortcoming to[10] the old type of sewing machine being used by your manufacturers. We feel sure this problem can easily be solved if a new type of machines is installed.

As requested, we enclose a catalogue and a price list for Model AN-CE Sewing Machine produced by Messrs. Juki & Co., Hong Kong. They have in stock 90 machines, which can be shipped to you promptly. This is the very machine suitable for making our poplin shirt, and the present price is HKD ... each FOB Hong Kong, which we can assure you is the lowest obtainable[11]. We wish to mention that we have not added anything to the price of the machine for our profit, and we are also prepared to ship the machines to you at cost with freight for your account[12]. The cost for the 90 machines will be advanced by us and can be repaid by you by installments, plus freight and interest at ... % per annum[13].

Please fax us as soon as possible if you are interested in these machines, and in the meantime let us have your best offer for the poplin shirts based on our order of 2,500 dozen per month. On receipt of your reply to our order of the sewing machines and your quotation for the shirts, we shall try our best to conclude the two deals as one package under compensation trade agreement[14].

We thank you in advance for an early reply and assure you of our full cooperation at all time.

Yours faithfully,
(Signature)

Letter 6: A confirmation reply to Letter 5

Dear Mr. Meier,

Through the friendly discussion between your Ms. Catherine and us, we are most pleased to have been able to conclude the said compensation trade[15]. We sincerely hope this deal will pave the way for further cooperation between us.

We are sending you three copies of Agreement on Compensation Trade, duly signed by[16] our manufacturers and us. Please countersign[17] two originals and return them to us for our record as well as for the record of our manufacturers.

We take this opportunity to express our thanks and appreciation for your cooperation in making our discussion a success, and hope that both of us will see the agreement be executed to the complete satisfaction of all parties concerned, and then the continuance of future business can be ensured.

Yours faithfully,
(Signature)

Letter 7: A reply to the request for the establishment of joint venture

Dear Mr. Leno,

We have received your fax of March 8, from which we learn that you are interested in establishing an auto parts factory in China in the form of joint venture and enquiring about its feasibility.

You are probably aware that China has always persisted in an open door policy and taken a positive stand with regard to introducing foreign investment, with a view to expanding economic cooperation and technical exchange with other countries on the basis of equality and mutual benefits[18]. China permits foreign firms, enterprises and other economic organizations or individuals to form joint ventures with Chinese firms, enterprises or other economic organizations.

In order to help you get fully acquainted with the various provisions in connection with the joint venture, we take pleasure in enclosing a copy of *The Law of the People's Republic of China on Joint Ventures Using Chinese and Foreign Investment* for your perusal and hope to have your comments.

Should you be interested in forming a joint venture with us, please let us know your tentative idea as to the type of commodity, quantity of production, material procurement, sales channels and principal machinery and equipment, so that we can make a thorough study of your plan and go further into the matter.

We look forward to your reply with interest.

Yours faithfully,
(Signature)
Tianzhi Shi
Business Director

Encl. As stated.

Letter 8: A reply to Letter 7

Dear Mr. Shi,

Thank you for your fax of March 18, enclosing a copy of *The Law of the People's Republic of China on Joint Ventures Using Chinese and Foreign Investment.*

Having gone through it carefully, we have now a better understanding about the establishment of a joint venture in China. However, there is still one point not clear to us. In Article 4, it states that in the registered capital of a joint venture, the proportion of the investment contributed by the foreign participants shall be in general not less than 25%, but no mention is made about the upper limit on the share of the registered capital of a joint venture contributed by a foreigner. As we have informed you previously, we are of the intention to make investment on 50% –50% basis and wonder if this is practicable.

Our investment, i. e. 50% of capital of the proposed joint venture, is to be made partly in cash and partly in machinery and equipment. As to the cash, it is to be converted from US dollars according to the exchange rate in effect on the date the agreement becomes effective[19]. We are well connected with the machinery suitable for the need in the course of production, which will be evaluated by both parties. In the meantime, we should like to know in what form your investment will be.

Upon hearing from you, we will go further into the matter or suggest a personal visit to have a face-to-face discussion so that problems can be cleared quickly.

We await your early reply.

Yours faithfully,
(Signature)

Notes to the specimen letters

1. marketing 营销
2. if it does 假若如此（即如果你方有兴趣达成协议的话）
3. last but not least 最后但并非最不重要的 = 同样重要的是
4. hinge upon 取决于，以……而定
5. for your perusal 供贵方细查
6. fall in with us on these essential points 在这些关键问题上与我方一致
7. processing after sample with supplied materials 来样来料加工
8. bear a brand designated by you 用贵方所指定的品牌
9. spoilage 损坏，rate of spoilage 损坏（耗）率
10. attribute this shortcoming to 将此种缺陷归咎于
11. the lowest obtainable 可获得的最低价格
12. We are also prepared to ship the machines to you at cost with freight for your account. 我方也准备将机器装船出运到贵方，其成本及运费计入贵方账户。
13. The cost for the 90 machines will be advanced by us and can be repaid by you by installments, plus freight and interest at ... % per annum. 90 台机器的成本将由我方先行支付，再由贵方以分期付款的方式进行冲抵，其中包含运费和……的年利息。
14. conclude the two deals as one package under compensation trade agreement 在补偿贸易协定下将两笔业务纳入一揽子交易
15. the said compensation trade 该补偿贸易
16. duly signed by 已由……正式签署
17. countersign 对签，会签
18. on the basis of equality and mutual benefits 在平等互利的基础上
19. As to the cash, it is to be converted from US dollars according to the exchange rate in effect on

the date the agreement becomes effective. 至于所支付的现金，将按合同生效之时的即期汇率把美元折算为人民币。

15.3 Focal Words（焦点词汇）

business

n. 商业；贸易；生意；公司，商行；业务

Another foreign bank has opened for business in Shanghai.（又有一家外商银行在上海开业。）

This company was doing a great business.（该公司生意兴隆。）

We have absorbed a small business.（我们已经兼并了一家小企业。）

I will make it my business to see that the money is paid promptly.（我将督促迅速付款。）

go into business 经商，从商

I have gone into business in partnership with him.（我已经和他合伙经营。）

go out of business 停止，歇业

The firm went out of business during the recession.（该公司已经在萧条时期停止营业了。）

in business 经营

He is in the real estate business.（他经营房地产业务。）

on business 因公，因事

The chairman is in New York on business.（董事长正在纽约出差。）

businessman：*n.* 商人，实业家，企业家

businesslike：*adj.* 有条理的；认真的；公事公办的

exchange

v. 交流，交换，兑换

We wish to exchange experience with you in business.（我们希望和你们交流业务经验。）

The customers need to exchange foreign currencies for Renminbi.（这些客户需要将外币兑换成人民币。）

This currency exchanges at par.（这种货币以平价兑换。）

n. 交换，兑换；汇率；交易所；总机

As a result of the exchange of e-mail between us, we have now come to terms.（通过双方电子邮件往来，我们现在已经达成了交易。）

Prices are liable to alteration in accordance with the fluctuation of exchange.（价格往往按汇率的波动而变化。）

stock exchange 交易所

commodity exchange 商品交易所

foreign exchange 外汇

telephone exchange 电话总机

exchangeable：*adj.* 可以兑换的，可以交换的，可以退换的

limit

n. **限制；限额，（价格）限度；价格**

They set a time limit for acceptance of the offer.（他们对接受报盘做了时间限制。）

Your limit is too high to work on.（贵方的限额太高，无法进行。）

We can not place orders at your limit.（我们无法按贵方的价格订货。）

v. **限制；限定**

They limit their business activities to textile.（他们的经营活动仅限于纺织品。）

limitation：*n.* **限制；限度，限额**

limited：*adj.* **有限的，受限制的**

As our stocks are limited, we recommend you to accept our offer immediately.（由于库存有限，我们建议贵方立即接受我方的报盘。）

negotiate

v. **谈判，协商；议付；谈妥；转让**

They are negotiating a transaction in woolen carpets.（他们正在洽谈一笔地毯交易。）

The exporters must present shipping documents when they negotiate payment with the bank.（出口商向银行议付时必须出示装运单据。）

Personally, I' m delighted with the terms negotiated.（我个人对已谈妥的各项条款均感满意。）

to negotiate a bill of lading **转让提单**

negotiable：*adj.* **可谈判的；可转让的；可流通的；可议付的**

The dispute is negotiable and can be settled amicably.（该争议可通过谈判友好解决。）

A bill of lading is a negotiable document.（提单是可以转让的单据。）

The draft drawn under this L/C shall be negotiable in Shanghai.（根据该信用证开立的汇票可在上海议付。）

negotiation：*n.* **谈判，磋商；议付**

We are still in negotiation with the parties concerned.（我们正与各有关方面进行磋商。）

We surrendered a clean on board bill of lading for the negotiation of payment.（议付时我们提交了清洁装运提单。）

15.4 Useful Sentences（实用语句）

(1) Being a reliable firm with wide and varied experience in the line, we offer to act as your sole (exclusive) agency in our territory.（作为一家在行内信誉卓著、经验丰富的公司，我们希望担任贵方在我地区的独家代理。）

(2) Regarding your proposal to represent us for the sale of our canned foods, we' d like to appoint you as our agent in Hong Kong on condition that you realize the annual turnover of USD500, 000.（关于贵方建议代理销售我方罐头食品一事，我们愿意指定贵方为我方在香港的代理，条件是贵方每年的销售额要达到50万美元。）

(3) Hearing from our correspondent that you are looking for an agent in this city, we are pleased to apply for the post.（从顾客处得悉，贵公司拟在本市寻找代理，我们特申请担任这

项工作，请酌定。）

（4）We would like to process garments according to supplied samples from you.（我们很愿意根据贵方来样加工服装。）

（5）We herewith take the liberty to offer you our services as forwarding agents in this port, hoping to be favored with your esteemed commands in the near future.（我公司希望成为贵公司在本港的运输代理。请早日赐予为荷。）

（6）With the components, auxiliary materials, and necessary equipment and tools supplied by your company, we shall assemble 36,000 refrigerators within a period of three years.（我公司在为期三年内用贵公司提供的零部件、辅料、必要的设备和工具可以装配3.6万台电冰箱。）

（7）We would like to do compensation trade with you for the construction of a plant with the production capacity of at least 12,000 M/T per year of MSP-3PVC Paste Resin Product in Hefei Chemical Works.（我们想与贵方以补偿贸易方式在合肥化工厂建一个年产至少1.2万公吨MSP-3PVC聚氯乙烯糊状树脂产品的化工厂。）

（8）I wish to proffer you my services, with the assurance that whatever claims and others you may be pleased to confide and recommend to my agency, shall be promptly and efficiently attended to.（不论任何要求或其他条件，只要委任或推荐本人为代理人，必能迅速有效地完成所赋任务。）

（9）We shall reimburse you the remaining value of the entire production line by five annual installments in a period of five years with the products turned out with the said production line.（我们将按五年分期平均付款的方法用该生产线所生产的产品偿还整个生产线的余额。）

（10）Herewith I have the pleasure to hand you an account sales of 150 bales textiles received per s. s. Henry, the net proceeds of which USD3,800 are passed to the credit of your account.（随函奉上亨利号货轮运来的150包纺织品的销售清单。贵公司应收额为3,800美元，现已记入贵公司贷方账户内。）

（11）Our joint venture law places no upper limit on the share of the registered capital of a joint venture contributed by a foreigner although generally speaking the minimum amount acceptable will not be less than 25%.（虽然我国合资企业法对合资企业的注册资本中外方所占的上限并未做出规定，但是，可接受的最低额度一般不应低于25%。）

（12）The profits, risks and losses of a joint venture shall be shared by the parties to the venture in proportion to their contribution to the registered capital.（合资企业的利润、风险和亏损按注册资本的投资比例由合资企业的各方承担。）

（13）We appreciate your suggestion that you sell our products on an exclusive basis, but we think it is premature for us to enter into agency agreement at the present stage.（感谢贵方独家销售我方产品的建议，但我们认为在现阶段签订代理协议为时过早。）

（14）We are willing to push the trade in your machines, and hope you will give us the sole agency for our place.（我们希望为贵公司拓销机械市场，请将贵公司在本地的独家代理赋予敝公司为盼。）

（15）Thank you very much for your letter of August 2nd enquiring about the possibility of manufacturing leather bags according to your samples.（感谢贵方8月2日来信询问来样生产皮包的

可能性。)

(16) Having heard that you are about to ship wine to this country, we offer our services as agents in Japan. (得悉贵公司准备到日本销售葡萄酒，请指定本公司为贵公司在该国的总代理。)

(17) At present, we have every prospect of rendering him good account sales, as cottons of all descriptions are in demand and the prices are rather on the advance. (目前，各类棉花销路很好，且价格渐涨。因此，我们有希望提出一个令人满意的销售账单。)

(18) I refer you to my signature at foot, also to that of Mr. G, who will sign per procuration. (我的签名如下，同时寄上将行使签名权的G先生的签名，请惠察。)

(19) We inform you that Mr. Y., who has held our procuration for the last fifteen years, will in future sign for the firm. (兹通知，过去15年中任我公司代理的Y先生今后将为本公司业务担任签名责任。)

(20) We would like to suggest for considering the following points to carry out compensation trade between us. (关于在我们之间做补偿贸易之事，我方建议考虑以下几个要点。)

(21) Your consignment of 30 cases textiles arrived in good condition. Cheap goods have a ready sale, and prices remain firm for the present. We shall be able to give you a good account sales. (贵公司寄售之30箱纺织品已安然抵达。廉价品的销路相当良好，且目前价格稳定。因此，我相信能向贵公司提出满意的销售报告书。)

(22) Our friends inform us that you have good connection in this trade, and that you import largely from this country, and acting entirely upon their advice, we are sending you a consignment as a trial. (据本公司客户告知，贵公司在此项贸易上有很好的关系，并且从我国大量进口。因此，我们按照他们的推荐，准备将该商品寄给贵公司，请代为试销。)

(23) We should be pleased to take care of any consignment of goods suitable for this market which you may be disposed to send us. (只要适合本地市场需求，贵公司委托的任何商品，我们都愿意接受。)

(24) We thank you for your letter of the 6th June, containing proposals for consignment business in cotton yarns, and we shall be pleased to act for you in this matter in the way manned. (贵公司6月6日函已收悉，关于委托销售棉纱一事，本公司愿按照贵公司的吩咐，尽力而为。特此致谢。)

(25) We take this opportunity to approach you in the hope that you will introduce us to any partner interested in forming joint ventures with us in producing chemical fertilizers in China. (我方借此机会与贵方联系，希望贵方给我们介绍任何有意和我们在中国合资生产化肥的伙伴。)

Exercises

1. Put the following English phrases into Chinese or Chinese phrases into English.

(1) 独家代理

(2) 代理佣金

(3) 明示同意

(4) 建立地位/立足
(5) 来样来料加工
(6) 来件装配
(7) 损耗率
(8) 资本货物
(9) 合资企业
(10) 注册资本
(11) 董事会
(12) 资产与负债
(13) 按比例均摊
(14) 多边贸易
(15) to entrust . . . with
(16) in view of . . .
(17) performance objective
(18) sale by sample
(19) CCPIT
(20) CEO
(21) compensation trade
(22) exporting resultant products
(23) in proportion to
(24) to spare no effort to do
(25) final and binding upon both parties
(26) resultant cost
(27) contracting parties
(28) PNTR

2. Multiple choice.

(1) If you appoint us as ________, we shall try to enlarge the sale of your products.

a. for your agent　　b. your agent

c. being your agent　　d. to be your agent

(2) ________ you mentioned in your letter in connection with the question of agency has had our attention.

a. Why　　b. When　　c. What　　d. That

(3) We appreciate your suggestion ________ establish agency relationship between our banks.

a. for　　b. that　　c. to　　d. we

(4) Forwarding agent service is valuable in foreign trade because of the complicated ________ that have to be made.

a. process　　b. procedures　　c. formalities　　d. arrangements

(5) The factory was awarded the contract for the ________ with supplied drawings.

a. processing gear boxes　　b. processing of gear box

c. process of gear box d. processing of gear boxes

(6) ________ compensation trade, we mean to pay for your machines with articles produced.

a. With b. For c. By d. In

(7) We have noticed the British producers ________ a joint venture agreement with Chinese companies.

a. interest in b. are interested in c. are interested d. interest

(8) In compensation trade, we will pay for the cost of technological imports by delivery of end products ________ in processing or assembly deals, and charge a fee for processing raw materials or assembly of parts.

a. while b. when c. whether d. if

(9) I am sorry ________ I don' t know anything about the joint venture agreement.

a. since b. for c. that d. because

(10) We should be obliged if you could furnish us ________ a detailed report ________ the financial position, business lines and other aspects of the joint venture.

a. with/on b. with/for c. on/for d. for/on

(11) If you find a barter business acceptable, don' t ________ to call.

a. submit b. notify c. regret d. hesitate

(12) In mass media, big advertising dollar rules. But by doing business on the Net, a small firm might just as effectively ________ through search engines.

a. get himself know b. get itself know

c. get itself known d. get known himself

(13) The joint venture should apply for the extension of the term ________.

a. six months expiration before b. before expiration six months

c. before six months expiration d. six months before expiration

(14) The two firms agreed to ________ a joint venture in China.

a. enter into b. intend c. engage d. embark on

3. Complete the following sentences with the following words or its corresponding forms.

negotiate, exchange, business, limit

(1) ________ prospects are likely to turn better.

(2) Now there are two kinds of e-mails ________ between our exporter corporations and their customers.

(3) The seller has set a time ________ for acceptance of his offer on July 5.

(4) The bank has ________ its credit, that is to say, it allows its customers only a certain amount of credit.

(5) We surrendered a clean on board bill of lading for the ________ of payment.

(6) They have concluded substantial ________ with that company.

(7) We are willing to ________ with you over your proposal to act as our agent.

(8) Without some kind of money, we could have only the most limited ________.

4. Translate the following letter into English.

先生，

贵方7月5日来信收悉，谢谢。关于向我方提供X光机装配线、技术资料、检验仪器和全部零件，由我方组装成成品的建议，我方甚感兴趣。

关于设备和技术的价款，我方愿意用装配费来支付。

希望能得到贵方的详细意见。相信我方定会密切合作。

敬上

5. Write a letter as per the following particulars.

(1) 告知已收到对方寄来的带有图片说明的小册子，并仔细研究了对方所要出售的机器的性能。

(2) 按照小册子说明，整套机器是3年前在瑞士制造的，设有自控系统和自动润滑装置；生产各种橡胶制品的功能给人以吸引力。

(3) 告知我方已同技术人员讨论过是否要进口的问题，得出的结论是：因急需资金重建厂房，无力购买任何新的东西，只得留待以后考虑。

(4) 表示感谢对方的联系，希望不久的将来开展业务交流。

Supplementary Reading

Part A

Processing and assembling are the two methods commonly used to promote foreign trade with the help of the use of foreign funds. By processing trade it means that the foreign merchant provides raw material or materials for the domestic enterprise to process them in a specified way and the finished products of the same quality, standard and specifications as required are thus made for the foreign merchant to sell them on his own account. Under assembling the trader supplies the domestic dealer with components or parts or elements that are to be assembled by the latter as per the requirements of the former.

With the development of the foreign trade, compensation trade is widely adopted in international business activities. It is a form using the resultant products or some other contracted commodities to pay for the equipment or technical know-how imported. It is a roundabout way to solve the problem of how a local company or manufacture can acquire foreign exchange necessary to finance essential imports.

Lease trade is concluded between a lessor and a lessee on the basis of a lease contract granting the lessee the use of the equipment or commodity for a specified term in return for a rent to the lessor with an adequate guarantee of guarantor usually provided. This is a special mode of raising funds for an enterprise to acquire equipment and articles ranging from large scale machinery, complete sets of equipment, electronic computers, airplanes and steamships to small precision instruments, containers and so on.

Notes

1. processing 来料加工
2. assembling 来件装配

3. compensation trade 补偿贸易
4. know-how 技术秘诀
5. roundabout 迂回的
6. lease trade 租赁贸易

Part B

How salespeople invest their sales time is a critical factor influencing territory sales. Due to the increasing cost of direct selling, high transportation costs, and the limited resource of time, salespeople have to focus on these factors. Proper time and territory management is an effective method for the salesperson to maximize territorial sales and profits.

A sales territory comprises a group of customers or a geographical area assigned to a salesperson. It is a segment out of the company' s total market. A salesperson within a territory has to analyze the various segments, estimate sales potential, and develop a marketing mix based on the needs and desires of the marketplace.

Companies develop and use sales territories for a number of reasons. One important reason is to obtain thorough coverage of the market to fully reach sales potential. Another reason is to establish salespeople' s responsibilities as territory managers.

Performance can be monitored when territories are established. A territory may also be used to improve customer relations so that customers receive regular calls from the salesperson. This helps to reduce sales expenses by avoiding duplicated effort in traveling and customer contacts. Finally, territories allow better matching of salespeople to customer needs and ultimately benefit salespeople and the company.

There also are disadvantages to developing sales territories. Some salespeople may not be motivated if they feel restricted by a particular territory. Also, a company may be too small to segment its market or management may not want to take time to develop territories.

Time and territory management is continuous for a salesperson; it involves seven key elements. The first major element is establishing the territory sales quota. The second element is account analysis, which involves identifying current and potential customers and estimating their sales potential. In analyzing these accounts, salespeople may use the undifferentiated-selling approach if they view accounts as similar; or, if accounts have different characteristics, they use the account-segmentation approach.

Developing objectives and sales quotas for individual accounts is the third element. How salespeople allocate time in their territories is another key element. Salespeople have to manage time, plan schedules, and use spare time effectively.

The fifth element of time and territorial management is developing the sales-call objective, profile, benefit program, and selling strategies for individual customers. Salespeople have to learn everything they can about customers and maintain records on each one. Once this is done, they can create the proper selling strategies to meet customers' needs.

Another major element is scheduling sales calls at specific times and places and routing the salesperson' s movement and travel pattern around the territory. Finally, established objectives and quotas are used to determine how effectively the salesperson performs. Actual performance is compared to these standards for evaluation purposes.

Part C

The telephone can be a great time-waster or time-saver, depending on how it is used. The increasing cost of a personal sales call, and the increasing amount of time spent traveling to make personal calls are reasons for the efficient territory manager to look to the telephone as a territory coverage tool.

With field sales costs still rising and no end in sight, more companies are developing telephone sales and marketing campaigns to supplement personal selling efforts. These campaigns utilize trained telephone communicators and well-developed telephone marketing techniques. Usually, they require a company wide effort.

Although each salesperson has to decide the types of calls and accounts that lend themselves to telephone applications, most people benefit from adopting the following practices as minimal territory coverage:

Satisfy part of the service needs of accounts by telephone.

Assign smaller accounts that contribute less than 5 percent of business to mostly telephone selling.

Do prospecting, marketing data gathering, and call scheduling by telephone.

Carefully schedule personal calls to distant accounts. If possible, replace some personal visits with telephone calls.

The telephone and the computer are important selling tools for salespeople. Many sales jobs require extensive travel. Out of the office, traveling salespeople can keep in contact with their offices, access computer files containing customer information, and record customer information.

Part D

Finding the Facts

Students aren't the only ones who need to sift through mountains of conflicting information on the Internet. Journalists use the Internet to gather data, collect background information, and verify facts. But how do professionals use the Internet wisely? The Des Moines Register offers four strategies:

(1) Use documents. Original documents, including public documents, e-mails, and videos tell you what really happened or was said, not what people say they said.

(2) Understand context. Expand your research to include how the information fits into the big picture. What you may see as important data may look different in the larger pattern.

(3) Use credible sources. Make sure the sources you use have good track records of accuracy and fair treatment of both sides of an issue.

(4) Present opinions as opinions. Forecasts of the future are almost always opinions.

Watch Your Language

The connotation of a phrase in a survey can unintentionally skew the way people react to a question. A survey used to learn about the leadership skills of managers asked employees whether their manager "takes bold strides" and "has a strong grasp" of complicated issues. Male managers tended to outscore female managers. In a literal sense, males on average take longer strides and have more muscle strength than females. The company changed the wording of a survey. "Has a strong grasp of complex problems" became "discusses complex problems with precision and clarity." After this change, the difference in ratings of female and male managers disappeared. Employees apparently stopped mixing images of size and strength into their ratings of intellectual insight.

Another word-related bias is that respondents tend to agree more than disagree with statements. If a survey about managers asks employees whether their manager is fair, ethical, intelligent, knowledgeable, and so on, they are likely to assign all of these qualities to the manager and to agree more and more as the survey goes along. To correct for this, some questions should be worded to generate the opposite response. For example, a statement about ethics can be balanced by a statement about corruption, and a statement about fairness can be balanced by a statement about bias or stereotypes.

Unit 16

Memo, Fax and E-mail

备忘录、传真与电子邮件

16.1 Introduction（简介）

在现代商务交往中，备忘录、传真和电子邮件已经成为除了商业信函外最主要的交流载体。备忘录是一种非正式的商务文件、便条，可用来解释政策、程序和指示，发布通知、提出信息和行动要求，以及答复要求。此外，备忘录可帮助人们提醒事物，并可对决定、电话交谈、会议提供书面记录。

传真又称传真电报，它是利用光电效应，通过安装在普通电话网络上的传真机，即刻对外发送或是接收外来的文件、书信、资料、图表、照片真迹的一种现代化的通信联络方式。利用传真通信的主要优点是操作简便、传送速度迅速、可将包括一切复杂图案在内的真迹传送出去，但缺点是自动发送性能差、需要专人操作、有时清晰度难以确保。

自20世纪90年代以来，电子邮件已发展成诸种电子通信手段中的“黑马”，成为当今商务名片上必不可少的一个部分。电子邮件又称电子信函，是利用电子计算机所组成的互联网络向交往对象所发出的一种电子信件。使用电子邮件进行对外联络，不但安全保密，节省时间，不受篇幅的限制，清晰度极高，而且还可以大大地降低通信费用。

本单元将介绍备忘录、传真和电子邮件在商务交往中的应用。

16.2 Memo（备忘录）

备忘录在本质上也是书信。事实上，memo 一词来自于拉丁语 memorandum，意指“必须记住的东西”。备忘录的特点是简明扼要，但同时也要做到适应受众，表达清楚且准确。

备忘录的格式一般较为固定，通常分为标题和正文两部分。标题包括 To（送交目标，即接受人）、From（写备忘录者）、Subject（主题句）和 Date（日期）。该四项顺序通常如上所示，但日期一项可置于最前面，也可置于 Subject 之前。

一些大公司或机构的备忘录纸笺上端通常印有公司或机构的名称、Memorandum 或 Memo 字样以及开头部分（包括 To，From，Date 和 Subject），但小单位可能不会有按以上格式打印出来的备忘录纸笺。

在打印或书写时，备忘录通常有两种格式：一种是每一行均顶左边齐；另一种是每段的第一行往后缩一定距离。备忘录正文之后通常没有签名。

1. 标题（Heading）

标题是写在备忘录开头的压缩信息。不同于书信，备忘录只有标题和正文，而没有收件人地址、称谓、结尾问候语或正式的签名。情况不同，标题格式可能不同，但是通常应采用下面这种格式：

Date：日期。日期的写法同书信里日期写法的要求完全一样，不要用数字来表示月份。如2009年12月24日应写成December 24, 2009。

To：收件人。这一标题后面应写收信人的姓名与职衔，姓名前可以用尊称或不用。

From：发件人。这一标题后应写发信人的姓名与职衔。职衔可根据需要决定写或不写，但姓名前不要用尊称。

Subject：主题句。好的主题句应符合以下三条标准：一是具体明确，即主题句应具体到足以区分该主题，同时也要足以涵盖所涉及的各个方面内容；二是简洁明了，即主题句应相对短些，以便吸引受众；三是主题句应与备忘录的组织模式相适应，即符合沟通情境方面的心理要求，同时也要适合撰写者的意图，力求使受众能迅速做出撰写者所期望的回复。

2. 正文（Body）

备忘录的正文部分和书信一样，只是省略其中的礼貌结尾，而且也不一定要齐头。此外，备忘录一般不需要结束语和签名。

备忘录正文使用的语气和词汇，取决于撰写人与收件人的关系。例如，若是与相同领域的人员沟通，便可以使用专有名词或术语。

3. 样函（Samples）

备忘录样函如图16-1、图16-2、图16-3所示。

MEMO

To: Annette T. Califero

From: Kyle B. Abrams

Date: March 18, 2009

Re: Spring Sales Promotion

Spring has sprung and we are celebrating the end of winter by putting on a special promotion for our customers on [list products to be included here].

Customers ordering [name of product] will be eligible for the following:

[Set out details of special pricing or discounts here.]

The promotion will start on [date] and end on [date].

To support you in your efforts, we will be [list any special advertising campaigns that will be launched in conjunction with the promotion].

As an incentive to our valued sales staff, we will reward our top performers during the promotion with [list details of incentives, prizes, or bonuses the company will be offering in conjunction with the promotion].

We will also enter all [name of department] employees' names in a draw for [type details of prize here].

Be sure to check out [newsletter, bulletin board, or e-mails] to see sales results as the promotion goes on.

I know all of you will give this promotion your very best effort. Let's all work together to make this our best promotion yet!

图16-1 备忘录样函一

MEMO

To: Dorothy N. Blasingham
From: Roger L. Trout
Date: February 18, 2010
Subject: Name Change for AARP Division of Ovations

Effective immediately, the AARP Divisions of Ovations are adopting new internal names. The three divisions will be known collectively as Ovations Partner Solutions, and each division name is changing as follows.

The AARP Insurance Division will be called Insurance Solutions.

AARP Pharmacy Services will change its name to Pharmacy Solutions.

Our catalog business will become Consumer Health Products.

We' re making this change because, at times, the placement of AARP in our division names has caused confusion for external audiences. This change will clarify to regulators, policymakers and other businesses that we are part of Ovations and, while we serve AARP members, we do not work directly for ASI or AARP.

The name change also strengthens our ties to Ovations and helps support the Ovations brand. As Ovations embarks on enterprise-wide initiatives to accelerate growth, we will continue to be a critical part and vital source for that success.

To ensure continuity and avoid any concern, we will still use our AARP marketing names with AARP member and customers, including AARP Pharmacy Services and AARP Health Care Options.

Please begin using the new names immediately for internal and corporate communication. More details will follow as we develop a new layout for business cards and letterhead using the Ovations logo. If you have any questions, please feel free to contact [name] at [phone] or [e-mail].

图 16-2 备忘录样函二

MEMO

Date: May 22, 2008
To: Records Section
From: P. Steelpes, Career Planning
Subject: Request for Paid Education Leave

In response to your request for one year of paid education leave to take a degree in English literature, I have to inform you that we cannot authorize this leave.

While we appreciate your desire to improve your knowledge, we feel that English literature is not directly related to your present position and to the goals of this organization.

I am aware of your great interest in literature, and I would like to point out that you could gain advantage to apply for leave without pay.

If you need the information on the above, do not hesitate to keep touch with me at any time.

图 16-3 备忘录样函三

16.3 Fax（传真）

作为一种成熟的通信手段，传真在商务交往中将继续扮演重要的角色。传真的最大优势在于简便，即使是传送一份文字、图片和图表兼具的文件，也不需要任何其他的硬件或者软件，只需把传真原件置入传真机中，拨通对方号码，发送即可。

使用传真时，通常有以下几点需要注意：

（1）尽量在工作时间发送传真，并且在发送前尽可能提前通知对方。

（2）传真原件的字体要稍大一些，因为很多时候，接收方收到的传真文本的字体会被缩小。

（3）尽管传真的页数并不受到限制，但是如果页数过多，就会长时间占用对方的线路，这在惜时如金的商界是很糟糕的现象。

（4）传真的文本内容尽量不要分布在纸张边缘，因为在传输时，纸张边缘的信息很可能会模糊不清。

1. 标题（Heading）

传真的格式并不固定，许多公司都有自己专门的传真格式（图 16-4）。传真的顶端一般会有显眼的字样，例如“TELEFAX”“TELEFAX MESSAGE”或者“FAX MESSAGE”。公司的传真一般都含有本公司名称和标志，并在传真的显眼位置以大字体突出。传真的标题一般包含以下信息：

TO：接收方信息，可以是注明地址的公司名，也可以指定具体接收人。传真中所给出的公司地址一般不如商业信函中那么详细。

ATTN：指定接收人。如果在 TO 栏中只给出了公司名，那么可以在此注明指定接收人；如果 TO 栏中已明确了指定接收人，则不必加入此项。

FAX NO.：接收方的传真号码。

FROM：发送方信息，可以是公司名，也可以是具体的发送人。

DATE：传真的发送日期，也可以改用 TIME 来标出具体的发送时间和日期。

FAX NO.：发送方传真号码。

PAGE：传真的页码信息，包含总页数和当前页数。传真的每一页必须清楚标出传真的总页数和当前页数，以确保接收方接收传真的完整性。

FAX MESSAGE

TO: Shanxi Textile Imp. & Exp. Corp

ATTN: Mr. Wu Wanlong, Manager　　　　160a Oak Avenue, New York, USA

FAX NO.: 0086-29-××××××××　　　　Tel: ×××××××× Fax: ××××××××

FROM: Trendsetters Inc.

DATE: Sep. 23, 2003

FAX NO.: ××××××××　　　　Page 1 of 3

PAGE: 1/3

……

Fax body

……

图 16-4　传真格式

通过传真发送的可以是一段信息，如商品报价等，也可以是一份文件。如果所发送的信息内容简短，那么这些信息会出现在传真的首页上；如果发送的是一份文件，那么还要在文件前发送一份封面（Cover Sheet），在封面上注明标题信息及“FAX COVER SHEET”字样（图16-5）。

Trendsetters Inc.

160a Oak Avenue, New York, USA

Tel: 78928666 Fax: 78928668

FAX COVER SHEET

TO: Shanxi Textile Imp. & Exp. Corp

ATTN: Mr. Wu Wanlong, Manager

FAX NO.: 0086-29-334876

FROM: Trendsetters Inc.

DATE: Sep. 23, 2003

FAX NO.: 78928668

PAGE: 4 INCLUDING COVER SHEET

图16-5 传真的封面

2. 正文（Text）

和商业信函相比，传真正文内容显得非正式一些，总体而言，与常用商业信函没有太大的区别。传真正文前也要用称呼语，如“Dear Mr. …”等，结束时也有“Best Regards”等，也使用商业信函中经常出现的程式化语句，如“Many thanks for your ... of ...”等。

必须注意传真所提供的信息，如价格、装运期等细节，要避免发生差错。其实，传真信息的法律重要性并不亚于普通商业信函。

在传真结尾，通常有发送方负责人的签名。通过普通传真机发送传真时，签名必须采用完整形式，而不用缩写形式。通过调制解调器发送的传真则不包含签名。

传真原件可以是打印机输出稿，也可以采用手写稿。

3. 样函（Samples）

传真样函分别如图16-6、图16-7所示。

F. Lynch & Co. Ltd.

(Head Office)，Nesson House，Newell Street，Birmingham B3 3EL

Tel：02-××××××××× Fax：02-××××××××× Telex：××××××××

FAX MESSAGE

Page 1/1

Message for：D. Causio

From：L. Crane

Address：Satex S. P. A. ，Via di pietra，0016 Roma

Date：19 September 1998

Fax number：(06) 4815473

Dear Mr. Causio，

This is an urgent request for a consignment to replace the damaged delivery that we received，and of which you have already been informed.

Please airfreight the following items：

Cat. No：	Quantity：
RN30	50
Ag20	70
L26	100

The damaged consignment will be returned to you on receipt of the replacement.

Yours sincerely，

L. Crane

L. Crane

Chief Buyer

图 16-6 传真样函一

FAX MESSAGE

To: Joseph Zhang
Sales Director
Island Silks
18, York Road
Kowloon
Hong Kong
Tel: (852) 9334275
Fax: (852) 9334530

Mayflowers Inc.
868a New Texas Avenue, New York, USA zip
Tel: 78925871 Fax: 78925870
Page 1 of 1
July 17, 2000

First of all, I would like to thank you for your hospitality during my stay in Hong Kong, and I am pleased to confirm our order for 9,000 Collection Silk Scarves. The details, as agreed in our discussion last week, are as follows:

Unit Price	USD50, inclusive of insurance and shipping
Delivery Date	November 28, 2000
No. of different patterns	15 (your "Cool Bear" selection)
No. of colours	10 (beige, peach, yellow, cream, white, rose, burgundy, russet, stone and azure)
Terms of payment	30 days presentation (irrevocable L/C)
Discount	3%

We look forward to doing more business with you in the future.

Best regards.

John Fagurson

John Fagurson
Chief Buyer

图 16-7 传真样函二

16.4 E-mail（电子邮件）

在20世纪的最后几年里，整个世界见证了一场由计算机网络在通信领域的应用所引起的革命。电子邮件服务作为最方便快捷的通信手段而迅速崛起，在商务领域也起到越来越重要的作用。由于电子邮件作为通信媒体处于不断发展之中，因此它的格式和用法也在不断变化中。当不知道所联系的具体公司所使用的电子邮件格式时，以下建议可作为撰写电子邮件的基本指导。

1. 标题（Heading）

由于所使用的软件和邮件服务提供商的不同，电子邮件的标题格式也各不相同。不过，一般而言，电子邮件的标题部分常常包含以下内容（图16-8）：

To：收件人地址栏，在此输入收件人的电子邮件地址。输入多个地址时，各电子邮件地址间用逗号隔开。

Cc：副本收件人（Carbon copy）地址栏。如果有多个副本收件人地址，就要用逗号隔开。副本收件人可收到这封邮件的副本，并且还可以知道有哪些人收到了相同的副本。

Bcc：匿名副本收件人（Blind carbon copy）地址栏。这些收件人同样会收到邮件副本，但是他们无法知道还有谁收到了副本。

Subject：邮件的主题栏。主题栏应当简明扼要地给出这封邮件的主旨，以使收件人能够一目了然并根据其轻重缓急加以处理。

Priority：优先度，即本邮件的紧急程度。如果设为高优先度，那么会在收件人端有所反映，如在邮件主题行前以“！”表明；如果没有注明优先度，则系统默认为普通邮件。有的邮件服务并没有这项功能。

Attachments：附件栏。附件栏能显示出随邮件发送的附件的文件名、文件类型和文件大小，由计算机自动根据附件情况载入。

Date：日期栏。一般由服务器端根据发送时间自动载入。

在上述这些栏目中，“To”栏和“Subject”栏必不可少，而其余栏目则为可选项，或者可以由系统自动载入。

To:	Ricardo@ hotmail. com
Cc:	
Bcc:	
Subject:	Meeting to Discuss 2005 Schedules
Attachments:	

图 16-8 电子邮件的标题格式

2. 正文（Text）

电子邮件的正文部分通常分为开头敬语（Salutation）、邮件主体（Body）、结尾敬语（Complementary Close）及署名（Signature）四个部分。

（1）开头敬语。电子邮件的行文风格较为随意，没有商业信函正式。一般而言，当只有单一收件人时，常常使用“Dear Mr. / Mrs. / Ms. + 姓”或者直接称呼对方全名或名字的形式，有时甚至会采用“Hi”“Hi + 名字”等较为随意的方法。当邮件发送给多人时，开头敬语通常使用“Hello all / folks”，“Hello everybody”或者“greetings”等形式，较少使用“Sirs”之类的正式称呼。此外，要尽量避免使用过时的或者有明显性别取向的称呼，如“Dear Sirs”“Gentlemen”等。最后，在书写开头敬语时，还要注意到文化之间的差异性。例如，“Dear Mr. . . . ”是比较符合中国和日本礼仪的称呼法，而“Hi . . . ”则是典型的西方式开头敬语。

(2) 邮件主体。电子邮件的主体即邮件的主要内容，通常只涉及一个主题，写作时应尽量简明一些，不要超过两个屏幕的长度。邮件主体一般由开头(Opening)、内文（Main body）和结束语（Closing）三部分构成。开头部分应该重申邮件的主旨，以便收件人在一开始就了解到邮件的大致内容或者用意。这里应该开门见山地说明来函的目的，不要绕弯子。内文部分则为开头的主旨提供了更为细节性的内容。结束语部分可以对上文进行总结，在此提出要求、观点等。一般而言，电子邮件的结束语可以给出一些实质性的要求或者说法，以求给对方留下深刻印象，例如：

Please submit your order by June 16 so that sufficient labels will be in stock for your peak sale season.

We will deliver the goods ASAP.

(3) 结尾敬语。商业信函的结尾一般用“Yours sincerely”“Yours faithfully”等敬语，较为正式。电子邮件的结尾敬语则可以用“Best wishes (Best regards)”“With best regards, Regards”“With best wishes”“Best wishes”“Thanks”“Best”“Cheers”等词语，显得较为随便、亲切一些。

(4) 署名。电子邮件软件通常会在信的末尾自动加上署名。例如：Maggie Wang（Maggiewang@ hotmail. com)。

正式一些的商务电子邮件的署名还包括发信人的职位或头衔，以及公司的相关信息。例如：

Maggie Wang（Maggiewang@ hotmail. com)

Chief Executive Officer

Timber Woods Inc.

(959) 123-4567

3. 写作要领（Writing guidelines)

(1) 邮件主题要精炼。你的邮件只是对方邮箱中众多邮件中的一封，所以要避免使用冗长的、含糊的主题，要使对方一眼就能看明白你的邮件主旨以便正确处理你的邮件。如果邮件内容紧急，可以提高优先度，或者在主题前加上“URGENT!”字样；如果是回信，加上“RE:”字样。

(2) 邮件的主体要简明。要做到：内容简短，一般4~7行为佳；措辞要直接，避免客套话和废话；主题要突出；段落层次要分明。不过，不要把电子邮件写作成电报那样，否则，就太矫枉过正了。

(3) 慎用强调符号、大写字母等，因为这样会影响对方的阅读流畅程度，并且有咄咄逼人的意味。

(4) 注意邮件安全，不要在其中加入隐秘的内容。

(5) 附件文件不宜过大，否则会大幅增加传输时间，从而浪费对方时间。

(6) 电子邮件在格式上不要太离谱，因为收件人的系统可能不支持不同的字体和颜色。

4. 首字母缩写词（Acronyms)

为了使内容简短，电子邮件中经常使用一些首字母缩写词来代表特定的含义，一些常见的缩写词见表16-1。

表 16-1 常见缩写词

首字母缩写词	含 义	首字母缩写词	含 义
GTG	got to go	TTYL	talk to you later
UR	you are	WRT	with respect to
VR	we are	MGR	manager
B/cuz	because	IOW	in other words
HV	have	INFO	information
HVB	have been	IMM，IMMD	immediate
PLS	please	TKS，THKS	thanks
TDY	today	BTW	by the way
OIC	oh，I see	SPEC	specifications
A/O	at once	ASAP	as soon as possible
MKT	market	TIA	thanks in advance
BIZ	business	FYR	for your reference
F2F	face to face	VG	very good
NBD	no big deal	FAQ	frequently asked questions

5. 样函（Samples）

电子邮件样函如图 16-9、图 16-10、图 16-11 所示。

To：lsimeon@hotmail.com

Subject：Recommendation

Cc：rochina@hotmail.com

Bcc：peace@usa.net

Dear Mr. Leung，

I have been a salesman for our company for quite a few years and have been to many countries in Europe，America and Asia. Our blankets have been selling very well in those areas.

This is the first time I have been to Africa as a salesman. During my dealings here I find that our blankets are welcome for their acceptable prices，fine workmanship and first class materials. However the turnover of our sales over the past few months was far from satisfactory. After my investigations I find out the reason. Many African customers don't like our dragon and moon pattern because snakes（very much like the dragon）are the taboo of some African nations，while the moon is worshiped as goddess by others. Australian blankets，much inferior to ours，have sold better here simply because of their patterns.

Therefore，I propose here that our company soon design some other patterns for sales in Africa while our old patterns can still be used for sales elsewhere.

The new patterns that might be welcomed here are：

1. Deer hunting
2. Corn fields
3. Pyramids
4. Camels and the desert

With all good wishes.

Yours sincerely，

G. Jones

Salesman of our company in Africa

图 16-9 电子邮件样函一

From: BethJ39903@ aat. co. jp < BethJ39903@ aat. co. jp >

To: Jackson < Jackson @ usa. net >

Date: Thursday, January 28, 1999 4: 53 PM

Subject: Invoice received, goods missing

Dear Jackson,

Thank you for your original invoice for 15 Bella Handbags under our order No. 123. But we haven' t yet received the goods. Would you please let us know whether it has been shipped or not?

Best regards,

Beth. J

图 16-10 电子邮件样函二

From: ipupdate@ ivey. uwo. ca

To: happystone@ hotmail. com

Cc: all. custser@ acme. com

Subject: December Issue AsiaLink-Ivey Business School

Date:

Greetings from London, Canada!

I am pleased to send you the latest issue of AsiaLink, the quarterly newsletter of the Asian Management Institute at the Richard Ivey School of Business. We welcome your comments and feedback.

http: //www. ivey. uwo. ca/ami/asialink

Progress on Ivey' s Asia-Pacific case development is updated on a regular basis. Feel free to download the latest issue of the Asia-Pacific Case Directory at:

http: //www. ivey. uwo. ca/ami/AP _ cases

Ivey is producing a significant and increasing amount of important Asia-related research. See the abstracts of articles dealing with Japanese Foreign Direct Investment and Joint Ventures & Alliances at:

http: //www. ivey. uwo. ca/ami/Research

Do you know people who might be interested in receiving AsiaLink on-line edition or print version? Subscription is free, so please forward this e-mail message to them.

Regards,

×××

图 16-11 电子邮件样函三

Supplementary Reading

Part A

Nowadays fax is one of the most popular methods of communication for many businesses. Since 1979 when the international fax transmission standards appeared, the fax has been receiving growing popularity in business community because of its fast speed, convenience and accuracy. Fax message comprises two parts: fax headings and fax body. Under the fax body, it ends with the signature of the sender. In constructing the body of a fax message, you may follow the layout of a formal business letter, but the salutation and complimentary close are normally omitted.

With the rapid development of the Internet, e-mail is increasingly used in business transactions. Compared with the traditional business letter, e-mail is much more efficient and economical. An e-mail message sent from one of them can reach another in seconds, while a business letter may take days of even longer. In addition, it saves money for papers and postage. In practice, e-mail is bringing about efficiency revolution in business.

Notes

1. layout 版式
2. salutation 称呼
3. complimentary close 信尾客套语

Part B

A salesperson who is promoted to sales manager becomes involved in sales planning, staffing, training, directing, and evaluating sales force activities. This article discussed the need to understand how to make sales forecasts and budgets, how to determine the number of salespeople to hire, how to recruit and train salespeople, and the legal aspects of staffing. The sales manager uses this knowledge to achieve the sales volume, profits, and growth of higher levels of management desire.

Today, firms structure their organizations to best serve their customers. Small companies use a simple line organizational design, whereas large firms design specialized structures based on geography, the products they market, customers, or a combination of these elements.

Sales managers are frequently involved in forecasting their firm' s sales. They are also involved in developing budgets and allocating money to various sales units, all of which ultimately serve as input into planning and aid in coordinating and controlling sales unit activities.

The contemporary sales manager is knowledgeable in personnel practices involving the recruiting and hiring of salespeople. Government laws need to be considered so that the firm can abide by EEOC guidelines. The staff function involves both personnel planning—the determination of the kind and number of needed salespeople—and employment planning—the locating, recruiting, evaluation, and hiring of applicants for the sales job.

Once the hiring is done, the sales manager becomes involved in training salespeople on things such as product knowledge and selling skills. Training begins immediately, usually in the salesperson' s territory and at company training facilities.

The sales manager is a salesperson first, but also something of a Jack-of-all-trades due to the various functions required for the job.

Part C

One of the biggest problems facing most new managers is their lack of preparation for the job.

There are several reasons why this happens. For example, a salesperson often is selected for promotion to a management position because of outstanding performance in their present job. The skills and abilities that help a person develop into a salesperson, however, are quite different from the skills needed by a manager. As a result, the new manager must acquire new attitudes, behaviors, and skills to succeed at managing others.

Adding to new managers' difficulties is the fact that companies generally expect them to step into the job and function effectively and immediately. This expectation exists even though many organizations offer them little help or support. Even formal training programs that teach essential new skills are not always offered until several months after a person is promoted into management. The sink-or-swim philosophy is still prevalent.

Finally, the new manager often lacks an immediate peer group. Former peers no longer regard the manager as one of them. Other managers may be hesitant to consider this person a member of their group until he or she has demonstrated the ability to think and act like management. This leaves the new manager belonging to neither group at a time when support from others is badly needed.

Given these and other problems, many new managers often feel inexperienced, uncertain, and overwhelmed by their new responsibilities. For example, Quaker Oats' Linda Slaby-Baker said, "The first week I started my new position [as district manager] I had to create a complete new district, train four new employees, and set up my district office."

Part D

Visuals That Translate Well

When preparing visuals, keep in mind cultural differences:

(1) Make sure any symbols in the visual will have the correct meaning in the culture of your audience. For example, a red cross symbolizes first aid in North America, but in Muslim countries the symbol with that meaning is typically a green crescent.

(2) If you use punctuation marks as symbols, be sure they are meaningful to your audience. A question mark in English and certain other languages might signal a help function or answers to questions. But in languages without this symbol, it has no meaning.

(3) In showing humans, respect the cultural norms of your audience. Europeans tend to accept images of nudity, but some cultures can be offended by images of even a bare leg or other body part.

(4) Organize the information according to the reading customs of the audience. North American and European audiences will tend to read visual information as they do text: from left to right. Asians view from right to left, and Middle Easterners in a rotation moving counterclockwise.

(5) Learn your audience's conventions for writing numbers. In the United States, a period indicates the decimal point, and commas separate groups of three digits. In much of Europe, a comma represents the decimal point, and a space goes between each group of three digits. For U. S. and French readers, 3, 333 would have different values.

Audience Feedback

Just as when you' re speaking with someone face-to-face, when you' re presenting in front of a group it' s important to look for feedback from your audience. Pay attention to body language, and ask your audience questions: the feedback that you get will help you build rapport with your audience so that you can express your message more clearly.

In some settings, such as when you' re presenting to a large group, you might use other tools to gather audience feedback. For example, you can build a group discussion into your presentation: give your audience some questions to discuss in small groups, then invite them to share their answers with the room. Give questionnaires to your audience, either before your presentation or during a break. Have a member of your team tabulate audience responses, then build them into the remainder of your talk.

Audience response devices give you another option for getting instant audience feedback. These devices—popular with training departments—allow your audience to respond quickly to multiply-choice or yes/no questions during presentations. Software tabulates the responses as numbers, charts, or graphs for all to see. These devices are particularly good for feedback in situations where people may want anonymity.

Avoiding Disastrous PowerPoint

Conference keynote presentations are notoriously boring, with long PowerPoint shows and droning presenters. Participants, bored, fiddle with smartphones and participate in electronic discussions. During one keynote presentation, bored audience members even designed a T-shirt and put it up for sale online. The shirt' s message? "I survived the keynote disaster of 2009."

How can you keep your presentations from ending up with their own T-shirts? Here are a few tips:

(1) Use visuals and words together. Your PowerPoint slides should augment and enhance your presentation, not distract from or displace it.

(2) Keep your slides simple. An audience should be able to completely understand each slide in two or three seconds.

(3) Break complex ideas into multiple slides. Don' t try to get all the information on a single slide. Use several slides that add up to something more complex.

(4) Use your slides as a mnemonic device. Your slides should make your presentation emotionally appealing and memorable to your audience.

Unit 17 Contracts 合 同

17.1 Introduction（简介）

词典上对合同的解释是："合同意味着人们之间、团体之间以及国家之间的约束性的一致表示；或对在固定的价格上提供货物、劳务的意思表示一致。"因此，合同可以理解为意思表示一致，这是合同的精髓。

当事人可以通过一方发出邀约，另一方接受的形式达成合同。如果另一方拒绝接受，就有必要做进一步的讨论，即商务谈判磋商的过程，这在实际工作中经常遇到。无论在进出口贸易中采取什么方式方法，双方最终都要按照国际贸易的要求达成或签订合同。

作为商务活动中双方当事人具有约束力的法律文体，合同的条款应内容完整、措辞严谨。当然，最重要的是一切都必须严格符合法律规定。

17.2 Structure of a Contract（合同的结构）

合同的结构一般包括三个部分：约首、约文和约尾。

约首（Head of the Contract）一般包括合同名称、合同号码以及双方当事人的名称、地址、电传或传真号码等。

约文（Body of the Contract）一般包括定义条款以及对各项交易条件的具体规定，包括品名条款、品质条款、数量条款、包装条款、价格条款、装运条款、保险条款、支付条款、商检条款、索赔条款、不可抗力条款、仲裁条款等。

约尾（End of the Contract）须指明合同的正本份数、使用的文字效力、合同的准据法等，并由双方当事人落款签字、盖印等。

17.3 Basic Clauses of Contracts（合同的基本条款）

合同一般应具备以下条款：

（1）合同当事人的名称或者姓名、国籍、主营业所或者住所（The corporate or personal names of the contract parties and their nationalities, principal place of business or residence addresses）。

（2）合同订立的日期、地点（Date and place of signature of the contract）。

（3）合同的类型和合同标的的种类、范围（Type of the contract and the kind, scope of the subject matter of the contract）。

（4）合同标的的技术条件、质量、标准、规格、数量（Technical conditions, quality, standard, specifications and quantities of the subject matter of the contract）。

（5）履行的期限、地点和方式（Time limit, place and method of performance）。

（6）价格条件、支付金额、支付方式和各种附带的费用（Terms of price, amount and way of payment, and various additional charges）。

（7）合同能否转让，或者合同转让的条件（Whether the contract could be assigned or conditions for assignment）。

（8）违反合同的赔偿和其他责任（Compensation and other liabilities for breach of the contract）。

（9）合同发生争议时的解决办法（Ways for settlement of disputes in case of disputes arising from the contract）。

（10）合同使用的文字及其效力（Languages to be used in the contract and their effectiveness）。

17.4 Specimen（合同样例）

Contract 1:

Sales Contract

No. SXR060702 Date: July 12, 2012 Place: Hangzhou

Sellers: Zhejiang ABC Trading Co., Ltd.

Add: No. 98 Wensan Road, Hangzhou, Zhejiang, China

Tel: ______ Fax: ______ E-mail: ______

Buyers: ENGROSS INC

Add: 146-36 68th Ave., Suite 398 Flushing, NY 11368

Tel: ______ Fax: ______ E-mail: ______

Whereas: the Sellers and the Buyers, each with full corporate authority, makes a commitment to sell and buy the commodity respectively on CIF terms, hereby certifies, represents and warrants, that each can fulfill the requirement of this contract and respectively provide the commodity and the funds referred to herein, in time and under the terms and conditions agreed to as follows:

(1) Commodity and pattern charge:

Item	Drawing No.	Qty	Unit price	Pattern charge
1	70146492	1	USD800.00 CIF Cleveland	USD2,500.00
2	51717612	1	USD1,200.00 CIF Cleveland	
TOTAL VALUE			USD4,500.00	

(2) Specifications: As per the drawings No. 70146492 & No. 51717612.

(3) Quality: As per the requirement of ASTM A 487/A and the drawing No. 70146492 & 51717612.

(4) Materials: ASTM A 487 Grade 4 Class B.

(5) Delivery Terms: 90 days after receiving the prepayment.

(6) Shipment: By sea during August, 2012.

(7) Ports of Shipment and Destination: FromHangzhou to Iowa.

(8) Inspection before shipment:

Chemical Analysis

Metal properties (Tensile, Yield, Elongation, Reduction, Hardness)

Dimension Test

Ultrasonic, X-Ray

(9) Payment Terms: T/T in advance

(10) Insurance: To be covered by the Sellers for 110% of invoice value against All Risks and War Risks as per the relevant Ocean Marine Cargo Clauses of the People's Insurance Company of China. If other coverage or an additional insurance amount is required, the Buyers must have the consent of the Sellers before shipment, and the additional premium is to be borne by the Buyers.

(11) Force Majeure: Neither party to this contract shall be held responsible for the breach of Contract caused by civil war, military operation or local emergency. The parties hereby accept the international provision of "Force Majeure" as published by ICC, Geneva, Switzerland.

(12) Discrepancy and Claim: Any claim by the Buyers on the goods shipped shall be filed within 30 days after arrival of the goods at port of destination and supported by a survey report issued by a surveyor approved by the Sellers. Claims in respect of matters within the responsibility of the insurance company or of the shipping company will not be considered or entertained by the Sellers.

(13) Arbitration: All disputes arising in connection with this contract or the execution thereof shall be settled by negotiation between two parties. If no settlement can be reached, the case in dispute shall then be submitted for arbitration in the country of defendant in accordance with the arbitration regulations of the defendant country. The decision made by the arbitration organization shall be taken as final and binding upon both parties. The arbitration expenses shall be born by the losing party unless otherwise awarded by the arbitration organization.

(14) Governing Law: This contract shall be governed by the United Nations Convention on Contracts for the International Sale of Goods.

(15) Others:

Sellers: Singed　　　Buyers: Signed

Contract 2:

Sales Confirmation

No. ________ Date: ________

To Messrs:

The undersigned Sellers and Buyers have agreed to close the following transactions on the terms and conditions stated below:

(1) Name of Commodity and Specifications: ________.

(2) Quantity: ________.

With ______% more or less.

(3) Unit Price: ________.

(4) Total Amount: ________.

(5) Packing and Shipping Marks: ________.

(6) Time of Shipment: Within ________ months after receipt of L/C allowing transshipment and partial shipments.

(7) Port of Shipment: ________.

(8) Port of Destination: ________.

(9) Terms of Payment: By confirmed, irrevocable, divisible, without recourse L/C of the full amount of ________, in favor of the Sellers, available against the Sellers' sight draft and valid for negotiation at the loading port until the 15th day after the aforesaid Time of Shipment.

The Buyers shall establish the covering Letter of Credit before ________, otherwise the Sellers may rescind the Sales Confirmation without further notice, and/or lodge claims for the losses thus sustained.

(10) Inspection: It is mutually agreed that the certificate of quality/quantity/weight issued by ________ at the port of ________ shall be regarded as final and binding upon both parties.

(11) Claims: Claims for quality discrepancy, if any, must be submitted within 2 months after the arrival of the goods at the port of destination, while claims for quantity discrepancy, if any, must be submitted within 15 days after the arrival of the goods at the port of destination. The Sellers shall not be liable for any discrepancy of the goods shipped due to causes for which the insurance company, shipping company, other transportation organizations and/or post offices shall be held responsible.

(12) Insurance: To be effected by ________, for 110% of invoice value against W. A., All Risks and War Risks.

If additional insurance value or coverage is required, the Buyers shall have the consent of the Sellers before shipment and the additional premium is to be borne by the Buyers.

(13) Settlement of Disputes: All disputes Arising from the execution of or in connection with this Confirmation shall be settled amicably through friendly negotiation. In case no settlement can be reached through negotiation, the case shall then be submitted to China International Economic and Trade Arbitration Commission of the China Council for the Promotion of International Trade, Beijing for arbitration in accordance with its Rules of Arbitration. The arbitrary award is final and binding upon both parties.

(14) Force Majeure: In case of Force Majeure, the Sellers shall not be held responsible for late delivery or non-delivery of the goods but shall notify the Buyers by cable, immediately of the Force Majeure accident and within ________ days thereafter the Sellers shall deliver to the Buyers by registered mail a certificate issued by the China Council for the Promotion of International Trade or other competent authorities.

(15) Applicable Law: This Sales Confirmation shall be governed by the laws of the People' s Republic of China as to its interpretation and performance.

(16) Address:

The Selles' Address: The Byers' Address:

The Sellers: (Signature) The Buyers: (Signature)

17.5 Useful Sentences（实用语句）

(1) 常用的合同名称。

Sales Confirmation/ Agreement/ Contract 售货确认书/协议/合同

PurchaseContract/ Agreement/ Confirmation 购货合同/协议/确认书

Import Contract 进口合同

Export Contract 出口合同

Agency Agreement/ Contract 代理协议/合同

Contract for Processing 加工合同

Lease Agreement/ Contract 租赁协议/合同

Agreement/ Contract of Consignment 寄售企业协议/合同

Joint-venture Agreement/ Contract 合资企业协议/合同

Compensation Trade Contract 补偿贸易合同

Contract for Civil Works 工程承包合同

(2) This contract is made by 15th of April, 2012 and between ABC Corporation, a Japanese corporation having its principal office at __________ Tokyo, Japan, who agrees to sell, and XYZ Corporation, a New York corporation having its principal office at __________ New York, N. Y. USA, who agrees to buy the following goods on the terms and conditions as below:（本合同于2012年4月15日由日本ABC公司，主营业所在日本东京__________，与XYZ公司，主营业所在美国纽约州市__________，所签订；按照下列条款，ABC公司同意出售，XYZ公司愿

意购买下述产品。)

(3) The goods must be shipped strictly within the period stipulated herein. In the event delay in shipment, the Buyers may cancel the contract and claim damages for breach of the contract; provided that shipment be delayed in whole or in part by reason of Force Majeure, the Buyers may extend the time of shipment to the extent of delay not exceeding one month. If shipment is delayed over one month, the Buyers shall have the option to cancel the contract at any time. In such case of cancellation, the Sellers shall refund all money paid in advance by the Buyers with respect to any undelivered goods. (必须按照合同规定的期限交货。若迟交，买方有权撤销合同，并向卖方提出由此造成损失的赔偿。如果是由于不可抗力导致的全部或部分货物迟交，买方同意延长交货期，但延长的期限不超过一个月，否则买方有权随时撤销合同。合同撤销后，卖方须退还买方预付的未交付货物的全部货款。)

(4) Inspection of quality, quantity, weight and packing of the contracted goods shall be performed at the time of loading at ____________ berth by an independent inspector appointed by the Buyers and acceptable to the Sellers. The inspector's certificate of quality, quantity, packing and weight shall be final, and inspection fee and charges shall be for the Sellers' account. (货物的质量、数量、重量和包装由买方指定、卖方同意的公证行在____________港装船对其进行检验，其质量、数量、重量和包装检验证书为最终依据，检验费由卖方负担。)

(5) The full particulars of such claim shall be made in writing and forwarded by registered airmail to the Sellers within 15 days after cabling. Buyers must submit such particulars as sworn public survey's report when quality or quantity of the merchandise is in dispute. (索赔须以书面形式提出，其详情文件须于发出电报后 15 天内航空邮寄给卖方。若纠纷系有关品质和数量，必须提交公证检验报告。)

(6) Quality to be strictly as per sample submitted by the Sellers on June 6, 2012. The Sellers shall guarantee all the shipments to conform to samples submitted with regard to quality. (质量完全以卖方 2012 年 6 月 6 日提供的样品为准。卖方必须保证交货质量与样品一致。)

(7) Shipment within the time stipulated shall be subject to shipping space being available. In case of FOB contract, the Buyers are bound to give shipping instruction in time and provide necessary shipping space; otherwise, the Sellers can dispose the goods for the Buyers' account and risk. (若订到舱位，则按期交货。若为 FOB 合同，则买方须及时发给卖方装船通知和租订舱位，否则，卖方可代买方处理货物，其风险由买方负担。)

(8) US $25 per dozen CIF New York, including your commission 3%. The commission shall be payable only after the Sellers have received the full amount of all payment due to the Sellers. The prices herein stated are based on current freight rates and any increase or decrease in freight rates at time of shipment is to be the benefit of the Buyers, with Sellers assuming the payment of all transportation charges to the point or place of delivery. (CIF 纽约到岸价每打 25 美元，包括你 3% 的佣金。卖方在收到全部货款之后支付佣金。合同价格按现行运费计算，装运时运费的增减均归买方。卖方承担至交货地的所有运费。)

(9) The trade terms shall be governed and construed under and by the latest INCOTERMS 2010. (贸易条款以最新的《2010 年国际贸易术语解释通则》的规定和解释为准。)

(10) The present contract is drawn in duplicate in the Chinese and English languages, both texts being equally authentic. In case of any divergence of interpretation, the Chinese text shall prevail. (本合同以中文和英文书就，两种文本均为正本。但在对其解释产生异议时，以中文本为准。)

Supplementary Reading

Part A

Long known as "the fastest way to send money", U. S. -based Western Union controls nearly 80% of the money-transfer market and is widely acknowledged as the world leader in wire transfers—electronic transfers of funds from one financial institution to another. In this case, it's a transfer from one Western Union office to another. Now, however, Western Union is facing stiff competition from banks threatening to encroach on its market share of the electronic money-transfer business.

Western Union was started in 1851 when a group of businessmen in Rochester, New York, formed the New York and Mississippi Valley Printing Telegraph Company. The name was changed to Western Union in 1861 when the first transcontinental telegraph line was completed. Western Union introduced its money transfer service in 1871; in 1989 it began offering it outside North America. Today, more than half a million Western Union agent locations are found in over 200 countries and territories around the world. Money transfers make up 85% of Western Union's revenues, with the company transferring about $80 billion annually.

Customers have many different options when sending money through Western Union office: in person, at an agent location, over the phone, or on line; via cash, debit cards, or credit cards. And they can use the service at a variety of locations: an actual Western Union office, a grocery store, a post office—just about anywhere people go to transact business. To send money to, say, India or Mexico using a Western Union agent location, the customer fills out a "Send Money" form and gets a receipt, which includes a Money Transfer Control Number to give to the person receiving the funds. To retrieve the funds, the receiver then fills out a "Receive Money" form and presents the Money Transfer Control number along with validation identification at a Western Union agent location.

Notes

1. Western Union 西联汇款
2. institution 机构
3. Money Transfer Control Number 汇款跟踪号

Part B

When in Rome, Do What the Romans Do

Imagine an American salesperson, Harry Slick, starting out on his overseas business trip. The following events occur on his trip:

(1) In England, he phones a long-term customer and asks for an early breakfast business meeting so that he can fly to Paris at noon.

(2) In Paris, he invites a business prospect to have dinner at La Tour d'Argent and greets him with, "Just call me Harry, Jacques."

(3) In Germany, he arrives 10 minutes late for an important meeting.

(4) In Japan, he accepts the business cards of his hosts and, without looking at them, puts them in his pocket.

How many orders is Harry Slick likely to get? Probably none, although his company will face a pile of bills.

International business success requires each businessperson to understand and adapt to the local business culture and norms. Here are some rules of social and business etiquette that managers should understand when doing business in other countries.

France	Dress conservatively, except in the south where more casual clothes are worn. Do not refer to people by their first names—the French are formal with strangers.
Germany	Be especially punctual. An American businessperson invited to someone's home should present flowers, preferably unwrapped, to the hostess. During introductions, greet women first and wait until they extend their hands before extending yours.
Italy	Whether you dress conservatively or go native in a Giorgio Armani suit, keep in mind that Italian businesspeople are style conscious. Make appointments well in advance. Prepare for and be patient with Italian bureaucracies.
United Kingdom	Toasts are often given at formal dinners. If the host honors you with a toast, be prepared to reciprocate. Business entertaining is done more often at lunch than at dinner.
Saudi Arabia	Although men kiss each other in greeting, they never kiss a woman in public. An American woman should wait for a man to extend his hand before offering hers. When a Saudi offers refreshment, accept; declining it is an insult.
Japan	Don't imitate Japanese bowing customs unless you understand them thoroughly—who bows to whom, how many times, and when. It's a complicated ritual. Presenting business cards is another ritual. Carry many cards, present them with both hands so your name can be easily read, and hand them to others in descending rank. Expect Japanese business executives to take time making decisions and to work through all of the details before making a commitment.

Part C

It may seem simple to develop an advertising campaign. Just pick the medium and develop a message. But it's not that easy. Effectiveness depends on using the "best" available medium and the "best" message considering ①promotion objectives, ② the target markets, and ③ the funds available for advertising.

Specific advertising objectives determine what kind of advertising to use product or institutional. If product advertising is needed, then the particular type must be decided pioneering, competitive (direct or indirect), or reminder. And advertising allowances and cooperative advertising may be helpful.

Many technical details are involved in mass selling, and specialists advertising agencies handle some of these jobs. But specific objectives must be set for them, or their advertising may have little direction and be almost impossible to evaluate.

Effective advertising should affect sales. But the whole marketing mix affects sales and the results of advertising usually can't be measured by sales changes alone. By contrast, sales promotion tends to be more action-oriented.

Sales promotion spending is big and growing. This approach is especially important in prompting action by customers, middlemen, or salespeople. There are many different types of sales promotion, and it is a problem area in many firms because it is difficult for a firm to develop expertise with all of the possibilities.

Advertising and sales promotion are often important parts of a promotion blend but in most blends personal selling also plays an important role. Further, promotion is only a part of the total marketing mix a marketing manager must develop to satisfy target customers.

Part D

Writing an Effective Business Plan

How do entrepreneurs raise the capital needed to launch a new business? They write a business plan. When you write one, you need to persuade an investor that your concept for an organization is solid and that you're the best person to carry it out. Venture capitalists and successful entrepreneurs give the following advice about writing a solid business plan:

(1) Keep it short and simple. A good business plan articulates what the company will do and how it it will benefit the customer. Specify the product or service. Begin with an executive summary.

(2) Introduce the management team. A good business plan explains the people behind the product.

(3) Anticipate problems and challenges. A good business plan answers the tough questions about your idea. Venture capitalists will already know the problem; they want to be sure you do too.

(4) Show there is a market. A good business plan identifies a target market and demonstrates that people will use the product or service offered.

(5) Show a path to profit. A good business plan explains how the business will make money.

(6) Make it personal. A good business plan is not a template; it shows passion about ideas.

In short, your business plans should answer these questions:

1. What is your product or service?
2. How well developed is it? Is a mock-up or demo available?
3. Who is your market? How large is it? Why does this market need your product or service?
4. How will you promote your product or service promoted?

5. Who are your competitors? How will you be better?

6. Who is also providing support for your business?

7. Who will be working with you? How many more employees will you need? What will you pay them? What benefits will you give them?

Keys to Successful Business Plans

Of the thousands of business plans presented to potential investors each year, only a few succeed. John W. Mullens, at the London Business School, offers five reasons why business plans fail.

(1) No problem. Plans must fix a problem or fill a need instead of just being examples of cool technology or good ideas.

(2) Unrealistic ambition. Successful business plans recognize a specific market, instead of aiming at the entire population.

(3) Flawed spreadsheets. Carefully prepared revenue models can work on paper, but successful business plans must work in the real economy.

(4) Wrong team. Investors are not necessarily impressed by education and work experience, unless those contribute to the success of the business.

(5) Perfect plan. Successful plans recognize realistic challenges to the business plan, instead of presenting everything in the best light.

Mullens suggests three keys for success: ①A clear problem and a logical solution; ②hard evidence that you have done your research; ③complete candor about challenges and risks associated with your plan.

Unit 18
Documents in International Trade
外贸单证

18.1 Introduction（简介）

国际贸易是跨国界、跨市场的国际商品流动。要顺利完成一笔国际贸易业务，除了买卖双方外，还必须至少由进出口双方所在国的海关、商检机构、银行、保险公司、海运或航空公司等十几乃至几十家国家机关、企业单位一起参与方能实现。因此，外贸单证是国际贸易活动中的一个重要组成部分。

国际商会将外贸单证划分为：金融单证（Financial documents）和商业单证（Commercial documents）两类，解释如下：

金融单证，是指汇票、本票、支票以及用于收款的其他单据。

商业单证，是指发票、提单、权利证书及其他不属于金融单证的所有单据。

根据在国际贸易中的使用频率，外贸单证可分为基本单证和附属单证。

基本单证，即出口商一般情况下必须提供的单据，包括发票、提单和保险单三大单据。

附属单证，即在某种特殊情况下，买方要求卖方协助提供的单据。这些单据又分为两类：一类是进口国官方要求的单证，如领事发票、海关发票、产地证、检疫证、黑名单证明以及出口许可证、装船证明等；另一类是卖方要求说明货物详细情况的单证，如装箱单、重量单和品质证等。

外贸单证是维系参与贸易各方权利和义务的重要凭证。单证工作质量的好坏关系到外贸业务能否顺利进行，关系到能否安全、迅速收汇或收货，也体现着外贸企业的业务素质和管理水平。因此，外贸单证的制作不仅要符合国际商业习惯和实际需要，而且要遵守国际贸易的法律、惯例和规则。外贸单证的缮制应做到正确、完整、及时、简明和整洁。

18.2 Commercial Invoice（商业发票）

商业发票简称发票，是出口商向进口商开立，凭以向买方收款的发货价目清单。商业发票是全套外贸单证的核心，其余单证均按此缮制，所以其为核心单证。发票的作用为：

（1）作为买卖双方收发货物、收付货款和记账的凭证。

（2）作为买卖双方办理报关的依据。

（3）作为卖方缮制其把单证的依据。

（4）在即期付款不出具汇票的情况下，卖方可凭发票向买方收款。

商业发票样单：

ABC INTERNATIONAL COMPANY
36 ZHONGSHAN ROAD
HANGZHOU, CHINA

COMMERCIAL INVOICE

INVOICE NO. 03-09116 DATE: March 28, 2012

To:
MARADONA COMPANY
BUENOS AIRES, ARGENTINA

MARKS & NOS	QUANTITIES and DESCRIPTIONS	UNIT PRICE	AMOUNT
	CHILDREN'S SCHOOL SHIRTS 4520 DZS CONSTRUCTION DELA TELEA: 65 0/0 POLIESTER Y 35 0/0 ALGODON 45 ×45 Y 96 ×87 TALLES 7/8 9/10 11/12 13/14 15/16 17/18 19/20	CFR BUENOS AIRES	
MARADONA	1 2 2 2 2 2 1		
BUENOS AIRES			
ITEM: CHILDREN'S SCHOOL SHIRTS			
QTY: 8DZS	4224 DZS	DEM 25.50/DZ	
COLOUR			
(WHITE OR LIGHT-BLUE)		DEM107 712.00	
BOX N#: 1-528			
TOTAL PACKED IN 528 CTNS			

ABC INTERNATIONAL COMPANY
HANGZHOU, CHINA
赵 高

18.3 Packing List（装箱单）

装箱单是商业发票的一种补充单证，是对商品的不同包装规格条件逐一分别详细列表的一种单证，也是买方收货时核对货物的品种、花色、尺寸、规格和海关验收的主要依据。

装箱单的主要作用是补充商业发票内容的不足，通过表内的包装件数、规格、唛头等项目，明确阐述商品的包装情况，便于买方掌握进口商品包装及数量，也便于在货物到达目的港时海关检查和核对货物。

装箱单样单：

Date：1st June，2013

Packing List

Commodity：Cigarette Lighters　　Destination：Hong Kong
Credit No：IFL/22571/KB/200/06　　Consignee：M/s. Ngal Company
Means of Transportation：By Vessel　　Mark & No.：

S. N. C.
HONGKONG
No. 1-13

"Fong Yuan" Brand Cigarette Lighters

Case No.	Art. No.	@ Qty.
1-5	0229	@ 100 doz.
6-7	0223	@ 100 doz.
8-9	0224	@ 100 doz.
10-11	723	@ 100 doz.
12-13	724	@ 100 doz.

Total：1,300 doz.（13 cases）

18.4 Certificate of Origin（原产地证书）

原产地证书是用以证明货物原产地或制造地，以便进口国海关采取不同的国别政策和关税待遇的书面证明文件。

我国出口商品所使用的原产地证书主要有以下四种：

（1）中华人民共和国原产地证书（Certificate of Origin of the People's Republic of China，C/O）。这是证明出口货物的原产地为中华人民共和国的证明文件，即证明有关出口货物是中国天然获得的产品或是在中国经过了主要的及最后的制造加工工序的产品，且该制造加工工序使所用的主要原材料的外形、性质、形态或用途产生了实质性的改变，符合《中华人民共和国出口货物进出口原产地条例》中的中国原产产品判定标准。

（2）普惠制产地证（Generalized System of Preferences Certificate of Origin，GSP）。目前给予我国普惠制待遇的国家主要有澳大利亚、新西兰、日本、加拿大、挪威、瑞士、俄罗斯及欧盟，还有部分东欧国家。凡是向给惠国出口受惠商品，均须提供普惠制产地证，才能享受关税减免的优惠，所以不管来证是否要求提供这种产地证，我国出口商均应主动提交。普惠制产地证的书面格式名称为格式 A（Form A）。但对新西兰还须提供格式 59A（Form 59A）；对澳大利亚不用任何格式，只需在商业发票上加注有关声明文句。在我国，普惠制产地证由出入境检验检疫局签发。

（3）纺织品产地证（Certificate of Origin of Textile Product）。对欧盟国家出口纺织品须提交该产地证，这是进口国海关控制配额的依据。在我国，该证由地方商务系统颁发。GSP 产地证是取得关税优惠的证明，而纺织品产地证是取得配额的证明。对欧盟出口有关产品时，须同时提交两种产地证。

（4）对美国出口的原产地声明书。凡属对美国出口的配额商品，如纺织品等，应由出口商填写原产地声明书。原产地声明书有三种格式：格式 A，单一国家产地声明书（Single Country Declaration），声明商品产地只有一个国家；格式 B，多国家产地声明书（Multiple Country Declaration），声明商品的原材料由两个或两个以上国家生产；格式 C，非多种纤维纺织品声明书，亦称否定声明书（Negative Declaration），凡纺织品的主要价值或主要重量属于麻或丝的原料或含羊毛量不超过 17%，则可填此格式，以说明该类商品为非配额产品。

原产地证书样单：

THE CHINA COUNCIL FOR THE PROMOTION OF INTERNATIONAL TRADE

CERTIFICATE OF ORIGIN

(Date: 21. 5. 2012)

(Consignor) Guangzhou Light Industrial Products I & E Corp.

(Consignee) M/S. Indian Bazaar (Nigeria) Ltd., P. O. Box 2773, Lagos/Nigeria.

(Port of Shipment) Guangzhou

(Destination) Cotonou W/T H. K.

(Mark & No.)	(Commodity)	(Place of origin)	(Quantity)	(Weight)
INDIAN BAZAAR U-2434 COTONOU IN TRANSIT TO LACO/APAPA No. 1-853	Kerosene Stoves	The People's Republic of China	853 Cartons	

(This is to certify that the above mentioned commodities were produced or manufactured in the People's Republic of China)

It is to certify that goods are neither of Israeli origin nor do they contain any Israeli materials.

The China Council for the Promotion of International Trade, Guangzhou Branch

(Sealed)

18.5 Weight Memo（重量单）

重量单也是商业发票的一种补充单证，其作用与装箱单基本相同。重量单一般列明每件货物的毛重和净重。

重量单样单：

Date: 2nd May, 2013

Weight Memo

Commodity: Porcelain Ware　　Destination: Beirut, Lebanon

Credit No. AF1859/36　　Consignee: M/s. Ramzi Chaha Co.

Means of Transportation: By Vessel　　Mark & No. ________

R. CHAHAL
815
BEITRUT

3000 doz.	C471	Coffee Cup/Saucer Barrel Shape dark brown gold stamped
1494 doz.	C472	Coffee Cup/Saucer fully decorated

	G. W. (kg.)	NETT (kg.)	MEASUREMENTS (cm.)
1-250 250 cartons@ 12 doz.			62.4×37.8×25.4
251-333 2 cartons@ 18 doz.	34	25	59×41×38

18.6 Bill of Lading（提单）

提单，也称海运提单（Ocean Bill of Lading），是用以证明海上货物运输合同和货物已由承运人接收或装船，以及承运人保证据以交付货物的单证。

海运提单的作用有两个方面：

（1）从法律规定的层面看，提单的基本作用为：①提单是海上货物运输合同的证明；②提单是货物已由承运人接收或装船的收货证据；③提单是承运人保证凭以交付货物的物权凭证。其中，根据提单中载明的收货人不同，承运人交付货物的对象有所不同，具体有三种情形：向记名人交付货物、按照指示人的指示交付货物、向提单持有人交付货物。

（2）从外贸业务和运输业务的层面看，提单的作用为：①提单是承运人对托运人货物运输要求给予有条件实现的书面确认；②提单是银行结汇文件中最重要的文件之一；③提单是货主与货代之间、货代与承运人之间或者货主与承运人之间支付及收取运费的凭证。

提单样单：

Shipper: Guangzhou Light Industrial Product I & E Corp.

Consignee or Assigns:

To Order Bank of Aroda

Notify M/s. C. P. Pa cl & Co.

P. O. Box 68, Ba, Fiji

中 国

海洋运输公司

CHINA OCEAN SHIPPING COMPANY

HEAD OFFICE: Beijing

BRANCHOFFICE: Guangzhou

Shanghai Tianjin

BILL OF LADING ORIGINAL

DIRECT OR WITH TRANSHIPMENT

S/O No. B/L No.

Vessel CARDROSS Voy.

Port of Loading Guangzhou

Port of Discharge Lautoka W/T Hong Kong

Nationality

Freight P ayable at

Particulars Furnished by the Shipper

Marks and Numbers	No. of Packages	Description of Goods	Gross Weight	Measurement
C. P. P. BA/LAUT OKA No. 1-18	18 P'kgs	Pocket Knives Sdetv Pins Press Butons Cigarette Lighters & Insec- ticide Sprayers Freight Prepaid		
Total Packages (in words)		SAY EIGHTEEN PACKAGES ONLY		

Shipped on board the vessel named above in apparent good order and condition (unless otherwise indicated) the goods or packages specked herein and to be discharged at the above mentioned port of discharge or as near thereto as the vessel may safety get and be always afloat.

The weight, measure, marks, numbers, quality, contents and value, being particulars furnished by the Shipper, are not checked by the carrier on loading.

The Shipper, Consignee and the Holder of this Bill of Lading hereby expressly accept and agree to all printed, written or stamped provisions, exceptions and conditions of this Bill of Lading, including those on the back hereof.

Freight and Charges:	In witness whereof, the Carrier or his Agents has signed THREE Bills of Lading all of this tenor and date, one of which being accomplished, the others to stand void.
Shippers are requested to note particularly the exceptions and conditions of this Bill of Lading with reference to the validity of the insurance upon their goods.	Date ________ at Guangzhou ________ For the Master

18.7 Draft (Bill of Exchange)(汇票)

汇票为资金单证，可以代替货币进行转让或流通，因此，汇票是一种很重要的有价证券。为了防止丢失，汇票一般都有两张正本：First Exchange 和 Second Exchange。根据票据法的规定，两张正本汇票具有同等效力，但付款人付一不付二，付二不付一，先到先付，后到无效。银行在寄送单证时，一般也要将两张正本汇票分两个邮次向国外寄发，以防在邮程中丢失。

汇票样单：

BILL OF EXCHANGE

No. S0001184　　　　Dated 2011-09-01

Exchange for JPY 1200000

At ________ Sight of this FIRST of Exchange (Second of exchange being unpaid)

Pay to the Order of BANK OF CHINA

The sum of JPY ONE MILLION TWO HUNDRED THOUSAND ONLY

Drawn under L/C No. 002/0000025　　　　Dated 2011-09-01

Issued by THE BANK of TOKYO-MITSUBISHI, LTD.

To THE BANK of TOKYO-MITSUBISHI

LTD. 2-10-22 2-10-22 Kayato Bldg 4F, Akebonocho

Tachikawa Shi, Tokyo　　　　ABC I&E Corp.

(Authorized Signature)

18.8 Letter of Credit（信用证）

信用证（Letter of Credit，L/C）是开证银行根据申请人的要求与指示，向受益人开立的承诺在一定期限内凭其规定支付一定金额的书面文件。

信用证的内容随不同交易的需要而定，各开证行习惯使用的格式也有所不同，信用证虽然没有统一的格式，但其基本内容是相同的，主要包括：

（1）对信用证本身的说明，包括信用证的种类、性质、金额及其有效期和到期地点等。

（2）对货物的要求，涉及货物的名称、品种规格、数量、包装、价格等。

（3）对运输的要求，涉及装运的最后期限、起运地和目的地、运输方式，可否分批装运以及可否中途转运等。

（4）对单据的要求。信用证要求的单据主要分为以下几类：①货物单据，以发票为中心，包括装箱单、重量单、原产地证、商检证明书等；②运输单据，如提单等，这是代表货物所有权的凭证；③保险单据，如保险单等。以 CIF、CIP 成交的合同，还可以进一步规定卖方应投保的险别及投保金额；

除了这三类单据外，还有可能提出其他的单证要求，如寄样证明、装船通知电报副本等。

（5）特殊要求与指示。根据每一笔具体交易的需要，做出不同的规定，并无一定标准，一般都是限制卖方不能做出或必须做出某种作为的规定。

（6）开证行保证付款的责任文句。即由开证行向受益人、议付行或其他汇票的持票人保证，银行在收到信用证所要求的单据后，将对按信用证开立的汇票承担付款的责任，以及遵守《跟单信用证统一惯例》的文句等。

信用证样单：

No. ____________

XIN HUA TRUST, SAVINGS & COMMERCIAL BANK, LTD

To Bank of China, INCORPORATED IN CHINA

Guangzhou HONG KONG BRANCH Date 15th January, 2013

OPENED BY MAIL

1011899A

Dear Sirs,

We hereby open our Irrevocable Commercial Letter of Credit No. ____________ in favor of Guangzhou Textile Imp. & Exp., Corp. for account of Arkai Silk Trading Co. up to an aggregate amount of RMB ¥ 16 200.00 (Say RENMINBI Sixteen Thousand Two Hundred Yuan Only.)

for 100% of the invoice value relative to the shipment of:

10000 yds. 11188 28" X50/52 yards per piece,

@ ¥1.62 per yard

as per Contract No. 03AK1334

From your port __________ to Hong Kong ______________ CIF Hong Kong Draft (s) to be drawn at 60 days sight on our bank & accompanied by the following documents, marked "X":

[X] Signed Commercial Invoice in duplicate

[X] Insurance Policy or Certificate for full invoice value plus 10% covering:

[X] FPA/WPA/All Risks and War Risk

&/or [X] Risks (including RFWD) Overland Transportation

[X] Full set of clean "On Board" ocean Bills of Lading made out to our order marked freight prepaid notify accountee

&/or [X] Full set of Forwarding Agents' Cargo Receipt made out to our order marked freight prepaid notify accountee

☐ Parcel Post Receipt showing parcels addressed to our Bank a/c accountee and mark with this L/C Number

[X] Other Documents in triplicate:

☐ Inspection and Testing Certificate issued by C. I. & T. B.

☐ Survey Report on Weight issued by C. I. & T. B.

☐ Certificate of Origin

[X] Packing List in duplicate

☐ Detailed Weight List

Partial shipments are permitted/prohibited

Transshipment is permitted/prohibited

Shipment (s) must be effected not later than 20th February, 20-

This L/C is irrevocable and valid in your port ________ until 25th February, 20-. inclusive.

Draft (s) so drawn must be inscribed with the number and date of this L/C

Other Conditions:

Amount and quantity 10% more or less allowed.

We hereby agree with the drawers, endorsers and bona-fide holders of the draft (s) drawn under and in compliance with the terms of this credit that such draft (s) shall be duly honored on due presentations and delivery of documents as herein specified.

Instructions of Negotiating Bank: The draft (s) and, documents taken up under this credit are to be forwarded direct to us by you.

For Reimbursement: [X] We hereby guarantee that the draft (s) under this credit will be duly paid by drawees at maturity and we shall credit your account or designated with us on the date (s) of such draft (s).

This Credit is subject to Uniform Customs and Practice for Documentary Credit (1974 Revision) International Chamber of Commerce, Publication No. 290.

Yours faithfully,

For XIN HUA TRUST, SAVINGS & COMMERCIAL BANK, LTD.

HONG KONG BRANCH

18.9 Letter of Guarantee（保函）

保函（Letter of Guarantee, L/G），又称银行保函，是银行根据申请人的要求向受益人开立的担保申请人正常履行合同义务的书面证明。保函是银行有条件承担一定经济责任的契约文件。当申请人未能履行其所承诺的义务时，银行负有向受益人赔偿经济损失的责任。由于银行信用代替或补充商业信用，保函的信用性更好、灵活性、更强，因此被广泛应用于外贸业务中。

保函作为第三方信用凭证，其出具的目的是使受益人能够得到一定保证，以消除其对申请人是否具有履行合同义务的能力或决心的怀疑，从而使交易顺利进行，保证货款和货物的正常交换，这是保函的基本功能。此外，保函还用来保证合约的正常履行、预付款项的归还、贷款及利息的偿还、合同标的物的质量完好、被扣财务的保释等。

银行保函的基本内容有：

（1）保函当事人（受益人、申请人、担保行、通知行或转开行）的完整名称和详细地址。

（2）保函的性质，即保函的种类。

（3）合同的主要内容。

（4）保函的编号和开立日期。

（5）保函金额。

（6）保函的有效期限和到期日。

（7）当事人的权利和义务。

（8）索偿条件。

保函样单：

ABC PUBLIC SECURITY
No. 66 Wenhua Road
HANGZHOU 310000
Zhejiang Province
P. R. CHINA

Milan 02/06/2011

Our Guarantee No. 6512289

Dear Sirs,

With reference to Contract No. 10DMAC/YSC889IT (hereinafter called the "Contract") signed between you—ABC PUBLIC SECURITY (hereinafter called "the Buyer") and Agusta S. p. A., Via Giovanni Agusta 520, Cascina Costa di Samarate (VA), Italy (hereinafter called "the Seller") for supply of one AW 139 Helicopter, one AW 119 MKII Helicopter, basic optional equipment, mission equipment logistics and services as stipulated in the said Contract (hereinafter called "the Goods"), we BANCA POPOLARE DI VICENZA Scpa, Via Btg. Framarin 18, 36100 Vicenza, Italy, at the request of the Seller, hereby open an irrevocable letter of guarantee No. 6512289 in an amount of USD5,728,195 (= U. S. Dollars five million seven hundred twenty eight thousand one hundred ninety five only), in favor of you.

We undertake the guarantee as follows:

(1) Our liability under this letter of guarantee shall be limited to USD5,728,195 (= U. S. Dollars five million seven hundred twenty eight thousand one hundred ninety five only) plus interest at the rate prevailing at the moment in which the refund is done per annum counting from the date on which we received the respective payment on account of Agusta S. p. A. up to the date on which the refund is made.

(2) If you declare that the contract has been terminated in accordance with the Contract clauses due to a breach of the Contract on the part of the Seller, specifying the reasons of the termination, we shall within seven days after receipt of your first written demand, unconditionally refund to you up to USD5,728,195 (= U. S. Dollars five million seven hundred twenty eight thousand one hundred ninety five only) plus the above mentioned interest per annum counting from the date on which we received the respective payment on the account of Agusta S. p. A. up to the date on which the refund is made and for which this letter of guarantee is still valid.

(3) This Letter of Guarantee shall become effective as soon as we receive the respective payment, and will remain valid till the date of the transfer of the title of the goods under the Contract covered by this payment.

(4) This guarantee shall in any case expire in full and automatically on 31st July 2011 (31/07/2011) should your above mentioned written demand for payment and your above mentioned written declaration together with a first class Chinese bank's confirmation of your signatures not be in our possession on or before that date.

The present Letter of Guarantee shall be automatically reduced, till full extinction, in proportion of the value of the down payment made based on the delivered amounts upon presentation by the Seller to ourselves of a copy of relative invoices showing the delivered amount and the down payment linked to this delivered amount as well as a copy of corresponding Final Acceptance Certificate.

This Letter of Guarantee has to be returned to us for the sake of administrative regularity after the date of validity expires.

Issued subject to the Uniform Rules for Demand Guarantees of the International Chamber of Commerce (Publication No. 456).

Sincerely yours,

BANCA POPOLARE DI VICENZA

Milan Branch 028

(Signature)

Supplementary Reading

Part A

A partnership is similar to a proprietorship, except that there are two or more owners (partners). In a general partnership, all the partners share in gains or losses, and all have unlimited liability for all partnership debts, not just some particular share. The way partnership gains (and losses) are divided is described in the partnership agreement. This agreement can be an informal oral agreement, such as "let's start a lawn mowing business," or a lengthy, formal written document.

In a limited partnership, one or more general partners will run the business and have unlimited liability, but there will be one or more limited partners who will not actively participate in the business. A limited partner's liability for business debts is limited to the amount that partner contributes to the partnership. This form of organization is common in real estate ventures, for example.

The advantages and disadvantages of a partnership are basically the same as those of a proprietorship. Partnerships based on a relatively informal agreement are easy and inexpensive to form. General partners have unlimited liability for partnership debts, and the partnership terminates when a general partner wishes to sell out or dies. All income is taxed as personal income to the partners, and the amount of equity that can be raised is limited to the partners' combined wealth. Ownership of a general partnership is not easily transferred, because a transfer requires that a new partnership be formed. A limited partner's interest can be sold without dissolving the partnership, but finding a buyer may be difficult.

Because a partner in a general partnership can be held responsible for all partnership debts, having a written agreement is very important. Failure to spell out the rights and duties of the partners frequently leads to misunderstandings later on. Also, if you are a limited partner, you must not become deeply involved in business decisions unless you are willing to assume the obligations of a general partner. The reason is that if things go badly, you may be deemed to be a general partner even though you say you are a limited partner.

Based on the discussion, the primary disadvantages of sole proprietorships and partnerships as forms of business organization are ①unlimited liability for business debts on the part of the owners, ②limited life of the business, and ③difficulty of transferring ownership. These three disadvantages add up to a single, central problem: the ability of such businesses to grow can be seriously limited by an inability to raise cash for investment.

Notes

1. proprietorship 独资企业
2. limited partnership 有限合伙企业

Part B

Respecting the Traditions of India

Lisa Hendrick walked briskly through the low door; the sound of her heels was muffled by the soft, thick rugs on the floor. She greeted her customer, Babu Jagjivan, with a wide smile and an outstretched hand. Babu Jagjivan was clad in a long, khaki cotton shirt with swirls of white cloth wrapped around his legs. He took her hand rather tentatively and gestured her to take a seat. Hendrick sat on the nearest available chair and crossed her legs. She was ready to negotiate prices with the help of her interpreter, who spoke Hindi. However, Babu Jagjivan did not appear ready to conduct business. Instead, he summoned a boy with a clap of his hands. Immediately, the boy brought two steel containers filled with hot, steaming tea. Being a hot, summer day with temperatures soaring to the 100s, Hendrick declined the tea. Babu Jagjivan seemed to be extremely reluctant to talk let alone negotiate a deal. Hendrick was puzzled. She had thought she was adjusting to India very well. Only yesterday, she had negotiated a good contract with Mr. Rajan in Bangalore, a large metropolitan city in south India. But here, in Kanpur (a major city in north India), she was not meeting with much success. Hendrick wondered what could be wrong.

In India, customers vary from Westernized, urban sophisticates like Mr. Rajan to the earthy Babu Jagjivan. Although people always seek to maximize economic benefits from a contract, the subtleties of negotiation and social mores cannot be overlooked. Babu Jagjivan was uncomfortable dealing with a woman. In the more traditional areas of India, it is not customary to shake hands with women—the traditional gesture of folding one's hands in respect (namaste) is the norm. The golden rule is to give the customer the pleasure of playing host, by accepting his tea and indulging in social pleasantries before getting down to business. Salespersons in India, as elsewhere, try to adapt to their customers by identifying with their customs. Hence, in urban India, the preferred language for business is English and customers are more apt to be familiar with Western customs. In smaller towns, customers are more comfortable in the regional language (there are 15 official languages in India). People would be distrustful of salespersons who do not respect their customs. Certain weekdays (usually Fridays) are considered auspicious for signing business contracts, although this may vary from one region to another. For instance, even though people in many parts of south India would not commence new business on Tuesdays, this may not be true in the north.

Part C

An important challenge of the sales manager is to motivate salespeople using financial and nonfinancial methods. Salary, commissions, contests, bonuses, and travel awards are common financial motivators. Achievement awards, challenging work assignments, recognition, leadership techniques, and performance evaluations are nonfinancial methods used as motivators.

Today, salespeople are paid by several methods, but most firms use a combination of salary and financial incentives rather than straight salary or straight commission plans. This provides salespeople with a guaranteed salary and helps motivate them to reach their sales goals to earn commissions and bonuses or to win contests.

The sales manager needs to understand the principles of leadership and apply them to salespeople based on their individual personalities and territorial situations. Managers need to be people oriented and job oriented toward salespeople to help them reach sales goals. This ultimately helps to reach the manager' s goals.

The performance of sales personnel is evaluated by comparing their quotas and objectives to actual sales and job activities to determine their success. The salesperson' s immediate manager implements periodic evaluations each year using both quantitative and qualitative performance criteria.

To effectively evaluate salespeople, managers should develop procedures to ensure fair treatment. By being prepared for the interview and having a positive attitude, the salesperson will be receptive to the manager' s critique. The manager should evaluate each performance criterion and explain the evaluation to the salesperson. A discussion of the salesperson' s past performance concludes the interview. Future performance quotas and objectives can now be established to serve as goals to reach for the upcoming sales period.

Part D

The Importance of Annual Reports

A survey, conducted by Withum Smith & Brown and MGT Design Inc., found that the annual report is the most important publication that a company produces. To understand the value of annual reports, the survey asked individual investors, portfolio managers, and securities analysts (the primary audiences for annual reports) about the ways they read and use the the reports to make decisions.

Here are some of their findings:

(1) Seventy-five percent said the annual report is the most important publication that a company produces.

(2) Seventy-nine percent said the annual report is an important tool for investment decisions.

(3) Sixty-six percent prefer photos and/or illustrations in annual report.

(4) Ninety percent said that important concerns facing the industry, such as environment issues and corporate governance, should be addressed in the report.

(5) Eighty-one percent prefer a print version over electronic versions. Respondents said the print documents were easier to read, highlight, annotate, and file.

Taken together, these findings suggest that the annual report is an important communication for organizations and well worth the time spent creating it.

Executive Summary of a Government Plan

On February 18, 2009, the Obama administration announced a "Homeowner Affordability and Stability" plan to counter the home mortgage crisis. The executive summary of the plan—given to the press—including the following:

(1) First, a statement of background, which included bullet points listing the effects of the crisis (for example, that nearly 6 million households will face foreclosure), and ending with the purpose of the plan (that the plan will help nearly 7 to 9 million families to "restructure" their mortgages to avoid foreclosure).

(2) Then, the two main components of the plan (affordability and stability) together with their subcomponents (a few subcomponents are given below as examples):

(3) Affordability:

1) Enabling refinancing.

2) Reducing monthly payments.

(4) Stability:

1) Helping homeowners stay in their homes.

2) Not aiding speculators.

3) Protecting neighborhoods.

The summary provided numbers and, where appropriate, examples to inform and explain the plan. A busy reader—or one who wanted to know the broad contours of the plan without going through its nuts and bolts—would likely benefit from reading the summary before deciding whether to read the whole plan.

Appendix

Appendix A Useful Phrases and Expressions

实用短语

A	
a copy of	一份/本/册
a commission (commission of)	佣金
a discount of (a discount)	折扣
a complete/ full set of documents	全套单据
a full range of samples	全套样品
a great number of	大量的
a parcel of	一批
a variety of	各种各样的
a wide range of	多种多样的
abide by	遵守
according to	根据
account for	解释
acquaint sb. with sth.	使某人熟悉某事
acknowledge an order	确认定单
additional cost	额外费用
adhere to one' s commitments	忠实履行某人的义务
advise sb. of sth.	通知某人某事
All Risks	一切险
allow/ give sb. a discount	给某人以折扣
amend L/C	修改信用证
apologize for	因……而道歉
appeal to	吸引
approve of	赞成
approach sb.	与某人联系
arrange insurance	办理保险
arrange for	安排
arrange with sb. about/for	与某人商定
ask for extension of	要求延长
assure sb. of sth.	向某人保证某事
as a special accommodation	作为特殊照顾

（续）

as a rule	作为惯例
as a result of	结果
as a matter of fact	实际上
as an exceptional case	破例
as agreed	按商定
as compared with	与……比起来
as far as	至于
as follows	如下
as long as	只要
as matters stand = as the matter stands	按照现状，照实际情况
as per	按照，根据
as regards	关于
as required	按要求
as specified/ stipulated	按规定
as soon/ early as possible	尽快，尽早
as to	就……而论，关于
at a time	同时，一次
at all times	一直，总是
at intervals	每隔一会
at intervals of	每隔……时间
at least	至少
at one' s disposal	由某人处理，支配
at one' s request	按某人要求
at other times	平时，在其他时候
at requested	按要求
at sight	即期
at the same time	同时
at . . . premium	按……保险费率
at . . . rate	按……率
at your end	在你处
at your request	应贵方要求
attribute . . . to . . .	把……归因于
avail oneself of	利用
B	
be acceptable to sb.	可以为某人所接受
be accustomed to	习惯于
be acquainted with	对……熟悉，了解

（续）

be assured of	请放心
be at a loss	困惑，不知道
be available for supply	可供货
be committed	接受订单，承担任务
be compelled/ forced/ obliged to do	被迫，不得不
be connected with	与……有联系
be desirous of	想要
be engaged in	从事
be familiar to	为……所熟悉
be familiar with	熟悉，通晓
be famous for	因……而闻名
be firm for/ be good/ open/ valid for...	有效期为……
be fully booked	订货已满
be heavily booked	订货太多
be interested in	对……感兴趣
be in the market for	欲购
be of high quality	高质量的
be only too glad to = be very glad to	十分乐意做某事
be on the high/low side	价偏高/低
be popular	畅销
be popular with/ among	受到……欢迎
be ready for shipment	备妥待运
be satisfied with	对……满意
be strictly confidential	严守机密
be sure of ...	肯定……；对……有把握
be used to	习惯于
be valid until	有效期至
be within the scope of	属于……业务范围
bid a price	递价
bilateral trade	双边贸易
blank endorsed	空白背书
book freight space = book shipping space	订舱
book/ place an order with sb.	向某人订货
book up	订完
bottom price	最低价格
bring down your price to	价格降至
bridge over the gap	弥补差距

（续）

bring up claim against	向……提出索赔
broaden the market	扩大市场
business entity	企业实体
buy. . . from	从……购买
by cable	用/通过电报
by joint efforts	通过共同努力
by request	应邀，按要求
by separate post/ mail = under separate cover	另寄，另封
by telex	用/通过电传
by weight	按重量（计）
C	
cable an inquiry for sth.	电报询盘
call at	停靠，停泊
call/ draw one' s attention to	请某人注意
cancel orders	撤销订单
cannot help doing	不得不，禁不住
captioned goods	标题货物
carry out orders	执行订单
cash account	现金账
cash against documents	凭单付款
cash against delivery	货到付款
cash payment	现金付款
cause trouble to sb.	给某人带来麻烦
charter ship	租船
check up	检查
classified catalogue	分类目录
clear off	清偿
close over the gap	弥补差距
come into effect/ force	生效
come to/ into the market	上市
come to terms = close a bargain/ deal	达成交易
come up to	达到，符合
compare favorably	比起来优于
compensation trade	补偿贸易
complain about/ of	抱怨
comply with	与……一致，符合
confirm an order	确认订单

（续）

conform to	与……一致，符合
coincide with	与……一致，符合
consist of	由……组/构成
Cost and Freight（CFR）	成本加运费（……指定目的港）
Cost，Insurance and Freight（CIF）	成本加保险费，运费（……指定目的港）
cover one’s loss	弥补……的损失
cover one’s demand/ request/ requirement	满足……的要求
cover insurance	保险
count on	指望，依靠
counter sample	对等样品
credit account	贷方账
credit standing/ status	信用状况
current price	现价，时价
current value	现值
customs broker	报关行，海关经纪人
customs duty	关税
customs entry	进口报关
customs formalities	海关手续
customary practice	习惯做法
D	
damage to the goods	货物的损失
date of delivery	交货日期
date of shipment	装运期
deal with	与……交易
deferred payment	延期付款
debit note	借方通知
delay in	在……耽搁
delay in shipment	装运方面的延误
delivery time/date	装运期
demurrage	滞期费
direct steamer	直达船
do business with	与……交易
do... on purpose	故意做某事
do one’s best/utmost = try one’s best	尽力，努力
depend on	依赖，依靠
double figures	两位数
dispatch money	速遣费

（续）

draw a draft on sb.	向某人开出汇票
draw one' s attention to	请某人注意
draw sample	抽样
draw up	起草，草拟
due to	由于
due to arrive	预计到达
E	
effect delivery	交货
effect payment	支付
enable sb. to do sth.	使某人能够做某事
enjoy fast sales	畅销
enjoy a good reputation	享有盛名
enjoy popularity	受欢迎，享有盛名
enlarge/ expand the market	扩大市场
equal to sample	与样品相同
enter into business relations with	与……建立业务关系
establish L/C	开立信用证
established practice	习惯做法
estimated time of arrival	预计到达时间
estimated time of departure	预计离港时间
Ex Works	工厂交货（……指定地）
existing market	目前的市场，现存市场
expedite L/C	催证
export declaration	出口申报单
export document	出口单据
export entry	出口报关
export license	出口许可证
export quota	出口配额
export volume	出口量
extend L/C	信用证展期
extend the market	扩大市场
ex S/S...	由……轮运来
F	
fail to	没有，未能
fall in line with	同意，符合
fall within the business scope of	属于……业务范围
favorable price	优惠价格

（续）

few and far between	（船）稀少
figure in	算进，包括进
figure out	算出，想出
figure up	合计
fill in/up	填写，填满
file a claim against	向……提出索赔
finalize a deal/ transaction	达成交易
financial standing/states	财务状况
find a market	找销路
find a way out	找（到）出路
find fault with	对……不满，挑剔
firm/ fixed price	固定价格
foreign freight forwarder	国际货运
forwarding agent	货运代理
for fear of	恐怕
for one' s account	由某人负担（费用）
for one' s approval	经某人同意
for the purpose of	为……目的/意图
for the sake of	为了……起见/缘故
for your file	供贵方存档
for your information/ reference/ consideration	供贵方参考
franchise	免赔率
Free Alongside Ship（FAS）	船边交货（……指定地）
Free from Particular Average（FPA）	平安险
Free on Board（FOB）	装运港船上交货（……指定装运港）
free of	免于……的，没有……的
free of charge	免费
from top to bottom	从头至尾，彻底
from now on	从现在起
from stock	供现货
frontier trade	边境贸易
furnish sb. with sth.	提供某人某物
G	
general average	共同海损
general open policy	预约总保单
get over	恢复，克服
get together	聚集，商谈，积累

（续）

give priority to	优先考虑……，给……以优先权
give up	放弃
go beyond	超出，超过，胜过
go over	检查
goods in question	标题货物
gross price	毛价，总价
gross weight	毛重
grow down	减少，缩小
guard against	防止，提防
H	
half price	半价
handle claims	理赔
hasten L/C	催证
have a share in	分担
have a confidence in	对……有信心
have a difficulty in	在……有困难
have extensive connections with	与……有广泛联系
have heavy commitments	订货太多
have/ feel/ take interest in	对……有兴趣
hear from	收到……信
have no choice but to	别无选择，只好
high quality	质优
highest price	最高价
hold one' s responsible for	使某人对……负责
honor one' s draft on presentation	见票承兑
I	
illustrated catalogue	有插图的目录
import license	进口许可证
in a large quantities	大量地
in accordance with	根据，按照，和……一致
in addition to	除……之外
in agreement with	符合，和……一致
in answer/ reply to	兹复
in bad/ poor condition	（表面）状况不好
in case of	假如，万一，如果
in charge of	负责，主管
in conformance/conformity with	符合，与……一致

（续）

inclusive of	包括，包含
in consideration of	考虑到
in detail	详细地
in due time/ course	及时地
in duplicate	一式两份
in error	错误地
in excessive of	超过
in fact	实际上
in future	将来
in line with the market	与市场价相符
out of line with the market	与市场价不符
in a position to	能够
in good condition	（表面）状况良好
in no case	决不
in one' s favor	以某人为受益人
in order	整齐，无误
in proportion	与……成比例
in order to	为了
in receipt of	收到
in reference to	参阅……
in regard to	关于
in reply (to one' s inquiry)	答复（某人询盘）
in short/ scarce supply	货少
in stock	有存货
in spite of	尽管
in strict confidence	严守机密
in terms of	就……而言
in this/ that case	既然这/那样
in the amount to	总金额达
in the line of	经营某商品
in/ under the circumstances	在这种情况下
in the event of	万一
in the meantime	同时
in the process of	在……过程中
in this respect	在这方面
in transit	运输途中
in two equal lots	同等数量两批

（续）

in view of	鉴于
in your place/ district	在贵处
inferior quality	质劣
inferior to	质量次于
inform sb. of sth.	通知某人某事
initial orders	首批订单
inquire for	询价
insist on	坚持
instead of	代替，而不
insure. . . for	按……金额投保
insure. . . with	向……投保
invite one' s attention to	请某人注意……
issue L/C = establish/ open L/C	开立信用证
	J
jerquer（customs officer attending clearance）	结关员
jerquer note	（海关）结关单
joint efforts	通过共同努力
joint venture	合资企业
	K
keep accounts	记账
keep apart	使……分离
keep doing	坚持……
keep in mind	记住
keep（in）touch with	与……保持联系
keep sb. advised/ informed/ posted of	随时通知某人……
	L
latent market	潜在市场
lead to	导致，导向
lie within the（business）scope of	属于……业务范围
liberal quantity	充足的数量
limited quantity	有限的数量
loading rate	装运效率
lodge a claim	索赔
look for	寻找
look forward to	盼望
look into	调查
look through	查阅，彻底调查
look up	查明

（续）

M	
make a counter-offer	还盘
make a mistake in	在……出错
make a reduction of . . . in price	减价
make allowance	折让
make an exception	破例
make an offer	报盘
make an apology for	因……抱歉
make an arrangement for	安排
make compensation for	赔偿
make customs declaration	报关
make. . . from	用……（原料）制成（看不出制作的原材料）
make of	用……（材料）制成（可以看出制作的原材料）
make the efforts	尽力，努力
make use of	利用
market potential	市场潜力
maximum quantity	最大数量
minimum quantity	最小数量
measure up to	符合，达到
meet one' s needs/ requirements	满足某人的要求
meet one' s obligation	履行义务、职责
meet with	（无意中）碰到
moderate quantity	中等数量
more or less	溢短装
N	
new order	新订单
non-negotiable copy of B/L	不可转让提单副本
not later than	不迟于
not less than	不少于
not only. . . but also	不但……而且
notify sb. of sth.	通知某人某事
O	
ocean marine cargo insurance	海洋运输货物保险
on a substantial of	大规模地
on arrival of	到达
on good terms with	与……关系良好
on/ under. . . terms	按……方式

（续）

on perusal	详阅之后
on... terms and conditions	在……条件下
on the basis of sample	根据样品
on the part of = on one's part	就……而言，在……方面
on the recommendation of	由……推荐/介绍
on the spot	现场
on the strength of	根据，凭借
on your side	在贵处
ocean B/L	远洋提单
only if	只有当……（才）
open an account	开立账户
open L/C	开证
order B/L	凭指示提单
original B/L	提单正本
outturn sample	到货样
overland insurance	陆运保险
owing to	由于
	P
packing list	装箱单
parent firm	母公司
partial loss	部分损失
partial shipment	分批/部分装运/船
particular average	单独海损
pass ... on to sb. for attention and reply	转交……办理答复
pay attention to	请注意……
pay by installment	分期付款
pay in advance	预付
pay on delivery	货到付款
payment by L/C	信用证支付
per metric ton = each metric ton	每公吨
perils of the sea	海上风险
place an order with	向……订货
point out	指出
poor (in) quality	劣质
present price = prevailing price	现行市价
press for L/C	催证
prior to	先于

（续）

product line	产品系列
production process	生产过程，工序
prompt attention	立即办理
prompt shipment	即期装运
push the sales of	推销
put forward	提出
put in a claim against	向……提出索赔
put. . . right	纠正
R	
raise a claim	索赔
reduce your price by	对……降价（多少）
refer to = referring to	参阅
refer. . . to. . .	请某人向某人了解……
refuse order	拒绝订单
regardless of	不顾，不管，不关心
relative/ relate to	有关的，关于
remind sb. of sth.	提醒某人某事
remit. . . by	以……方式汇款
repeat order	续订单
replace A with B	用 B 代替 A
resent/ revoke order	取消订单
result from	产生于
result in	导致
revert to	重提；复原
rough handling	野蛮装运
ruling price	现价
run the risk of	冒……风险
rush L/C	催证
S	
sell fast/ well	畅销
send by separate mail/ post = send separately	另寄/ 函
send herewith = enclose	随函
set forth	规定
shipping advice	装运通知
shipping instruction	装运须知
shipping mark	装运标记
sign a contract	签合同

（续）

sight L/C	即期信用证
so as to (do)	以便，为了
specialize in	专门经营
stand competition	经得起竞争
standard quality	标准质量
state terms of	说明……的条款
step up	加速
subject to	以……为条件
subject goods	标题货物
such being the case	情况既然如此
suffer from	遭受
superior quality	优质
supply from the stock	供现货
survey report	鉴定报告
	T
tax return	税单，纳税申报表
take effect = come into effect/ force	生效
take delivery	提货
take out insurance	投保，办理保险
take place	发生
take... into consideration/account	考虑到
take the liberty of	冒昧
technical know-how	专门知识，技术诀窍
thanks to	幸亏，承蒙
the quoted price	所报价格
time of shipment/ date	装运期
to one' s order	凭……指定
to our mutual benefit/ interest/ advantage	相互有利
to the contrary	相反
top priority	最优先考虑的事
top quality	上等质量
trade in = deal in	经营，买卖
trade mark	商标
trade practice	贸易惯例，贸易习惯
trade term	贸易术语，贸易条件
trade with	进行交易
transit trade	转口贸易，过境贸易

（续）

turn down an order	拒绝订货
turn out to be	结果是
two items of commission	两笔佣金
U	
unclean B/L = foul/ dirty B/L	不清洁提单
under cover	随函附上
undertaking	保证，承担，许诺
unit price	单价
unloading charges	卸货费，卸车费
unloading point	卸货地点
unloading port	卸货港
unless otherwise provided for	除非另有规定
unless otherwise notice	除非另有通知
up-to-date	最新的，现代的
up to standard	达到标准
urgent consignments	急运货物
urgent shipments	急运
usance/ term/ time Letter of Credit	远期信用证
usual quality	通常的质量
V	
valuable to/for	对……重要，有价值
vary from	不同于
vary with	随……变化
volume of exports	出口量
volume of freight traffic	货运量
volume of goods arrived	到货量
volume of trade	贸易额
W	
War Risks	战争险
warehouse keeper	仓库管理员
warehouse receipt	仓（库）单
with the consent of	经……同意
wholesale distribution	批发商
wholesale price	批发价
wholly owned subsidiary	独资子公司
with a view to = with the view of = with an eye to	为了，目的在于
with best regards	谨致问候
With Particular Average（WPA）	水渍险

（续）

within the validity of	在……有效期内
write off	购销，注销
withdraw an order	取消订单
without engagement	无约束力
world market price	世界市场价格
world-wide	遍及全球的，世界范围的
world-wide influence	世界性的影响
work out	算出，拟订（计划）
Y	
yield up	放弃

Appendix B Abbreviations Commonly Used in International Trade

国际贸易中常用缩略词

A		
A. A. R.	against All Risks	担保全险，担保一切险
Abbr.	abbreviation	缩写字
Abs.	abstract statement	摘要说明书
acc.	acceptance, accepted	承兑，承诺
a/c	account	账户，客户
A/C	account current	来往账户
ackmt	acknowledgement	承认，收条
a/d	after date	出票后限期付款（票据）
ad. , advt.	advertisement	广告
A. D.	Anno Domini	公元
adv.	advice	通知（书）
ad val.	ad valorem (according to value)	从价税
Al	first class	一级
AID	Agency for International Development	美国国际开发总署
A. M. , a. m.	ante meridiem (before noon)	上午
A. M. T.	Air Mail Transfer	信汇
amt.	amount	金额
A. N.	arrival notice	到货通知
ans.	Answer, answered	回答，已答
A/o	account of	记入……账目
A. p.	account payable	应付账款
A/P	Authority to Purchase	委托购买证
a. p.	additional premium	附加保费
A. R.	All Risks	全险，一切险
Arr.	arrival	到达
Art.	article	条款，项
A/S	account sales	销售清单
a/s	after sight	见票后限期付款
Assmt.	assignment	转让
assn.	association	协会

（续）

Asst.	assistant	助理，助手
asstd.	assorted	各色具备的，各种各样（混在一起）的
att.，attn.	attention	注意
Auct.	auction	拍卖
av.，a/v	average	平均，海损
a/v	a vista（at sight）	见票即付
Ave.，Av.	Avenue	街道
A/W	actual weight	实际重量
	B	
B/ –，b/ –	bale，bag	包，装
bal.，balce.	balance	余额
BB	bill book	出纳簿
B. C.	Before Christ	公元前
B/C	bill for collection	托收票据
B/D	bank draft	银行汇票
b/d	brought down	承前页
bd.	bond	债券
bds.	boards	董事会
b' dle，bdl.	bundle	束，把
B/E	bill of exchange	汇票
b. f.	bona fide	善意的
B/F	brought forward	承前页，转下页
bg	bag	袋
BIS	Bank for International Settlement	国际清算银行
bk.	bank book	账簿
bkg.	banking	银行业
B/L	Bill of Lading	提单
B/N	bank note	银行纸币
B/O	bought over	多买
bot.	bottle	瓶
B/P	bill purchased，bills payable	买入票据，出口押汇，应付票据
B/R	bills receivable，bank rate	应收票据，银行贴现率
brl.，barl.	barrel	桶，樽
B/S	balance sheet	资产负债表
bsh.，b/s	bushel	蒲式耳
BTN	Brussels Tariff Nomenclature	布鲁塞尔税则分类
bx	box	箱，盒

（续）

C		
c.	cent，centigrade	（美）分，百分度（寒暑表）
C/A	capital account	资本账户
CAD	cash against documents	凭单证付现金
carr.	carriage	运费
cat.	catalogue	货品目录
C. B.	clean bill，cash book	光票，现金账簿
c. c.	carbon copy，cubic centimeter	副本，立方厘米
C/C	Chamber of Commerce	商会
CCC	The Commodity Credit Corporation	美国商品金融公司
C/D	cash against document，customs declaration	凭单据付款，报关单
cert.	certificate	证明
cf.	confer	对照，协商
C/F	carried forward	转下页
CFR	cost and freight	运费在内价
CFRC	cost，freight and commission	运费及佣金在内价
C. F. S.	container freight station	货柜集散场
chq.	cheque，check	支票
cge.	carriage	运费
CH	custom house	海关
c. i. a.	cash in advance	预付现金
CIF	cost，insurance and freight	运费保险费在内价
CIFC	cost，insurance，freight and commission	运费、保险费、佣金在内价
ck.	cask	樽
C/N，C. N.	credit note，covering note	贷方通知，保险承保单
	consignment note	寄售通知书
C/O	certificate of origin，cash order	原产地证，现款支票
c/o	care of，carried over	烦转，转下页
Co.	company	公司
COD	cash on delivery	货到付款
Con. Inv.	Consular Invoice	领事发票
cont.	contract	合同
Corp.	corporation	法人，公司
COS	cash on shipment	付款装运
C/P	charter party	租船契约
Cr.	credit	贷方，债权人
cs	case	箱
csk.，ck	cask	樽

（续）

C. T. L.	constructive total loss	推定全损
CTN	carton	纸箱
cur.	current	本月，现付
C. W. O.	cash with order	现金订货
cwt.	hundredweight	英担
C. Y.	container yard	货柜集散场
cy.	currency	货币
	D	
D/A	documents against acceptance	承兑交单
	days after acceptance	承兑后……日付款
	deposit account	存款账户
D/D. , D. D.	demand draft, documentary draft	即期汇票，跟单汇票
dd.	delivered	交付
d/d	... days after date	出票后……日付款
de.	deferred	延期
deg.	degree	等级
d. f.	dead freight	空载运费（船）
dft.	draft	汇票
Dis.	discount	折扣
Div.	dividend	红利，股息
D/N	debit note	借方通知
D/O	delivery order	卸货通知书
do.	ditto (the same)	同上
DOC	document	单据
DOZ	dozen	一打
D/P	documents against payment	付款交单
Dr.	debit debtor	借方，债务人
d. r.	deposit receipt	存款收据
d/s. , d. s.	days after sight	见票后……日付款
D/W	dock warrant	码头交单
	E	
ea.	each	每，各
e. e. , E. E.	error excepted	错误除外
EEC	The European Economic Community	欧洲经济共同体
e. g.	example gratia (for example)	例如
EIB	Export-Import Bank	进出口银行（美国）
EMS	express mail special	特快专递

(续)

Enc. , encl.	Enclosure	附件
E. & O. E.	errors and omissions excepted	错误或遗漏不在此限
Esq.	Esquire	先生（信内尊称）
ETA	estimated time of arrival	预定到达日期
etc.	et cetera (and so forth)	等等
Ex	out of, without	自，无，交货
ex.	example, executive, exchange, extract	例子，执行官，外汇交换，摘要
	F	
f	foot, franc	尺，法郎
f. a. , f. a. a.	free of all average	全损赔偿
FAC	facsimile	传真
F. A. Q.	fair average quality	良好平均品质
FAS	free alongside ship	船边交货价
F. B. E.	foreign bill of exchange	国外汇票
f. c. l.	full container load	集装箱整箱货物
F/D	Forward delivery, free docks	定期交货，船坞交货
f. d.	free discharge	免费卸货
f. g. a.	free of general average	不保共同海损
f. i.	free in/ for instance	装卸船方不负责/ 例如
f. i. o.	free in and out	装卸货船均不负责
f. i. o. s. t.	free in, out, stowed and trimmed	装卸、理仓、平仓船方均不负责
f. o.	free out	卸货船方不负责
f. o. , f/o	firm offer	规定时限的报价
FOB, f. o. b.	free on board	船上交货价
f. o. c.	free of charge	免费
f. o. r.	free on rail, free on road	火车上交货价
f. o. s.	free on steamer	轮船上交货价
f. o. t.	free on truck	货车上交货价
FP, f. p.	fully paid	付讫
FPA	free of particular average	单独海损不保
frt.	freight	运费
F/P	floating policy	流动保单
F. R. B.	Federal Reserve Bank	美联储
FX	foreign exchange	外汇
FY	fiscal year	会计年度
	G	
g. , gm.	gramme	公克

（续）

G/A	general average	共同海损
gall.	gallon	加仑
GATT	General Agreement on Tariffs and Trade	关贸总协定
GBP	Great Britain Sterling Pound	英镑
g. m. b.	good merchantable brand	品质良好适合买卖之货品
g. m. q.	good merchantable quality	良好可售品质
G. P. O.	General Post Office	邮政总局
gr. wt. , GW	gross weight	毛重
G. S. P.	Generalized system of preference	普惠制
g. s. w.	gross shipping weight	装输总重量
	H	
h.	hour, height	小时，高度
H. O.	Head Office	总公司
h. p.	horse power	马力
hr.	hour	时
	I	
IATA	International Air Transport Association	国际航空运输协会
IBRD	International Bank for Reconstruction and Development	国际复兴开发银行（世界银行）
ICC	International Chamber of Commerce	国际商会
id.	idem (the same)	同上
i. e.	id est (that is)	即是
I/L	import license	进口许可证
IMF	International Monetary Fund	国际货币基金组织
Inc.	incorporated	有限责任公司
Incoterms	International Commercial Terms	国际商业用语
inst.	instant (this month) / installment	本月/分期付款
int.	interest	利息
in trans.	in transit	运输中
inv.	invoice	发票
IOP	irrespective of percentage	免赔额不适用条款
IOU	I owe you	借据
I. Q.	import quota	进口配额
ISB	International Settlement Bank	国际清算银行
ISIC	International Standard Industrial Classification	国际行业标准分类
it	item	项目

（续）

J		
j. , jour.	journal	流水账
J/A	joint account	共同账户
Jr.	Junior	年少者
K		
k.	carat	克拉
kg.	kilogramme	千克，公斤
kl.	kiloliter	公升
km.	kilometer	公里
K. W.	kilo watt	千瓦
L		
lb.	libra (pound or pounds in weight)	磅（ 重量单位）
lbs.	pounds	磅（重量单位）；英镑（货币单位）
L/C	letter of credit	信用证
LCL	less than carload lot	零担货物
L/I	letter of indemnity	赔偿保证书
L/G	letter of guarantee, loss and gain	保证函，损益
l. t.	long ton	长吨
LS	locus sigil (place of seal)	盖印处
L/T	Letter Telegram	书信电报
Ltd.	Limited	有限责任公司
M		
m.	mile, mark, month, minute	米，记号，月，分
M.	Monsieur	先生
max.	maximum	最大限度
m/d	month after date	出票后……月付款
Mdme	Madame (Madam)	太太，夫人
memo.	memorandum	备忘录，便条纸
Messrs	Messieurs	先生（复数），贵公司
Mgr.	manager	经理
min.	minimum, minute	最低限额，分钟
M. I. P.	marine insurance policy	海上保险单
misc.	miscellaneous	杂项
mks.	marks	商标
mkt	market	市场
M/L	more or less	增或减
MM.	Messieurs	先生（多数）

（续）

Mme	Madame	夫人
MO	Money Order	拨款单，汇款单
Mr.	Mister	先生
MR	Mate' s Receipt	大副收据
Mrs.	Mistress	太太，夫人
m/s	months after sight	见票后……月付款
m. s.	mail steamer, motor ship	邮船，轮船
MSS.	manuscripts	原稿，手抄本
M. T.	metric ton, mail transfer	公吨，信汇
	N	
N/A	no account, new account	无存款，新账户
N. B.	Note bene (take notice)	注意
N/D	no dated	未注明日期
n/f, n. f.	no funds	无款
NL	night letter	夜间拍发电报
NM	no mark	无商标
No.	number	号码
n. o. p.	not otherwise provided for	无其他规定者，未列名者
n. o. s.	not otherwise specified for	无其他说明（规定）者
n/p	non-payment	拒付
N/S	Not sufficient fund	存款不足
Nt. Wt., NW	Net Weight	净重
	O	
O.	Order	订单，订货
o/a	on account of	因为，在……账户
O. B/L	order bill of lading	批示式提单
O. C. P.	Overland Common Point	通常陆上运输可到达地点
O/d	overdraft, on demand	透支，见票即付
OECD	Organization for Economic Cooperation and Development	经济合作与开发组织
OEEC	Organization for European Economic Cooperation	欧洲经济合作组织
O. K.	all correct, approved	无误，同意
O/No.	order number	订单编号
o. p.	open policy	预约保单
ORD	ordinary telegram	寻常电报
O/S	on sale, out of stock, old style	廉售，无存货，旧式

（续）

o. t.	old term	旧条件
oz	ounce	盎司
	P	
P/A, P. A.	particular average	单独海损
p. a.	per annum (by the year)	每年
p. c.	per cent, petty cash	百分比，零钱
PCE	piece	只，个，支等
PCT	percent	百分比
Per Pro. , p. p.	per procuration	代理的
PKG, pkg.	package	包裹
P/L	packing list	装箱单
p. l.	partial loss	单独损失
P. & L.	profit and loss	损益
pm. , prem.	premium	保险费
p. m.	post meridiem (afternoon)	下午
P. M. O.	postal money order	邮政汇票
P/N	promissory note	本票，期票
P. O. B.	postal office box	邮政信箱
P. O. D.	payment on delivery	付款交货
p. p. a.	percent per annum	年利率
ppd.	prepaid	预付
p. p. s.	post postscript	后记
P/R	parcel receipt	邮包收据
PRC	price	价格
pro forma	for form' s sake	估计的，形式的
prox.	proximo (next month)	下月的
PS. , p. s.	postscript	附笔
pt.	pint	品脱
PTL	private tieline service	电报专线业务
P. T. O.	please turn over	转阅背面，转下页
	Q	
Q.	quantity	数量
qty	quantity	数量
quotn	quotation	报价
quty	quality	品质
qy	quay	码头

（续）

R		
re.	with reference to	关于
recd	received	收讫
recpt	receipt	收据
ref.	reference	参考，关于
RFWD	rain，fresh water damage	雨水及淡水险
remit.	remittance	汇款
rm	ream	令
r. m.	ready money，ready-made	备用金，现成的
RMB	renminbi	人民币
R. P.	reply paid，return of post	邮费或电费预付，请即回示
R. S. D.	receiving，storage and delivery	港务局装卸费用
R. S. V. P.	Repondez s' il vous plait（please reply）	请回覆
rt.	rate	率
S		
S. A.	Statement of Account	账单
s. a.	subject to approval	以承认（赞成，批准）为条件
S/C	Sales contract	销售确认书
S/D	sight draft	即期汇票
S/D	sea damage	海水损害
secy	secretary	秘书
sig.	signature	签名
Sir	Signor（mr.）	先生
S/M	shipping mark	装船标记
S/N	shipping note	装运通知
S. O.	shipping order	装船通知书
S. O. S	save our ship or souls	求救信号
s. p. a.	subject to particular average	以不保单独海损为条件
Sr.	Senior	年长者
SRCC	strike，riot，civil commotions	罢工、暴动、内乱条款
S/S，s/s，ss，s. s.	steamship	轮船
s. t.	short ton	短吨
st.	street	街
STL.	style	式样
s. v.	sailing vessel	帆船
T		
T.	ton，tare	吨，皮重

（续）

T/A	telegraphic address	电报挂号
TC	collated telegram	校对电报
T& Dft.	tare and draft	皮重和包含物
T. D. O.	transshipment delivery order	转船提货单
T. L. O.	total loss only	只担保全损（分损不赔）
T. M. O.	telegraphic money order	电报汇款
TPND	theft, pilferage and non-delivery	盗窃、提货不着险
T. R.	trust receipt	信托收据
T. T. , T/T	telegraphic transfer	电汇
	U	
ult.	ultimo	上个月
u/w	underwriter	保险商
	V	
v. , vs.	versus	对于
vid	vide (see)	参阅
VIP	very important person	贵宾
viz	videlicet (namely)	即是
voy.	voyage	航次
v. v.	vice versa	反之亦然
	W	
w. a.	with average	水渍险（单独海损赔偿）
war	with all risk	担保一切险
W/B	way bill, warehouse book	货运单，仓库簿
wgt	weight	重量
whf	wharf	码头
W/M	weight or measurement	重量或尺寸量
W. O.	waiting order	等候订单
W. P. A.	with particular average	单独海损赔偿
W. R.	War Risks, warehouse receipt	战争险，仓单
w. r. t.	with regard to	关于
wt, WT	weight	重量
w. w.	warehouse warrant	仓单
w. w. d.	weather working day	良好天气工作日
	X	
x	ex (out of without) exclusive	除外，无
x. d.	ex divident	无红利
x. in.	ex interest	无利息

（续）

XX	good quality	良好品质
XXX	very good quality	极佳品质
XXXX	best quality	最佳品质
	Y	
Y. A. R.	york-Antwerp Rules	约克—安特卫普规则
yd.	yard	码
yr.	your, year	你的，年
Yr. B.	year book	年鉴

Appendix C Writing Correctly
正确写作

商务信函写作的正确性往往会影响到撰写者及其所在组织的专业形象。因此，撰写者必须多花些精力来纠正那些会影响受众阅读的错误。然而，如果在写作商务信函第一稿和第二稿时就担心语法和标点问题，那么撰写者就很容易思维中断。所以，撰写者应等到成文后再来检查初稿中的语法、标点、数字和日期的书写和词语的使用是否正确。

（一）语法

1. 一致性

主语和谓语在单数或复数时要一致。当主语和谓语之间出现其他单词时，主语和谓语经常会不一致。修改文章时要注意找出句子的主谓语，检查是否一致。

美式英语中公司名称、company 和 government 之类的单词常常被看作单数名词，而英式英语中则被视为复数。

正确的：The accountants who conducted the audit were recommended highly.

正确的（美式）：State Farm Insurance trains its agents well.

正确的（英式）：Lloyds of London train their agents well.

当两个或两个以上的单数主语用 and 连在一起时，要用动词的复数形式；当两个或两个以上的单数主语用 or，nor 或 but 连在一起时，要用动词的单数形式；当句子以 here 或者 there 开头时，动词应该与动词后面的主语一致；注意尽管有些单词以 s 结尾，但应该当作单数，动词仍然要用单数形式。

正确的：Larry Mc Greevy and I are planning to visit the client.

正确的：Either the shipping clerk or the superintendent has to sign the order.

正确的：Here is the booklet you asked for.

正确的：There are the blueprints I wanted.

正确的：A series of meeting is planned.

如果遇到与规则不相符的情况，或者当遵循规则会使句子读起来拗口时，那么应修改句子。

有问题（的）：The Plant Manager in addition to the sales representation (was/were) pleased with the new system.

正确的：The Plant Manager and the sales representation were pleased with the new system.

代词所指代的数字或人与其所指代的不一致时，就会出现名词与代词一致性错误。

错误的：A manager has only yourself to blame if things go wrong.

正确的：As a manager, you have only yourself to blame if things go wrong.

以下单词要求使用动词和代词的单数形式：everybody，either，each，nobody，either，a person 与 everyone。

正确的：Everyone should bring his or her copy of the manual to the next session on changes in law.

当为了避免可能产生的性别歧视而使用的代词组合显得笨重时，应当避免使用上述单词词组。相反，可使用复数代词或第二人称 you。

每个代词必须指代一个特定的词。如果代词并不指代特定的词，那么就应通过加一个词来更正错误。

错误的：We open three new stores in the suburbs. This will bring us closer to our customers.

正确的：We will open three new stories in the suburbs. This strategy will bring us closer to our customers.

提示：要明确 this 和 it 指代前面句子中的特定的词。如果指代的是某个观点，则在句子中加一个名词（this strategy）来使句子符合语法要求。

用 who 和 whom 指代人，用 which 指代物。that 可以指代任何对象：人、动物、组织或物体。

正确的：The new Executive Director, who moved here from Boston, is already making friends.

正确的：The information which she wants will be available tomorrow.

正确的：This confirms the price that I quoted you this morning.

2. 格

格是指名词和代词中所起的语法作用。在主语从句中使用主格代词。使用所有格代词表示谁的或者东西的归属；使用宾格代词表示动词或介词宾语；使用反身代词或强调格代词来指代或强调句子中已经提到过的名词或代词。

正确的：Shannon Weaver and I talked to the customer, who was interested in learning more about integrated software.

正确的：Microsoft Office will exactly meet her needs.

正确的：When you send in the quote, thank her for the courtesy she showed Shannon and me.

正确的：I myself think the call was a very productive one.

不要使用反身代词作为从句的主语或作为动词或介词的宾语。注意第一人称代词放在指代其他人的名字或代词后面。

错误的：Elaine and myself will follow up on this order.

正确的：Elaine and I will follow up on this order.

错误的：He gave the order to Dan and myself.

正确的：He gave the order to Dan and me.

3. 悬垂的修饰语

修饰语是能为句子中的主语、谓语和宾语提供更多信息的词或词语。悬垂修饰语是指在句子中使用不当的词。解决的办法是修改该修饰语的措辞，使其在语法上正确。

错误的：Confirming our conversation, the truck will leave Monday. (The speaker is doing the confirming. But the speaker isn' t in the sentence. 讲话者要确认某事，但句子中该讲话者并不存在。)

错误的：At the age of eight, I began teaching my children about American business. (This sentence says that the author was eight when he or she had children who could understand business.

句子的意思是当他或她有懂经营的孩子时，作者才8岁。）

可用以下方法来改正悬垂修饰语：①将修饰语改为从句；②修改主句使其主语或宾语与现有的悬垂修饰语相配。

正确的：As I told you, the truck will leave Monday.

正确的：When they were eight, I began teaching my children about American business.

正确的：Confirming our conversation, I have scheduled the truck to leave Monday.

正确的：At the age of eight, my children began learning about American business.

提示：无论何时当你使用以-ing结尾的动词或形容词时，要确保它所修饰的是句子语法上的主语。否则，就要修改句子的措辞。

4. 误用的修饰语

误用修饰语是指错误修饰了作者本不打算修饰的其他句子成分。修改误用的修饰语时，可以让修饰语更为靠近它所修饰的词或者通过加标点来明确你的意思。如果修饰语修饰的是整个句子，不妨将它放在句首作为引导词或引导句；当然，其后应加上逗号。

错误的：Customers who complain often alert us to changes we need to make. (Does the sentence mean that customers must complain frequently to teach us something? Or is the meaning that frequently we learn from complaints? 句子是否想说：要教授我们某些事情，顾客必须经常申诉？或者我们经常从申诉中吸取教训？)

正确的：Often, customers who complain alert us to change we need to make.

5. 并行结构

并列成分或列表成分必须采用相同的语法结构。

不并列的：In the second month of your internship, you will... （在你实习期间的第二个月，你会……）

①Learn how to resolve customers' complaints. （学习如何处理顾客的申诉。）

②Supervision of desk staff. （对办公室职员的管理。）

③Interns will help plan store displays. （实习生可帮助商店计划产品陈列。）

并列的：In the second month of your internship, you will...（在你实习期间的第二个月，你会……）

①Learn how to resolve customers' complaints. （学习如何处理顾客的申诉。）

②Supervise desk staff. （管理办公室职员。）

③Plan store displays. （计划商店中产品的陈列。）

其他并列方法：Duties in the second month of your internship include resolving customers' complaints, supervising desk staff, and planning store displays. （你实习期间第二个月的任务包括处理顾客的抱怨、管理办公室职员以及计划商店中产品的陈列。）

提示：当列表项目有两三项（无论是横句的还是纵句的）时，要确保它们所用语法形式的统一。用纵向列表列出项目往往更方便阅读。

6. 谓语错误

句子中的谓语在语法上和逻辑上都要与主语一致。在句子中使用is或其他系动词时，补足语必须是名词、形容词或名词从句。另外，要确保动词修饰的行为是主语所为或施加于主语的。

错误的：The reason for this change is because the SEC now requires fuller disclosure.

正确的：The reason for this change is that the SEC now requires fuller disclosure.

错误的：Our goals should begin immediately.

正确的：Implementing our goals should begin immediately.

（二）断句

每个句子至少包含一个主句。主句或独立句都是完整的句子。非独立句或从句都包含主语和动词，但不是完整的句子，不能独立存在。短语是一组没有主语和动词的词。正确运用标点符号可以避免犯四种主要句子错误：逗号连逗号、句连句、多意句和残句。

1. 逗号连逗号

如果两个主句由一个逗号（不是用逗号和并列连词）连接起来，就会发生逗号连逗号或逗号错误。例如：The contest will start in June, the exact date has not been set（错误的）. 运用以下方法来改正逗号连逗号：

（1）如果两个分句联系密切，那么使用分号替代逗号；如果两个分句联系不密切，则分成两个句子。例如：The contest will start in June; the exact date has not been set.

（2）加并列连词。例如：The contest will start in June, but the exact date has not been set.

（3）将其中一句改为从句。例如：Although the contest will start in June, the exact date has not been set.

切忌在以下连词中只用逗号：however，nevertheless，therefore 与 moreover。相反，应该使用分号断句或分成两个句子。

错误的：Computer grammar checkers do not catch every error, however, they may be useful as a first check before an editor reads the material.

正确的：Computerized grammar checkers do not catch every error. However, they may be useful as a first check before an editor reads the material.

2. 句连句

句连句是指将几个主句用 and，but，or，so 与 for 连接起来。句连句和逗号连逗号的错误刚好相反。逗号连逗号只用了逗号而没有用连词，句连句则只用了连词而没用逗号。因此，加入逗号可以修改短的句连句。对于较长的句连句，可以将其分成两个或多个句子。还可以考虑将一个或多个句子变成从句。

错误的：We will end up with a much smaller markup but they use a lot of this material so the volume would be high so try to sell them on fast delivery and tell them our quality is very high.

正确的：Although we will end up with a much smaller markup, volume would be high since they use a lot of this material. Try to sell them on fast delivery and high quality.

3. 多意句

如果两个或多个句子直接合在一起，既没有用标点符号也没有用连词，那么就会形成多意句。可以通过加标点或连词，或将其中一句改成从句来修改多意句方面的错误。

错误的：The advantages of Intranets are clear the challenge is persuading employees to share information.

正确的：The advantages of Intranets are clear; the challenge is persuading employees to share information.

正确的：Although the advantages of Intranets are clear，the challenge is persuading employees to share information.

4. 残句

在残句中，实际上并不构成完整句子的一组词被标点符号分开，看起来似乎像一个完整的句子。要修改残句，既可以加入句子中缺少的部分，也可以将残句合并到位于其前后的句子中。

错误的：Observing these people，I have learned two things about the program. The time it takes. The rewards it brings.

正确的：Observing these people，I have learned that the program is timer-consuming but rewarding.

（三）标点符号

标点符号起到路标的作用，可以帮助读者推测下文。常见的标点符号及其作用如下所示：

标点符号	传达的信息
句号/句点	到此停止
分号	接下来的内容与刚说的内容紧密相关
冒号	接下来的内容是关于刚才所说内容的一个例子
破折号	接下来的内容是关于刚才所说内容的一个有趣例子或要发生转折
逗号	接下来的内容可能有一些小变化，但基本主题仍然不变

阅读时一般从主语到谓语，中间不会停顿，所以不需要逗号。看完引导词或引导句，使用逗号可告诉读者引言结束，将进入主句部分。当一些词语插在了主句之前，就像现在这样，使用逗号可告诉读者以最短途径转向主句以及何时返回。

有时需要用逗号来告知读者什么地方该停顿。这一方法并不好。多久停顿一次取决于读者肺活量的大小，读者的朗读速度和音量，以及读者想强调的内容。逗号不是停顿；相反，与其他标点符号一样，逗号类似于路标。

因此，优秀的商务函电撰写者应当知道如何使用以下标点符号：撇号、冒号、逗号、破折号、连字号、括号、句号、分号等。

1. 撇号“’”

（1）用来表示被省略的字母或符号。例如：

We’ re trying to renegotiate the contract. （我们想就这个合同重新谈判。）

The ’90s were years of restructuring for our company. （20 世纪 90 年代是公司进行重组的时期。）

（2）用“’s”来表示所有格。当比较中一方名词被省略时，经常使用这种方法。当一个单词以 s 结尾时，直接加撇号来表示所有格。在许多短语中，名词后面加撇号可表示该名字是单数还是复数。例如：

正确的：The corporation’ s home office is in Houston，Texas. （公司总部设在得克萨斯州的休斯敦。）

正确的：This year' s sales will be higher than last year' s.（今年的销售额会比去年高。）

正确的：The meeting will be held at New Orleans' convention center.（会议将在新奥兰斯的国际会议中心举行。）

错误的：The program should increase the participant' s knowledge.（暗示了在这个活动中只有一个参与者。）

正确的：The program should increase the participants' knowledge.（在这个活动中有很多参与者。）

需要注意的是，物主性代词（如 his，ours 等）通常不用撇号。唯一例外的是 one' s。

The company needs the goodwill of its stockholders.（这家公司需要股东的支持。）

His promotion was announced yesterday.（昨天宣布了他被晋升之事。）

One' s greatest asset is the willingness to work hard.（一个人最大的优点是积极主动地努力工作。）

（3）使用撇号将复数、名词与其他词区分开来。但是，其他的复数名词都不使用撇号。

I earned A' s in all my business courses.（所有的商务课程我都得了 A。）

2. 冒号

冒号用于分开主句与解释主句最后部分所提及内容的列表。列表项目是对冒号前内容的具体说明。当列表内容按纵向排列时，每一项的首字母都要大写。

Please order the following supplies（订购以下材料）：

Printer cartridges（打印机墨水盒）

Computer paper（20-1b. white bond）（计算机用纸）

Bond paper（25-1b.，white，25% cotton）（文件纸）

Company letterhead（印有公司抬头的信笺）

Company envelopes（印有公司名称的信封）

当这些项目依次排列在句子里时，冒号后面的内容不需要大写。例如：

正确的：Please order the following supplies：printer cartridges，computer paper（20-1b. white bond），bond paper（25-1b.，white，25% cotton），company letterhead，and company envelopes.

如果列表在语法上是主句的一部分，那么不必使用冒号。

错误的：The rooms will have coordinated decors in natural colors such as：eggplant，moss，and mushroom.

正确的：The rooms will have coordinated decors in natural colors such as eggplant，moss，and mushroom.

正确的：The rooms will have coordinated decors in a variety of natural colors：eggplant，moss，and mushroom.

3. 逗号

（1）可以用逗号将主句与引导性从句、某人姓名或者插入主句中的词语分离开来。注意：该插入信息前后都要使用逗号。

非限制性定语从句对于被修饰的名词而言并不是必需的。因为它提供了额外的信息，所以需要加逗号。

正确的：Sue Decker，who wants to advance in the organization，has signed up for the company training program in sales techniques.（为了在公司得到提升，休·戴克已签字要参加公司的销售技巧培训课程。）

不要用逗号将限制名词或者代词的信息分开。限制性定语从句提供的是必需的信息，而不是额外的信息。

正确的：Anyone who wants to advance in the organization should take advantage of on-the-job training.（想在公司里得到发展的人都应该利用好这次在职培训。）

不要用逗号将主语和谓语分开，即使读完很长的主语后想停顿。

错误的：Laws requiring anyone collecting $5,000 or more on behalf of another person，apply to schools and private individuals as well to charitable groups and professional fund-raisers.

正确的：Laws requiring anyone collecting $5,000 or more on behalf of another person apply to schools and private individual as well to charitable groups and professional fund-raisers.

（2）如果从句很长或有不同的主语，那么就在复合句中的第一个从句后加逗号。不要在没有使用连词的情况下用逗号连接两个独立的从句。否则，会发生逗号连逗号的错误。

正确的：This policy eliminates all sick-leave credit of the employee at the time of retirement，and payment will be made only once to any individual.（这项政策取消了员工退休后所享有的病假赊账，任何人都要一次性付款。）

（3）可用逗号来分离并列项目。有些权威人士认为在 and 和 or 前面不需要使用逗号，但用逗号会使内容更加清晰。如果这些并列项目本身已经包含单词 and，那么就要使用逗号。

正确的：The company pays the full cost of hospitalization insurance for eligible employees，spouses，and unmarried dependent children under age 23.（公司为合格员工及其配偶与23岁以下的未婚孩子支付全部医疗保险费。）

4. 破折号

用破折号来强调思维的中断。打印破折号时，使用1个连字号，且前后都不要有空格。

正确的：Ryertex comes in 30 grades—each with a special use.（热固性塑料板分30类——每种都有专门用途。）

5. 连字号

用连字号表示一个单词被分开在两行中。分割单词时，要注意单词的音节；如果不能确定音节从哪里中断，不妨在词典中查询。若一个单词有多个音节，那么在元音之后或两个辅音之间将之分开，不要将只有一个音节的单词拆分开来（如 acre）。

可用连字号将两个或多个单词连接起来组成一个独立的形容词。用连字号可以防止误读。在下面第一个例子里，需要5个，并不是需要长度是5、10或12英尺的产品。在第二个例子中，若没有连字号，读者可能会认为 computer 是主语，而 prepared 是动词。

正确的：Order five 10- or 12-foot lengths.（订购五个长度为10或12英尺的产品。）

正确的：The computer-prepared Income and Expense statements will be ready next Friday.（计算机制作的收支报表下周五可完成。）

6. 括号

括号用于将那些解释或评价主要观点的单词、短语或句子分开。如果标点符号是针对整个句子的，任何其他的标点符号都应放在后括号外。如果标点符号只是针对括号内的词语，那么就要放在括号内。

正确的：For the thinnest Ryertex（.015”）only a single layer of the base material may be used，while the thickest（10”）may contain over 600 greatly compressed layers of fabric or paper. By varying the fabric used（cotton，asbestos，glass，or nylon）or the type of paper，and by changing the kind of resin（phenol，melamine，silicone，or epoxy），we can produce 30 different grades.（最薄的热固性塑料板（.015”）也只使用基本的单层材料，最厚的（10”）包含600层经压缩的织物和纸。通过变化使用的织物（棉花、石棉、玻璃或者尼龙）或纸张规格，以及通过改变树脂类型（酚、三聚氰胺、硅树脂或者环氧），我们可以生产出30种不同类别的产品。）

正确的：Please check the invoice to see if credit should be issued.（A copy of the invoice is attached.）（请核对发票，看是否应该开立信用证。）（附发票一份。）

7. 句号/句点

在句子结尾处使用句号/句点。英文中，句点与后面的句子之间要保留一个空格。在一些缩写单词后面使用句点。如果用句点代替人名时，在句点与后一个单词之间，要留一个空格。在其他缩写形式中，不需要留空格。不过，现在的趋势是尽量减少标点符号的使用。

正确的：R. J. Tebeaux has been named Vice President for Marketing.

正确的：The U. S. division plans to hire 300 new M. B. A. s in the next year.

正确的：The US division plans to hire 300 new MBAs in the next year.

8. 分号

如果两个独立句语意联系密切，就用分号将它们连接起来。用分号可以表示两个观点非常紧密。用句号并重新另起一句也是正确的，但这意味着这两个句子之间没有多大关系。此外，若一个系列中的项目本身包含逗号，那么可以用分号将这些项目分开。

正确的：The final choices for the new plant are EI Paso，Texas；Albuquerque，New Mexico；Salt Lake City，Utah；Eureka，California；and Eugene，Oregon.（工厂的最后选址是：得克萨斯州的埃尔帕索市；新墨西哥州的阿尔伯克基市；犹他州的盐湖城；加利福尼亚州的尤利卡市；俄勒冈州的尤金市。）

正确的：Hospital benefits are also provided for certain specialized care services such as diagnostic admissions directed toward a definite disease or injury；normal maternity delivery，Caesarean section delivery，or complications of pregnancy；and inpatient admissions for dental procedures necessary to safeguard the patient' s life or health.（医疗福利也提供某些特殊的医疗服务。例如：直接针对一种疾病或伤害的诊断；正常的分娩、剖腹产或者怀孕并发症；保障病人生命和健康所必需的牙病住院保障。）

9. 引号

（1）宣传手册、说明书和杂志文章的名字需加引号。在美式标点符号中，句号/点和逗号放在引号里面，冒号和逗号放在引号外面。如果问号是所引用资料的内容，就把问号放在引号里面。

Enclosed are 30 copies of our pamphlet“Saving Energy”.（所附的是30本《节约能源》小册子。）

You' ll find articles like "How to Improve Your Golf Game" and "Can You Keep Your Eye on the Ball?" in every issue. （在每一期刊物中你都可以找到如《如何提高你的高尔夫水平》和《在舞会上你能尽兴吗》这样的文章。）

（2）为了避免误导，有时可以把所引用的词语用引号标出来；对所要讨论的词语，可使用引号；在引用别人的词语或者句子时，要使用引号。

These "pro-business policies" actually increase corporate taxes. （这些"前企业的政策"事实上增加了公司的税负。）

Forty percent of the respondents answered "yes" to the first question. （对第一个问题，40%的被调查者回答了"是"。）

Use "Ms" as a courtesy title for a woman unless you know she prefers another title. （如你不知道一位女士喜欢何种称呼，那就用小姐这个礼貌的方式。）

10. 方括号

如果你想对引用的材料进行补充或者更改，则使用方括号。下例中的方括号表示史密斯并没有说这些话。为了读者理解引文，你在文件中添加了该内容。

Senator Smith' s statement: "These measures will create a deficit. "（史密斯参议员说，"这些措施会导致出现赤字。"）

Your use of Smith' s statement: According to Senator Smith, "These measures [in the new tax bill] will create a deficit. "（你引用史密斯参议员的话：史密斯参议员说，"这些措施［新的税收法案］会导致出现赤字。"）

11. 省略号

英文中，省略号是一组有间隔的点。打印时，空格隔开的三个点就能组成一个省略号。用省略号表示引用内容中有一个或多个词被省略了。在引用的开头或结尾处，不必使用省略号。另外，在广告和直接邮件中，使用省略号来表示讲话的节奏。

The "Wall Street Journal" notes that Japanese magazines and newspapers include advertisements for a " $2. 1 million home in New York' s posh Riverdale section. . . 185 acres of farmland [and]. . . luxury condos on Manhattan' s Upper East Side" . （《华尔街日报》注意到日本的杂志和报纸上有广告称"纽约豪华区价值210万美元的房子……185英亩的农场……曼哈顿东部的豪华公寓。"）

If you' re ever wanted to live on a tropical island. . . cruise to the Bahames. . . or live in a castle in Spain. . . you can make your dreams come true with Vacations Extraordinaire. （如果您想去热带岛园生活，或是乘船去巴哈马群岛畅游……或是去领略西班牙城堡的风光，选择假日奇妙公司就可梦想成真。）

12. 下划线和斜体

在报纸、杂志和书名下加下划线或用斜体；宣传手册和说明书的题目要加引号。此外，加下划线或用斜体字可表示强调。

<u>The Wall Street Journal</u>《华尔街日报》

<u>Fortune</u>《财富》

<u>The Wealth of Nations</u>《国富论》

Here' s bulletin that gives you, in handy chart form, <u>workable data</u> on over 50 different types of tubing and pipe.（这里有一个公告，在这个图表里，有50种不同规格的管子的可用数据。）

（四）数字和日期

对1~9要拼写出来；在大多数情况下，10与超过10以上的数量可直接用数字。钱的数量也可直接使用数字。

如果数字位于句首，则要把数字拼写出来。若拼写这个数字不合适，则修改该句，使其不以数字开头。

Fifty students filled out the survey.（50名学生填写了调查表。）

In 2002, euro notes and coins entered circulation.（2002年，欧元开始流通。）

如果两个数字相连，则拼写小的数字，大的仍以数字形式表示。

在写日期的时候，用数字表达日期和年份，月份通常是拼写出来的。在国际商务函电中，必须将月份拼写出来。美国人通常将月份放在前面，因此1/10/10就表示2010年1月10日。欧洲人通常将日期放在前面，所以1/10/10就表示2010年10月1日。在现代标点符号中，只有在有日期和月份的情况下才在年份的前面加逗号：

May 1, 2010

但是

Summers 2007-10

August 2010

Fall 2009

在军事和欧洲用法中，不用标点符号。在这些用法中，将日期放在最前面，例如：13 July 2009。在用于分开日期的斜线前后不要留空格，例如：10/05 –5/09。

用连号连接包含的时间：

March-August 2010（或写成 March to August 2010）

'08 –'09

1999-2001

注意在连字号后面不必使用表示世纪的数字，如：2008~2009年可写为2008 –09。

（五）易混淆的单词

以下列出了一些经常易混淆的单词。掌握这些单词，就能正确地运用它们。

(1)	accede: to yield exceed: to go beyond, surpass	I accede to your demand that we not exceed the budget.
(2)	accept: to receive except: to leave out or exclude; but	I accept your proposal except for point 3.
(3)	access: (noun) the right to use; admission to excess: (adjective) surplus	As supply clerk, he had access to any excess materials.
(4)	adept: (adjective) skilled adopt: to take as one's own	She was adept at getting people to adopt her ideas.
(5)	advice: (noun) counsel advise: (verb) to give counsel or advice to someone	I asked him to advise me, but I didn't like the advice I got.

(续)

(6)	affect: (verb) to influence or modify effect: (verb) to produce or cause; (noun) result	He hoped that his argument would affect his boss's decision, but so far as he could see, it had no effect. The tax relief effected some improvement for the citizens whose incomes had been affected by inflation.
(7)	affluent: (adjective) rich, possessing in abundance effluent: (noun) something that flows out	Affluent companies can afford the cost of removing pollutants from the effluents their factories produce.
(8)	a lot: many (informal) allot: to divide or give to	A lot of players signed up for this year's draft. We allotted one first-round draft choice to each team.
(9)	among: use with more than two choices between: use with only two choices	This year the differences between the two candidates for president are unusually clear. I don't see any major differences among the candidates for city council.
(10)	amount: (use with concepts that cannot be counted individually but can only be measured) number: (use when items can be counted individually)	It's a mistake to try to gauge the amount of interest he has by the number of questions he asks.
(11)	attributed: was said to be caused by contributed: gave something to	The rain probably contributed to the accident, but the police officer attributed the accident to driver error.
(12)	cite: (verb) to quote sight: (noun) vision, something to be seen site: (noun) location, place where a building is or will be built	She cited the old story of the building inspector who was depressed by the very sight of the site for the new factory.
(13)	complement: (verb) to complete, to finish; (noun) something that completes compliment: (verb) to praise; (noun) praise	The compliment she gave me complemented my happiness.
(14)	compose: to make up, to create comprise: to consist of, to be made up of, to be composed of	The city council is composed of 12 members. Each district comprises an area 50 blocks square.
(15)	confuse: to bewilder complicate: to make more complex or detailed exacerbate: to make worse	Because I missed the first 20 minutes of the movie, I didn't understand what was going on. The complicated plot exacerbated my confusion.
(16)	dependant: (noun) someone for whom one is financially responsible dependent: (adjective) relying on someone else	IRS regulations don't let us count our 27-year-old son as a dependant, but he is still financially dependent on us.
(17)	describe: to list the features of something, tell what something looks like prescribe: to specify the features something must contain	The law prescribes the priorities for making repairs. This report describes our plans to comply with the law.
(18)	different from/ different than: almost always different from (try changing the adjective different to the verb differs); the most common exception is the indirect comparison.	Bob's job description is different from mine. Susan has a different attitude than you and I [do is implied].

（续）

(19)	elicit: (verb) to draw out illicit: (adjective) not permitted, unlawful	The reporter could elicit no information from the senator about his illicit love affair.
(20)	disinterested: impartial uninterested: unconcerned	Because our boss is uninterested in office spats, she makes a disinterested referee.
(21)	fewer: (use for objects that can be counted individually) less: (use for objects that can be measured but not counted individually)	There is less sand in this bucket; there are probably fewer grains of sand, too.
(22)	forward: ahead foreword: preface, introduction	The author looked forward to writing the foreword to the book.
(23)	farther: use for physical difference further: use for metaphoric difference; also use for additional or additionally	As I traveled farther from the destruction at the plant, I pondered the further evidence of sabotage presented to me today.
(24)	i. e.: (*id est*—that is) introduces a restatement or explanation of the preceding word or phrase e. g.: (*exempli gratia*—for the sake of an example; for example) introduces one or more examples	Although he had never studied Latin, he rarely made a mistake in using Latin abbreviations, e. g., i. e., and etc., because he associated each with a mnemonic device (i. e., a word or image used to help one remember something). He remembered *i. e. as in effect*, pretended that *e. g. meant example given*, and used etc. only when examples to *continue* would fit.
(25)	imply: to suggest, to put an idea into someone's head infer: to deduce, to get an idea out from something	She implied that an announcement would be made soon. I inferred from her smile that it would be an announcement of her promotion.
(26)	lectern: raised stand with a slanted top that holds a manuscript for a reader or notes for a speaker podium: platform for a speaker or conductor to stand on	I left my notes on the lectern when I left the podium at the end of my talk.
(27)	lie: to recline; to tell a falsehood (never takes an object) lay: to put an object on something (always takes an object)	He was laying the papers on the desk when I came in, but they aren't lying there now.
(28)	loose: (noun) not tight lose: to have something disappear	If I lose weight, this suit will be loose.
(29)	It's: it is, it has its: belonging to it	It's clear that a company must satisfy its customers to stay in business.
(30)	objective: goal rationale: reason, justification	The objective of the meeting was to explain the rationale behind the decision.
(31)	personal: individual, to be used by one person personnel: staff, employees	All personnel will get personal computers by the end of the year.
(32)	possible: (adjective) something that can be done possibly: (adverb) perhaps	It is possible that we will be able to hire this spring. We can choose from possibly the best graduating class in the past five years.

（续）

(33)	precede: (verb) to go before proceed: (verb) to continue; (noun: proceeds) money	Raising the money must precede spending it. Only after we obtain the funds can we proceed to spend the proceeds.
(34)	principal: (adjective) main; (noun) person in charge; money lent out at interest principle: (noun) basic truth or rule, code of conduct	*The Prince*, Machiavelli's principal work, describes his principles for ruling a state.
(35)	quiet: not noisy quite: very	It was quite difficult to find a quiet spot anywhere near the floor of the stock exchange.
(36)	regulate: to control relegate: to put (usually in an inferior position)	If the federal government regulates the size of lettering on country road signs, we may as well relegate the current signs to the garbage bin.
(37)	residence: home residents: people who live in a building	The residents had different reactions when they learned that a shopping mall would be built next to their residence.
(38)	respectfully: with respect respectively: to each in the order listed	When I was introduced to the queen, the prime minister, and the court jester, I bowed respectfully, shook hands politely, and winked, respectively.
(39)	role: part in a play or script, function (in a group) roll: (noun) list of students, voters, or other members; round piece of bread; (verb) move by turning over and over	While the teacher called the roll, George—in his role as class clown—threw a roll he had saved from lunch.
(40)	simple: not complicated simplistic: watered down, oversimplified	She was able to explain the proposal in simple terms without making the explanation sound simplistic.
(41)	stationary: not moving, fixed stationery: paper	During the earthquake, even the stationery was not stationary.
(42)	unique: sole, only, alone unusual: not common	I believed that I was unique in my ability to memorize long strings of numbers until I consulted *Guinness World Records* and found that I was merely unusual: someone else had equaled my feat in 1993.
(43)	verbal: using words oral: spoken, not written	His verbal skills were uneven: his oral communication was excellent, but he didn't write well. His sensitivity to nonverbal cues was acute: he could tell what kind of day I had just by looking at my face.
(44)	whether: (conjunction) used to introduce possible alternatives weather: (noun) state of the atmosphere: wet or dry, hot or cold, calm or storm	We will have to see what the weather is before we decide whether to hold the picnic indoors or out.

Appendix D Keys to Exercises
参考答案

Keys to Unit 1

1.

Beijing Textiles Import & Export Corporation
43 Tian An Men Street
Beijing 100053
P. R. China

Mr. Williams Smith
Sunlight Company
23 Oxford Street
London SE5, 6JD
U. K.

2.

China's National Garment Corp.
260 Zhujiang Road, Nanjing 210018, P. R. China
Tel: 86 - 25 - 83838388

March 13, 2005

Walkman Co.
2561 California Avenue
Seattle, WA889
U. S. A.

Dear Gentlemen,

Re: Gent's Shirt

Message

Yours faithfully,
Dong Gang
Dong Gang
Manager

Encl. Catalogue

Keys to Unit 2

1.

(1) 利用，使用
(2) 由于……得知某人的姓名和地址
(3) 由……推荐
(4) 业务范围

(5) 希望

(6) establish business relations

(7) on the basis of equality and mutual benefit

(8) inform of

(9) Chamber of Commerce

(10) specialize in

2.

(1) c (2) a (3) c (4) d (5) a (6) a (7) c (8) a (9) a (10) b

3.

(1) We have come to know the name of your corporation and are pleased to write to you in the hope of establishing business relations with you.

(2) We specialize in the export of Chinese arts and crafts.

(3) It will be appreciated if you can give us your cooperation.

(4) Enclosed are two copies of our price list.

(5) Our company is thinking of expanding its business relations with China.

(6) We have been in this line of business for many years.

4.

Dear Sir or Madam,

We are writing to you at the suggestion of our Commercial Counselor' s Office of the Embassy in your country. We take the liberty to introduce ourselves as exporters of silk piece goods, which we have been exporting to Japan and Europe. We are specialized in the above business. We are desirous of establishing direct business relations with your corporation, knowing that you are the importer of silk piece goods. We shall be grateful if you will let us know whether you are interested in the above items. If so, please inform us of the quantity required.

Yours sincerely,

(Signature)

5.

Having obtained your name and address from the Internet, we are writing to you in the hope of establishing business relations between us. We have been importers of arts and crafts for many years. At present, we are interested in various kinds of Chinese arts and crafts and would appreciate your catalogues and pricelists. We are looking forward to receiving your early reply.

Keys to Unit 3

1.

(1) 信用状况

(2) 财务状况

(3) 绝对保密

(4) 经营方式

(5) 开立账户
(6) small business engagement
(7) overtrading
(8) trade reference
(9) standing credit
(10) delay payment

2.

(1) d (2) c (3) c (4) a (5) b (6) a (7) b (8) c (9) a

3.

(1) The firm with whom we intend to deal has referred us to you for particulars respecting their business standing and trustworthiness.

(2) We should be most grateful if you would furnish us with your opinion on the financial status and reliability of the above company.

(3) As far as we know, their financial standing is sound.

(4) They are a firm of high reputation and have large financial reserves.

(5) We advise you to proceed with every possible caution in dealing with the firm in question.

(6) Any information you may be able to pass on to us will be treated as confidential.

4.

Dear Sir,

We are thinking of granting credit to Messrs . . . of . . . of whom we have only slight knowledge gained during a few months of trading on a cash basis. If you can find out anything about their financial and credit standing, we shall be very grateful to you. They give us only their bankers, the Bank of . . . as a reference, and they estimate their monthly orders at about 800 pounds. We hope that you will be able to assist us.

Yours sincerely,

(Signature)

5.

Would you please be kind enough to obtain for us in confidence all the information possible respecting the financial standing, the capacity of doing business and so on, of ABC Company? The only reference they give us is the Bank of America, their banker. Any information you may give us will be treated as strictly confidential. We thank you for your assistance.

Keys to Unit 4

1.

(1) 定期供应
(2) 合理的价格
(3) 优惠折扣
(4) 激烈竞争
(5) 大量购买

(6) place an order with

(7) by return

(8) available from stock

(9) rock bottom

(10) competitive price

2.

(1) a (2) c (3) d (4) b (5) a (6) c (7) d (8) a (9) b (10) c

3.

(1) We are interested in your computers and should be glad if you would send us by return prices of computers available from stock.

(2) We are confident that we could place regular orders with you provided your prices are competitive.

(3) Please quote us your lowest price for the undermentioned, CIF Shanghai, and the earliest shipment.

(4) The article we require should be durable in quality, bright and attractive in color.

(5) We will appreciate it if you will let us have your comments on our products after trial use.

(6) Another supplier in your market offered us the similar article at a price 3% lower.

4.

Dear Sirs,

We learn from Thomas H. Pennie of New York that you are producing hand-made gloves in a variety of artificial leathers. There is a steady demand here for gloves of high quality at moderate prices. Will you please send me a copy of your glove catalogue, with details of your prices and terms of payment? I should find it most helpful if you could supply samples of these gloves.

Yours sincerely,

(Signature)

5.

We have seen your advertisement in *The Financial Times*. We are considering the purchase of table-cloths. Please send us your catalogue, price list and your best delivery date. We may be able to place a large order if your prices are competitive and deliveries prompt. We are looking forward to receiving your early reply.

Keys to Unit 5

1.

(1) 以……为准

(2) 能保兑的

(3) 通过即期汇票

(4) 按照某人的要求

(5) 收到电子邮件确认书

(6) offering period
(7) revocable offer
(8) firm offer
(9) free sample
(10) offerer

2.

(1) b (2) d (3) c (4) b (5) d (6) b (7) d (8) a (9) c (10) a

3.

(1) We are glad to receive your letter dated Nov. 14 for our bicycles. In reply to your inquiry, we are pleased in making you the following offer.

(2) We are making you, subject to your acceptance reaching us not later than Sep. 15, the following offer.

(3) We are sending you separately a copy of our latest price list giving CIF Amsterdam Price together with an illustrated catalogue for your reference.

(4) Please state terms of payment and discounts you allow on purchases of not less than 10,000 washing machines of Little Swan brand.

(5) You will be interested to hear that we can offer a further supply of the best quality products at the lowest price.

(6) We have here cabled to you a firm offer until May 31.

4.

Dear Sirs,

We acknowledge with thanks the receipt of your inquiry of Sep. 18, and are pleased to make you an offer regarding our Changhong color TV sets in the size you required. All sizes can be supplied by the beginning of next month subject to our receiving your order. The price for Changhong brand color inch 34 is USD450 each at CIF Copenhagen. Our price is very competitive for other good quality TV sets. We look forward to receiving of your large number of order.

Yours sincerely,
(Signature)

5.

We are pleased to receive your inquiry dated May 25, 2015 and as requested, we are sending you under separate cover, a copy of our catalogue, latest price list, together with our sample books. Details of our condition of sale and terms of payment are stated therein. Our cotton tablecloths are enjoying fast sales in the United States and Europe because they are both excellent in quality and reasonable in price. We are looking forward to your order.

Keys to Unit 6

1.

(1) 发盘不能接受

(2) 以立即答复为准的发盘

(3) 转向

(4) 按照样品

(5) 悬殊太大

(6) counter-suggestion

(7) strike a bargain

(8) cut down the price

(9) make it a deal

(10) market fluctuation

2.

(1) b (2) d (3) d (4) c (5) b (6) a (7) b (8) a (9) b (10) a

3.

(1) While appreciating the quality of your bicycles, we find your prices are too high to be acceptable.

(2) To accept your present quotation would mean a heavy loss to us, not to speak of profit.

(3) We suggest your placing orders without delay, so that we may guarantee the supply, and would not miss the chance.

(4) We like the quality of your goods and also the way in which you have handled our inquiry, and would welcome the opportunity to do business with you.

(5) We regret to inform you that we are not in a position to accept your counter-offer or those terms.

(6) We hope you will agree that our prices are very competitive for these good quality clothes, and we look forward to receiving your initial order.

4.

Dear Sir or Madam,

Thank you for your counter offer of May 18 for cotton shirts. We are pleased to confirm the following cable we have just dispatched: YOUR COUNTEROFFER MAY 18TH ACCEPTED. Please note, however, that we have specially accepted your request solely because we wish to make this the forerunner of many future orders from you. We hope you will send us your formal order by return, which we will execute with our best attention.

Yours Sincerely,

(Signature)

5.

Thank you very much for your offer of May 4 for our laser printer. We regret to inform you that our clients find your price on the high side and hesitate to place orders. Although we enjoy the design and style of your laser printer and the way you have handled our inquiry, we are not in the position to accept your offer at the price quoted, since the competitors are quoting a lower price. If your prices were reduced by 10%, we would place a substantial order with you. We are looking forward to your favorable reply.

Keys to Unit 7

1.

(1) 很受欢迎

(2) 试订单

(3) 做某事对某人有利

(4) 比……更好

(5) 商业折扣

(6) to meet one' s demand

(7) moderate in price

(8) unique in style

(9) excellent in quality

(10) skillful in craftsmanship

2.

(1) b (2) c (3) d (4) c (5) b (6) a (7) b (8) b (9) a (10) a

3.

(1) We specialize in the import of chemicals.

(2) Orders are pouring in. We fear that you will miss the chance by sitting on the fence.

(3) Owing to its superior quality and reasonable price, our product has met with a warm reception.

(4) A trial order would convince you of the excellent quality of our products.

(5) A simple comparison will no doubt induce you to let us have your order.

(6) As the type required is out of supply, we will replace it by the following type.

4.

Dear Sirs,

With reference to your enquiry of 30th, we confirm that we can supply any quantity and any size. Our silk products are famous for super quality, excellent craftsmanship, moderate in price are unique in design and are met with warm reception all over the world.

We are attaching a copy of our quotation sheet and the latest catalogue to our letter.

Owing to the large number of orders we are receiving, we would advise you to work fast and place an order with us as soon as possible.

Yours sincerely,

(Signature)

5.

Dear Sir or Madam,

We take the liberty of introducing our new TV which is unique in style and moderate in price. We can send you a sufficient supply of our new product to enable you to test on its quality. For owners of old type TV, our TV is a must for all who prefer to enjoy a perfect home life.

With this letter, we enclose illustrated catalogues and sales literature. We are pleased to inform you that we can supply any quantity straight from stock and delivery is guaranteed within a month.

We look forward to your reply.

Yours faithfully,

(Signature)

Keys to Unit 8

1.

(1) 试购订单
(2) 重复订单
(3) 未完成订单
(4) 达成交易
(5) 订货单
(6) initial order
(7) stock list
(8) accept an order
(9) cancel an order
(10) carry out an order

2.

(1) a (2) d (3) b (4) c (5) d (6) c (7) a (8) d (9) d (10) b

3.

(1) As to a trial order, we are delighted to give you a small order for 150 sets of your air conditioners AC106. Please note that the goods are to be supplied in accordance with your samples.

(2) Although prevailing prices are somewhat higher, in view of our long-standing relationship, we are prepared to accept the order on the same terms as before.

(3) As we find both quality and prices satisfactory, we place an order with you for the following.

(4) We are sending you our Sales Contract No. 123 in duplicates for your signature. Please sign and return one copy for our file.

(5) We are sorry to say that because orders for the item required have been booked up to the end of this year, we are unable to accept any fresh order for shipment within this year.

(6) It is our hope that this order is the first step in the establishment of a long and pleasant business relationship.

4.

Dear Sirs,

Re: Canada Oat

We thank you for your letter of November 10, 1998 together with one copy of your Order Confirmation No. P/756 for 1,000 tons of Canada oats.

Enclosed are two copies each of the original and duplicate of our Contract No. FM-4321 for your signature. Please sign and return one signed copy each thereof for our files.

So far as the delivery is concerned, we will try our utmost to ship the total quantity promptly, if your L/C arrives here in time. Therefore, in order to enable us to make early shipment, you are requested to arrange the establishment of L/C at your earliest convenience.

We take this opportunity to express our gratitude for your confidence in our company.

Faithfully yours,

(Signature)

5.

Dear Sirs,

Thank you for your letter of 12th July sending us patterns of cotton prints. We find both quality and prices satisfactory and are pleased to give you an order for the following items on the understanding that they will be supplied from current stock at the prices named:

Quantity	Pattern No.	Prices (net)
300 yards	72	33p per yard
450 yards	82	38p per yard
300 yards	84	44p per yard
		CIF Lagos

We expect to find a good market for these cottons and hope to place further and larger orders with you in the near future.

Please send us your confirmation of sales in duplicate.

Yours faithfully,

(Signature)

Keys to Unit 9

1.

(1) 电开信用证

(2) 修改信用证

(3) 延展信用证有效期

(4) 增加信用证面额

(5) 拒绝偿还

(6) confirmed L/C

(7) transferable L/C

(8) with recourse L/C

(9) credit balance

(10) to establish a credit through a bank

2.

(1) b (2) b (3) b (4) c (5) a (6) a (7) c (8) a (9) d (10) c

3.

(1) Please make amendments of the L/C as soon as possible so that we may arrange shipment.

(2) We are pleased to inform you that we have been requested to open a credit in your favor.

(3) L/C No. 357 which expires on April 17 has been extended to May 2.

(4) Delete the word "long" and insert the word "metric" before "ton".

(5) In consideration of our long friendly relations, we accept 60 days L/C for this transaction.

(6) We urged you many times to open the L/C, but up to now it still hasn' t been received.

4.

Dear Sirs,

Re: L/C No. 4654 Issued by District Bank

We acknowledge receipt of your letter of August 6 and wish to express our sincere apologies for the error (mistake) in the captioned L/C, which is mainly due to an unfortunate oversight.

We have, this morning, instructed our bank to amend the L/C No. 4654 by cable and trust the cable amendment will reach you in due course. As we are badly in need of the goods, we shall highly appreciate it if you will arrange immediate shipment.

Should this shipment prove satisfactory to our customers, repeat orders will be possibly placed before long.

Thank you in anticipation for your close cooperation in this respect.

Yours faithfully,

(Signature)

5.

Dear Sirs,

We are in receipt of your letter of April 5, contents of which have been duly noted.

With regard to L/C No. 20888, we have already instructed the opening bank to extend the dates of shipment and validity to the 15th and 30th of May respectively. The cable extension, we trust, must have reached you now. Please contact the shipping company and book the shipping space so as to ensure that the shipment will be effected before the 15th of May.

Should this order prove satisfactory to our users, we can assure you that repeat orders in increased quantities will be placed.

Your close cooperation in this respect will be highly appreciated. In the meantime, we await your shipping advice by cable.

Yours truly,

(Signature)

Keys to Unit 10

1.

(1) 付款交单

(2) 承兑交单

(3) 汇票

(4) 支付方式

(5) 向……开汇票

(6) as an exception case

(7) on receipt of

(8) easier terms

(9) in consideration of . . . / in view of . . .

(10) in every respect

2.

(1) b (2) a (3) b (4) d (5) c (6) b (7) c (8) d
(9) a (10) b

3.

(1) With regard to Contract No. 25, we are agreeable to D/P payment terms.

(2) In consideration of our long friendly relations, we accept T/T.

(3) We regret to have to decline your request for D/A terms.

(4) In compliance with your request, we will accept delivery against 30 days' D/A as an exceptional case.

(5) We will appreciate it if you can make a concession in payment terms, such as D/P at sight.

(6) We will send our draft at 60 days' for acceptance by separate posts.

4.

Dear Sirs,

We are the largest supermarket in India and have recently received a number of enquiries of your bicycles. We think there are good prospects for the sale of this product, but at present it is little known here and as we can' t count on regular sales we don' t feel able to make purchases at our own expenses.

We are therefore writing to suggest that you send us a trial delivery for sale on D/A terms. We make the proposal hoping to place firm orders when the market is established.

We believe our proposal offers good business chances and hope you will be willing to accept.

Yours sincerely,

(Signature)

5.

Dear Sir or Madam,

We would like to place an order for 500 computers at our price.

In consideration of our long cooperation, we would like to pay for this order by D/P.

We much appreciate the support you have given us in the past and would be most grateful if you could extend this favor to us. If you are agreeable, please send us your contract.

Yours faithfully,

(Signature)

Keys to Unit 11

1.

(1) 防水

(2) 木箱

(3) 完好无损

(4) 注册商标

(5) 包装要求

(6) 标准出口包装

(7) packing list

(8) gross for net

(9) customary packing

(10) neutral packing

(11) seaworthy packing

(12) shipping mark

2.

(1) c (2) b (3) c (4) b (5) b (6) a (7) c (8) d (9) a (10) b

3.

(1) Cement is to be packed in double craft-paper bags, each containing 50 kilos.

(2) Full details regarding packing and marking must be strictly observed.

(3) Please make sure you use leak-proof packing.

(4) All the bags are beautifully designed to come in line with local market preference at your end.

(5) The cases are to be marked with our initials in a diamond as usual.

(6) Our way of packing has been widely accepted by other clients, and we have received no complaints what so ever so far.

4.

Dear Sirs,

We regret to inform you that 20 of the 200 cartons of iron nails you shipped in Dubai on February 12 were badly damaged, which of course is not your fault.

But we have to write to you in regard to the packing of these nails, which we feel necessary to clarify so as to avoid the same damages in the future transactions.

The packing for Dubai is to be in wooden cases of 112lbs. net, each containing 7lbs. 16 packets. For Malta, we would like you to have the goods packed in double gunny bags of 50/60 kilos each. As for British market, our buyers prefer 25-kilo cartons.

We should be grateful if you let us have your opinions about these requirements.

Yours truly,

(Signature)

5.

Dear Sirs,

Thank you for your packing instructions, but regret our inability to comply with your request for special packing.

In order to finalize this initial trade activity between us, we would like to make the following suggestions for your consideration.

(1) The bed sheets will be packed 8 dozen to a packet, 6 packets to a carton and 10 cartons to a crate.

(2) Your initials will be printed in a diamond instead of the full name.

(3) The name of the country of origin of the good will be marked on the carton and crate, not on every packet.

(4) Special directions and warnings will be stenciled on the crate, not on every carton.

Please let us know your comments by return fax.

Yours faithfully,

(Signature)

Keys to Unit 12

1.

(1) 代表某人

(2) 由某方付费

(3) 请……参看，参照

(4) 将保险费退还给你

(5) 没有明确指示

(6) franchise

(7) insurance premium

(8) arrange insurance

(9) insurance certificate

(10) warehouse to warehouse clause (w/w clause)

2.

(1) b (2) c (3) d (4) a (5) d (6) a (7) c (8) d (9) c (10) b

3.

(1) Premium for breakage is 5%. If you desire to cover breakage, we will arrange it on your behalf.

(2) Please arrange the insurance as per our request and in the meantime we await your shipping advice.

(3) We shall take out insurance at this end under open policy.

(4) If you like, you may draw on us at sight for the amount required.

(5) In the absence of your definite instructions, we will cover insurance FPA and War Risks according to usual practice.

(6) We know that according to your usual practice, you insure the goods only for 10% above invoice value, therefore the extra premium will be for our account.

4.

Dear Sirs,

We refer to our Purchase Confirmation No. 123 for 500 pieces of White Rabit Blanket. We are notifying that we have opened through Citi Bank a confirmed irrevocable letter of credit No. 567, totaling USD4,400, the L/C shall remain in force till 31st, August.

Please see to it that the above mentioned articles would be shipped before the end of August and the goods should be covered insurance for 130% of the invoice value against All Risks.

We know that according to your usual practice, you insure the goods only at invoice value plus 10%. Therefore, the extra premium will be for our account.

Please arrange insurance as per our requirements and we await your advice of shipment.

Yours faithfully,

(Signature)

5.

Dear Sirs,

We thank you for your L/C NO. 157 covering wall tiles. Please note it that we do not cover breakage. Therefore we hope you will delete the word breakage from the insurance clause in the credit. Furthermore, we have to inform you that for such articles as window glass, porcelains, etc., even if additional Risk of Breakage has been insured, the insurance is subject to a franchise of 5%. In other words, if the breakage is surveyed to be less than 5%, no claims for damage will be entertained.

We believe you have now made our position clear. Please fax the amendment at once.

Yours faithfully,

(Signature)

Keys to Unit 13

1.

(1) 滞期费率

(2) 速遣费

(3) 卸货港

(4) 装货港

(5) 托运单

(6) 运费预付
(7) 分批装运
(8) notice of readiness
(9) charter party
(10) shipping mark
(11) on board bill of lading
(12) liner transport
(13) freight collect
(14) liner' s freight tariff

2.

(1) d (2) a (3) d (4) a (5) a (6) b (7) b (8) a (9) c (10) a

3.

(1) As is stipulated under the contract, the seller should cable the shipping advice to the buyer as soon as the goods are on board of the ship.

(2) We are under the necessity of requesting you to allow transshipment in Paris.

(3) For some special reasons we request you to advance shipment of the consignment under order No. 579 from October to September.

(4) We shall book shipping space on that vessel on receipt of your L/C amendment.

(5) We shall do our best to make delivery of the goods next month.

(6) We will hand over a set of clean shipped bills of lading, made out "to order", in triplicate, to Commercial Bank of Midland, who will forward them to you.

4.

Dear Sirs,

We have received your letter of April 4.

In respect of the remaining 500 tons of steel plates, as it is extremely difficult to book a vessel at present, we cannot inform you of the exact departure of a vessel for the time being. If you can book a vessel for us, we can ship the goods at an early date, otherwise kindly apply for the extension of your import license. As soon as we have the opportunity to book a vessel, we will let you know.

Sincerely yours,

(Signature)

5.

Dear Sirs,

Re: Order No. 8901

The above order was shipped on 17 October 2015 on the S. S. Tiantan which is due in Liverpool on 27 October.

We have informed your agent, Eddis Jones, who will make arrangements for the consignment to be sent to you, as you requested.

Our bank's agents, Westorland Bank Ltd., High Street, Nottingham, will hand over the documents which consist of bill of lading (No. 517302), invoice (No. EH3314) and insurance certificate (AR1184531), once you have accepted our bill.

We are sure you will be delighted when you see the machines, and that they will find a ready market in your country. We look forward to hearing from you again in the near future.

Yours faithfully,

(Signature)

Keys to Unit 14

1.

(1) 中国国际贸易促进委员会

(2) 经调查此事

(3) 不负赔偿责任

(4) 着手处理这个问题

(5) 由某人做主，由某人支配

(6) 补偿某人的损失

(7) the public surveyor

(8) Force Majeure

(9) Arbitration Award

(10) without recourse

(11) assume responsibility

(12) Foreign Trade Arbitration Commission

2.

(1) a (2) b (3) c (4) d (5) a (6) a (7) b (8) d (9) b (10) c

3.

(1) Upon examination, we found that many of the goods were severely damaged, though the cases themselves show no trace of damage.

(2) We hereby register a claim with you on the basis of the SCIB's survey reports.

(3) We now lodge/register a claim with you for short weight and inferior quality.

(4) It is just and fair to propose a reduction of 30% in the contractual price, otherwise the buyer has the right to reject the goods and lodge a claim according to the contract stipulations.

(5) Since you sent us complaints, we have taken measures to overcome the shortcomings. Now, we have satisfied ourselves that the goods were in sound condition before they were packed.

(6) We regret these faulty sets of equipment were sent to you, and have today sent a replacement of 12 sets. We hope you will be pleased with the new lot.

4.

Dear Sirs,

Re: Your claim on 1,000 Metric Tons Chemical Fertilizer

With reference to your letter of September 6 in which a claim has been lodged for a short delivery of 1,800 lbs. chemical fertilizer, we express our deepest regret over the unfortunate incident. You must have had difficulty in executing the orders of your clients.

After a check-up by our warehouse staff, it was found that 40 bags had not been packed in 5-ply strong paper bags as stipulated in the contract, resulting in breakage during transit. This was due entirely to negligence on the part of the warehouse managers, for which we, the exporters, tender our apologies.

We therefore enclose our check No. XX for USD1,146 in full and final settlement of your claim. Please acknowledge receipt in due course.

We hope this matter will not affect our good relations in our future dealings.

Yours faithfully,

(Signature)

5.

Dear Sirs,

We have just received the 50 cases of porcelain shipped by M/S President under our order No. 123 but regret to inform you that 7 cases are broken and their contents are badly damaged.

As you see, our Survey Report stated the damage was attributed to improper packing. We must therefore lodge a claim against you for damage and inspection fee of the goods amounting to USD8 650. We hope the matter will call your best attention.

Yours faithfully,

(Signature)

Keys to Unit 15

1.

(1) sole (exclusive) agent

(2) agent commission

(3) express consent

(4) to gain a foot in

(5) assembling after sample with supplied material

(6) assembling with supplied parts and components

(7) rate of spoilage

(8) capital goods

(9) Joint Venture

(10) registered capital

(11) the Board of Directors

(12) assets and liabilities

(13) prorate average

(14) multilateral trade

(15) 将……委托于
(16) 鉴于
(17) 业绩目标
(18) 凭样销售
(19) 中国国际贸易促进委员会
(20) 首席执行官
(21) 补偿贸易
(22) 出口成果产品
(23) 按……比例
(24) 不遗余力
(25) 终局的且对双方都有约束力
(26) 综合成本
(27) 合同各方
(28) 永久性正常贸易关系

2.

(1) b (2) c (3) c (4) d (5) d (6) c (7) b (8) a (9) c (10) a (11) d (12) c (13) d (14) a

3.

(1) Business
(2) exchanged
(3) limit
(4) limited
(5) negotiation
(6) business
(7) negotiate
(8) exchange

4.

Dear Sirs,

We thank you for your letter of July 5 and we are very much interested in your proposal that you supply us with the assembly line of X-Ray, technical information, testing instruments and complete sets of components and parts for us to assemble them into finished products.

As for the cost of the equipment and technology, we will use the assembling fee to pay for it.

We hope you will go into details and be assured of our close cooperation.

Yours faithfully,
(Signature)

5.

Dear Sirs,

We have received the illustrated pamphlets you sent us and have carefully studied the characteristics of the machine you intend to sell.

According to the illustration stated in the pamphlets, this complete set of machine was manufactured in Switzerland three years ago. It has an automatic control system and an automatic lubricating device. Its function to manufacture all kinds of gum products offers many attractions.

We have discussed with our technical engineers the question whether or not to import this machine to revamp our production. Recently we have come to the conclusion that seems too costly to buy the machine especially at the present time when we are in urgent need of funds for reconstructing our factory premises. Under such circumstances, we can not make any fresh purchase but leave the matter for further consideration.

Nevertheless, we thank you for keeping us in touch and hope that someday in the near future we will do some successful business.

Yours truly,

(Signature)

Bibliography

参考文献

[1] John D Daniels，Lee H Radebaugh，Daniel P Sullivan. International Business [M]. San Antonio：Pearson Education，2015.

[2] 基蒂 O 洛克，唐娜 S 科恩茨乐尔. 商务与管理沟通 [M]. 赵银德，等译. 北京：机械工业出版社，2009.

[3] 芮艳萍. 领先商务英语函电 [M]. 北京：高等教育出版社，2013.

[4] 菲利普 R 凯特奥拉，玛丽 C 吉利，约翰 L 格雷厄姆. 国际市场营销学 [M]. 赵银德，沈辉，张华，译. 北京：机械工业出版社，2012.

[5] 程同春，程欣. 新编国际商务英语函电 [M]. 南京：东南大学出版社，2011.

[6] 姚大伟，鲁丹萍. 国际商务单证实务 [M]. 北京：清华大学出版社，2009.

[7] 滕美荣，许楠. 外贸英语函电 [M]. 北京：首都经济贸易大学出版社，2008.

[8] 易露露，王娜娜，陈原. 外贸英语函电 [M]. 北京：清华大学出版社，2008.

[9] 查尔斯 M 富特雷尔. 销售学基础 [M]. 赵银德，译. 北京：机械工业出版社，2006.

[10] 郑敏. 商务英语函电与合同 [M]. 北京：清华大学出版社；北京交通大学出版社，2005.

[11] 王丰，陈沄沄. 国际商贸英语信函写作教程 [M]. 北京：清华大学出版社，2005.

[12] 冯祥春，隋思忠. 外经贸函电核心英语 [M]. 北京：中国商务出版社，2005.

[13] 檀文茹，徐静珍. 外贸函电 [M]. 北京：中国人民大学出版社，2004.

[14] 胡鉴明. 商务英语函电 [M]. 北京：中国商务出版社，2004.

[15] 齐智英. 商务英语函电 [M]. 北京：机械工业出版社，2004.

[16] 胡鉴明. 商务英语写作 [M]. 广州：华南理工大学出版社，2003.

[17] 谢金领，徐以敬. 新编国际商务英语函电 [M]. 太原：山西经济出版社，1999.

[18] 冯云霞. 国际商务函电教程 [M]. 南京：南京大学出版社，1995.

[19] 郁福敏，郭珊琏. 国际商务英语函电 [M]. 上海：上海交通大学出版社，1994.

[20] 吴林康. 实用外贸英语 [M]. 北京：外语教学与研究出版社，1988.

《外贸函电　第3版》（赵银德主编）

信息反馈表

尊敬的老师：

您好！感谢您多年来对机械工业出版社的支持和厚爱！为了进一步提高我社教材的出版质量，更好地为我国高等教育发展服务，欢迎您对我社的教材多提宝贵意见和建议。另外，如果您在教学中选用了本书，欢迎您对本书提出修改建议和意见。

一、基本信息

姓名：__________ 性别：__________ 职称：__________ 职务：____________

邮编：__________ 地址：____

任教课程：________________ 电话：____—__________（H）_________（O）

电子邮件：______________________________________ 手机：_____________

二、您对本书的意见和建议

（欢迎您指出本书的疏误之处）

三、您对我们的其他意见和建议

请与我们联系：

100037　机械工业出版社·高教分社　常编辑 收

Tel：010-8837 9721（O），6899 7455（Fax）

E-mail：changay@126.com